The Song of the Talking Wire

Eyewitness to the Old West

First-Hand Accounts of Exploration, Adventure, and Peril

Richard Scott

A Roberts Rinehart Book

TAYLOR TRADE PUBLISHING

Lanham • New York • Dallas • Boulder• Toronto • Oxford

A Roberts Rinehart Book
Taylor Trade Publishing
An imprint of The Rowman & Littlefield Publishing Group, Inc.
4501 Forbes Boulevard, Suite 200
Lanham, MD 20706

Distributed by National Book Network

The hardcover edition of this book was previously cataloged by the Library of Congress
as follows:

Scott, Richard, 1941–
  Eyewitness to the Old West : first-hand accounts of exploration, adventure, and peril /
Richard Scott.
    p. cm.
  Includes bibliographical references.
  ISBN 1-57098-407-7 (cloth : alk. paper)
  1. West (U.S.)—History—Sources. 2. West (U.S.)—Discovery and
exploration—Sources. 3. Frontier and pioneer life—West (U.S.)—Sources. 4. West
(U.S.)—Biography. 5. Pioneers—West (U.S.)—Biography. I. Title.
  F591 .S4 2002
  978'.02—dc21   2002004909

  ISBN 1-57098-407-7 (cloth : alk. paper) — 1-57098-426-3 (pbk. : alk. paper)

♾™ The paper used in this publication meets the minimum requirements of American
National Standard for Information Sciences—Permanence of Paper for Printed Library
Materials, ANSI/NISO Z39.48-1992.

Manufactured in the United States of America.

Dedicated to
my Mother,
Mae Melissa (neé Burdett) Scott
who loved history's stories, but whose own story can never be
adequately told, yet her courage, endurance and determination to hold
fast to her ideals and to protect her children, makes her a woman to be
remembered and admired.

This book is also dedicated to
the Burdett Family:
Eva (Little Mother)
William (Uncle Buddy)
Marsada (Aunt Sadie)
Charles (Uncle Buster)
who, by their love and attention, uplifted my brothers, sisters, and I.

Acknowledgments

First, I want to acknowledge the authors of the vignettes contained in this anthology. These authors lived their stories in one way or another, either as direct participants in the events conveyed, or as observers. It took years of research for me to locate the sources of these vignettes. The research trail led me to numerous repositories such as the Denver Public Library, Idaho Springs Public Library, Auraria Higher Education Center Library, Santa Fe Public Library, Jefferson County Public Library, Southern Utah University Library, New Mexico State University Library, University of Arizona Library, and many others. Aside from the libraries that I searched, I located a number of rare Old West stories in new and used bookshops throughout Colorado, New Mexico, Texas, Arizona, Wyoming, Montana, Utah, California, and South Dakota. In a few cases I found published vignettes on the Internet and Ebay online auctions. Good sources all.

Second, most published works flow from a compilation of effort and support from a large number of people. In selecting, editing, and writing the introductions to the stories contained in this book, I especially owe the following people a huge debt of gratitude: Judith DeLouche Scott—my wife, bush buddy, and professorial colleague; Salvatore T. DeFatta—my motorcycle-riding chum and direction-finding guru who rode side-by-side with me as we explored many of the Old West locations from where the stories in this book sprung; Ron Scott—my motorcycle-riding little brother who loves Old West history as much as I do, such that he has to not only see it, but needs to touch it, feel it, smell it, and commune with it; and Charles and David Scott, my motorcycling sons and fellow adventurers, who can run the roads as good as their old man and who always appreciate a good story; William Scott—my number three son and a modern-day teamster who pilots his heavy loads down the outback highways of Colorado, Wyoming, South Dakota and Montana; Kristin Scott Williams—my only daughter and teacher of Arizona high schoolers; and to my other siblings, Dorothy, Bobby, Linda, and Janis for helping to build a firm family foundation for all of us.

Contents

Illustrations

Preface

When, where, and what is the Old West? To me, the Old West is not just a geographical region locked into a chronology of time, but it is a period of American history that loosely began with some of the earliest contacts between Europeans and the indigenous peoples west of the Mississippi River. That is why my first selection in this book begins with the cultural collision between the hapless Spanish adventurer, Cabeza de Vaca, and the Indians he bumped into in the early-sixteenth century in the area that we now call Texas and New Mexico.

To my way of thinking, the end of the Old West was just about as abrupt and unplanned as its beginning. I see its end as occurring in southern South Dakota, at a place called Wounded Knee. There, on a cold and blustery December day in 1890, the U.S. Army unleashed its firepower on some piteous Lakota reservation-bound Indians. This event marked the end of the era when the plains Indians of the Old West would rise up against its relentless American foe.

Where was the Old West? Like its lifetime, its location is conjectural. It depends on where you want to put it. If, for example, you live in New York City, anything west of there is west to you. But, I believe that the Old West can be defined more definitively than its lifetime. Thus, in this book I have only chosen stories that emanate within that vast area lying west of the Mississippi River and spreading all the way to the Pacific coastline, and bordered on the north by Canada and on the south by Mexico.

What is the Old West? I'm sure that you would agree that the Old West is not just a time, or a compass direction or a geographic location; it is a state of mind, a concept, a culture, and an orientation. I know what it is. I can see it plainly. It is a conjured and vivid panorama of covered wagons filled with hopeful emigrants following the ruts on a worn trail; it is Indians lurking just over the rise astride their quick ponies; it is tired and dusty cowboys shepherding their herds of longhorns north to the railroad trailheads; it is fast-draw gunslingers nursing a whiskey in a musty saloon where gamblers and soiled doves ply their trades; it is youthful Cavalry troopers following an evaporating trail made by plundering Indian war parties; it is work-worn miners with the gleam of gold fading in their tired eyes; and, it is clapboard towns with muddy streets filled with hungry-eyed men looking for who-knows-what.

One westerner, Ladd Haystead, said that the West was the "place where you climb for water, dig for wood, look farther and see less [and] it's a land of fable, myth, tradition and the lack of it, of extremes of heat and cold, wetness and dryness, lowness and highness, of promise and bitter disappointment." No doubt that *your* mind's eye conjures up vivid scenes that represents the Old West to you. But, I'll bet that you agree with me that the Old West is a state of mind as well as a time and a place.

The stories in this book were primarily obtained from the published diaries and journals of real-life people who experienced the Old West firsthand. The more than one-hundred selections that I chose for this book were mainly drawn from hundreds of published works, many lying dormant on library shelves or in out-of-the-way bookstores throughout the West. Finding these sources took a lot of effort and took several years. From those sources, I have only used selections for this book that I thought that readers would find interesting. In addition, I also tried to choose vignettes that would give readers a cross-section of human interest stories, penned by a diversity of authors. The book, therefore, contains a mix of stories rendered by males and females, Native Americans, Hispanics, African-Americans, as well as Whites, who found themselves in all sorts of situations. Some of the stories are funny, some are tragic, and some are just reflections of everyday life. But they are all real. Their chroniclers are all gone.

The stories in this book are presented in chronological order. In many cases the precise date of the event is known and is therefore recorded. In some cases, the actual date of the event is lost to history, yet an approximation of the month, season or year can usually be determined. But in a few stories, even the year had to be estimated from information contained in the story or the story's setting or, more likely, from my own guesswork.

In almost all the first-hand accounts, the previously published sources where the selections were published were copied verbatim. That is, no editorial work was done on those selections. In a few excerpts, however, slight editorial additions were made when the document was either illegible or where the words, descriptions, locations, used by the author rendered the meaning doubtful. The indication [*sic*] or an explanatory addendum was inserted in brackets [ ] only when I felt that there may be uncertainty in the reader's mind about a strange spelling, a date, or a fact. I tried to keep these editorial intrusions to a minimum.

I also made a conscious effort to maintain consistency in the spelling of proper names, localities, Indian tribes, and the like as they were provided in the published source. Thus, I did not attempt to "correct" the spelling, punctuation, capitalization, or structure of the vignettes. Although some of the authors of the stories produced a written product that sorely needed editorial help, their writing style is nonetheless interesting and delightful. I do not believe that you will find any of the stories hard to grasp. Sometimes, however, your reading of a story may be slowed due to the writing errors encountered in a few of these first-hand accounts. It was sometimes necessary, however, to delete extraneous material in an attempt to keep the story on track. When material was eliminated from the original source of the vignette, it is so indicated by the customary ellipsis (. . .).

It is important to note that the people of the Old West were not as attuned to socially acceptable niceties as we, who now live in a supposedly more enlightened age. In that light a few of the book's stories may contain racial or ethnic slurs that are not considered appropriate today. I wondered if I should eliminate all such references with my editor's pen and make them more "politically correct" for today's readers. After all, I reasoned, my job is to inform and entertain the readers of the book, not to offend them. Yet, at the same time, I felt I had an honest obligation to present the vignettes with as little editorial interference as possible. After contemplation, I decided that I would remain true to the wording contained in the sources that I used for the stories in this book. My decision was based on the belief that the stories really belong to those who penned them in the age when they lived. Thus, I determined that I would not be unduly swayed by today's notion of political correctness. Part of my motivation is my belief that modern readers are sophisticated and they understand that although what may have been acceptable in one time period may not be in another—but we should not necessarily re-write history to conform to a present viewpoint. You can use the filter of your mind to eliminate words or phrases that you may find offensive or inappropriate.

Through their stories that I republish in this book, I hope that you can hear the faraway voices of the authors who are speaking to you across the ages. It is my sincere desire that you enjoy reading my book as much as I enjoyed writing it.

Richard Scott
Denver, Colorado

Foreword

Richard Scott has brought together wonderfully vivid true-life stories of a cross-section of Old West characters. This book shows us that the history of the U.S. West is not one linear story about America's step-by-step exploration and seizure of the land west of the Mississippi, which can be a bland account that lulls students to sleep. Rather, the West was (and still is) a site for conflicting stories, a dynamic place of what Scott calls a "cultural collision."

The opening writer, Cabeza de Vaca, is literally lost in America, where in the desert he loses his way and his clothes, symbolically becoming a baby in the New World: "Through all that country we went naked, and not being accustomed to it, like snakes we shed our skin twice a year." The closing writer, Black Elk, recalls his Plains Indian youth from his vantage point as "a pitiful old man" who recalled the 1890 massacre at Wounded Knee. He laments, "for the nation's hoop is broken and scattered. There is no center any longer, and the sacred tree is dead." In the "contact zone" of the West, one person's opening of the frontier is another's closing of a cherished era.

In between the bookends of these two compelling accounts lay wonderfully interesting stories of miners, traders, newlyweds, explorers, and much, much more. Some are told in polished language meant to impress while others contain idiosyncratic diary spelling that gives us a hint of how the person actually pronounced his words such that the reader can almost hear the words spoken.

Thus, these eyewitness accounts let us "hear" the authentic voices that form the cacophony of American history in the western wilderness, for host Richard Scott introduces us to a variety of characters, each insistent on being heard, each bound by his or her own perspective. Scott has not censored their voices, their prejudices, or their fear. And yet there are moments when the cacophony moves to common understanding, in which some of the writers who encounter other cultures show genuine compassion and curiosity. For example, when Cabeza de Vaca departs from some of his Indian hosts who enslaved him, they cry. And writing in her diary while at Bent's Fort, Susan Magoffin ironically notes the "heathenish customs" that keep an Indian mother healthy while the coddled Susan lies abed sick.

In his Preface, Richard Scott describes the panorama of the Old West that he imagines. And in his book he gives us much more and shows us a more complicated and interesting West, indicating that there are *many* Wests and many perspectives. Scott is himself a great storyteller and he couldn't resist a good story about the West for this collection when he discovered it. You will find some of the voices entertaining, some irritating, some naive, but none tiresome. For those readers interested in digging up the books from which the eyewitness excerpts are taken Scott has generously left a bibliographic trail marker at the end of his collection.

Think of *Eyewitness to the Old West* as an invitation to a party of gregarious people who have had incredible experiences. I guarantee there are some you will be delighted to encounter and some you will want to get to know better.

Judy Nolte Temple
Tucson, Arizona

Judy Nolte Temple is a professor at the University of Arizona, and is editor of *Open Spaces, City Places; Contemporary Writers on the Changing Southwest* and author (under surname Lensink) of *'A Secret to be Buried:' The Diary and Life of Emily Hawley Gillespie, 1858–1888.*

Living among the Indians, c. 1531

Alvar Nuñez Cabeza de Vaca

A hapless trailblazer into the Old West, de Vaca was born into Spanish nobility about 1490. He became a soldier in his teens, serving the Spanish army in Italy. In 1527, he was appointed second-in-command of the Pánfilo de Narváez expedition to occupy the mainland of the New World. Because of this expedition, de Vaca became the first European to describe America, from Florida, Texas, Arizona, and northern Mexico. In March 1528 the expedition landed near what is now Tampa Bay. Initially welcomed by the Indians, the party overstayed their welcome and were violently attacked and expelled by their hosts. Trying to escape the Indians, the expedition survivors traveled north into what we now call the panhandle of Florida. There, in a bay of the Gulf of Mexico, they constructed crude rafts that they hoped to sail to Cuba, and their salvation. But, unable to control the raft's direction, they were grounded near present-day Galveston, Texas. Local Indians helped them initially, but after the natives began to die of a mysterious disease, they blamed the newcomers, and de Vaca and several surviving Spaniards headed west. By 1532, only de Vaca and two other members of the original expedition were still alive. They continued west in hopes of reaching the Spanish outposts in Mexico. In July, 1536, they finally made contact with a group of fellow Spaniards in northern Mexico and their ten-year odyssey was ended. In 1537 de Vaca returned to Spain and in 1542, de Vaca wrote an official report of his piteous adventures in the New World with the title, La Relación.

When the Indians saw us they clustered together, after having talked among themselves, and each one of them took the one of us whom he claimed by the hand and they led us to their homes. While with those we suffered more from hunger than among any of the others. In the course of a whole day we did not eat more than two handfuls of the fruit, which was green and contained so much milky juice that our mouths were burnt by it. As water was very scarce, whoever ate of them became very thirsty. And we finally grew so hungry that we purchased two dogs, in exchange for nets and other things, and a hide with which I used to cover myself. . . . Through all that country we went naked, and not being accustomed to it, like snakes we shed our skin twice a year. Exposure to the sun and air covered our chests and backs with big sores that made it very painful to carry the big and heavy loads, the ropes of which cut into the flesh of our arms.

The country is so rough and overgrown that often after we had gathered firewood in the timber and dragged it out, we would bleed freely from the thorns and spines which cut and slashed us wherever they touched. Sometimes it happened that I was unable to carry or drag out the firewood after I had gathered it with much loss of blood. In all that trouble my only relief or consolation was to remember the passion of our Savior, Jesus Christ, and the blood He shed for me, and to ponder how much greater His sufferings had been from the thorns, than those I was then enduring. I made a contract with the Indians to make combs, arrows, bows and nets for them. Also we made matting of which their lodges are constructed and of which they are in very great need, for, although they know how to make it, they do not like to do any work, in order to be able to go in quest of food. Whenever they work they suffer greatly from hunger.

Again, they would make me scrape skins and tan them, and the greatest luxury I enjoyed was on the day they would give me a skin to scrape, because I scraped it very deep in order to eat the parings, which would last me two or three days. It also happened to us, while being with these Indians and those before mentioned, that we would eat a piece of meat which they gave us, raw, because if we broiled it the first Indian coming along would snatch and eat it; it seemed useless to take any pains, in view of what we might expect; neither were we particular to go to any trouble in order to have it broiled and might just as well eat it raw. Such was the life we led there, and even that scanty maintenance we had to earn through the objects made by our own hands for barter.

After we had eaten the dogs it seemed to us that we had enough strength to go further on, so we commended ourselves to the guidance of God, Our Lord, took leave of these Indians, and they put us on the track of others of their language who were nearby. While on our way it began to rain and rained the whole day. We lost the trail and found ourselves in a big forest, where we gathered plenty of leaves of tunas which we roasted that same night in an oven made by ourselves, and so much meat did we give them that in the morning they were fit to be eaten. After eating them we recommended ourselves to God again, and left, and struck the trail we had lost.

Issuing from the timber, we met other Indian dwellings, where we saw two women and some boys, who were so frightened at the sight of us that they fled to the forest to call the men that were in the woods. When these came they hid behind trees to peep at us. We called them and they approached in great fear. After we addressed them they told us they were very hungry and that nearby were many of their own lodges, and they would take us to them. So that night we reached a site where there were fifty dwellings, and the people were stupefied at seeing us and showed much fear. After they had recovered from their astonishment they approached and put their hands to our faces and bodies also. We stayed there that night, and in the morning they brought their sick people, begging us to cross them, and gave us of what they had to eat, which were leaves of tunas and green tunas baked.

For the sake of this good treatment, giving us all they had, content with being without anything for our sake, we remained with them several days, and during that time others came from further on. When those were about to leave we told the first ones that we intended to accompany them. This made them very sad, and they begged us on their knees not to go. But we went and left them in tears at our departure, as it pained them greatly.

From: *The Journey of Alvar Nuñez Cabeza de Vaca*, translated by Fanny Bandelier (1905), and *Adventures in the Unknown Interior of America*, translated and edited by Cyclone Covey from the original 1542 edition and from later English translations (Albuquerque, NM: University of New Mexico Press, 1998)

Coronado Makes an Impression, c. December 1540

Pedro de Castañeda

About sixty-seven years before the English established their little colony in Jamestown, Spaniards led by Francisco Vásquez de Coronado marched north in a large loop beginning in the populous valley of Mexico and reconnoitering the unknown reaches of today's American Southwest in search of the elusive "Seven Cities of Gold." Conflicting statements put his force as between 250 to 300 horsemen, 70 to 200 footmen, and from 300 to 1000 Indian servants. The author of the following story was a common soldier of this expedition. This incident occurred in present-day New Mexico.

One who I will not name, out of regard for him, left the village where the camp was and went to another village about a league distant, and seeing a pretty woman there he called her husband down to hold his horse by the bridle while he went up; and as the village was entered by the upper story, the Indian supposed he was going to some other part of it. While he was there the Indian heard some slight noise, and then the Spaniard came down, took his horse, and went away. The Indian went up and learned that he had violated, or tried to violate, his wife, and so he came with the important men of the town to complain that a man had violated his wife, and he told how it had happened. When the general [Coronado] made all the soldiers and the persons who were with him come together, the Indian did not recognize the man, either because he had changed his clothes or for whatever other reason there may have been, but he said he could tell the horse, because he had held his bridle, and so he was taken to the stables, and found the horse, and said that the master of the horse must be the man. He denied doing it, seeing that he had been recognized, and it may be that the Indian was mistaken in the horse; anyway, he went off without getting any satisfaction. The next day one of the Indians, who was guarding the horses of the army, came running in, saying that a companion of his had been killed, and that the Indians of the country were driving off the horses toward their villages. The Spaniards tried to collect the horses again, but many were lost, besides seven of the general's mules.

The next day Don Garcia Lopez de Cardenas went to see the villages and talk with the natives. He found the villages closed by palisades and a great noise inside, the horses being chased as in a bull fight and shot with arrows. They were all ready for fighting. Nothing could be done, because they would not come down on to the plain and the villages are so strong that the Spaniards could not dislodge them. The general then ordered Don Garcia to go and surround one village with all the rest of the force. This village was the one where the greatest injury had been done and where the affair with the Indian woman occurred. Several captains who had gone on in advance with the general, Juan de Saldivar and Barrionuevo and Diego Lope and Melgosa, took the Indians so much by surprise that they gained the upper story, with great danger, for they wounded many of our men from within the houses. Our men were on top of the houses in great danger for a day and a night and part of the next day, and they made some good shots with their crossbows and muskets. The horsemen on the plain with many of the Indian allies from New Spain smoked them out from the cellars into which they had broken, so that they begged for peace.

Pablo de Melgosa and Diego Lopez, the alderman from Seville, were left on the roof and answered the Indians with the same signs they were making for peace, which was to make a cross. They then put down their arms and received pardon. They were taken to the tent of Don Garcia, who, according to what he said, did not know about the peace and thought that they had given themselves up of their own accord because they had been conquered. As he had been ordered by the general not to take them alive, but to make an example of them so that the other natives would fear the Spaniards, he ordered 200 stakes to be prepared at once to burn them alive. Nobody told him about the peace that had been granted them, for the soldiers knew as little as he, and those who should have told him about it remained silent, not thinking that it was any of their business. Then when the enemies saw that the Spaniards were binding them and beginning to roast them, about a hundred men who were in the tent began to struggle and defend themselves with what there was there and with the stakes they could seize. Our men who were on foot attacked the tent on all sides, so that there was great confusion around it, and then the horsemen chased those who escaped. As the country was level, not a man of them remained alive, unless it was some who remained hidden in the village and escaped that night to spread throughout the country the news that the strangers did not respect the peace they had made, which afterward proved a great misfortune. After this was over, it began to snow, and they abandoned the village and returned to the camp just as the army came from Cibola.

From: *The Journey of Coronado*, translated by George Parker Winship from earlier Spanish and English translations (New York: Dover Publications, Inc., 1990)

Explorers Draw Blood, July 27, 1806

Meriwether Lewis

In 1803 President Thomas Jefferson completed the Louisiana Purchase for $15 million. This added to the United States, the territory from west of the Mississippi River to the Rocky Mountains and the country in between the Mexican and Canadian borders. Mainly unexplored by white men, Jefferson commissioned his private secretary, Meriwether Lewis, to command an overland expedition to the newly-acquired lands. Lewis chose a military officer, William Clark, to share the command with him. Thus, the expedition became known as the Lewis and Clark journey of discovery and took place between 1804 and 1806. In the following story, Lewis had split off from the main party taking only nine men with him to look for a short-cut to the Missouri River. His small party met up with a few Blackfeet Indians with whom they shared a night camp. The next morning things took a turn for the worse as Lewis' diary indicates. Hopefully, the reader will not be too troubled by Lewis' difficulty with spelling, grammar, and punctuation. Overlooking these writing problems, the reader should be able to see the vivid pictures that Lewis' words describe.

This morning at daylight the indians got up and crouded around the fire, J. Fields who was on post had carelessly laid his gun down behi[n]d him near where his brother was sleeping, one of the indians the fellow to whom I had given the medal last evening sliped behind him and took his gun and that of this brother unperceived by him, at the same instant two others advanced and seized the guns of Drewyer and myself. J. Fields seeing this turned about to look for his gun and saw the fellow just runing off with her and his brother's he called to his brother who instantly jumped up and pursued the indian with whom they overtook at the distance of 50 or 60 paces from the camp s[e]ized their guns and rested them from him and R. Fields as he seized his gun stabed the indian to the heart with his knife the fellow ran about 15 steps and fell dead; of this I did not know untill afterwards, having recovered their guns they ran back instantly to the camp.

Drewyer who was awake saw the indian take hold of his gun and instantly jumped up and s[e]ized her and rested her from him but the indian still retained his pouch, his jumping up and crying damn you let go my gun awakened me I jumped up and asked what was the matter which I quickly learned when I saw drewyer in a scuffle with the indian for his gun. I reached to seize my gun but found her gone, I then drew a pistol from my holster and terning myself about saw the indian making off with my gun I ran at them with my pistol and bid him lay down my gun which he was in the act of doing when the Fieldses returned and drew up their guns to shoot him which I forbid as he did not appear to be about to make any resistance or commite any offensive act, he droped the gun and walked slowly off, I picked her up instantly, Drewyer having about this time recovered his gun and pouch asked me if he might no kill the fellow which I also forbid as the indian did not appear to wish to kill us, as soon as they found us all in possession of our arms they ran and indeavored to drive off all the horses I now hollowed to the men and told them to fire on them if they attempted to drive off our horses, but accordinly pursued the main party who were dr[i]ving the horses up the river and I pursued the man who had taken my gun who with another was driving off a part of the horses which were to the left of the camp. I pursued them so closely that they could not take twelve of their own horses but continued to drive mine with some others; at the distance of three hundred paces they entered one of those steep nitches in the bluff with the horses before them being nearly out of breath I could pursue no further, I called to them as I had done several times before that I would shoot them if they did not give me my horse and raised my gun, one of them jumped behind a rock and spoke to the other who turned arround and stoped at the distance of 30 steps from me and I shot him through the belly, he fell to his knees and on his wright elbow from which position he partly raised himself up and fired at me, and turning himself about crawled in behind a rock which was a few feet from him. He overshot me, being bearheaded I felt the wind of his bullet very distinctly.

Not having my shotpouch I could not reload my piece and as there were two of them behind good shelters from me I did not think it prudent to rush on them with my pistol which I had discharged I had not the means of reloading untill I reached camp; I therefore returned leasurly towards camp, on my way I met with Drewyer who having heared the report of the guns had returned in surch of me and left the Fieldes to pursue the indians, I desired him to haisten to the camp with me and assist in catching as many of the indian horses as were necessary and to call to the Fields if he could make them hear to come back that we still had a suffcent number of horses, this he did but they were too far to hear him. We reached the camp and began to catch the horses and saddle them and put on the packs. The reason I had not my pouch with me was that I had not time to return about 50 yards to camp after getting my gun before I was obliged to pursue the indians or suffer them to collect and drive off all the horses. We had caught and saddled the horses and began to arrange the packs when the Fieldses returned with four of our horses; we left one of our horses and took four of the best of those of the indian's; while the men were preparing the horses I put four sheilds and two bows and quivers of arrows which had been left on the fire, with sundry other articles; they left all their baggage at our mercy. They had but 2 guns and one of them they left The others were armed with bows and arrows and eyedaggs. The gun we took with us. I also retook the flagg but left the medal about the neck of the dead man that they might be informed who we were. We took some of their buffaloe meat and set out ascending the bluffs by the same rout we had decended last evening leaving the ballance of nine of their horses which we did not want.

The Fieldses told me that three of the indians whom they pursued swam the river one of them on my horse, and that two others ascended the hill and escaped from them with a part of their horses, two I had pursued into the nitch one lay dead near the camp and the eighth we could not account for but suppose that he ran off early in the contest. Having ascended the hill we took our course through a beatifull level plain a little to the S. of East. My design was to hasten to the entrance of Maria's river as quick as possible in the hope of meeting with the canoes and party at that place having no doubt but that they [the Indians] would pursue us with a large party and as there was a band near the broken mountains or probably between them and the mouth of that river we might expect them to receive inteligence from us and arrive at that place nearly as soon as we could, no time was therefore to be lost and we pushed our horses as hard as they would bear. At 8 miles we passed a large branch 40 yds. wide which I called battle river. At 3 P.M. we arrived at rose river about 5 miles above where we had passed it as we went out, having traveled by my estimate compared with our former distances and cou[r]ses about 63 ms. here we halted an hour and a half took some refreshment and suffered our horses to graize; the day proved warm but the late rains had supplied the little reservors in the plains with water and had put them in fine order for traveling, Our whole rout so far was as level as a bowling green with but little stone and few prickly pears.

After dinner we pursued the bottoms of rose river but finding [it] inconvenient to pass the river so often we again ascended the hills on the S. W. side and took the open plains; by dark we had traveled about

17 miles further, We now halted to rest ourselves and horses about 2
hours, we killed a buffaloe cow and took a small quantity of the meat, after refreshing ourselves we again set out by moonlight and traveled lea-
surely, heaving thunderclouds lowered around us on every quarter but
that from which the moon gave us light. We continued to pass immence
herds of buffaloe all night as we had done in the latter part of the day. We
traveled until 2 oCk in the morning having come by my estimate after
dark about 20 ms. we now turned out our horses and laid ourselves down
to rest in the plain very much fatiegued as may be readily conceived. My
indian horse carried me very well in short much better than my own
would have done and leaves me with but little reason to complain of the
robery.

From: *Original Journals of the Lewis and Clark Expedition*, edited by Reuben Gold
Thwaites (New York: Dodd, Mead & Company, 1904)

The Pawnees Choose a Flag, September 29, 1806

Zebulon Pike

Born in New Jersey in 1779, Pike led exploration parties to the headwaters of the Mississippi, Arkansas, and Red Rivers and explored new areas of the Southwest. In 1806 Pike was assigned to examine the Spanish territory in what is now New Mexico. Pike set up camp near present-day Pueblo, Colorado. From there, he led his party into the Rocky Mountains. At the Front Range of the Rockies, he discovered the peak now known as Pikes Peak. He tried to climb the mountain but was unsuccessful. Pike served in the War of 1812, attaining the rank of brigadier general. He was killed in battle in an attack on York (now Toronto), Ontario, in 1813. The following narrative was taken from his journals of his exploration of the Southwest.

Held our grand council with the Pawnees, at which were present not less than 400 warriors, the circumstances of which were extremely interesting. The notes I took on my grand council held with the Pawnee nation were seized by the Spanish government, together with all my speeches to the different nations. But it may be interesting to observe here (in case they should never be returned) that the Spaniards had left several of their flags in this village; one of which was unfurled at the chief's door the day of the grand council, and that amongst various *demands* and *charges* I gave them, was, that the said flag should be delivered to me, and one of the United States' flags be received and hoisted in its place. This probably was carrying the pride of nations a little too far, as there had so lately been a large force of Spanish cavalry at the village, which had made a great impression on the minds of the young men, as to their power, consequence, &c. which my appearance with 20 infantry was by no means calculated to remove. After the chiefs had replied to various parts of my discourse, but were silent as to the flag, I again reiterated the demand for the flag, adding that "it was impossible for the nation to have two fathers; that they must either be the children of the Spaniards or acknowledge their American father." After a silence of some time, an old man rose, went to the door, and took down the Spanish flag, and brought it and laid it at my feet, and then received the American flag and elevated it on the staff, which had lately borne the standard of his Catholic majesty. This gave great satisfaction to the Osage and Kans, both of whom, decidedly avow themselves to be under the American protection. Perceiving that every face in the council was clouded with sorrow, as if some great national calamity was about to befall them, I took up the contested colors, and told them that as they had now shewn themselves dutiful children in acknowledging their great American father, I did not wish to embarrass them with the Spaniards, for it was the wish of the Americans that their red brethren should remain peaceably round their own fires, and not embroil themselves in any disputes between the white people: and that for fear the Spaniards might return there in force again, I returned them their flag, but with an injunction that it should never be hoisted during our stay. At this there was a general shout of applause and the charge particularly attended to.

Living Off of Paradise, c. April 1810

Thomas James

Born in Maryland in 1782, Thomas James' family moved west—first to Kentucky and then to southern Illinois. Then, Thomas and his brother and father acquired a piece of land near St. Louis. They were living there when Lewis and Clark returned through St. Louis after their exploration to the Pacific Ocean. Their return triggered a rush of traders and trappers into the Upper Missouri country. Thomas joined the nearly-formed St. Louis Missouri Fur Company and signed a three-year contract to assist in transporting, trapping, hunting, and collecting meats and furs. Later in life he was elected General of the Second Brigade, First Division, Illinois Militia and was also elected to serve in the Illinois state legislature. The year before his death, Three Years among the Indians and Mexicans, *was published. Thomas died in 1847. In the following narrative, Thomas describes the beauty of the Upper Missouri River as he saw it in the spring of 1810.*

We arrived at the Forks of the Missouri on the third day of April, 1810, ten months after leaving St. Louis and two months and one day after quitting my cabin above the Gros Ventre village. We had now reached our place of business, trapping for beaver, and prepared to set to work. Dougherty, Brown, Ware and myself agreed to trap in company on the Missouri between the Forks and the Falls, which lie several hundred miles down the river to the north, from the Forks. We made two canoes by hollowing out the trunks of two trees and on the third or fourth day after or arrival at the Forks we were ready to start on an expedition down the river. The rest of the Americans with a few French, in all eighteen in number, determined to go up the Jefferson river for trapping and the rest of the company under Col. Menard remained to complete the Fort and trading house at the Forks between the Jefferson and Madison rivers. On parting from Cheek, he said in a melancholy tone, "James you are going down the Missouri, and it is the general opinion that you will be killed. The Black-feet are at the falls, encamped I hear, and we fear you will never come back. But I am afraid for myself as well as you. I know not the cause, but I have felt fear ever since I came to the Forks, and I never was afraid of anything before. You may come out safe, and I may be killed. Then you will say, there was Cheek afraid to go with us down the river for fear of death, and now he has found his grave by going up the river. I may be dead when you return."

His words made little impression on me at the time, but his tragical end a few days afterwards recalled them to my mind and stamped them on my memory forever. I endeavored to persuade him to join our party, while he was equally urgent for me to join his, saying that if we went in one company our force would afford more protection from Indians, than in small parties, while I contended that the fewer our numbers the better would be our chance of concealment and escape from any war parties that might be traversing the country.

We parted never to meet again, taking opposite directions and both of us going into the midst of dangers. My company of four started down the river and caught some beaver on the first day. On the second we passed a very high spur of the mountain on our right. The mountains in sight on our left, were not so high as those to the east of us.

On the third day we issued from very high and desolate mountains on both sides of us, whose tops are covered with snow throughout the year, and came upon a scene of beauty and magnificence combined, unequaled by any other view of nature that I ever beheld. It really realized all my conception of the Garden of Eden. In the west the peaks and pinnacles of the Rocky Mountains shone resplendent in the sun. The snow on their tops sent back a beautiful reflection of the rays of the morning sun. From the sides of the dividing ridge between the waters of the Missouri and Co-lumbia, there sloped gradually down to the bank of the river we were on, a plain, then covered with every variety of wild animals peculiar to this region, while on the east another plain arose by a very gradual ascent, and extended as far as the eye could reach. These and the mountain sides were dark with Buffalo, Elk, Deer, Moose, wild Goats and wild Sheep; some grazing, some lying down under the trees and all enjoying a perfect mil-lennium of peace and quiet. On the margin the swan, geese, and pelicans, cropped the grass or floated on the surface of the water. The cotton wood trees seemed to have been placed by the hand of man on the bank of the river to shade our way, and the pines and cedars waved their tall, majes-tic heads along the base and on the sides of the mountains. The whole landscape was that of the most splendid English park. The stillness, beauty and loveliness of this scene, struck us all with indescribable emotions. We rested on the oars and enjoyed the whole view in silent astonishment and admiration. Nature seemed to have rested here, after creating the wild mountains and chasms among which we had voyaged for two days. Dougherty, as if inspired by the scene with the spirit of poetry and song, broke forth in one of Burns' noblest lyrics, which found a deep echo in our hearts. We floated on till evening through this most delightful country, when we stopped and prepared supper on the bank of the river.

We set our traps and before going to rest for the night, we examined them and found a beaver in every one, being twenty-three in all. In the evening we were nearly as successful as before and were cheered with thoughts of making a speedy fortune.

From: *Three Years among the Indians and Mexicans* (St. Louis: Missouri Historical Society, 1916)

Encounter with Indians, May 10, 1810

John Bradbury

Scotsman John Bradbury and Englishman Thomas Nuttall were the two earliest professional botanists to explore the Missouri River floodplain. Working independently of one another, Bradbury and Nuttall met up in early-1810 in St. Louis. There, they got permission to travel with a party of trappers and traders of John Jacob Astor's American Fur Company who were headed for Oregon territory. Although they covered much of the same landscape and saw much of the same flora, the two made independent collections. Because Bradbury was delayed by the War of 1812, Nuttall was able to return to England much sooner. Thus, Nuttall's botanical research was published before Bradbury's, and Nuttall became Britain's most celebrated botanist of his day. Bradbury, however, had a very unique experience which became a part of American geologic history. On December 15, 1811, Bradbury was heading down the Mississippi River with a party of boatmen. They had tied up for the night just upstream from Chickasaw Bluffs (now the site of the city of Memphis, Tennessee) and Bradbury was fast asleep when "a most tremendous noise" woke him and his companions. "All nature seemed running into chaos," he later wrote, "as wild fowl fled, trees snapped and river banks tumbled into the water." What Bradbury experienced is now called the New Madrid Earthquake. Bradbury was closer to the epicenter than almost anyone. He recorded a total of twenty-seven aftershocks. Aside from his interest in botany and geology, Bradbury also was keen to observe the native people that he encountered during his journey. In the following vignette, Bradbury describes his first face-to-face encounter with native inhabitants of the Missouri River region.

When on the bluffs yesterday, I observed in the river an extensive bend, and determined to travel across the neck. I therefore did not embark with the boats, but filled my shot pouch with parched corn, and set out, but not without being reminded that we were now in an enemy's country. In about two hours I had entirely passed the range of hills forming the boundary of the Missouri; and as I had before experienced, I found the soil and face of the country to improve very much as we proceed from the river. The hills here are only gentle swellings, and, together with the intervening valleys, were covered with the most beautiful verdure.

I [travelled] through this charming country till near the middle of the afternoon, when I again came to the bluffs of the Missouri, where, amongst a number of new plants, I found a fine species of currant. As it was now time to look for the boats, I went to the river and proceeded down the bank, in the expectation of meeting them. I had probably travelled about two miles, when suddenly I felt a hand laid upon my shoulder, and turning round, saw a naked Indian with his bow bent, and the arrow pointed towards me. As I had no expectation of meeting any Indians excepting the Sioux, and as with them the idea of danger was associated, I took my gun from my shoulder, and by a kind of spontaneous movement put my hand towards the lock, when I perceived that the Indian drew his bow still farther. I now found myself completely in his power; but recollecting that if an enemy, he would have shot me before I saw him, I held out my hand, which he took, and afterwards laid his hand on my breast, and in the Osage language said *"Moi-he ton-ga de-ah,"* literally in English, "Big Knife you?" which I luckily understood and answered, *"Hoya,"* (Yes) and laying my hand on his breast, said, *"Nodo-wessie de-ah,"* (Sioux you?)" He replied, *"Honkoska ponca we ah"* (No, Poncar me.) He then pointed up the river, and I saw two other Indians running towards us, and not more than fifty yards distant. They soon came up, and all three laid hold of me, pointing over the bluffs, and making signs that I should go with them. I resisted and pushed off their hands. As the river had overflowed where we stood, I pointed to a sand-hill a small distance from us, to which we went and sat down. I amused them with my pocket compass for some time, when they again seized me, and I still resisted, and took out a small microscope. This amused them for some time longer, when on a sudden one of them leaped up and gave the war whoop. I laid hold of my gun, with an intention to defend myself, but was instantly relieved from apprehension by his pointing down the river, and I perceived the mast of one of the boats appear over the willows. The Indians seemed very much inclined to run away, but I invited them to accompany me to the boats, and shewed them by signs that I would give them something to drink, which they complied with, but soon after disappeared.

From: *Travels in the Interior of America in the Years 1809, 1810, and 1811* (London: Sherwood, Neely, and Jones, Publishers, 1819)

Rambling through an Indian Village, June 13, 1811

Henry Marie Brackenridge

Born in Pittsburgh, Henry Marie Brackenridge (1786–1871) moved to St. Louis after he was admitted to the Pennsylvania bar. In St. Louis he practiced law and also became a journalist of sorts. In 1811 Brackenridge accompanied a party of trappers contracted to the Missouri Fur Company up the Missouri River. Brackenridge's journal of these adventures were published in a book called Views of Louisiana, Together with a Journal of a Voyage up the Missouri River. *The following journal entry was extracted from that book and paints a vivid word picture of everyday life in an Indian village.*

This morning, found ourselves completely drenched by heavy rains, which continued the whole night. The Indian women and girls, were occupied all this morning, in carrying earth in baskets, to replace that which the rains had washed off their lodges. Rambled through the village, which I found excessively filthy, the "villainous smells," which everywhere assailed me, compelled me at length, to seek refuge in the open plain. The lovers of Indian manners, and mode of living, should contemplate them at a distance. The rains had rendered their village little better than a hog pen; [with cleaning people] extremely negligent.

Some of the ancient cities of the old world, were probably like this village, inattentive to that cleanliness so necessary to health, where a great mass of beings are collected in one place; and we need not be surprised at the frequency of desolating plagues and pestilence.

The village is swarming with dogs and children. I rank these together, for they are inseparable companions. Wherever I went, the children ran away, screaming, and frightened at my outre and savage appearance. Let us not flatter ourselves with the belief, that the effect of our civilization and refinement, is to render us agreeable and lovely to the eyes of those whom we exclusively denominate! The dogs, of which every family has thirty or forty, pretended to make a show of fierceness, but on the least threat, ran off. They are of different sizes and colors. A number are fattened on purpose to eat, others are used to draw their baggage. It is nothing more than the domesticated wolf. In wandering through the prairies, I have often mistaken wolves for Indian dogs. The larger kind has long curly hair and resembles the shepherd dog. There is the same diversity amongst the wolves of this country. They may be more properly said to howl than bark. . . .

I entered several lodges, the people of which received us with kindness, placed mats and skins for us to sit on, and after smoking the pipe, offered us something to eat; this consisted of fresh buffalo meat served in a wooden dish. They had a variety of earthen vessels, in which they prepared their food, or kept water. After the meat, they offered us hominy made of corn dried in milk, mixed with beans, which was prepared with buffalo marrow, and tasted extremely well. . . . The prairie turnip, is a root very common in the prairies, with something of the taste of the turnip but more dry; this they eat dried and pounded, made into gruel.

In one of the lodges which I visited, I found the doctor, who was preparing some medicine for a sick lad. He was cooling with a spoon a concoction of some roots, which had a strong taste and smell. He showed us a variety of samples which he used. The most of them were common plants with some medicinal properties, but rather harmless than otherwise. The boy had a slight pleurisy. The chief remedy for their diseases, which they contrive to be owing to a disorder of the bowels, is rubbing the belly and sides of the patient, sometimes with such violence, as to cause fainting. When they become dangerous, they resort to charms and incantations, such as singing, dancing, blowing on the sick, &c. They are very successful in the treatment of wounds. When the wound becomes very obstinate, they commonly burn it, after which it heals more easily.

From: *Views of Louisiana, Together with a Journal of a Voyage up the Missouri River, in 1811* (Pittsburgh, PA: Cramer, Spear and Eichbaum, Publishers, 1814)

"I Heard My Skull Brake," November 13, 1821

Jacob Fowler

In the late-1890s, Colonel R. T. Durrett of Louisville, Kentucky, stated that he had obtained Jacob Fowler's (1765–1850) journal from the great-granddaughter on Fowler's maternal side, Mrs. Ida Symmes Coates. Mrs. Coates told Colonel Durrett that although Fowler was an educated man, "he wrote a very bad hand." In 1897 Colonel Durrett sent Fowler's journal to Dr. Elliott Coues to edit and to see if it could be published. The manuscript sent to Dr. Coues was titled, "memorandom of the voige by land from fort Smith to the Rockey mountains." Because of Fowler's "very bad hand," Dr. Coues found the manuscript very difficult to decipher, both in the syntax it employs as well as its spelling and punctuation. Although a major undertaking, Dr. Coues called it deciphering "hieroglyphics," he overcame the challenge and brought Fowler's adventures to light. Hopefully, readers will also overcome the syntax and grammatical errors and read Fowler's narrative for the vividness and energy that flows from it.

We stoped Heare [on the Purgatory River, near to present-day Fort Lyon, Colorado] about one oclock and Sent back for one Hors that Was not able to keep up—We Heare found some grapes among the brush—While Some Ware Hunting and others Cooking Some Picking grapes a gun Was fyered off and the Cry of a White Bare [grizzly bear or 'silvertip'] Was Raised We Ware all armed in an Instent and Each man Run His own Cors to look for the desperet anemel—the Brush in Which We Camped Contained from 10 to 20 acors Into Which the Bare Head [bear had] Run for Shilter find[ing] Him Self Surrounded on all Sides—threw this Conl glann With four others atemted to Run But the Bare being In their Way and lay Close in the brush undiscovered till the Ware With in a few feet of it—When it Sprung up and Caught Lewis doson [Dawson] and Pulled Him down In an Instent Conl glanns gun mised fyer or He Wold Have Releved the man But a large Slut Which belongs to the Party atacted the Bare With such fury that it left the man and persued Her a few steps in Which time the man got up and Run a few steps but Was overtaken by the bare When the Conl maid a second atempt to shoot but His [gun] mised fyer again and the Slut as before Releved the man Who Run as before—but Was Son again in the grasp of the Bare Who Semed Intent on His distruction—the Conl again Run Close up and as before His gun Wold not go off the Slut makeing an other atack and Releveing the man—the Conl now be Came alarmed lest the Bare Wold pusue Him and Run up Stooping tree—and after Him the Wounded man and Was followed by the Bare and thus the Ware all three up on tree—but a tree standing in Rich [reach] the Conl steped on that and let the man and Bare pas till the Bare Caught Him [Dawson] by one leg and drew Him back wards down the tree. While this Was doing the Conl Sharpened His flint Primed His gun and Shot the Bare down While pulling the man by the leg be fore any of the party arived to Releve Him—but the Bare Soon Rose again but Was Shot by several other [men] Wo Head [who had] got up to the place of action—it Is to be Remarked that the other three men With Him Run off— and the Brush Was so thick that those on the out Side Ware Som time geting threw—

I Was my Self down the Crick below the brush and Heard the dredfull Screems of man in the Clutches of the Bare—the yelping of the Slut and the Hollowing of the men to Run in Run in the man Will be killed and noing the distance So grate that I Cold not get there in time to Save the man So that it Is much Easeer to Emagen my feellings than discribe them but before I got to the place of action the Bare Was killed and [I] met the Wounded man with Robert Fowler and one or two more asisting Him to Camp Where His Wounds Ware Examined—it appeers His Head Was In the Bares mouth at least twice—and that When the monster give the Crush that Was to mash the mans Head it being two large for the Span of His mouth the Head Sliped out only the teetch Cutting the Skin to the bone Where Ever the tuched it—so that the Skin of the Head Was Cut from about the Ears to the top in Several derections—all of Which Wounds Ware Sewed up as Well as Cold be don by men In our Situation Haveing no Surgen nor Surgical Instruments—the man Still Retained His under Standing but Said I am killed that I Heard my Skull Brake—but We Ware Willing to beleve He Was mistaken—as He Spoke Chearfully on the Subgect till In the after noon of the second day When He began to be Restless and Some What delereous—and on examening a Hole in the upper part of his Wright temple Which We believed only Skin deep We found the Brains Workeing out—We then Soposed that He did Heare His Scull

Brake He lived till a little before day on the third day after being Wounded—all Which time We lay at Camp and Buried Him as Well as our meens Wold admit Emedetely after the fattal axcident and Haveing done all We Cold for the Wounded man We turned out atention [to] the Bare and found Him a large fatt anemel We Skined Him but found the Smell of a polcat so Strong that We Cold not Eat the meat—on examening His mouth We found that three of His teeth Ware broken off near the gums Which We Sopose Was the Caus of His not killing the man at the first Bite—and the one not Broke to be the Caus of the Hole in the Right [temple] Which killed the man at last—the Hunters killed two deer Cased the Skins for Baggs We dryed out the Bares oil and Caryed it with us the Skin Was all so taken Care of—

Fur Trappers in the Western Wilderness

An Artist's Description of a Sioux Home, c. Summer 1832

George Catlin

Born in 1796 in Pennsylvania, Catlin's parents wanted him to study law. After passing his bar examinations, Catlin practiced law. But art had always been a main interest and having taught himself how to draw and paint, Catlin gave up the practice of law and opened a portrait studio. Catlin met a group of Indians passing through Philadelphia to visit President Andrew Jackson. Then, his life's goal became clear to him: to become the Indians' artist-historian. In 1830 he traveled West in the company of William Clark of Lewis and Clark fame. In 1832 Catlin traveled to the Upper Missouri painting Indian scenes and portraits. After returning to the eastern states, Catlin opened a gallery and tried to sell his works. Catlin was unable to make enough money to support his family so he left the United States and opened a gallery in London. After years of ups and downs, Catlin died penniless in New Jersey in 1872. In the following narrative Catlin's artistic eye captures the essence of the Sioux at home.

There is no tribe better clad, who live in better houses (wigwams), or who are better mounted, than the Sioux. They catch an abundance of wild horses, which are grazing on the prairies, oftentimes in groups of several hundreds, and from their horses' backs, at full speed, they deal their deadly arrows, or wield their long and fatal lances in the chase of the buffaloes, and also in war with their enemies.

These people, living mostly in a country of prairies (meadows), where they easily procure the buffalo skins, construct their wigwams with them, in form of tents, which are more comfortable than rude huts constructed of timber, are more easily built, and have the advantage of being easily transported over the prairies; by which means the Indians are enabled to follow the migrating herds of buffaloes during the summer and fall seasons, when they are busily engaged in drying meat for their winter's consumption, and dressing robes for their own clothing, and also for barter to the fur traders.

From [my] view . . . of a Sioux village, on the Upper Missouri, my little readers will get a very correct notion of the manner in which these curious people live. There were in this village about four hundred skin tents, all built much in the same manner: some fifteen or twenty pine poles forming the frame, covered with one entire piece of fifteen or twenty buffalo-skins sewed together, and most curiously painted and embroidered, of all colours; presenting one of the most curious and beautiful scenes imaginable.

Inside of these tents, the fire is placed in the centre, the smoke escaping out at the top; and at night the inmates all sleep on buffalo-skins spread upon the ground, with their feet to the fire; a most safe, and not uncomfortable mode. When you enter one of these wigwams you have to stoop rather awkwardly; but when you are in, you rise up and find a lofty space of some twenty feet above your head. The family are all seated, and no one rises to salute you, whatever your office or your importance may be. All lower their eyes to your feet, instead of staring you in the face, and you are asked to sit down.

A robe or a mat of rushes is spread for you, and as they have no chairs you are at once embarrassed. It is an awkward thing for a white man to sit down upon the ground until he gets used to it, and when he is down, he don't know what to do with his legs.

The Indians, accustomed to this from childhood, sit down upon, and rise from, the ground with the same ease and grace that we sit down in, and rise from, a chair. Both men and women lower themselves to the ground, and rise, without a hitch or a jerk, and without touching their hand to the ground. This is very curious, but it is exceedingly graceful and neat. The men generally sit cross-legged; and to sit down they cross their feet, closely locked together, and extending their arms and head forward, slowly and regularly lower their bodies quite to the sitting posture on the ground: when they rise they place their feet in the same position, and their arms and head also, and rise to a perfectly straight position, apparently without an effort.

The women always sit with both feet and lower legs turned under and to the right or the left, and, like the men, lower and raise themselves without touching the ground.

When you are seated, to feel at ease your legs must be crossed, and your heels drawn quite close under you, and then you can take the pipe when it is handed to you, and get a fair and deliberate glance at things around you.

The furniture in these wigwams is not much, but it is very curious in effect, and picturesque, when we look at it. The first startling thing you will meet on entering will be half-a-dozen saucy dogs, barking, and bristling, and showing their teeth, and oftentimes as many screaming children, frightened at your savage and strange appearance.

These hushed, you can take a look at other things, and you see shields, and quivers, and lances, and saddles, and medicine bags, and pouches, and spears, and cradles, and buffalo masques (which each man keeps for dancing the buffalo dance), and a great variety of other picturesque things hanging around, suspended from the poles of the tent, to which they are fastened by thongs; the whole presenting, with the picturesque group around the fire, one of the most curious scenes imaginable.

In front of these wigwams the women are seen busily at work, dressing robes and drying meat. The skin-dressing of the Indians, both of the buffalo and deer-skins, is generally very beautiful and soft. Their mode of doing this is curious: they stretch the skin either on a frame or on the ground, and after it has remained some three or four days with the brains of the buffalo or elk spread over the fleshy side, they grain it with a sort of adze or chisel, made of a piece of buffalo bone.

Men are seen coming in from the hunt, with their horses loaded with meat and skins, to keep the poor women at work. It is proverbial in the civilized world that "the poor Indian woman has to do all the hard work." Don't believe this, for it is not exactly so. She labours very hard and constantly, it is true. She does most of the drudgery about the village and wigwam, and is seen transporting heavy loads, etc. This all looks to the passer-by as the slavish compulsion of her cruel husband, who is often seen lying at his ease, and smoking his pipe, as he is looking on.

His labors are not seen, and therefore are less thought of, when he mounts his horse, with his weapons in hand, and working every nerve and every muscle, dashes amongst the herds in the chase, to provide food for his wife and his little children, and scours the country both night and day, at the constant risk of his life, to protect them from the assaults of their enemies.

We see the Indian women in the full enjoyment of their domestic happiness, with their little children and dogs around them, the villagers dressed in their ordinary costumes, and the little cupids taking their first lessons in archery, which is the most important feature in their education. This happens to be "scalp-day;" from which are suspended the scalps which have been taken, which is the signal for all the warriors to do the same; so that the chief and every person in the village can count them, and understand each warrior's standing and claims to promotion, which are estimated by the number of scalps he has taken.

How curious it is that these ingenious people, who have invented so many ways of constructing their dwellings, never yet have adopted the mode of building with stone. This is probably not the result of ignorance or want of invention, but from their universal policy of leaving no monuments. All the American tribes are more or less migratory; and when they move, they destroy all their marks, by burning their wigwams, if they cannot take them with them, and smoothing over the graves of their parents and children.

From: *Life among the Indians* (London: Gall & Inglis, Publishers, 1875)

"Creasing" a Wild Horse, c. 1832

John B. Wyeth

John B. Wyeth went on a westward adventure in 1832 with his cousin, Nathaniel J. Wyeth. After a number of misadventures, the party made it to Rendezvous that summer. There, John Wyeth and about half of the party quit the expedition and returned to Boston. Shortly after his return, John published a book relating his thoughts about the expedition in general and his negative opinion of trying to settle Oregon in particular. In his book, Wyeth relates an unusal approach for capturing wild horses—creasing the neck with a bullet—which is repeated here. It is interesting to note that Wyeth does not say what happens to the horse when the marksman misses his mark.

The wild horses are a great curiosity. They traverse the country, and stroll about in droves from a dozen to twenty or thirty; and always appear to have a leader, like a gander to a flock of geese. When our own horses are fettered around our encampments, the wild horse would come down to them, and seem to examine them, as if counting them; and would sometimes come quite up to them if we kept out of sight; but when they discovered us they would one and all give a jump off and fly like the wind.

There is a method of catching a wild horse, that may appear to many "a traveller's story." It is called *creasing* a horse. The meaning of the term is unknown to me. It consists in shooting a horse in the neck with a single ball so as to graze his neck bone, and not to cut the pith of it. This stuns the horse and he falls to the ground, but he recovers again, and is as well as ever, all but a little soreness in the neck, which soon gets well. But in his short state of stupefaction, the hunter runs up, and twists a noose around the skin of his nose, and then secures him with thong of buffalo-hide. I do not give it merely as a story related; but I believe it, however improbable it may appear, because I saw it done. I saw an admirable marksman, young Andrew Sublet, fire at a fine horse, and after he fell, treat him in the way I have mentioned; and he brought the horse into camp, and it turned out to be a very fine one. The marvel of the story is, that the dextrous marksman shall shoot so precisely as only to graze the vital part; and yet those who know these matters better than I do, say, that they conceive it possible.

From: *Oregon, or A Short History of a Long Journey from the Atlantic Ocean to the Region of the Pacific by Land, drawn up from the Notges and Oral Information of John B. Wyeth, One of the Party who left Mr. Nathaniel J. Wyeth, July 28th 1832, Four Days March Beyond the Ridge of the Rocky Mountains and the Only One Who Has Returned to New England* (Cambridge, MA, 1833)

The Effect of a Meteor Shower on the Crows, c. October 1832

James P. Beckwourth

Little is known about Beckwourth's early life, but it is probable that he was a person of mixed blood, the son of a Virginia planter and a female slave. In 1823, young Beckwourth joined a Rocky Mountain Fur Company trapping expedition to the West, headed by General William Henry Ashley. The experiences noted by Beckwourth in his 1856 published work, The Life and Adventures of James P. Beckwourth, *have been strongly criticized by some of his contemporaries. For example, Francis Parkman (author of* The Oregon Trail*), Hiram M. Chittenden (author of* The American Fur Trade of the Far West*), and Charles Godfrey Leland (editor of an 1892 "Adventure Series"), speculate that Beckwourth was a liar, especially in his claim that he spent thirty years as the titular head of the Crow nation. More recent researchers believe that Beckwourth can be reliable except when it comes to "numbers, romance, and personal grandeur." The following narrative does not fall into one of these areas, so it seems "safe" to conclude that the events of, and following, the meteor storm, actually transpired. But, who's to know? It makes a good story.*

On our way to Little Box Elder we observed a remarkable meteoric shower, which filled us all (more particularly my followers) with wonder and admiration. Although my warriors were ready to face death in any form, this singular phenomenon appalled them. It was the wrath of the Great Spirit showered visibly upon them, and they looked to me, in quality of medicine chief, to interpret the wonder. I was as much struck with the prodigious occurrence, and was equally at a loss with my untutored followers to account for the spectacle. Evidently I must augur some result therefrom, and my dejected spirits did not prompt me to deduce a

30

very encouraging one. I thought of all the impostures that are practiced upon the credulous, and my imagination suggested some brilliant figures to my mind. I thought of declaring to them that the Great Spirit was pleased with our expedition, and was lighting us on our way with spirit lamps; or that these meteors were the spirits of our departed braves, coming to assist us in our forthcoming fight. But I was not sanguine enough to indulge in any attractive oratory. I merely informed them I had not time to consult my medicine, but that on our return to the village I would interpret the miracle to them in full.

On our arrival, I found the people's minds still agitated with the prodigy. All were speaking of it in wonder and amazement, and my opinion was demanded respecting the consequences it portended. Admonished by my defeat, I had no trouble in reading the stars. I informed them that our people had evidently offended the Great Spirit; that it was because of his wrath I had suffered defeat in my excursion, and returned with the loss of twenty-three warriors. I thence inferred that a sacrifice must be made to appease the wrath of the Great Spirit, and recommended that a solemn assembly be convened, and a national oblation offered up.

I was fully confident that by thus countenancing such pagan superstitions I was doing very wrong, but, like many a more prominent statesman in civilized governments, I had found that I must go with the current, and I recommended a measure, not because it was of a nature to benefit the country, but simply because it was popular with the mass.

The camp in which we then were was a mourning-camp, in which medicine would have no effect. Therefore we moved to Sulphur River, ten miles distant, in order to offer up our sacrifice. All the leading men and braves assembled, and I was consulted as to the kind of offering proper to make for the purpose of averting the wrath that was consuming us. I ordered them to bring the great medicine kettle, which was of brass, and capable of holding ten gallons, and was purchased at a cost of twenty fine robes, and to polish it as bright as the sun's face. This done, I ordered them to throw in all their most costly and most highly-prized trinkets, and whatsoever they cherished the most dearly. It was soon filled with their choicest treasures. Keepsakes, fancy work on which months of incessant and patient toil had been expended, trinkets, jewels, rings to highly prized by them that the costliest gems of emperors seemed poor by their side—all these were thrown into the kettle, along with a bountiful contribution of fingers, until it would hold no more. I then had weights attached to it, and had it carried to an air-hole in the ice where the river was very deep, and there it was sunk with becoming ceremony. Three young maidens, habited like May queens, carried the burden.

This great sacrifice completed, the minds of the people were relieved, and the result of the next war-party was anxiously looked forward to see if our oblation was accepted. Their crying, however, continued unabated, so much to the derangement of my nervous system that I was fain to retire from the village and seek some less dolorous companionship.

From: *The Life and Adventures of James P. Beckwourth, Mountaineer, Scout, and Pioneer, and Chief of the Crow Nation Indians*, as dictated to T. D. Bonner (New York: Harper and Brothers, 1856)

James Beckwourth—Black Mountain Man

Suffering in a "Desolate Wilderness," c. February 1833

Zenas Leonard

Born in Pennsylvania in 1809, Leonard left his parent's home in 1830 to work in Pittsburgh for a year. From there, in 1831, Leonard joined an expedition across the Rocky Mountains to Spanish California. After not having heard from him in 5 years, his parents lamented him dead, but were happily awe-struck when he returned to Pennsylvania in the autumn of 1835. Finding his adventures very interesting, Leonard had his stories published in book form in 1839. Later in life, Leonard operated a boat between St. Louis and western Missouri, carrying merchandise up-river and furs down stream. He died in 1858. In the narrative that follows, Leonard recounts tough times in the Rocky Mountains.

Here we are, in a desolate wilderness, uninhabited (at this season of the year) by even the hardy savage or wild beast–surrounded on either side by huge mountains of snow, without one mouthful to eat, save a few beaver skins—our eyes almost destroyed by the piercing wind, and our bodies at times almost buried by the flakes of snow which were driving before it. Oh! how heartily I wished myself at home; but wishing, in such a case appeared useless—action alone could save us. We had not even leather to make snow shoes, but as good fortune would have it, some of the men had the front part of their pantaloons lined with deer skin, and others had great coats of different kinds of skin, which we collected together to make snow shoes of. This appeared to present to us the only means of escape from starvation and death. After gathering up every thing of leather kind that could be found, we got to making snow shoes, and by morning each man was furnished with a pair. But what were we to subsist upon while crossing the mountain, was a painful question that agitated every bosom, and employed every tongue in company. Provision, we had none, of any description; having eaten every thing we had that could be eat with the exception of a few beaver skins, and, after having fasted several days, to attempt to travel the distance of the valley, without any thing to eat, appeared almost worse than useless. Thinking, however, that we might as well perish one place as another, and that it was the best to make an exertion to save ourselves; and after each man had selected two of the best beaver skins to eat as he traveled along, we hung the remainder upon a tree, and started to try our fortune with the snow shoes. Owning to the softness of the snow, and the poor construction of our snow shoes, we soon found this to be a difficult and laborious mode of traveling. The first day after we started with our snow shoes we traveled but three or four miles and encamped for the night, which, for want of a good fire, we passed in the most distressing manner. Wood was plenty but we were unable to get it, and it kept one or two of the men busy to keep what little fire we had from going out as it melted the snow and sunk down. On the Morning [30th Jan.] After roasting and eating some of our beaver skins, we continued our journey through the snow. In this way we continued to travel until the first day of February, in the afternoon, when we came to where the crust on the snow was sufficiently strong to carry us. Here we could travel somewhat faster, but at the best not much faster than a man could crawl on his hands and feet, as some of the men from hunger and cold were almost insensible of their situation, and so weak that they could scarcely stand on their feet, much less walk at speed. As we approached the foot of the mountain the snow became softer and would not carry us. This caused the most resolute despair, as it was obviously impossible, owing to extreme weakness, for us to wade much further through the snow. As we moved down the mountain plunging and falling through the snow, we approached a large spruce or cedar tree, the drooping branches of which had prevented the snow from falling to the ground about its trunk—here we halted to rest. While collected under the sheltering boughs of this tree, viewing, with horrified feelings, the way-worn, and despairing countenances of each other, a Mr. Carter, a Virginian, who was probably the nighest exhausted of any of the company, burst into tears and said, "here I must die." This made a great impression upon the remainder of the company, and they all, with the exception of a Mr. Hockday and myself, despaired of going any further. Mr. Hockday, however, after some persuasion, telling them that if they had strength to follow us we would break the road as far as possible, if not out to the valley, succeeded in getting them started once more. —Mr. Hockday was a large muscular man, as hardy as a mule and as resolute as a lion; yet kind and affectionate. He was then decidedly the stoutest man in the company, and myself, probably, the next stoutest. As for our Captain, Mr. Stephens, he was amongst the weakest of the company.

We resumed our journey, and continued to crawl along through the deep snow slowly till the evening of the fourth, when we arrived in the plain at the foot of the mountain. Here we found the snow shallow that we could dispense with the use of our snow shoes; and while in the act of taking them off some of the men discovered, at the distance of 70 or 80 yards; two animals feeding in the brush, which they supposed to be buffaloe, but from blindness, caused by weakness and pine smoke, could not be positive. Mr. Hockday and I were selected to approach and kill one of the animals without regard to what they might prove to be, while the remainder of the company were to go to a neighboring grove of timber and kindle a fire. Having used our guns as walking canes in the snow, we found them much out of order, and were obliged to draw out the old loads and put in new ones, before attempting to shoot. After taking every precaution we deemed necessary to insure success, we started and crawled along on our hands and knees, until we approached within ten or fifteen steps of the animals, when Mr. Hockday prepared to shoot; but upon finding that he would not see the sight of the gun or hold it at arms length, forbore, and proposed to me to shoot. I accordingly fixed myself and pulled trigger. My gun missed fire! I never was so wrecked with agitation as at that moment. "There," said I, "our game is gone, and we are not able to follow it much further;" but as good fortune had it, the Buffaloe, (for such we had discovered them to be), did not see nor smell us, and after raising their heads out of the snow, and looking around for a few moments for the cause of the noise, again commenced feeding. I then picked the flint of my gun, fired and broke the back of one of the Buffaloe, my ball not taking effect within 18 inches of where I thought I aimed. —The men in the grove of timber, on hearing the report of my rifle came staggering forth to learn the result, and when they received the heart-cheering intelligence of success they raised a shout of joy. It was amusing to witness the conduct of some of the men on this occasion. Before we had caught the buffaloe they appeared scarcely able to speak—but a moment after that, were able to holler like Indians at war. I will not describe the scene that followed here—the reader may imagine it—an account of it would be repulsive and offensive rather than agreeable. This was the ninth day since we had eaten anything but dried beaver skins. We remained at this place four days feasting upon the carcass of this Buffaloe, during which time we recruited considerably in strength and spirits, and on the 8th we resumed our journey down the river . . . and but little snow to obstruct our march. We continued our journey, killing plenty of game and living well, without any strange occurrence.

From: *The Adventures of Zenas Leonard, Fur Trader and Trapper, 1831-1836* (Cleveland, OH: W. F. Wagner, 1904)

A Grave for a Trapper, c. September 1833

Warren Angus Ferris

New York-born and raised, Warren A. Ferris (1810–1873) left the east in 1828 and traveled west in the employ of the American Fur Company. He mapped the Yellowstone country and kept a journal of his five adventurous years (1830–1835) in the West, first serialized in the Western Literary Messenger, *and later published as a book titled,* Life in the Rocky Mountains. *Ferris moved to Texas at the time when it became a Republic, and was elected surveyor. During that time, Ferris acquired large sections of land, some of it later becoming part of metropolitan Dallas. In the following story Ferris vividly describes some of his early experiences in the Rocky Mountains and the death and burial of a fellow trapper, a man named Fraiser, a French-Iroquois from Canada. Ferris described Fraiser as "upright and fair in all his dealings, and very generally esteemed and respected by his companions." As the reader will determine from this vignette, although he died a lonely death, Fraiser was properly laid to rest and mourned by his faithful companions.*

We departed southeastward for the Jefferson River on the morning of the fifteenth, accompanied by all the Indians; and picturesque enough was the order and appearance of our march. Fancy to yourself, reader, three thousand horses of every variety of size and color, with trappings almost as varied as their appearance, either packed or ridden by a thousand souls from squalling infancy to decrepid age, their persons fantastically ornamented with scarlet coats, blankets all colors, buffalo robes painted with hideous little figures, resembling grasshoppers quite as much as men for which they were intended, and sheep-skin dresses garnished with porcupine quills, beads, hawk bells, and human hair. Imagine this motley collection of human figures, crowned with long black locks gently waving in the wind, their faces painted with vermillion, and yellow ochre. Listen to the rattle of numberless lodgepoles [carried] by packhorses, to the various noises of children screaming, women scolding, and dogs howling. Observe occasional frightened horses running away and scattering their lading over the prairie. See here and there groups of Indian boys dashing about at full speed, sporting over the plain, or quietly listening to traditional tales of battles and surprises, recounted by their elder companions. Yonder see a hundred horsemen pursuing a herd of antelopes, which sport and wind before them conscious of superior fleetness—there as many others racing towards a distant mound, wild with emulation and excitement, and in every direction crowds of hungy dogs chasing and worrying timid rabbits, and other small animals. Imagine these scenes, with all their bustle, vociferation and confusion, lighted by the flashes of hundreds of gleaming gun-barrels, upon which the rays of a fervent sun are playing, a beautiful level prairie, with dark blue snow-capped mountains in the distance, and you will have a faint idea of the character and aspect of our march, as we followed old Guignon (French for bad-luck) the Flathead slowly over the plains, on the sources of Clark's River. Exhibitions of this description are so common to the country that they scarcely elicit a passing remark, except from some comparative stranger.

Next day we separated into two parties, one of which entered a cut in the mountains southward, while the other (of which was I) continued on southeastward, and on the 17th crossed a mountain to a small stream tributary to the Jefferson. In the evening a Pen-d'oreille from the other division, joined us and reported that he had seen traces of a party of footmen, apparently following our trail. We ourselves saw during our march, the recent encampment of a band of horsemen, and other indications of the vicinity of probable foes. Pursuing our route, on the following day we reached and descended into the valley of the Jefferson twenty-five miles below the forks. This valley extended below us fifteen or twenty miles to the northward, where the river bending to the East, enters a narrow passage in the mountain between walls of cut rock. The plains are from two to five miles in breadth, and are covered with prickly pear—immediately bordering the river are broad fertile bottoms, studded with cottonwood trees. The River is about one hundred yards wide, is clear, and has a gentle current—its course is northward till it leaves the valley. We found the plains alive with buffalo, of which we killed great numbers, and our camp was consequently once more graced with piles of meat, which gave it something the appearance of a well stored market place. From starvation to such abundance the change was great, and the effect was speedily apparent. Indians, children, and dogs lay sprawling about, scarcely able to move, so gorged were they with the rich repast, the first full meal which they had, perhaps, enjoyed for weeks. The squaws alone were busy, and they having all the labour of domestic duty to perform, are seldom idle. Some were seen seated before their lodges with buffalo skins spread out before them, to receive the fat flakes of meat they sliced for drying. Others were engaged in procuring fuel, preparing scaffolds, and making other preparations for curing and preserving the fortunate supply of provisions thus obtained. Even the children were ususually quiet and peaceable, and all would have been exempt from care or uneasiness, had not the unslumbering cautiousness of the veteran braves discovered traces of lurking enemies.

On the morning of the 19th several of our men returned from their traps, bearing the dead body of Frasier, one of our best hunters, who went out the day previous to set his traps, and by his not returning at night, excited some alarm for his safety. His body was found in the Jefferson, about five miles below camp, near a trap, which it is supposed he was in the act of setting when fired upon. He was shot in the thigh and through the neck, and twice stabbed in the breast. His body was stripped, and left in the water, but unscalped.

In the afternoon we dug his grave with an axe and frying pan, the only implements we had that could be employed to advantage in this melancholy task, and prepared for the sad ceremony of committing to the earth the remains of a comrade, who but yestermorn was among us in high health, gay, cheerful, thoughtless, and dreaming of nothing but pleasure and content in the midst of relations and friends. Having no coffin, nor the means to make one, we covered his body in a piece of new scarlet cloth, around which a blanket and several buffalo robes were then wrapped and lashed firmly. The body thus eveloped was carefully laid in the open grave, and a wooden cross in token of his catholic faith placed upon his breast. Then there was a pause. The friends and comrades of the departed trapper gathered around to shed the silent tear of pity and affection over a companion so untimely cut off; and the breeze as if in sympathy with their sorrow, sighed through the leaves and brances of an aged cottonwood, which spread its hoary arms above his last resting place, as though to protect it from intrusion; while in contrast with this solemnity merry warblers skipped lightly from limb to limb, turning their little pipes to lively strains, unmindful of the touching and impressive scene beneath. At length the simple rite was finished, the grave closed, and with saddened countenances and heavy hearts the little herd of mourners retired to their respective lodges, where more than one of our ordinarily daring and thoughtless hunters, thus admonished of the uncertainty of life, held serious self-communion, and perhaps resolved to make better preparations for any event that might come at almost any moment, after which there can be no repentance. But it may be doubted if these resolutions were long remembered. They soon recovered their light heartedness, and were as indifferent, reckless, and mercurial as ever.

From: A series of installments originally published in the *Western Literary Messenger* from July 13, 1842 to May 4, 1844 by J.S. Chadbournes & Co., in Buffalo, New York

The Power of a Pawnee Bow, May 22, 1834

John Kirk Townsend

The early American Indian lived by his bow. It was his weapon of choice that he ably used against his enemies. It was also his superb hunting tool that was capable of bringing down a buffalo, a symbol of warrior status. The arrival of Europeans introduced the Indian to primitive trade guns, then more sophisticated percussion arms, and finally fast-loading cartridge guns—all of which supplanted the bow in a blink of history's eye. Townsend discovered the power of the Indian bow when he was on an expedition across the Rocky Mountains to the Columbia River in 1834. An ornithologist by occupation, Townsend was among the first naturalists to study these regions. In 1839, Townsend published a narrative of his Western adventures in his book, Narrative of a Journey across the Rocky Mountains to the Columbia River.

When the men were packing the horses, after breakfast, I was . . . engaged with my Indian friend. I took his bow and arrows in my hand, and remarked that the latter were smeared with blood throughout: upon my expressing surprise at this he told me, by signs, that they had passed through the body of a buffalo. I assumed a look of incredulity; the countenance of the savage brightened, and his peculiar and strange eyes actually flashed with eagerness, as he pointed to a dead antelope lying upon the ground about forty feet from us, and which one of the guards had shot near the camp in the morning. The animal lay upon its side with the breast towards us: the bow was drawn slightly, without any apparent effort, and the arrow flew through the body of the antelope, and skimmed to a great distance over the plain.

Reprinted from *Narrative of a Journey across the Rocky Mountains to the Columbia River* courtesy of the University of Nebraska Press.

Getting Acquainted with a Grizzly, August 20, 1834

Osborne Russell

Osborne Russell, a fur trapper, was a member of a forty-person party whose mission was to traverse the West from Independence, Missouri, to the mouth of the Columbia River. Once there, he and his companions were commissioned to establish the Columbia River Fishing and Trading Company. This company was to trade for salmon and fur. The party was led by Nathaniel Wyeth, "a persevering adventurer and lover of Enterprise"—according to Russell. The incident described here happened in the valley of the Snake River where the party had stopped and built a fort. Russell's diary was first published in 1914.

We left the Fort and travelled abot 6 miles when we discovered a Grizzly Bear digging and eating roots in a piece of marshy ground near a large bunch of willows. The Mullattoe approached within 100 yards and shot him thro the left shoulder he gave a hideous growl and sprang into the thicket. The Mullattoe then said "let him go he is a dangerous varmint" but not being acquainted with the nature of these animals I determined on making another trial, and persuaded the Mullattoe to assist me we walked round the bunch of willows where the Bear lay keeping close together, with our Rifles ready cocked and presented towards the bushes untill near the place where he had entered, when we heard a sullen growl about 10 ft from us, which was instantly followed by a spring of the Bear toward us; his enormous jaws extended and eyes flashing fire. Oh Heavens! Was ever anything so hideous? We could not retain sufficient presence of mind to shoot at him but took to our heels separating as we ran the Bear taking after me, finding I could out run him he left and turned to the other who wheeled about and discharged his

Rifle covering the Bear with smoke and fire the ball however missing him he turned and bounded toward me—I could go no further without jumping into a large quagmire which hemmed me on three sides, I was obliged to turn about and face him he came within about 10 paces of me then suddenly stopped and raised his ponderous body erect, his mouth wide open, gazing at me with a beastly laugh at this moment I pulled trigger and I knew not what else to do and hardly knew that I did this but it accidentally happened that my Rifle was pointed towards the Bear when I pulled and the ball piercing his heart, he gave one bound for me uttered a deathly howl and fell dead: but I trembled as if I had an ague fit for half an hour after, we butchered him as he was very fat packed the meat and skin on our horses and returned to the Fort with the trophies of our bravery, but I secretly determined in my own mind never to molest another wounded Grizzly Bear in a marsh or thicket.

From: *Journal of a Trapper: or, Nine years in the Rocky Mountains, 1834-1843: being a general description of the country, climate, rivers, lakes, mountains, etc., and a view of the life by a hunter in those regions* (Boise, ID: Syms-York, Publishers, 1914)

Why She Ran Away,
June 10, 1835

Wife of a Blackfoot Warrior

While camping and enjoying excellent pasturage just east of the Wind River Mountains in present-day Wyoming, the exploring party of Captain B. L. E. de Bonneville was approached by a solitary rider who asked for Bonneville's assistance to save a young white trapper and his companion, a beautiful young Blackfoot woman. Bonneville learned that the couple had been abandoned by the trapping party they had been traveling with and left in the midst of a "desolate prairie" without the wherewithal to survive. Bonneville sent horses out from his camp to rescue the couple. After the couple was brought to the campsite, Bonneville found the woman to be especially quick-witted and communicative. Questioning her, Bonneville learned of the circumstances that had brought the white trapper and the woman together. The woman said that her husband had constantly treated her horribly, and thus, she ran away from him and sought protection and asylum with a neighboring Nez Perce tribe. There she met, and eventually took up with, the white trapper. In the following narrative the woman explains why she left her husband. Her story is compelling and bespeaks of a woman who has tried everything to be appreciated by a thoughtless, uncaring, and cruel husband. Bonneville recorded her story in his journal which was later published by Washington Irving (noted American author of books and short stories) in 1848 with the title, The Adventures of Captain Bonneville.

I was the wife of a Blackfoot warrior, and I served him faithfully. Who was so well-served as he? Whose lodge was so well provided, or kept so clean? I brought wood in the morning and placed water always at hand. I watched for his coming; and he found his meat cooked and ready. If he rose to go forth, there was nothing to delay him. I searched the thought that was in his heart, to save him the trouble of speaking. When I went abroad on errands for him, the chiefs and warriors smiled upon me, and the braves spoke soft things, in secret; but my feet were in the straight path, and my eyes could see nothing but him.

When he went out to hunt, or to war, who aided to equip him but I? When he returned I met him at the door; I took his gun; and he entered without further thought. While he sat and smoked, I unloaded his horses; tied them to stakes, brought in their loads, and was quickly at his feet. If his moccasins were wet I took them off and put on others which were warm and dry. I dressed all the skins that were taken in the chase. He could never say to me, why is it not done? He hunted the deer and the antelope, and the buffalo, and he watched for the enemy. Everything else was done by me. When our people moved their camp; it was I who packed the horses and led them on the journey. He mounted his horse and rode away; free as though he had fallen from the skies. He had nothing to do with the labor of the camp. When we halted in the evening, he sat with other braves and smoked, it was I who pitched his lodge; and when he came to eat and sleep, his supper and bed were ready.

I served him faithfully; and what was my reward? A cloud was always on his brow, and sharp lightning on his tongue. I was his dog; and not his wife. Who was it scarred and bruised me? It was he.

From: *The Adventures of Captain Bonneville* (Chicago: Belford, Clarke & Company, Publishers, 1848)

A Buffalo Dance,
July 29, 1835

Samuel Parker

In 1835, the Methodist Episcopal Missionary Board sent Rev. Samuel Parker and Dr. Marcus Whitman to prepare for missionary work in the northwest. Parker and Whitman joined forces at Independence, Missouri, the jumping off point for the West. From there they traveled with a caravan of hardened men bound for the annual rendezvous of mountain men and trappers held on the Green River. The journey was not a pleasant one, especially for Witman, who felt that Parker considered him little more than a servant. Nor was the journey pleasurable for their traveling companions because as Christian missionaries, they did not permit the consumption of alcoholic spirits. The following story was extracted from Parker's book, Journal of an Exploring Tour Beyond the Rocky Mountains, *first published in 1838. The buffalo dance described took place in the Black Hills, homeland of the Blackfeet and Sioux Indians who traversed the Great Plains before the advent of Europeans. The lives of the Indians were closely tied to the comings and goings of the great buffalo herds. The bison provided their chief food and material needs. The most exciting event of the year's festival was the buffalo dance. During the ceremony, the old men of the tribe beat upon drums and chanted prayers for successful buffalo hunting. As noted in the following story, the Rev. Parker took issue with the ceremony.*

On the 29th, the Indians had a buffalo and dog dance. I witnessed the former, and was content to dispense with the latter. In the buffalo dance, a large number of young men, dressed with the skins of the neck and head of buffalos, with their horns on, moved around in a dancing march. They shook their heads, made the low bellowing of the buffalo, wheeled, and jumped. At the same time men and women sung a song,

46

accompanied with the beating of a sort of drum. I cannot say I was much amused to see how well they could imitate brute beasts, while ignorant of God and salvation. The impressive enquiry was constantly on my mind, what will become of their immortal spirits? Rational men imitating beasts, and old gray-headed men marshaling the dance! And enlightened whites encouraging them by giving them intoxicating spirits, as a reward for their good performance. I soon retired, and was pleased to find, that only a small part of the Indians took any part in the dance.

From: *Journal of an Exploring Tour Beyond the Rocky Mountains, Under the Direction of the A.B.C.F.M. Performed in the Years 1835, '36, and '37; Containing a Description of the Geography, Geology, Climate, and Productions; and the Number, Manners, and Customs of the Natives with a Map of Oregon Territory* (Minneapolis: Ross & Haines, reprinted in 1967 in limited edition from the 1838 edition)

Surrounded at the Alamo, February 23, 1836

Davy Crockett

Tennessee-born in 1786, David Crockett worked two days a week in return for four days of school when he was in his teens. According to him, his education amounted to "100 days of study." His lack of education, however, did not hold him back. Elected to the Tennessee Legislature in 1821 at age 35; he made a bid for the U.S. Congress in 1825, but was soundly defeated. Not one to give up, Crockett won a seat in the Congress in 1827. Then, after being defeated to keep his seat in 1830 in a close election, he won it back in 1832, but lost it again in 1834. Disgusted with politics, Crockett said of his detractors, "They can go to hell. I'm going to Texas." Then, with a few coon-skin capped, diehard supporters and carrying their long-rifles, Crockett set out for Texas in 1835 hoping for a role in the political leadership in what he thought would soon gain independence from Mexico. In early 1836 Crockett found himself in San Antonio de Bexar, besieged by a hostile Mexican Army led by General Antonio Lopez de Santa Anna. On March 6, 1836, Santa Anna's troops overwhelmed the Alamo and its defenders were killed to the man. Legend holds that Crockett was one of the first defenders killed and died heroically outside of the Alamo chapel. In the 1990s, however, a diary allegedly penned by one of Santa Anna's officers, Lt. Col. José Enrique de la Peña, tells that Crockett and six other defenders surrendered during the final battle, but were subsequently tortured and executed by order of Santa Anna. Because de la Peña's account flies in the face of Texas lore, it has been soundly criticized and dismissed as a fake. But tests on the diary's paper date it from around the period of the Alamo's fall. Moreover, the handwriting matches that of letters written by de la Peña. Whatever the true events, Crockett did die at the Alamo. The following diary entry was extracted from a 1902 version of The Life of David Crockett, *etc.*

Early this morning the enemy came in sight, marching in regular order, and displaying their strength to the greatest advantage, in order to strike us with terror. But that was no go; they'll find that they have to do with men who will never lay down their arms as long as they can stand on their legs. We held a short council of war, and, finding that we should be completely surrounded, and overwhelmed by numbers, if we remained in the town, we concluded to withdraw to the fortress of Alamo, and defend it to the last extremity. We accordingly filed off, in good order, having some days before placed all the surplus provisions, arms, and ammunition in the fortress. We have had a large national flag made; it is composed of thirteen stripes, red and white, alternatively, on a blue ground with a large white star, of five points, in the center, and between the points the letters Texas. As soon as all our little band, about one hundred and fifty in number, had entered and secured the fortress in the best possible manner, we set about raising our flag on the battlements.

From: *The Life of David Crockett, etc.* (New York: A.L. Burt Company, 1902)

The Attack on the Alamo

Captured by Comanches, April 4, 1836

Sarah Ann Horn

English-born (c. 1809), at the age of eighteen Sarah Ann was wed to a fellow countryman, John Horn, in 1827. To better their condition, the young couple emigrated to New York in 1833. John obtained employment in New York City as a clerk but longed to move to the American frontier. After the defeat of Mexican forces which resulted in Texas becoming a Republic, the new nation offered great inducements to obtain settlers. A fellow Englishman who was practicing medicine in New York, Dr. John Charles Beales, obtained a grant to raise a settlement on the Rio Grande. To entice settlers, each family was offered 177 acres of land plus a town lot for building a home. The location of the town, La Villa de Dolores, did not give it protection from the Indians. John and Sarah Horn and their two young children joined in the venture. On New Year's Day 1836 the Horns and their accompanying settlers—eleven men, two women, and three children— started for the Rio Grande. In West Texas, near the Nueces River, the company was attacked by Comanche warriors. The following narrative describes the first hours of her captivity and was taken from her book of the event that was first published in 1839. Eventually Sarah was ransomed by traders in New Mexico and returned to the United States via the Santa Fe Trail.

We had turned out the teams to feed—some of the men were cooking dinner (from a fine deer)—some were fishing, and others fixing their guns, and reading. Mrs. Harris was a short distance off, gathering some wild fruit, and my husband was sitting on the ground near me, with our little sons . . . I had just washed Mrs. Harris' babe, and as I was stepping up on the fore part of the wagon to get a clean dress to put on it, I saw a large company of strange-looking men mounted on mules, armed, and nearly naked. I was terribly frightened, and running back to my husband as soon as possible, told him what I had seen, and expressed my fears that they were Indians. He looked up in my face, and, smiling, said he thought there could be no danger, and wished me to dress the babe that I held naked in my arms; but while he was speaking the Indians came in sight, and the work of death had commenced. The first thing I perceived, an arrow had found its way into the breast of one of our men standing by my side. He drew it out with his own hands, when the blood flowed in a stream, and he fell on his face and expired. By this time our little company was falling in every direction. I flew to my husband, who was standing a short distance from me with our children, one on each side, holding them by the hand. I still had Mrs. Harris' babe in my arms; she being a short distance off, and dreadfully frightened, had hid herself in the bushes. As I approached my husband, I caught hold of my little Joseph by the hand, and by this time the Indians were in the midst of us. They instantly tore me and my children from my dear husband, when one of the savages struck him on the back of his head with a double barrel gun, and he fell to the ground upon his face. I saw him draw his arms up under him, and raise his head once from the ground, when he uttered a deep sigh, and the mortal agony was past with him forever. My children were much frightened, as may well be supposed; but neither they nor their wretched mother were permitted to linger near the scene of their murdered father, as the Indians immediately conducted us to the wagon. By this time they had found Mrs. Harris, and led her also to the same spot, where I gave her her babe. My dear little children were frantic with grief and fear, while I was endeavoring in my distracted condition to do all I could to console them; but the savages took every precaution to prevent me from doing so. They immediately tore the little trembling creatures from me, and producing their instruments of death, showed them, by signs most appalling, that they would kill them if they went near me. There were between forty and fifty of the Indians, but these were but a small part of the whole band, as will shortly appear. Having thrown everything out of the wagon, they selected such things as they were disposed to take away at this time. They then placed myself and Mrs. Harris behind two of the party on horseback, she having her babe in her arms, and two of the men took charge of my children.

Thus arranged we left the spot, where, in one short moment, we had buried our fondest earthly hopes; and what was to be my fate, or that of my dear children, I was utterly at a loss even to conjecture; and but for my orphan babes, my heart had been almost insensible to life or death. As we could not understand a word of the language of our captors, so we were unable to learn where they were going, or what disposition was to be made of us. We soon learned, however, that their camp was only about two miles from the place where they found us, and when we had got within about a quarter of a mile of the spot, a scene presented itself that defies all description. We were met by several hundred of their companions, in files of six or eight abreast, who, with the most horrid yells, and varied contortion of body and limbs, expressed their barbarous joy. We were soon conducted to the camp, which was formed in the midst of an almost impenetrable thicket, for the purpose of concealment. Having reached this dreadful place, we were almost suffocated with the stench arising from the stale horse-meat which lay in and about the camp. Here we were seated on the ground, under a guard, when they commenced stripping us of our bonnets, handkerchiefs, combs and rings. They took everything from my children, leaving them as naked as they were born. Mrs Harris' babe, the reader will recollect, was naked in my arms at the time we were taken, and so it remained, although I begged them to let me put a blanket on it before we left the scene of conflict, which they would not permit. By this time night was coming on, when the Indians partook of the offensive meat of which I have spoken; but they offered neither us nor our children a morsel of anything, though they had plenty of the provisions of which they had plundered us, nor did they ever after permit us or our children to taste of it. Before they laid down for the night, Mrs. Harris and myself were bound by passing a cord about our ankles and arms, so as to bring the latter close to our sides. In this condition we were placed upon the naked ground, with a blanket thrown over us, and the whole of that dreadful night, my agonized heart seemed ready to burst, as I listened to the cries of my orphan babes, as they called for their murdered father, and for water to quench their thirst; and as though my cup of anguish was not otherwise complete, the mosquitoes, of enormous size, were annoying me at every point, without the use of a single limb with which to defend myself. It is infinitely beyond the power of language to express the horrors of this painfully memorable night. The babe lay quiet till near day-light, when it began to cry with cold and hunger, as its mother's breasts were in such a condition that she had not been able to give it suck, and it had been brought thus far upon food by hand. I had bestowed a mother's care upon it, but had no chance to prepare it any food since the day previous. As soon as we were permitted to rise, I asked the Indians for some flour with which to make the babe something to eat. They said, "yes, it shall have something to eat;" a smile accompanied the reply, and a tall, muscular Indian came to me and taking hold of it, swung it by its arms, and threw it up as high as he could, and let it fall upon the ground at his feet. This barbarous act having been repeated three time, its sufferings were at an end.

Reprinted from *Comanche Bondage* by Carl Coke Rister by permission of the University of Nebraska Press. Copyright 1955 by the Arthur H. Clark Company. Renewal copyright © 1983 by the Arthur H. Clark Company.

Christmas Frolicking at Fort Union, c. 1838

Charles Larpenteur

For decades Larpenteur was a fur trader for the American Fur Company, organized by John Jacob Astor. Mostly, Larpenteur spent his years in the Upper Missouri region and at his beloved Fort Union—located at the confluence of the Yellowstone and Missouri Rivers. A devoted diarist, Larpenteur's journals from the 1830s, 1860s and early-1870s survived. They were first published in a two-volume set in 1898 and carried the title, Forty Years a Fur Trader.

Thanks to kind Providence, here I am again in good old Fort Union, at a splendid table, with that great prairie appetite to do it justice. The day after my arrival I was reinstated in the liquor shop, and as it was the height of the meat trade I had enough to do, night and day. Excepting plenty of buffalo, deer, and rabbit hunting, nothing took place worth mentioning until Christmas. On this anniversary a great dinner is generally made, but that was never the case here, as it was always taken out in drinkables instead of eatables; and I, who did not drink, had to do without my dinner. At the height of the spree the tailor and one of the carpenters had a fight in the shop, while others took theirs outside, and toward evening I was informed that Marseillais, our hunter, had been killed and thrown into the fireplace. We immediately ran in, and sure enough, there he was, badly burned and senseless, but not dead yet. We were not at first sure whether this was the mere effect of liquor, or had happened from fighting; but we learned that a fight had taken place, and on examination we found that he had been stabbed in several places with a small dirk. Knowing that the tailor had such a weapon, we suspected him and demanded it. He was at that time standing behind his table; I saw him jerk the dirk out of his pocket and throw it under the table. I immediately picked it up; it was bloody, and from its size we judged it to be the weapon with which the wounds had been inflicted. Having learned that the carpenter had also been in the fight, they both were placed in irons and confined to await their trial. As such Christmas frolics could not be brought to a head much under three days, the trial took place on the fourth day, when a regular court was held. Everything being ready, the criminals were sent for, the witnesses were well examined, and after a short session the jury returned a verdict, "Guilty of murder." The judge then pronounced sentence on the convicted murderers, which was that they be hanged by the neck, until they were "dead, dead, dead!" But, not considering it entirely safe to have this sentence executed, he changed it to thirty-nine lashes apiece. John Brazo was appointed executioner.

Always ready for such sport, he immediately went in quest of his large ox-whip, and, not making any difference between men and oxen, he applied it at such a rate that Mr. Mitchell, the judge, had now and then to say, "Moderate, John, moderate"; for had John been suffered to keep on, it is very likely that the first sentence would have been executed.

After this everything went on perfectly smooth.

Reprinted from *Forty Years a Fur Trader on the Upper Missouri*, courtesy of the Uiversity of Nebraska Press.

The Yearly Rendezvous, c. July 1839

Fredrick A. Wislizenus

Spreading out from the original routes of the pathfinders Lewis and Clark, Ameri-can trappers found beaver aplenty in the clear and pristine waters that flowed out of the Rocky Mountains. But they encountered a major problem: how to get their pelts to market in St. Louis, more than a thousand miles away? As a solution, groups of these men formed 'Companies,' who would transport the bundled furs on the haz-ardous journey back east to sell. The next summer, these same companies of men would make the long journey back to the mountains, bringing goods and supplies to trade with the trappers for their fall and spring catch. This trading would take place at a predetermined location, called the Rendezvous. Fredrick Wislizenus (1810–1889), a German-born physician and amateur botanist living in St. Louis, took a trip down the Oregon Trail, and on his return travels stopped off at the Ren-dezvous site—south-central Wyoming—in 1839. His account, originally published in German in 1840, was translated into English and published by the Missouri His-torical Society in 1912. It makes for interesting reading.

Our objective was the upper Green River valley, which is thrust like a bay or prairie between the main chain of the Rockies and the projecting Wind River Mountains. Our direction was northeast. The road thither leads over sand hills and plateaus. The Wind River Mountains lay to our right, permitting a closer view of the precipitous, weather-beaten granite forma-tions cut by deep ravines. As intervening bulwark, there were foothills, dark with evergreens, but void of snow. To our left new snow peaks came into view, the Grand River Mountains. We crossed several streams, first the Little Sandy and the Big Sandy, then the New Fork; all having their sources in the Wind River Mountains and flowing into the Green River. The water is clear and cool, the river bed pebbly. The shores are usually fringed with willows.

On the second day we found traces of whites and Indians, that had journeyed ahead of us through this region a short time before, probably to the rendezvous, which takes place yearly about this time, though our leaders did not know precisely what place had been chosen for it this year, some of our men were sent out for information. They returned the next day while we were camping on the New Fork, with two agents of the fur company, Trips and Walker. These agents were accompanied by their Indian wives and a lot of dogs. The two squaws, quite passable as to their features, appeared in highest state. Their red blankets, with the silk kerchiefs on their heads, and their gaudy embroideries, gave them quite an Oriental appearance. Like themselves, their horses were bedight with embroideries, beads, corals, ribbons and little bells. The bells were hung about in such number that when riding in their neighborhood, one might think one's self in the midst of Turkish music. The squaws, however, behaved most properly. They took care of the horses, pitched a tent, and were alert for every word of their wedded lords.

From the agents we learned that this year's meeting place had been fixed on the right bank of the Green River at the angle formed by its junction with Horse Creek. We were now about a day's journey from the place. Starting off in company in the afternoon, we covered, at a more rapid pace than usual, about twelve miles, and then camped on a branch of the New Fork, whose shore were framed with fine pines. It was the Fourth of July, the great holiday of the United States. Our camp, however, presented its humdrum daily appearance. We stretched out around the fires, smoked and, in expectation of what the morrow would bring, went quietly asleep.

The next morning we started early, and reached toward noon the Green River, so long desired. The Green River rises in the northwestern slope of the Wind River Mountains, flows in southwestern direction, and empties into the Gulf of California. Where we first saw it, it is a clear, rippling streamlet, abounding in trout; neither very broad, nor very deep; but later on it becomes a broad, rushing stream. Its navigation is said to present enormous difficulties.

We reached the camping place. What first struck our eye was several long rows of Indian tents, extending along the Green River for at least a mile. Indians and whites were mingled here in varied groups. Of the Indians there had come chiefly Snakes, Flatheads and Nezperces, peaceful tribes, living beyond the Rocky Mountains. Of whites the agents of the different trading companies and a quantity of trappers had found their way here, visiting this fair of the wilderness to buy and to sell, to renew old contracts and to make new ones, to make arrangements for future meetings, to meet old friends, to tell of adventures they had been through, and to spend for once a jolly day.

These trappers are such a peculiar set of people that it is necessary to say a little about them. The name in itself indicates their occupation. They either receive their outfit, consisting of horses, beaver traps, a gun, powder and lead, from trading companies, and trap for small wages, or else they act on their own account, and are then called freemen. The latter is more often the case. In small parties they roam through all the mountain passes. No rock is too steep for them; no stream too swift. They are in constant danger from hostile Indians, whose delight it is to ambush such small parties, and plunder them, and scalp them. Such victims fall every year. One of our fellow travelers, who had gone to the mountains for the first time nine years ago with about one hundred men, estimated that by this time half the number had fallen victims to the tomahawks of the Indians. But this daily danger seems to exercise a magic attraction over most of them. Only with reluctance does a trapper abandon his dangerous craft; and a sort of serious home-sickness seizes him when he retires from his mountain life to civilization.

In manners and customs, the trappers have borrowed much from the Indians. Many of them, too, have taken Indian women as wives. Their dress is generally of leather. The hair of the head is usually allowed to grow long. In place of money, they use beaver skins, for which they can satisfy all their needs at the forts by way of trade. A pound of beaver skins is usually paid for with four dollars worth of goods; but the goods themselves are sold at enormous prices, so-called mountain prices. A pint of meal, for instance, costs from half a dollar to a dollar; a pint of coffee-beans, cocoa beans or sugar, two dollars each; a pint of diluted alcohol, four dollars; a piece of chewing tobacco of the commonest sort, which is usually smoked, Indian fashion, mixed with herbs, one to two dollars. Guns and ammunition, bear traps, blankets, kerchiefs, and gaudy finery for the squaws, are also sold at enormous profit.

At the yearly rendezvous the trappers seek to indemnify themselves for the sufferings and privations of a year spent in the wilderness. With their hairy bank notes, the beaver skins, they can obtain all the luxuries of the mountains, and live for a few days like lords. Coffee and chocolate is cooked; the pipe is kept aglow day and night; the spirits circulate; and whatever is not spent in such ways the squaws coax out of them, or else it is squandered at cards. Formerly single trappers on such occasions have often wasted a thousand dollars. But the days of their glory seem to be past, for constant hunting has very much reduced the number of beavers. This diminution in the beaver catch made itself noticeable at this year's rendezvous in the quieter behavior of the trappers. There was little drinking of spirits, and almost no gambling. Another decade perhaps and the original trapper will have disappeared from the mountains.

The Indians who had come to the meeting were no less interesting than the trappers. There must have been some thousands of them. Their tents are made of buffalo hides, tanned on both sides and sewed together, stretched in cone shape over a dozen poles, that are leaned against each other, their tops crossing. In the front and on top this leather can be thrown back, to form door and chimney. The tents are about twelve feet high and twenty feet in circumference at the ground, and give sufficient protection in any kind of weather. I visited many tents, partly out of curiosity, partly to barter for trifles, and sought to make myself intelligible in the language of signs as far as possible. An army of Indian dogs very much resembling the wolf, usually beset the entrance.

From some tents comes the sound of music. A virtuoso beats a sort of kettle drum with bells around with all his might, and the chorus accompanies him with strange monotone untrained sounds that showed strong tendency to the minor chords. A similar heart-rending song drew me to a troop of squaws that were engrossed in the game of "the hand," so popular with the Indians. Some small object, a bit of wood, for instance, is passed from hand to hand among the players seated in a circle; and it is some one's part to guess in whose hands the object is. During the game the chorus steadily sings some song as monotonous as those to which bears dance. But the real object is to gamble in this way for some designated prize. It is a game of hazard. In this case, for example, a pile of beads and corals, which lay in the midst of the circle, was the object in question. Men and women are so carried away by the game, that they often spend a whole day and night at it.

Other groups of whites and Indians were engaged in barter. The Indians had for the trade chiefly tanned skins, moccasins, thongs of buffalo leather or braided buffalo hair, and fresh or dried buffalo meat. They have no beaver skins. The articles that attracted them most in exchange were powder and lead, knives, tobacco, cinnabar, gaily colored kerchiefs, pocket mirrors and all sorts of oraments. Before the Indian begins to trade he demands sight of everything that may be offered by the other party to the trade. If there is something there that attracts him, he, too, will produce his wares, but discovers very quickly how much or how little they are coveted. If he himself is not willed to dispose of some particular thing, he obstinately adheres to his refusal, though ten times the value be offered him. The peltry bought from the Indians must be carefully beaten and aired, at peril of having objectionable troops billeted on you. . . .

The rendezvous usually lasts a week. Then the different parties move off to their destinations and the plain that today resounded with barbarous music, that was thronged with people of both races, with horses and dogs, returns to its old quiet, interrupted only now and then by the muffled roar of the buffalo and the howl of the wolf. . . .

From: *A Journey to the Rocky Mountains in 1839* (St. Louis, MO: Missouri Historical Society, 1912)

Walks-Galloping-On Falls from Grace, c. 1840

Stephen R. Riggs

In the 1830s American missionaries focused their efforts on the Sioux Nation. The term "Dakota" is the term that the Sioux used to refer to themselves. In 1837, Riggs (1812–1883), an ordained-Presbyterian minister, took his bride, Mary, to Lac qui Parle, Minnesota, to begin their life as missionaries among the Dakotas. Later, Riggs founded a new missionary station at Traverse des Sioux, a river ford near St. Peter, Minnesota. Riggs worked diligently and in 1852 published, Grammar and Dictionary of the Dakota Language. *Later, working with his missionary colleagues, Riggs succeeded in translating the entire Bible into the Dakota language and had it published in 1880.*

Among the encouraging events . . . was the conversion of Simon Anawangmane. He was the first full-blood Dakota man to come out on the side of the new religion. Mr. Renville and his sons had joined the church, but the rest were women. It came to be a taunt that the men used when we talked with them and asked them to receive the gospel, "Your church is made up of women;" and, "If you had gotten us in first, it would have amounted to something, but now there are only women. Who would follow after women?" Thus the proud Dakota braves turned away.

But God's truth has sharp arrows in it, and the Holy Spirit knows how to use them in piercing even Dakota hearts.

Anawangmane (Walks-Galloping-On) was at this time not far from thirty years old. He was not a bright scholar—rather dull and slow in learning to read. But he had a very strong will-power and did not know what fear was. He had been a very dare-devil on the war-path. The Dakotas had a curious custom of being *under law* and *above law*. It was always competent for a Dakota soldier to punish another man for a misdemeanor, if the other man did not rank above him in savage prowess. As for example: If a Dakota man had braved an Ojibwa with a loaded gun pointed at him, and had gone up and killed him, he ranked above all men who had not done a like brave deed. And if now one in the community had done such an act of bravery, then this man could not be punished for any thing, according to Dakota custom. . . .

This young man, Anawangmane, had reached that enviable position of being above Dakota law. He . . . was the chief. And so when he came out on the side of the Lord and Christianity, there was a propriety in calling him Simon when he was baptized. He was ordinarily a quiet man—a man of deeds and not of words. But once in a while he would get roused up, and his eyes would flash, and his words and gestures were powerful. Simon immediately put on white man's clothes, and made and planted a field of corn and potatoes adjoining the mission filed. No Dakota brave dared to cut up his tent or kill his dog or break his gun; but this did not prevent the boys, and women too, from pointing the finger at him, and saying, "There goes the man who has made himself a woman." Simon seemed to care for it no more than the bull-dog does for the barking of a puppy. He apparently brushed it all aside as if it was only a straw. So far as any sign from him, one looking on would be tempted to think that he regarded it as glory. But it did not beget pride. . . .

And yet, as time rolled by, it was seen, by the unfolding of the divine plan, that Simon could not be built up into the best and noblest character without suffering. Naturally, he was the man who would grow into self-sufficiency. There were weak points in his character which he perhaps knew not of. It was several years after this when Simon visited us at the Traverse, and made our hearts glad by his presence and help. But alas! he came there to stumble and fall! "You are a brave man—no man so brave as you are," said the Indians at the Traverse to him. And some of them were distantly related to him. While they praised him and flattered him, they asked him to drink whiskey with them. Surely he was man enough for that. How many times he refused Simon never told. But at last he yielded, and then the very energy of his character carried him to great excess in drinking "spirit water."

From: *Mary and I: Forty Years with the Sioux* (Chicago: Congregational S.S. and Publishing Society, 1887)

A Flood's Aftermath, c. Summer 1846

Samuel C. Reid, Jr.

Many historians believe that Samuel Chester Reid, Jr., a Texas Ranger, wrote the definitive work of the U.S.–Mexican War of 1846. The following extract from his book, however, does not address the war with Mexico, but is presented to underscore the problem of natural disasters, as opposed to human conflicts, that the people in the Old West had to contend with. Even to this day, the Rio Grande valley is notorious for its rapid and devastating floods. But the river system provided good crop lands and gave superb yields of cotton, citrus, vegetables, and sorghum. The town of Comargo still exists and is adjacent to its larger neighbor in Texas, Rio Grande City. Both communities were founded by men and women of stubborn stock who were able to face droughts, floods, savage Indians, poor and inaccessible markets, and raiding outlaw bands.

Some two miles above the city of Rio Grande, on the left bank of the San Juan, is situated the town of Comargo, which but a few weeks ago was one of the finest built towns in this section of country, and contained a population of nearly three thousand.

On ascending the bank, we were struck with the desolation and ruin which had spread itself on every side. The late flood, which had been the cause of it, came on rapidly in the night, while the inhabitants were wrapped in their peaceful slumbers, and many had not the least intimation of it, until the waters had actually floated them out of their beds. From a description which we received from a Mexican, who was here at the time, it must have been heart-rending in the extreme. Mothers were seen wading waist-deep, carrying their children in their arms, hurrying to places of safety, filling the air with shrieks of dismay. The men were engaged saving the children, many of whom were clinging to floating materials, and carrying them to the tops of the houses for safety, which had become the only resort among the poorer classes, who lived in huts, and slept on the ground floor—while those who occupied two-story houses were in greater peril, for the walls becoming saturated, gave way and fell in with a crash, frequently drowning a whole family, while others were carried away by the flood, or drowned in their beds. There were many lives lost, and the destruction of property was very great, about two hundred houses having been ruined. The town was once very beautiful, and from the ruined walls we saw, the houses must have been quite pretty. It contains three plazas, in the middle one of which is situation the finest buildings, and where still stands a neat little church.

From: *The Scouting Expeditions of McCulloch's Texas Rangers; or the Summer and Fall Campaign of the Army of the United States in Mexico 1846; Including Skirmishes with the Mexicans and an Accurate Detail of the Storming of Monterey; Also, the Daring Scouts at Buena Visa Together with Anecdotes, Incidents, Descriptions of Country, and Sketches of the Lives of the Celebrated Partisan Chief, Hays, McCulloch, and Walker* (Philadelphia: John E. Potter and Company, 1859)

Birthing at Bent's Fort
July 31, 1846

Susan Shelby Magoffin

Only eighteen-years-old and married less than a year, Magoffin was the first American woman to go down the Santa Fé Trail. She traveled with her trader husband's (Samuel Magoffin) baggage train which was moving, nip and tuck, with Stephen W. Kearny's military force that was to occupy and take from Mexico what we now know as the State of New Mexico. Her diary records the scenes of the Santa Fé Trail, Mexican life and customs, Kearny's conquest of New Mexico, and the progress of the Mexican War. In the following vignette, Magoffin compares the still-born birth of her first child with the simultaneous birth of a child by an Indian woman also housed at Bent's Fort. Magoffin died in 1855, at the age of twenty-eight. Her diary was first published in 1926.

My pains commenced and continued till 12 o'c. At night, when after much agony and severest of pains, which were relieved a little at times by medicine given by Doctor Mesure, *all was over*. I sunk off into a kind of lethargy, in *mi alma's* [literally, "my soul's," referring to her husband's] arms. Since that time I have been in my bed till yesterday a little while, and a part of today.

My situation was very different from that of an Indian woman in the room below me. She gave birth to a fine healthy baby, about the same time, *and in half an hour after she went to the River and bathed herself and it*, and this she has continued each day since. Never could I have believed such a thing, if I had not been here, and *mi alma's* own eyes had not seen her coming from the River. And some gentleman here tells him, he has often seen them immediately after the birth of a child go to the water and *break the ice* to bathe themselves!

It is truly astonishing to see what customs will do. No doubt many ladies in civilized life are ruined by too careful treatments during childbirth, for this custom of the heathen is not known to be disadvantageous, but it is a *"heathenish custom."*

From: *Down the Santa Fé Trail and into Mexico* (New Haven, CT: Yale University Press, 1926)

We're Taking Your Country, August 15, 1846

Stephen Watts Kearny

Still smarting from its defeat at the Battle of San Jacinto and the subsequent loss of Texas, Mexico attempted to return Texas back into its fold by military action. As a result, the United States declared war on Mexico on May 13, 1846. At that time, Colonel Stephen Watts Kearny was stationed at Fort Leavenworth, Kansas, as commander of the 1ˢᵗ United States Dragoons. In late-June, 1846, armed with orders from President James K. Polk, Kearny left Fort Leavenworth at the head of the Army of the West. The army consisted of over 1,600 soldiers and had a two-fold mission: to take New Mexico first, and then to march to California and take it for the United States too. At eight o'clock on the morning of August 15ᵗʰ, re-cently-promoted Brigadier General Kearny rode into the village plaza of Las Ve-gas, New Mexico, climbed to the roof of a building, and spoke to an awe-struck assembly of Las Vegas citizens. Kearny's speech is duplicated in the following narrative.

Mr. Alcalde [the mayor] and the People of New Mexico:

I have come amongst you by the orders of my government, to take pos-session of your country, and extend over it the laws of the United States. We consider it, and have done so for some time, a part of the territory of the United States. We come amongst you as friends—not as enemies; as protectors—not as conquerors. We come among you for your benefit—not for your injury.

Henceforth, I absolve you from all allegiance to the Mexican govern-ment, and from all obedience to General Armijo. He is no longer your governor; I am your governor. I shall not expect you to take up arms and follow me, to fight your own people who may oppose me; but I now tell you, that those who remain peaceably at home, attending to their crops and their herds, shall be protected by me in their property, their persons, and their religion; and not a pepper, nor an onion, shall be disturbed or taken by my troops without pay, or without the consent of the owner. But listen! he who promises to be quiet, and is found in arms against me, I will hang.

From the Mexican government you have never received protection. The Apaches and Navajos come down from the mountains and carry off your sheep, and even your women, whenever they please. My government will correct all this. It will keep off the Indians, protect you in your persons and property; and, I repeat again, will protect you in your religion. I know you are all great Catholics; that some of your priest have told you all sorts of stories—that we should ill-treat your women, and brand them on the cheek as you do your mules on the hip. It is all false. My government respects your religion as much as the Protestant religion, and allows each man to worship his Creator as his heart tells him is best. Its laws protect the Catholic as well as the Protestant; the weak as well as the strong; the poor as well as the rich. I am not a Catholic myself—I was not brought up in that faith; but at least one-third of my army are Catholics, and I respect a good Catholic as much as a good protestant.

There goes my army—you see but a small portion of it; there are many more behind—resistance is useless.

Mr. Alcalde, and you two captains of militia, the laws of my country require that all men who hold office under it shall take the oath of allegiance. I do not wish for the present, until affairs become more settled, to disturb your form of government. If you are prepared to take oaths of allegiance, I shall continue you in office and support your authority.

From: *Notes of a Military Reconnaissance, from Fort Leavenworth, in Missouri, to San Diego, in California, including part of the Arkansas, Del Norte, and Gila Rivers* (Washington, DC: 30th Congress, 1st Session, 1848)

General Stephen Watts Kearny—Las Vegas, New Mexico

A Funeral in Santa Fé, c. August 1846

Frank S. Edwards

Born in England, but raised in New York, Francis ("Frank") S. Edwards found himself in St. Louis when the U.S.–Mexican war broke out in 1846. There, he joined up with an artillery company and soon thereafter marched to fight the Mexicans in what is now called, New Mexico. After the war, Frank returned to New York where he worked as a physician and a pharmacist. His book, A Campaign in New Mexico with Colonel Doniphan, *published in November, 1847, was one of the first works published on the U.S.–Mexican war. In the following story extracted from his book, Frank describes a typical child's funeral in Santa Fé.*

Although there are . . . churches, there is no burying-ground, and the dead are interred by the side of the road, just out of the city, with simply a pile of stones, and a small wooden cross on the top of it. I did not witness any grown Mexican buried while I was in Santa Fé, with the exception of an officer, and he was interred with military honors; persons of both nations following to the grave. But our troops had brought the measles with them, and it was soon communicated to the children of the inhabitants, and carried off many of them; therefore, funerals among the young were common. In these processions, two men went first, bearing spades with which to dig the grave; next music, consisting, generally, of a violin and clarinet played to some lively tune; after these came the bier, upon which was placed the body, generally without coffin—the latter, (black, with white tape crossed all over it), being borne empty by two children across their shoulders, walking behind; the body was usually in its best clothes, strewed with flowers, and lying upon a white pall; the bier was borne on the shoulders of four children, generally girls; and after these came the friends, without any order, dressed in their most showy clothes, and most of them provided with a bottle of *aguadiente*, or homemade brandy. After the ceremonies in the church were ended, the poor little innocent was buried by the roadside, and a pile of stones raised over it; and if the father was too lazy to make a cross for his child's grave, he stole one from and adjoining stone-pile. And the funeral party went home pretty tipsy.

From: *A Campaign in New Mexico with Colonel Doniphan* (Philadelphia: Carey and Hart, Publishers, 1847)

The Power of the Black-Robes, September 12, 1846

Pierre-Jean de Smet

Father de Smet, a Jesuit ("black robe") priest, was born in Belgium in 1801. He emigrated to America in 1821 and entered the Jesuit novitiate in Maryland because of a missionary zeal. His first Indian missionary work was to establish St. Joseph's Mission at Council Bluffs for the Pottawatomies. Curiously, in 1831, some Rocky Mountain Indians, influenced by Iroquois descendants of converts of one hundred and fifty years before, sent delegations to St. Louis begging to have "Black-robes" sent to their country. In 1840, Father de Smet set off for the Rocky Mountains and the far west. There, he worked with the Flatheads, Crows, Gros Ventres. He established St. Mary's Mission on the Bitter Root River, thirty miles north of present-day Missoula. Father de Smet was respected throughout the Indian nations and it was reported that he "alone of the entire white race could penetrate to these cruel savages and return safe and sound." Father de Smet died in St. Louis in 1873.

Some of the hunters are sent out to look for game; for scarcity was making itself felt in the camp. One of these scouts soon spies in the distance immense herds of buffalo, appearing as little black dots. He returns toward camp to announce the glad news and mounts a high hill, whence he can be seen, standing on his horse, holding the stock of his gun high in the air; it is a signal to announce the presence of the animals. Then the chief proclaims a great hunt; the hunters rope their best running horses, which are jumping and prancing with joy. We start at a gallop; but when they are about to rush upon their prey, the horsemen stop, to recite, after the example of the Flatheads, three Ave Marias, in honor the Holy Virgin. (Some of them know it in Flathead.) Can I express the joy I felt at hearing this prayer under these circumstances? I shall not try; pious souls will feel it sufficiently. The prayer ended, the hunters get to horse again and pursue the animals, which lead them to a great distance. Each killed one, two or three, according to the strength of his horse. There was an abundant supper in every lodge and all the fires were surrounded with numerous beef-steaks; mine was garnished with a wreath of tongues, humps and kidneys, which the hunters had reserved for the Black-robes, and which we shared like brothers with all who came to call.

After supper a splendid evening entertainment, given in our lodge by a Blackfoot, so good, so sensible and at the same time so original, that it was a real pleasure in every respect to us to hear him. All communication was by signs. Here are some of the observations he had made during his stay in the Flathead camp. "When we arrived," he said, "we had plenty of meat. The Flatheads and the Nez Percés were short: they visited us and we gave them to eat according to custom. The Flatheads, before they would touch anything, put their hands to their foreheads, made the sign of the cross, then a good prayer; whereas the Nez Percés fell upon the food like starved animals. Sunday the Flatheads sat quiet in their lodges, thought only of praying to God and encouraging one another in well-doing; while the Nez Percés put on their fine clothes and scattered here and there, for more harm than good. I noticed especially that the Nez Percés maintained no such reserve toward our young people as did the Flatheads; so, in the fight with the Crows, it was only the Nez Percés who had any losses to mourn; I saw by this that the white men's God is good to the good; but also that when he chooses, he knows how to find the wicked, to punish them as they deserve."

The astonishing successes of the Flatheads, in the wars that have been forced on them the last three years, have confirmed their enemies in the belief that they have held of late, that the medicine of the Black-robes is stronger than theirs.

From: *Life, Letters and Travels of Father Pierre-Jean de Smet, S.J., 1801-1873* (New York: Francis P. Harper, Publishers, 1905)

Night Sounds of an Oglala Village, c. 1846

Francis Parkman

A former Harvard student from a wealthy Bostonian family, Francis Parkman set out in 1846 at age twenty-three to experience the West first-hand and to "observe the Indian character." To accomplish his purpose he felt that to really know the Indians it was necessary to "live in the midst of them, and become, as it were, one of them." Living his purpose, Parkman took up life in an Oglala village of the Teton Dakota Sioux. In 1849, Parkman published his adventures under the title, The Oregon Trail. In the narrative that follows, Parkman paints a vivid word picture of the sounds emanating from an Indian village in the evening.

The camp was filled with the low hum of cheerful voices. There were other sounds, however, of a different kind; for from a large lodge, lighted up like a gigantic lantern by the blazing fire within, came a chorus of dismal cries and wailings, long drawn out, like the howling of wolves, and a woman, almost naked, was crouching close outside, crying violently, and gashing her legs with a knife till they were covered with blood. Just a year before, a young man belonging to this family had been slain by the enemy, and his relatives were thus lamenting his loss. Still other sounds might be heard; loud, earnest cries often repeated from amid the gloom, at a distance beyond the village. They proceeded from some young men who, being about to set out in a few days on a war party, were standing at the top of a hill, calling on the Great Spirit to aid them in their enterprise. While I was listening, Rouleau, with a laugh on his careless face, called to me and direct my attention to another quarter. In front of the lodge, another squaw was standing, angrily scolding an old yellow dog, who lay on the ground with his nose resting between his paws, and

73

his eyes turned sleepily up to her face, as if pretending to give respectful attention, but resolved to fall asleep as soon as it was all over.

"You ought to be ashamed of yourself!" said the old woman. "I have fed you well, and taken care of you ever since you were small and blind, and could only crawl about and squeal a little instead of howling as you do now. When you grew old, I said you were a good dog. You were strong and gentle when the load was put on your back, and you never ran among the feet of the horses when we were all traveling together over the prairie. But you had a bad heart! Whenever a rabbit jumped out of the bushes, you were always the first to run after him and lead away all the other dogs behind you. You ought to have known that it was very dangerous to act so. When you had got far out on the prairie, and no one was near to help you, perhaps a wolf would jump out of the ravine; and then what could you do? You would certainly have been killed, for no dog can fight well with a load on his back. Only three days ago you ran off in that way, and turned over the bag of wooden pins with which I used to fasten up the lodge. Look up there, and you will see that it is all flapping open. And now tonight you have stolen a great piece of fat meat which was roasting before the fire for my children. I tell you, you have a bad heart, and you must die!"

So saying, the squaw went into the lodge, and coming out with a large stone mallet, killed the unfortunate dog at one blow. This speech is worthy of notice, as illustrating a curious characteristic of the Indians, who ascribe intelligence and a power of understanding speech to the inferior animals, to whom, indeed, according to many of their traditions, they are lined in close affinity; and they even claim the honor of a lineal descent from bears, wolves, deer, or tortoises.

From: *The Oregon Trail: Sketches of the Prairie and Rocky-Mountain Life* (Boston: Little, Brown and Company, 1892)

A Sioux Village

A Blizzard in South Park, c. Winter 1847

George Frederick Ruxton

Already having traveled to Spain, Africa, Canada, and Mexico by the time he arrived in the American West, England-born George Frederick Ruxton (1821–1848) joined a group of mountain men in the high mountain plateau of central Colorado, known as South Park. There, Ruxton and his acquaintances experienced life to the fullest and had hair-raising escapes from Indians as well as from the weather. Ruxton apparently loved the wilderness and he wrote about it with an illuminating relish. He chronicled his adventures in a diary which was published in 1847 with the title, Adventures in Mexico and the Rocky Mountains. *Ruxton died in St. Louis in 1848 at the youthful age of twenty-seven. In this vignette, Ruxton tells of a life-threatening encounter with a blizzard in the Colorado high country known as South Park.*

The sky had been gradually overcast with leaden-colored clouds, until, when near sunset, it was one huge inky mass or rolling darkness: the wind had suddenly lulled and an unnatural calm, which so surely heralds a storm in these tempestuous regions, succeeded. The ravens were winging their way towards the shelter of the timber, and the coyote was seen trotting quickly to cover, conscious of the coming storm.

The black threatening clouds seemed gradually to descend until they kissed the earth, and already the distant mountains were bidden to their very bases. A hollow murmuring swept through the bottom, but as yet not a branch was stirred by wind; and the huge cottonwoods, with their leafless limbs, loomed like a line of ghosts through the heavy gloom. Knowing but too well what was coming, I turned my animals towards the timber, which was about two miles distant. With pointed ears, and actually trembling with fright, they were as eager as myself to reach the shelter; but, before we had proceeded a third of the distance, with a deafening roar the tempest broke upon us. The clouds opened and drove right in our faces a storm of freezing sleet, which froze upon us as it fell. The first squall of wind carried away my cap, and the enormous hailstones, beating on my unprotected head and face, almost stunned me. In an instant my hunting-shirt was soaked, and as instantly frozen hard; and my horse was a mass of icicles. Jumping off my mule—for to ride was impossible— I tore off the saddle-blanket and covered my head. The animals, blinded with the sleet, and their eyes actually coated with ice, turned their sterns to the storm, and, blown before it, made for the open prairie. All my exertions to drive them to the shelter of the timber was useless. It was impossible to face the hurricane, which now brought with it clouds of driving snow; and perfect darkness soon set in.

Still the animals kept on, and I determined not to leave them, following, or rather being blown after them. My blanket, frozen stiff like a board, required all the strength of my numbed fingers to prevent it being blown away, and, although it was no protection against the intense cold, I knew it would in some degree shelter me at night from the snow. In half an hour the ground was covered on the bare prairie to the depth of two feet, and through this I floundered for a long time before the animals stopped. The prairie was as bare as a lake; but one little tuft of greasewood bushes presented itself, and here, turning from the storm, they suddenly stopped and remained perfectly still. In vain I again attempted to turn them towards the direction of the timber, huddled together, they would not move an inch; and, exhausted myself, and seeing nothing before me but, as I thought, certain death, I sank down immediately behind them, and, covering my head with the blanket, crouched like a ball in the snow.

I would have started myself for the timber, but it was pitch dark, the wind drove clouds of frozen snow into my face, and the animals had so turned about in the prairie that it was impossible to know the direction to take; and although I had a compass with me, my hands were so frozen that I was perfectly unable, after repeated attempts, to unscrew the box and consult it. Even had I reached the timber, my situation would have been scarcely improved, for the trees were scattered wide about over a narrow space, and, consequently, afforded but little shelter; and if even I had succeeded in getting firewood—by no means an easy matter at any time, and still more difficult now that the ground was covered with three feet of snow—I was utterly unable to use my flint and steel to procure a light, since my fingers were like pieces of stone, and entirely without feeling.

The way the wind roared over the prairie that night—how the snow drove before it, covering me and the poor animals partly—and how I lay there, feeling the very blood freezing in my veins, and my bones petrifying with the icy blasts which seemed to penetrate them—how for hours I remained with my head on my knees, and the snow pressing it down like a weight of lead, expecting every instant to drop into a sleep from which I knew it was impossible I should ever awake—how every now and then the mules would groan aloud and fall down upon the snow, and then again struggle on their legs—how all night long the piercing howl of wolves was borne upon the wind, which never for an instant abated its violence during the night—I would not attempt to describe. I have passed many nights alone in the wilderness, and in a solitary camp have listened to the roarings of the winds and the howling of wolves, and felt the rain or snow beating upon me, with perfect unconcern: but this night threw all my former experiences into the shade, and is marked with the blackest of stones in the memoranda of my journeyings.

Once, late in the night, by keeping my hands buried in the breast of my hunting-shirt, I succeeded in restoring sufficient feeling into them to enable me to strike a light. Luckily my pipe, which was made out of a huge piece of cottonwood bark, and capable of containing at least twelve ordinary pipefuls, was filled with tobacco to the brim; and this I do believe kept me alive during the night, for I smoked and smoked until the pipe itself caught fire, and burned completely to the stem.

I was just sinking into a dreamy stupor, when the mules began to shake themselves, and sneeze and snort; which hailing as a good sign, and that they were still alive, I attempted to lift my head and take a view of the weather. When with great difficulty I raised my head, all appeared dark as pitch, and it did not at first occur to me that I was buried deep in snow; but when I thrust my arm above me a hole was thus made, through which I saw the stars shining in the sky and the clouds fast clearing away. Making a sudden attempt to straighten my almost petrified back and limbs, I rose, but, unable to stand, fell forward in the snow, frightening the animals, which immediately started away. When I gained my legs I found that day was just breaking, a long grey line of light appearing over the belt of timber on the creek, and the clouds gradually rising from the east, and allowing the stars to peep from patches of blue sky. Following the animals as soon as I gained the use of my limbs, and taking a last look at the perfect cave from which I had just risen, I found them in the timber, and jump[ing] upon my horse . . . galloped back to the Arkansas [River], which I reached in the evening, half dead with hunger and cold.

From: *Adventures in Mexico and the Rocky Mountains* (London, 1847) with part of that book reprinted as *Wild Life in the Rocky Mountains* (New York: The MacMillan Company, 1916)

"You Don't [K]now What Trubel Is Yet," May 16, 1847

Virginia Reed

The ill-fated Donner Party took the so-called Hastings' Cutoff and became bogged down in the snow in the Sierra Nevada Mountains for almost six months. Without food, members of the emigrant group stooped to cannibalism after about half of them had perished from starvation. After being rescued and safe on the west side of the mountains, twelve-year-old Virginia Reed penned a letter to her cousin, Mary C. Keyes, in Springfield, Illinois. Without concern for spelling or grammar, Virginia told Mary the remarkable story of The Donner Party. On December 16, 1847, Virginia's letter was published by Springfield's Illinois Journal *with the title, "Deeply Interesting Letter." Interestingly, Virginia advises her cousin, Mary, "to never take no cutofs and hury along as fast as you can." In 1850, Virginia married John Murphy, settled in San Jose, California, and had nine children. Although Virginia's father allegedly checked her letter over to correct its spelling and grammar before it was mailed, modern readers should try their best to overlook those errors and read the letter for the vivid story it conveys.*

Napa Vallie
California
May 16th 1847

My Dear Cousin May the 16 1847

I take this oppertunity to write to you to let you now that we are all Well at present and hope this letter may find you all well to My Dear Cousin I am going to write to you about our trubels geting to Callifornia. We had good luck til we come to big Sandy thare we lost our best yoak of oxens we come to Brigers Fort & we lost another ox we sold some of our provisions & baut a yoak of Cows & oxen and thay pursuaded us to take Hastings

cutof over the salt plain thay said it saved 3 Hundred miles. We went that
road & we had to go through a long drive of 40 miles With out water Hastings said it was 40 but I think 80 miles We traveld a day and night & a
nother day and at noon pa went on to see if he could find Water. He had
not bin gone long till some of the oxen give out and we had to leve the
wagons and take the oxen on to water one of the men staid with us and the
others went on with the cattel to water pa was a coming back to us with
water and met the men & thay was about 10 miles from water pa said thay
[would] get to water that nite and the next day to bring the cattel back for
the wagons and bring some water pa got to us about noon the man that
was with us took the horse and went on to water We wated thare [think-
ing] he [would] come we wated till night and We thought we [would] start
and walk to Mr. Donners wagons that night we took what little water we
had and some bread and started pa caried Thomos and all the rest of us
walk we got to Donner and thay were all a sleep so we laid down on the
ground we spred one shawl down We laid down on it and spred another
over us and then put the dogs on top it was the couldes night you most
ever saw the wind blew and if it haden bin for the dogs we would have
Frosen As soon as it was day we went to Mrs Donners she said we could
not walk to the Water and if we staid we could ride in thare wagons to the
spring so pa went on to the water to see why thay did not bring the cattel
when he got thare thare was but one ox and cow thare None of the rest had
got to water Mr. Donner come out that night with his cattel and brought
his wagons and all of us in we staid thare a week and Hunted for our cattel and could not find them so some of the compania took thare oxens and
went out and brougt in one wagon and cashed the other tow and a grate
many things all but What we could put in one wagon we Had to devied
our provisions out to them to get them to carie it We got three yhoak with
our ox & cow so we went on that way a while and we got out of provisions
and pa had to go on to Callifornia for provisions we could not get along
that way. in 2 or 3 days after pa left we had to cash our wagon and take Mr
graves wagon and cash some more of our things. well we went on that
way a while and then we had to get Mr eddies wagon we went on that way
a while and then we had to cash all our close except a change or 2 and put
them in Mr Bri[ns] Wagon and Thomos & James rode the other 2 horses
and the rest of us had to walk. we went on that way a While and we come
to nother long drive of 40 miles and then we went with Mr Donner We had
to walk all the time we was a travling up the truckee river we met a man
and to Indians that we had sent on for provisions to Suter Fort thay had
met pa not fur from Suters Fort he looked very bad he had not ate but 3
times in 7 days and the three last days without any thing his horse was not
abel to carrie him thay give him a horse and he went on so we cashed some
more of our things all but what we could pack on one mule and we started

Martha and James road behind the two Indians it was a rain[in]g then in the Vallies and snowing on the montains so we went on that way 3 or 4 days till we come to the big mountain or the Callifornia Mountain the snow then was about 3 feet deep thare was some wagons thare thay said thay had atempted to croos and could not. well we thought we would try it so we started and thay started again with those wagons the snow was then up to the mules side the farther we went up the deeper the snow got so the wagons could not go so thay pack thare oxens and started with us carring a child a piece and driving the oxens in snow up to thare wast the mule Martha and the Indian was on was the best one so thay went and broak the road and that indian was the Pilet so we wint on that way 2 miles and the mules kept faling down in the snow head formost and the Indian said he could not find the road we stoped and let the indian and man go on to hunt the road thay went on and found the road to the top of the mountain anc come back and said thay thought wo could git over it did not snow any more well the Weman were all so tirder caring there Children that thay could not go over that night so we made a fire and got something to eat & ma spred down a bufalo robe & we all laid down on it & spred somthing over us & ma sit up by the fire & it snowed one foot on top of the bed so we got up in the morning & the snow was so deep we could not go over & we had to go back to the cabin & build more cabins & stay thar all winter without Pa we had not the first thing to eat

Ma maid arrangements for some cattel giving 2 for 1 in callifornia we seldom thot of bread for we had not any since I [remember] & the cattel was so poor thay could not git up when thay laid down we stoped thare the 4th of November & staid till March and what we had to eat I cant hardley tell you & we had that man & Indians to feed to well thay started over a foot and had to come back so thay made snowshoes and started again & it come on a storm & thay had to come back it would snow to days before it would stop thay wated till it stoped & started again I was a going with them & I took sick & could not go. thare was 15 started & thare was 7 got throw 5 weman & 2 men it come a storme and thay lost the road & got out of provisions & the ones that got throwe had to eat them that Died not long after thay started we got out of provisions & had to put matha at one cabin James at another Thomas at another & Ma and Elizia & Milt Eliot & I dried up what little meat we had and started to see if we could get across & had to leve the childrin o Mary you may think that hard to leve theme with strangers & did not now wether we would see them again or not we couldnt harle get a way from them but we told theme we would bring them Bread & then thay was willing to stay we went & was out 5 days in the mountains Eliza giv out & had to go back We went on a day longer we had to lay by a day & make snowshows & we went on a while and coud not find the road so we had to turn back I could go on

verry well while I thout we were giting along but as soone as we had to
turn back I coud hadley get along but we got to the cabins that night & I
froze one of my feet verry bad that same night thare was the worst storme
we had that winter & if we had not come back that night we would never
got back we had nothing to eat but ox hides o Mary I would cry and wish
I had what you all wasted Eliza had to go to Mr. Graves cabin & we staid
at Mr Breen thay had meat all the time. & we had to kill littel cash the dog
& eat him we ate his entrails and feet & hide & every thing about him o
my Dear Cousin you don't now what trubel is yet. Many a time we had
on the last thing a cooking and did not now wher the next would come
from but there was awl weis some way provided there was 15 in the cabin
we was in and half of us had to lay a bed all the time thare was 10 starved
to death then we was hadly abel to walk we lived on little cash a week and
after Mr. Breen would cook his meat we would take the bones and boil
them 3 or 4 days at a time ma went down to the other cabin and got half
a hide carried it in snow up to her wast it snowed and would cover the
cabin all over so we could not git out for 2 or 3 days we would have to cut
pieces of the logs in sied to make the fire with I coud hardly eat the hides
and had not eat anything 3 days Pa sta[r]ted out to us with provisions and
then come a storm and he could not go he cash his provision and went
back on the other side of the bay to get a compana of men and the San
Wakien [Joaquin] got so hye he could not cross well thay Made up a Compana at Suters Fort and sent out we had not ate any thing for 3 days & we
had onely half a hide and we was out on top of the cabin and we seen
them a coming

O my Dear Cousin you don't now how glad I was we run and met them
one of them we knew we had traveled with him on the road thay staid
thare 3 days to recruit us a little so we could go thare was 21 started All
of us started and went a piece and Martha and Thomas give out and the
men had to take them back Ma and Eliza & James and I come on and o
Mary that was the hades thing yet to come on and leiv them thar did not
now but what thay would starve to Death Martha said well Ma if you
never see me again do the best you can the men said they could hadly
stand it it maid them all cry but they said it was better for all of us to go
on for if we was to go back we would eat that much more from them thay
give them a little meat and flore and took them back and we come on we
went over great hye mountain as strait as stair steps in snow up to our
knees litle James walk the hole way over all the mountain in snow up to
his waist. he said every step he took he was a gitting nigher Pa and something to eat the Bears took the provision the men had cashed and we had
but very little to eat when we had traveld 5 days travel we me[t] Pa with
13 men going to the cabins o Mary you do not now how glad we was to
see him we had not seen him for 6 months we thought we woul never see

him again he heard we was coming and he made some s[w]eet cakes to give us he said he would see Martha and Thomas the naxt day he went in tow days what took us 5 days some of the compana was eating them that Died but Thomas & Martha had not ate any Pa and the men started with 17 people Hiram G. Miller carried Thomas and Pa caried Martha and thay wer caught in [storms] and thay had to stop two days it stormed so they could not go and the Bears took their provisions and thay were 4 days without any thing Pa and Hiram and all the men started one Donner boy [sentence unfinished] Pa a carring Martha Hiram caring Thomas and the snow was up to thare wast and it a snowing so thay could hadly see the way. thay [w]rap[p]ed the children up and never took them out for 4 days thay had nothing to eat in all that time Thomas asked for somthing to eat once them that thay brought from the cabins some of them was not able to come and som would not come that was 3 died and the rest eat them thay was 11 days without any thing to eat but the Dead Pa braught Tom and pady on to where we was none of the men was abel to go there feet was froze very bad so thay was a nother Compana went and brought then all in thay are all in from the mauntains now but four thay was men went out after them and was caught in a storm and had to come back thare was a nother compana gone thare was half got through that was stoped thare thare was but [2] families that all of them got [through] we was one O Mary I have not rote you half of the truble we have had but I have rote you anuf to let you now that you don't now what truble is but thank god we have all got throw and the onely family that did not eat human flesh we have left everything but I don't coir for that we have got thuow with our lives but Don't let this letter dish[e]a[r]ten anybody never take no cut-ofs and hury along as fast as you can. . . .

My Dear casons

Virginia Elizabeth B Reed

The Donner Party—at Donner Lake, November 1846

Hanging Mexican Murderers, c. Spring 1847

Lewis H. Garrard

Lewis Garrard was only seventeen when he left his home in Cincinnati to seek adventure in the West. Soon thereafter he found himself at Bent's Fort on the Santa Fé Trail. He lived at the fort for a few months. Garrard joined a little company of volunteers recruited by William Bent, chief of the fort and brother of Governor Charles Bent of New Mexico Territory. Governor Bent was murdered in a Mexican-Indian revolt at Taos shortly after the Mexican War ended and the United States claimed New Mexico Territory as its own. The purpose Garrard and his fellow volunteers was "kill and scalp every Mexican to be found." In the following vignette, some of the Mexicans who participated in Governor Bent's murder are about to be hung for the crime. Garrard's book, Wah-to-Yah and the Taos Trail *was first published in 1850 and is the only contemporaneous source for the trial and execution of those responsible for Governor Bent's murder.*

On Friday, the ninth, the sky was unspotted, save by hastily-fleeting clouds; and, as the rising sun loomed over the Taos Mountain, the bright rays, shining on the yellow and white mud houses, reflected cheerful hues, while the shades of the toppling peaks receding from the plain beneath drew within themselves. The humble valley wore an air of calm repose. The plaza was deserted; woe-begone donkeys drawled forth sacrilegious brays as the warm sunbeams roused them from hard, grassless ground to scent among straw or bones their breakfast: a *señora* in her nightdress and disheveled hair—which, at the *fandango*, was the admiration of the moustached *señors* and half-wild *voluntarios*—could here and there be seen at this early hour, opening her house, previous to the preparation of the fiery *chile colorado*.

85

As onward sped the day, so did the crowd of morning drinkers at Estis's tavern to renew their libations to Bacchus. Poor Mexicans hurried to and fro, casting suspicious glances around; *los Yankees* at *El casa Americano* drank their juleps and puffed their cigarillos in silence.

The sheriff (Metcalfe, formerly a mountaineer, son-in-law to Estis) was in want of the wherewith to hang the criminals, so he borrowed our rawhide lariats and two or three hempen picket cords of a teamster. In a room adjoining the bar, we put the hangman's noose on one end, tugging away quite heartily. . . .

The prison was at the edge of town; no houses intervened between it and the fields to the north. One hundred and fifty yards distant a scaffold of two upright posts and a crossbeam was erected.

At the portal were several *compañeros*, discussing, in a very light way, the "fun," as they termed it, on hand—they almost wishing a rescue would be attempted so as to gratify their propensity for excitement.

The word was passed, at last, that the criminals were coming. Eighteen soldiers received them at the gate, with their muskets at port arms—the six abreast, with the sheriff on the right—nine soldiers on each side. Hatcher, Loyu Simonds, Chadwick, myself, and others, eight in all, formed in line a pace behind, as the rear guard, with our trusty mountain rifles at rest in the bended elbow of the left arm, the right hand resting on the stock, to be drawn up to the face, and all ready to fight on our own responsibility at the least intimation of danger.

The poor *pelados* marched slowly, with down-cast eyes, arms tied behand, and bare heads, with the exception of white cotton caps stuck on the back part, to be pulled over the face as the last ceremony.

The *azoteas*—roofs—in our vicinity, were covered with women and children, to witness the first execution by hanging in the valley of Taos, save that of Montojo, the insurgent leader. No men were near; a few, afar off, stood moodily looking on.

On the flat jail roof was placed a mountain howitzer, loaded and ranging the gallows. Near was the complement of men to serve it, one holding in his hand a lighted match.

The two hundred and thirty soldiers (deducting the eighteen forming the guard) were paraded in front of the jail and in sight of the gibbet, so as to secure the prisoners awaiting trail. Lieutenant Colonel Willock, on a handsome charger, from his position commanded a view of the whole.

When within fifteen paces of the gallows, the side guard, filing off to the right and left, formed, at regular distances from each other, three sides of a hollow square; the mountaineers and myself composed the fourth and front side, in full view of the trembling prisoners, who marched up to the tree, under which was a government wagon with two mules attached. The driver and sheriff assisted them in, ranging them on a board, placed across the hinder end, which maintained its balance, as they were six–and even number—two on each extremity and two in the middle. The gallows was so narrow they touched. The ropes, by reason of size and stiffness despite the soaping given them, were adjusted with difficulty; but, though the indefatigable efforts of the sheriff and a lieutenant, all preliminaries were arranged. The former, officiating as deputy sheriff for the occasion, seemed to enjoy the position—but the blue uniform looked sadly out of place on a hangman.

With rifles grounded, we awaited the consummation of the fearful tragedy. No crowd was around to disturb; a death-like stillness reigned. The spectators on the *azoteas* seemed scarcely to move–their eyes directed to the painful sight of the doomed wretches, with harsh halters now circling their necks.

The sheriff and assistant sat down; and, succeeding a few moments of intense expectation, the heart-wrung victims said a few words to their people.

But one said that they had committed murder and deserved death. In their brief, but earnest appeals, which I could but imperfectly comprehend, the words, *"mi padre, mi madre,"* could be distinguished. The one sentenced for treason showed a spirit of martyrdom worthy of the cause for which he died—the liberty of his country; and, instead of the cringing, contemptible recantation of the others, his speech was firm asseverations of his own innocence, the unjustness of his trial, and the arbitrary conduct of his murderers. With a scowl, as the cap was pulled over his face, the last words he uttered between his gritting teeth were, *"Caraho, los Americanos!"*

Bidding each other *"adios,"* with a hope of meeting in Heaven, at word from the sheriff the mules were started, and the wagon drawn from under the tree. No fall was given, and their feet remained on the board till the ropes drew taut. The bodies swayed back and forth, and, coming in contact with each other, convulsive shudders shook their frames; the muscles, contracting, would relax, and again contract, and the bodies writhed most horribly.

While thus swinging, the hands of two came together, which they held with a firm grasp till the muscles loosened in death.

From: *Wah-To-Yah and the Taos Trail* (Cincinnati, OH: A. S. Barnes and Company, Publishers, 1850)

A Scout's Experience
Saves Lives, c. June 1848

George Douglas Brewerton

George Brewerton, a 19-year-old second lieutenant of the New York Volunteers and a veteran of the Mexican War, was ordered to leave Los Angeles to join a new regiment as a newly appointed U.S. Army regular officer. To join his new regiment in Mississippi with as little delay as possible, he had to cross the plains via the Old Spanish Trail and the Santa Fé Trail. At the same time, the famous mountaineer and guide, Christopher "Kit" Carson, was preparing to head East. Carson had been contracted to be the guide and to carry official dispatches and ordinary mail from Los Angeles to St. Louis where it could then be placed in the U.S. postal system. Brewerton joined the Carson expedition and traveled with him as far as Santa Fé where Brewerton became ill. Carson continued his journey and later Brewerton joined an eastward-bound commercial wagon train to complete his trek. The following event took place in the Taos Valley in northern New Mexico. It was published in Brewerton's 1853 book of his adventures.

During the night great uneasiness among the animals betokened the presence or close vicinity of lurking Indians; and Kit, whose long acquaintance with the savages had taught him a perfect knowledge of their modes of warfare, believing that they would attack us about daybreak, determined to steal a march upon the enemy. In pursuance of this object, we saddled our beasts at midnight, and departed as noiselessly as possible, traveling by starlight until the first glimmer of the dawn, when we paused for a few moments to breathe our tired animals, and then continued on.

We had, upon leaving our last night's camp, nearly one hundred miles to travel before reaching the first settlements in New Mexico, the nearest place of safety; and it was now determined to make the distance without delay. Accordingly we pressed on as rapidly as the condition of our cattle would permit, stopping only to shift our saddles in one of the loose animals when those we rode showed signs of giving out. Late in the afternoon we had, by the free use of whip and spur, reached a point some eighteen miles distant from the first Mexican habitations.

I was just beginning to feel a little relieved from the anxious watchfulness of the last few days, and had even beguiled the weariness of the way by picturing to myself the glorious dinner I would order upon reaching Sante Fé, when Carson, who had been looking keenly ahead, interrupted my musings, by exclaiming: "Look at that Indian village; we have stumbled upon the rascals, after all!" It was but too true—a sudden turning of the trail had brought up full in view of nearly two hundred lodges, which were located upon a rising ground some half a mile distant to the right of our trail. At this particular point the valley grew narrower, and hemmed in as we were upon either hand by a chain of hills and mountains, we had no resource but to keep straight forward on our course, in the expectation that by keeping, as sailors say, "well under the land," we might possibly slip by unperceived. But our hope was a vain one; we had already been observed, and ere we had gone a hundred yards, a warrior came dashing out from their town, and, putting his horse to its speed, rode rapidly up to Carson and myself: he was a finely formed savage, mounted upon a noble horse, and his fresh paint and gaudy equipments looked anything but peaceful. This fellow continued his headlong career until almost at our side, and then, checking his steed so suddenly as to throw the animal back upon its haunches, he inquired for the "capitán" (a Spanish word generally used by the Indians to signify chief); in answer to which, I pointed first to Carson, and then to myself. Kit, who had been regarding him intently, but without speaking, now turned to me, and said: "I will speak to this warrior in Eutaw, and if he understands me it will prove that he belongs to a friendly tribe; but if he does not, we may know the contrary, and must do the best we can: but from his paint and manner I expect it will end in a fight anyway."

Kit then turned to the Indian, who, to judge from his expression, was engaged in taking mental but highly satisfactory notes of our way-worn party with their insufficient arms and scanty equipments; and asked him in the Eutaw tongue, "Who are you?" The savage stared at us for a moment; and then, putting a finger into either ear, shook his head slowly from side to side. "I knew it," said Kit; "it is just as I thought, and we are in for it at last. Look here, Thomas!" added he (calling to an old mountain man)—"get the mules together, and drive them up to that little patch of chaparral, while we follow with the Indian." Carson then requested me in a whisper to drop behind the savage (who appeared determined to accompany us), and be ready to shoot him at a minute's warning, if necessity required. Having taken up a position accordingly, I managed to cock my rifle, which I habitually carried upon the saddle, without exciting suspicion.

Kit rode ahead to superintend the movements of the party who, under the guidance of Thomas, had by this time got the pack and loose animals together, and were driving them toward a grove about two hundred yards further from the village. We had advanced thus but a short distance, when Carson (who from time to time had been glancing backward over his shoulder) reined in his mule until we again rode side-by-side. While stooping, as if to adjust his saddle, he said, in too low a tone to reach any ears but mine: "Look back, but express no surprise." I did so, and beheld a sight which, though highly picturesque, and furnishing a striking subject for a painting, was, under existing circumstances, rather calculated to destroy the equilibrium of the nerves. In short, I saw about a hundred and fifty warriors, finely mounted, and painted for war, with their long hair streaming in the wind, charging down upon us, shaking their lances and brandishing their spears as they came on.

By this time we had reached the timber, if a few stunted trees could be dignified with the name; and Kit, springing from his mule, called out to the men, "Now, boys, dismount, tie up your riding mules; those of you who have guns, get round the caballada, and look out for the Indians; and you who have none, get inside, and hold some of the animals. Take care, Thomas, and shoot down the mule with the mail bags on her pack, if they try to stampede the animals."

We had scarcely made these hurried preparations for the reception of such unwelcome visitors, before the whole horde were upon us, and had surrounded our position. For the next fifteen minutes a scene of confusion and excitement ensured which baffles all my powers of description. On the one hand the Indians pressed closely in, yelling, aiming their spears, and drawing their bows, while their chiefs, conspicuous from their activity, dashed here and there among the crowd, commanding and directing their followers. On the other side, our little band, with the exception of those who had lost their rifles in Grand River, stood firmly round the caballada; Carson, a few paces in advance, giving orders to his men, and haranguing the Indians, His whole demeanor was now so entirely changed that he looked like a different man; his eye fairly flashed, and his rifle was grasped with all the energy of an iron will.

"There," cried he, addressing the savages, "is our line, cross it if you dare, and we begin to shoot. You ask us to let you in, but you won't come unless you ride over us. You say you are friends, but you don't act like it. No, you don't deceive us so, we know you too well; so stand back, or your lives are in danger."

It was a bold thing in him to talk thus to these blood-thirsty rascals; but a crisis had arrived in which boldness along could save us, and he knew it. They had five men to our one; our ammunition was reduced to three rounds per man, and resistance could have been but momentary; but among our band the Indians must have recognized mountain men, who would have fought to the last, and they knew from sad experience that the trapper's rifle rarely missed its aim. Our animals, moreover, worn out as they were, would have been scarcely worth fighting for, and our scalps a dear bargain.

Our assailants were evidently undecided, and this indecision saved us; for just as they seemed preparing for open hostilities, as rifles were cocked and bows drawn, a runner, mounted upon a weary and foam-specked steed, came galloping in from the direction of the settlements, bringing information of evident importance. After a moment's consultation with this new arrival, the chief whistled shrilly, and the warriors fell back. Carson's quick eye had already detected their confusion, and turning his men, he called out, "Now, boys, we have a chance, jump into your saddles, get the loose animals before you, and then handle your rifles, and if these fellows interfere with us we'll make a running fight of it."

In an instant each man was in his saddle, and with the caballada in front we retired slowly; facing about from time to time, to observe the movements of our enemies, who followed on, but finally left us and disappeared in the direction of their village, leaving our people to pursue their way undisturbed. We rode hard, and about midnight reached the first Mexican dwellings which we had seen since our departure from the Pacific coast. This town being nothing more than a collection of shepherds' huts, we did not enter, but made camp near it. Here also we learned the secret of our almost miraculous escape from the Indians, in the fact that a party of two hundred American volunteers were on their way to punish the perpetrators of recent Indian outrages in that vicinity; this then was the intelligence which had so opportunely been brought by their runner, who must have discovered the horsemen while upon the march.

From: *A Ride with Kit Carson through the Great American Desert and the Rocky Mountains* (New York: Harper & Brothers, 1853)

The Painted Ladies of Santa Fé, c. Summer 1848

George Douglas Brewerton

In the previous story, Brewerton, a young lieutenant, traveled overland from Los Angeles, California, to Santa Fé, New Mexico, with Kit Carson. In Santa Fé Brewerton became ill with influenza and remained there, while Carson continued on his eastward trek. It was during his period of recovery that Brewerton noticed the interesting cosmetics worn by the women of Santa Fé.

During my sojourn in Santa Fé I was struck with the very peculiar taste which the young ladies of that city display in their fondness for cosmetics. Indeed, when I first entered the town, it appeared to me that every woman under the age of five-and-thirty was afflicted with an inflammation of the face, which I had mentally concluded might be "catching;" in this belief I continued until my fears were relieved by the kindness of a friend, who elucidated the mystery by letting me into the secret. It seems that the "*señoritas*," and for that matter, the "*señoras*" too, occasionally are in the habit of disfiguring themselves, by covering one or both cheeks with some kind of colored paste, which gives even to their village belles any thing but an attractive appearance. This painting might to the casual observer, seem intended as an ornament, got up in imitation of their Indian neighbors, or, it may be, of our own fashionable fair ones. But it is not so; for I am assured, by those whose opportunities of judging are undeniable, that it is put on as a preservative to the complexion. So that a New Mexican beauty is not only willing to forego the luxury of the bath, but even to appear hideous for a month at a time, for the sake of exhibiting a clean face and ruddy cheeks while gracing some grand *fandango* or *fiesta*.

From: *A Ride with Kit Carson through the Great American Desert and the Rocky Mountains* (New York: Harper & Brothers, 1853)

Southwestern Mirages, September 1, 1848

Alexander Majors

*One of the differences between the rolling green hills of the East and the West-
ern desert landscapes are mirages—tricks that your eyes play on you. In the
West, one can see vast distances, unhindered by forests, and through clear, dry
air. The light is bent and the eyes think they see either what does not exist, or
a changed appearance of something that does. It is these mirages that Majors
writes about. Majors played an important role in developing the West. Born in
Kentucky in 1814, Majors operated a freighting firm that carried goods on the
Santa Fé Trail and started the Pony Express as well as the Overland Stage
Company. Eventually he employed over 4,000 people—among them a teen-
aged Pony Express rider named William F. Cody (Buffalo Bill). In 1865 Majors sold out his remaining businesses and moved to Colorado. There, thirty
years later, old and poor, Buffalo Bill found Majors and gave him a job in the
Wild West Show. In 1893 Majors published his memoirs and died in Kansas
City in 1900.*

On my way from Independence, Mo., to Santa Fé, N.M., I met some of
the soldiers of General Donaldson's regiment returning from the
Mexican War on the Hornather or dry route, lying between the crossing
of the Arkansas and Cimarron. It was about noon when we met. I saw
them a considerable distance away. They were on horseback, and when
they first appeared, the horses' legs looked to be from fifteen to eighteen
feet long, and the body of the horses and the riders upon them presented
a remarkable picture, apparently extending into the air, rider and horse,
forty-five to sixty feet high. This was my first experience with mirage, and
it was a marvel to me.

At the same time I could see beautiful clear lakes of water, apparently not more than a mile away, with all the surroundings in the way of bulrushes and other water vegetation common to the margin of lakes. I would have been willing, at that time, to have staked almost anything upon the fact that I was looking upon lakes of pure water. This was my last experience of the kind until I was returning later on in the season, when one forenoon, as my train was on the march, I beheld just ahead the largest buffalo bull that I ever saw. I stopped the train to keep from frightening the animal away, took the gun out of my wagon, which was in front, and started off to get a shot at the immense fellow, but when I had walked about eighty yards in his direction, I discovered that it was nothing more nor less than a little coyote, which would not have weighed more than thirty pounds upon the scales.

The person who imagines for a minute that there is nothing in the great desert wastes of the Southwest but sand, cacti, and villainous reptiles is deluded. It is one of the most common fallacies to write down these barren places as devoid of beauty and usefulness. The rhymester who made Robinson Crusoe exclaim, "Oh, solitude, where are the charms that sages have seen in thy face?" never stood on a sand-dune or a pile of volcanic rock in this Southwestern country just at the break of day or as the sun went down, else the rhyme would never have been made to jingle.

To one who has never seen the famous mirages which Dame Nature paints with a lavish hand upon the horizon that bounds an Arizona desert, it is difficult to convey an intelligent portrait of these magnificent phenomena. And one who has looked upon these incomparable transformation scenes, the Titanic paintings formed by nature's curious slight-of-hand, can never forget them. They form the memories of a lifetime.

From: *Seventy Years on the Frontier: Alexander Majors' Memoirs of a Lifetime on the Border* (Chicago: Rand, McNally & Co., Publishers, 1893)

The Disaster of Frémont's Fourth Expedition, February 10, 1849

Edward M. Kern

Georgia-born in 1813, John Charles Frémont had successfully made three expeditions into the American West; first to the Rocky Mountains in 1842, then to Oregon in 1843–1844, and finally to California in 1845–1846. In 1848 he led a fourth expedition that turned out to be a disastrous effort that was intended to locate passes for a future transcontinental railroad. Because of judgment errors, mismanagement of time and food, and hampered by bad weather, the expedition suffered severe loss of human and animal life. In the following letter that Kern wrote to his older sister, Mary, many of the hardships of Frémont's fourth expedition are detailed. Later, Kern would strongly condemn Frémont for the disaster.

TAOS February 10, 1849

Mary, I have just arrived in this place about an hour ago and as there will be an opportunity of sending [mail] to the States in the morning I hasten to write you a few lines to relieve you of any apprehensions as regards our safety and our future movements.

I have not time to enter into detail nor dates with me but must leave that for some future letter–therefore can only give you a general outline of our miseries–You received among you I suppose letters from us at Bent's–at least we wrote from there–some time in November, about the 20th–from that place we went to the Pueblo on the Fontaine Qui Bouit the ground covered slightly with snow–from thence to the upper Pueblo where we procured corn for our animals and the services of Bill Williams as a pilot–We all left this point on foot packing our riding animals with corn and entered the mountains by the same creek on which the Pueblo is situated from thence to the Rio del Norte. leaving this river we attempted to cross the divide between it and the river St. John [actually, the river is the Gunnison] a tributary of the Colorado. Here commenced our difficulties the snow deepened every day our corn failed and the animals became so much weakened that we lost one after another, and still were travelling in search of the divide that we might cross to a more promising country— Somewhere about the 18 or 20 of December we arrived at a bald ridge supposed to be the Divide.—To get to it men were obliged to be sent ahead to break a road for the animals—and once we start to cross it but were obliged to return to our camp on account of the storm—I was impossible to see 5 yds ahead for the drift & had we remained ? an hour on the top we would certainly have perished as it was we lost several animals and had a number of the men frozen hand & feet & faces You can have no conception of the way it storms here. The next day we tried it again and reached a small clump of Pines about sundown—the snow about 5 feet deep our animals were driven to a bald place on a neighboring hill in hopes of their finding a little feed—from this place they never moved. Storm after storm continued and from hunger and the severity of the weather they perished—nearly a hundred head of as fine animals as ever entered the mountains 'Twas a melancholy sight to see the poor brutes standing shivering with the cold, without sufficient strength to reach a place of shelter. From this camp we commenced making portages to the hill top each man carrying 60 to 70 pounds hard work I can assure you. I carried 70 pounds on my back for 3 miles to the next camp. The baggage was then gradually worked down towards the Del Norte entirely by the men—Our food was failing us fast though we started with an excellent outfit sufficient for the whole journey the unexpected delays had used it up—On Christmas we made us pies from mule meat—not quite mince but very good for the Country we were in—On the first of January we reached a camp about 6 miles of the River. Frémont continuing on Doc & I returned to the mountains where we spent 3 days in trying to get down our clothing and materials. We were successful in reaching this camp. Mr. King started on the 26 for Abacue [Abiqiu, New Mexico] in hopes of obtaining relief for us but did not return. On the 11th January the Col started down the river in hopes of meeting the relief party—with his mess—We were if possible to get our baggage to the river and follow him—We all arrived on the River on the 14th glad to get there with our bedding and arms—Camp was left in charge of a man by the name of Vincenthaller a weak & cowardly person to whose imbecility and cowardice may be laid the subsequent deaths of most of the men who were lost. On the 16th we made our little packs took our rifles and started down the river with no particular place ahead that we could arrive at with any degree of certainty. Our provisions had already failed and we were reduced to parflesh (scraped buffalo hides used by the Indians in making their bales) raw hide ropes—Here commenced our severest suffering—reduced already by continued exertion and low diet we had but a poor prospect of reaching any place our only chance lay in the arrival of relief to us—A deer was killed by so divided as to do but little good to us—and then the Camp divided—the strongest and most experienced men went ahead—leaving the weaker ones to get along as they could. Our mess joined with one and concluded to help one another as long as there was a possibility of doing any thing—to this junction we owe our lives. Taplin the head of the other mess fortunately killed a couple of Prairie hens and found a dead wolf there, though starving themselves they divided with us, and to this we owe our lives—We continued down the river until the 19th when we made a camp to rest and hunt. Our sight was fast failing from the snow and the gradual exhaustion of our strength—In truth we were just able to crawl about to gather a little wood to keep from perishing with the cold—My food for 4 days consisted of the thigh of a hen that I cooked and recooked for breakfast and supper 8 times during those days rather meager soup that you would say. I had long passed the craving of hunger, and was gradually sinking into a sleep that would have required loud bawling to have awakened me from—I felt happy and contented sitting nearly all day by the fire in a kind of stupor listless and careless of when my time would come—for I was expecting it and in anticipation of it had written and closed all my business—But luckily on the 28th Relief arrived in shape of *Alek Godey*. he had reached the settlements and returned immediately with a supply of provisions—a day later and it would have been useless some people would say there was a special providence in it but we think it was management & luck Here ended our troubles—on the next day we mounted animals and started for this place. Of 33 that left the mountain 10 have perished from hunger—dying along the river where they sat down to rest and from their utter exhaustion were unable to rise. I smoked a pipe with an old French Voyageur on the side of the trail who 3 or 4 hours after was stiff and stark. Others who were strong in limb failed and died from the fear of that death—Among those who have perished was poor Proulx You may remember him being in Philada with me.

There never has been a more total defeat of any party in these mountains in pecuniary way and loss of life. Frémont's loss must be from 8 to 10,000 dollars—To the perseverance of Godey must be accredited the salvation of those of us that remain and he was the only man capable of performing such an exploit—

As for the Relief party sent under King they were picked up by the Col on his way down—King was dead and the rest in a most horrid state of starvation—some of them frozen as high as their hips. had we have waited for them we would have perished to a certainty as they themselves had given up all hopes of returning to us—The whole business may be laid down to error in judgment to whom attributable I am not now prepared to say.

The Col is in town though I have not yet seen him. He proceeds I understand on his journey—how or by what route I do not know—

Dick and Doc will return to the States by the earliest opportunity for myself I cannot say at least for a few days—I am nearly flat broke and scarcely know what to do—Though I do not think I will venture to butt another mountain this winter any how but I must close as it near 12 o'-clock and I am anxious to enjoy the luxury of a clean pair of *Sheets*

So Á Dios   NED

Reprinted from *Fremont's Fourth Expedition* edited by LeRoy R. Hafen and Ann W. Hafen, by permission from The Arthur H. Clark Company. Copyright © 1960.

Being Apprehensive around Apache Warriors, c. February 1849

William Henry Chase Whiting

On February 12, 1849, twenty-four-year old Whiting left San Antonio, Texas, accompanied by just over a dozen men, to explore a western pathway to ascertain if there was a practicable route "for military and commercial purposes between El Paso and the Gulf of Mexico, passing by or near Austin or San Antonio de Béxar in Texas." After the expedition moved west of the Pecos River, they had an interesting encounter with Apache Indians. Born in Biloxi, Mississippi, Whiting had no previous experience in dealing with Indians or prairie travel but this journey honed his knowledge of the West. The route located by Whiting, was extensively traveled in later years and today, it closely follows the railway tracks westward from San Antonio to El Paso. The following story of the expedition's encounter with Apaches west of the Pecos was excerpted from Whiting's journal.

At three we left this trail and took another nearly on our course southwest, but at four o'clock I spied . . . at some distance beyond, a large *caballada*. The valley in which we were was narrow; the hills prevented an extended view. Upon this the train was halted, but before any preparation could be made our scouts came galloping in from the front closely pursued by a large band of Apache, and simultaneously we were enveloped front, rear, and left flank by five different parties. Issuing from every gorge hard by, the painted devils came crowding up at full speed, and looking about us we could see them on every hill. They advanced upon us with bows strung and brandishing their lances, [and] appeared as if they wished by their hostile gestures and wild cries to frighten both ourselves and our animals. On our right was a little recess between two spurs of the boundary ridge of the valley. Wishing to avoid, if possible, a collision, yet if obliged to fight, to do it to the utmost, I remained alone among them, while Smith and Howard with the party moved gradually to this point, extricating themselves coolly from their dangerous neighbors. They crowded close upon me and upon the party. To gain a little time for the men to tie their mules together and make their few preparations, I called out to the chiefs to stop and parley. . . .

They sternly demanded who we were and whether we came to the Apache country for peace or war. I answered Americans, *en route* for Presidio. We came peaceable; if we remained so, depended on them. In the meantime the mules had been tied up, their heads together; and in front of them appeared the Texans, squatted to the ground, their rifles cocked, their mouths filled with bullets, and their faces showing every variety of determined expression from the cool indifference of the veteran of San Jacinto and the men of Mier and Monclova. They waited but a signal. Howard, more fluent in Spanish than myself, came down to interpret.

We were enveloped by an angry crowd of the painted devils. On our right and left, parties stripped to the breechclout, with bows strung and fingers full of arrows, were ready to take us in flank. The remainder . . . were ready to charge. Their numbers were upwards of two hundred. The prospect was gloomy. Gómez [a feared Apache war chief] insisted we should go to their camp, and adding if we didn't move, he'd make us; [he] called out: "You are afraid." But the defiant reply of our intrepid young guide and interpreter and the significant cocking of pistols and rifles which accompanied it, changed the tone of the cowardly and treacherous crowd. . . .

It was decided that they should precede us to the springs hard by, where they were encamped; we would follow, take our position, and decide our future relations by a council.

Cautiously and with much apprehension on the part of my men of treachery from the savages, we followed the yelling bands. It was an exciting and picturesque scene. Two hundred Apache, superbly mounted, set off by their many colored dresses, their painted shields, and hideous faces, galloping to and fro at full speed and brandishing their long lances, moved in advance down the valley. Behind, at some distance, mounted humbly on jaded mules, close together and watchful, [came] the little band of Texans. This swart and bearded party, with their resolute and rugged aspect and cautious advance, was not the least impressive feature of the scene. Between the two parties rode Howard, Smith, and myself, accompanied by the five chiefs. We had made this arrangement in view of treachery, that at the first movement of hostility the revolvers with which unfortunately we alone were armed, might do their work upon the chiefs. Turning to the right, we shortly came upon a spring of clear, cool water issuing from the hillside. Here was the *caballada* of the Indians and their large drove of cattle, all, of course, with Mexican brands.

We took our posts in a little rocky gully which seemed, in the treeless valley, to afford the best chance. Each man, unsaddling his mule with one hand while the other held the rifle, placed his packs together; and closed we sat down, our movements curiously watched by the Indians. Gómez, riding up, insultingly demanded why we made no fires, why we didn't scatter, and collect wood (here very scarce), and go to cooking. But observing his band still mounted, their bows still strung, he was answered that we held wood enough in our hands; and we all remained together, gloomy and almost despondent of escape.

At eight o'clock the chiefs appeared, unarmed, to talk. Through the medium of Mr. Howard . . . I explained to them that towards all friendly Indians the intentions of the United States were friendly, that agents would probably be sent among them, and they would, while they continued peaceable and well disposed, be put upon the same footing with other Indian tribes; that we were an advance party of the army soon to appear on the frontier for the purposes of carrying out the United States intentions. They asked if they would be disturbed in the possession of their lands. I told them no, provided they were peaceable. They were curious as to our relations with Mexico. I satisfied them as far as I could, but prudently refrained from touching on all points, for the slightest allusion to that part of our treaty which relates to the restraining of Indian depredations and the restoration of stolen captives and property would have been the signal to fight. I was in no condition to enforce what I said; and when it is considered that we were but thirteen armed men, and five of these provided with but a single shot, our scanty stock of provisions reduced to short allowance, badly armed and mounted, and important public information dependent upon our return, this concealment on my part will be pardoned.

The chiefs, each making a short speech, which one who spoke Spanish interpreted to me, declared themselves satisfied. They spoke to the effect that they wished to be friendly with the United States. The old chief Cigarito . . . addressed me to this end, as near as I could gather: "Stranger, your words are good. You come of a great people. We have heard of you in Mexico. You have conquered the Mexicans in many battles, and your warriors are many and braver than theirs. We do not believe you speak two ways like them. I live in these mountains; my relations and my tribe is here. We wish to be undisturbed and to be at peace with your people. I and my band are friends to yours." He concluded by requesting a paper, or safeguard, for himself to the great chief (meaning General Worth) who commanded the army. The others said nearly the same thing, with the exception of Gómez, who preserved throughout his fierce and insulting demeanor, proudly declaring he was the greatest man in his country or in Mexico and that he didn't care for Americans or any nation—he was not afraid.

We separated there. Hungry, supperless, and anxious, we lay down on the rocks, our arms in our hands. The chill air of the mountains and the cold wind from the north increased our discomfort. Desperate beggars and accomplished thieves as these Indians are, our tobacco and the small articles which in the darkness of the council they could lay hands on, suffered.

Unexpected Party Guests, July 4, 1849

Catherine Margaret Haun

Much of the history of nineteenth-century America is the story of people chasing a dream. Certainly this was the case of westward migration. Between 1840 and 1870, about a quarter of a million people crossed the plains and mountains to find their El Dorado in the California Gold Rush. Catherine Haun and her lawyer husband were a part of this great American internal migration. They were freshly married and longing for a "romantic wedding tour" and felt that in California they could quickly pick up sufficient gold to start their marriage off right financially. The Hauns left their native Iowa and joined a wagon train of other like-minded Gold-Rushers. On the fourth of July, having reached the Laramie River, the wagon train celebrated the American Independence in an evening celebration. It was at the height of the celebration that the Hauns and their traveling companions and celebrants were flabbergasted when a distraught young woman and her daughter burst into their midst.

The young folks decorated themselves in all manner of fanciful and grotesque costumes—Indian characters being most popular. To the rollicking music of violin and Jew's harp we danced until midnight. There were Indian spectators, all bewildered by the (to them) weird war dance of the Pale Face and possibly they deemed it advisable to sharpen up their arrow heads. During the frolic when the sport was at its height a strange white woman with a little girl in her sheltering embrace rushed into the corral. She was trembling with terror, tottering with hunger. Her clothing was badly torn and her hair disheveled. The child crouched with fear and hid her face within the folds of her mother's tattered skirt. The woman could give no account of her forlorn condition but was only able to sob:

"Indians," and "I have nobody nor place to go to." After she had partaken of food and was refreshed by a safe night's rest she recovered and the next day told us that her husband and sister had contracted cholera on account of which her family consisting of husband, brother, sister, herself and two children had stayed behind their train. The sick ones' died and while burying the sister the survivors were attacked by Indians, who, as she supposed, killed her brother and little son. She was obliged to flee for her life dragging with her the little five year old daughter.

She had been three days walking back to meet a train. It had been necessary, in order to avoid Indians, to conceal herself behind trees or boulders much of the time and although she had seen a train in the distance before ours she feared passing the Indians that were between the emigrants and herself. She had been obliged to go miles up the Laramie to find a place where she could get across by wading from rock to rock and the swift current had lamed her and bruised her body.

Raw fish that she had caught with her hands and a squirrel that she killed with a stone had been their only food. Our noise and campfire had attracted her and in desperation she braved the Indians around us and trusting to the darkness ventured to enter our camp. Martha, for that was her name, had emigrated from Wisconsin and pleaded with us to send her home; but we had now gone too far on the road to meet returning emigrants so there was no alternative for her but to accept our protection and continue on to California. When she became calm and somewhat reconciled to so long and uncertain a journey with strangers she made herself useful and loyally cast her lot with us. She assisted me with the cooking for her board; found lodgings with the woman whose husband was a cripple and in return helped the brave woman drive the ox team. Mr. & Mrs. Lamore kept her little girl with their own. . . .

Upon the second day of our resumed travel, still following up the North Platte, Martha spied a deserted wagon some little distance off the road which she recognized as her own. Mr. Bowen went with her to investigate, hoping to find her brother and son. The grave of her sister was still open and her clothing as well as that of her husband, who was in the wagon where he had died, were missing. The grewsome sight drove her almost mad. Mr. Bowen and she did not bury the bodies lest they might bring contagion back to us. No trace of either brother or son could be found.

Reprinted from an entry of Catherine Haun's 1849 Manuscript Diary by permission of The Huntington Library, San Marino, CA.

A Gift for a Gift,
c. Summer 1849

Hermann B. Scharmann, Sr.

In 1904, Scharmann's son, Hermann B. Scharmann, Jr., found a copy of the New Yorker Staats Zeitung *issued during the year 1852. He was surprised to find a story describing his family's 1849 journey to California. Hermann Scharmann, Sr., had taken his wife, three-year old daughter, and two sons on the overland adventure across the United States to satisfy his "wanderlust and by a desire for gold." Scharmann Jr., had his father's account published in 1918.*

About 115 miles from Fort Laramie we met a band of Indians which, counting women and children, numbered 230 persons. The chief handed us a document, signed by the commander of the fort, which stated that the Indians of this branch of the Sioux were not hostile, but most friendly, and that therefore every traveler should avoid insulting them. We soon learned that they had come in order to get some of our provisions, but our company was not very abundantly provided and could give them very little. I camped about fifty yards away from the general camp, with my wagon of provisions. Soon I counted thirty-six Indians around my wagon. Among them was the chief, with his squaw and three children. Naturally I was curious to learn something of their customs. So I gave orders that the wash-kettle should be filled with tea and all other available vessels with coffee; also I had three large pancakes baked. My cows still gave quite a bit of milk, and so a supper was prepared for the Indians. The chief thought that he had more rights than the others, so he and his family sat close to the wagon. The others lay around the fire in a circle.

When the other Indians saw that these were being feasted, they all came running up. I indicated to the chief that this was unwelcome to me, whereupon he immediately arose, held up his hand and cried aloud: "Womeski!" As though struck by lightning, the approaching Indians stopped short and then turned back.

After the meal my guests left with many expressions of gratitude; only the chief and his family remained. I was very much drawn to this man, because of his unusual physiognomy and behavior. We sat together some time and smoked. Our conversation consisted of silence and signs., Meanwhile his wife brought my wife a pair of deerskin shoes, finely embroidered in pearls. I made them a few presents in return.

The following morning, before we resumed our journey, I visited their camp. My youngest son drove the wagon and my oldest son accompanied me. Here I verified the truth that all good deeds are rewarded, for these savages strive earnestly to repay everything that they had received at my hands. Their huts are round, narrowing toward the top and covered with large skins; the camp is circular and in the midst of it is the chief's dwelling. As soon as the chief caught sight of me he shook hands and then took me into his tent and presented to me some dried buffalo meat. All the women that I saw were busily making shoes and embroidering dresses with pearls. The chief's daughter, who was about nineteen years old, threw a rope of pearls around my son's neck while I gazed at her long and admiringly. My son was fifteen years old, of a strong, manly stature, yet he did not seem to guess at the thoughts which one might surmise were running through the girl's head. I experienced real regret at having to leave these savages who appeared to me to be more civilized than many so-called civilized men.

From: *Scharmann's Overland Journey to California* (Freeport, NY: Books for Library Press, 1918)

Inability to Save Mrs. White, c. October 1849

Kit Carson

Born Christopher Houston Carson in Missouri in 1809, Carson was apprenticed to a saddle-maker when he turned fourteen. He ran away from the apprenticeship in 1826 and became employed as a hunter at Bent's Fort. Carson lived among Indians and his first two wives were Arapaho and Cheyenne women. Carson met the explorer John C. Fremont in 1842 and was employed by him as a guide to Oregon and California. His service to Fremont, celebrated in Fremont's widely-read reports, made Carson a national personality hailed in popular fiction as a rugged mountain man. In the time of the incident contained in the following narrative, Carson had settled down in Rayado, about fifty miles east of Taos, New Mexico, because he was "getting old" and wanted to better provide for his family. In Carson's narrative of the incident involving the White family, Carson makes no mention on the fate of the child taken prisoner at the same time that Mrs. White was captured. The U.S. Congress appropriated $1,500 to be used to ransom the little girl, and provided a search party to search for her but she was never found.

In October, the train of a Mr. White was attacked by the Jicarilla Apache. White was killed, and his wife and child were taken prisoners. A party was organized in Taos, with Leroux and Fisher as guides, to rescue them. When they reached Rayado, I was also employed as a guide. We marched to the place where the depredation had been committed, and then followed the trail of the Indians. I was the first man to discover the camp where the murder had been perpetrated. The trunks of the unfortunate family had been broken open, the harnesses cut to pieces, and everything else that the Indians could not carry away with them had been destroyed. We tracked them for ten or twelve days over the most difficult trail that I have ever followed. Upon leaving their camps they would separate in small groups of two or three persons and travel in different directions, to meet again at some appointed place. In nearly every camp we found some of Mrs. White's clothing, and these discoveries spurred us to continue the pursuit with renewed energy.

We finally came in view of the Indian camp. I was in the advance, and at once started for it, calling to our men to come on. The commanding officer ordered a halt, however, and no one followed me. I was afterwards informed that Leroux, the principal guide, had advised the officer to halt us, as the Indians wished to have a parley. The latter, seeing that the troops did not intend to charge, commenced packing up in all haste. Just as the halt was ordered, the commanding officer was shot; the ball passed through his coat, his gauntlets that were in his pocket, and his shirt, stopping at the skin, and doing no other damage than making him a little sick at the stomach. The gauntlets had saved his life, sparing a gallant officer to the service of his country. As soon as he had recovered from the shock given him by the ball, he ordered the men to charge, but it was too late to save the captives. There was only one Indian left in the camp, who was promptly shot while he was running into the river in a vain effort to escape. At a distance of about 200 yards, the body of Mrs. White was found, still perfectly warm. She had been shot through the heart with an arrow not more than five minutes before. She evidently knew that some one was coming to her rescue. Although she did not see us, it was apparent that she was endeavoring to make her escape when she received the fatal shot.

I am certain that if the Indians had been charged immediately on our arrival, she would have been saved. They did not know of our approach, and as they were not paying any particular attention to her, perhaps she could have managed to run towards us, and if she had, the Indians would have been afraid to follow her. However, the treatment she had received from them was so brutal and horrible that she could not possibly have lived very long. Her death, I think, should never be regretted by her friends. She is surely far more happy in heaven, with her God, than among her friends on this earth.

I do not wish to be understood as attaching any blame to the officer in command of the expedition or to the principal guide. They acted as they thought best for the purpose of saving Mrs. White. We merely differed in opinion at the time, but I have no doubt that they now see that if my advice had been taken, her life might have been saved, for a least a short period.

We pursued the Indians for about six miles on a level prairie. We captured all their baggage and camp equipage, many of them running off without any of their clothing. We also took some of their animals. One warrior was killed, and two or three children were captured. We found a book in the camp, the first of the kind I had ever seen, in which I was represented as a great hero, slaying Indians by the hundred. I have often thought that Mrs. White must have read it, and knowing that I lived nearby, must have prayed for my appearance in order that she might be saved. I did come, but I lacked the power to persuade those that were in command over me to follow my plan for her rescue. They would not listen to me and they failed. I will say no more regarding this matter, nor attach any blame to any particular person, for I presume the consciences of those who were the cause of the tragedy have severely punished them ere this.

Reprinted from *Kit Carson's Autobiography* courtesy of the University of Nebraska Press.

Christopher "Kit" Carson

Business Dealings in San Francisco, c. January 1850

Benjamín Vicuña MacKenna

Born in Santiago in 1831, Vicuña MacKenna was forced to leave Chile in 1850 because of his involvement in an attempted revolution. His first port was San Francisco, still in its Gold Rush heyday. Vicuña MacKenna traveled the world and finally returned to Chile in late-1855. Then, he founded a newspaper, El Mercurio. *Later, Vicuña MacKenna became a part of the faculty of the National University and was elected to serve the Republic of Chile as a senator. He died in 1886. The diary that he kept was published in 1862 under the title,* Páginas de mi Diario durante tres Años de Viaje. *The following story comes from an English version of his diary.*

At dawn I went up on deck. The city, strewn over the hills, was silent. A gas lamp still burned in the lighthouse, but in a little while the sun dimmed its flame and the city began to stir. The steamships fired up their boilers and wagons began to arrive at the docks. I was thinking about this curious new world at whose gates I stood. Four years ago this broad bay was only a lonely lake, disturbed occasionally by keels of small fishing barks. Now I saw a lighthouse and a telegraph line, and heard the sharp hiss of steam. All the great discoveries of the age were in use here. I looked at the tranquil bay, my view obstructed by piers lined with ships. The city is the most beautiful in the Pacific. It rises on hills where yesterday tents were set up, and where the day before that there were the huts of fishermen. I recalled cities I had seen that were more than three hundred years old and compared them with this child of yesterday. They seemed old without ever having been young. . . .

I had come to San Francisco with two thousand sacks of Chilean wheat as a cargo. My consignee sold them all in a few hours at twenty-nine and a half dollars a sack. They had cost only eight dollars in Valparaiso, so that made us a profit of thirty-five thousand dollars. But I, who thought I knew so much about San Francisco, discovered I knew nothing. In the first place, the pilot lost two of my anchors in the mouth of the bay and made me pay eighty dollars, or five cents a day for each unit of the ship's tonnage. The towing of the ship two or three miles cost fifty dollars more. When I got finally tied up to one of the hundreds of public or private piers on the bay, the owner, a butcher, told me there would be no charge provided I bought all the meat for the crew from him. The ship was unloaded, but the bill for about a month came to two hundred forty-nine dollars, or about five cents a day for each ton of the ship's total tonnage of two hundred fifty.

When we got moored at the pier, the customs service sent on board an inspector whom we had to feed as well as paying six dollars a day. After the cargo was sold, other men came to make an official quality inspection. Every sack was marked good, bad, or very bad, according to the amount of damage each sack showed. One ounce of damaged flour got the whole sack stamped as bad; but our official, a man of the highest rank in the service, marked a large part of the cargo as very bad, and there was an eight dollar difference in price between that and the good. He had obviously been bribed by the purchaser—as had happened in the case of the ship *Castor*, which arrived when flour was selling at forty dollars a sack; not one was found to be good. The stamping of the sacks dropped the value of my cargo six thousand dollars. I wanted to make some comments, but the officials would not listen. I raised my voice, but they remained unmoved.

What was I to do? I knew that one of the legal tricks in vogue then in California was to provoke someone to strike you. That carried a fine of ten thousand dollars; and the court orders were so strict that a man's ship was legally attached at once if he was found guilty, and he was subjected to other harassment—except that of being sent to jail, because there they would have to feed him, and that cost too much! My venture was going onto the rocks in every sense. The price of flour fell in eight days from thirty dollars to nine dollars, and the purchaser refused to accept the second half of the flour. I had to be patient. How was I to lodge a complaint against an American merchant? Could a lawyer help me? I remembered that one day I had gone with my consignee, Señor Lorca, to confer with a lawyer about some lots he had to reclaim in the town of Benicia. We met the lawyer coming down the stairs, hat on head and with a book under his arm. He waited two minutes while I explained my situation; but when I tried to give a fuller explanation, my friend, Lorca took my arm and said goodbye for us. "Don't you realize," he told me, "that if you held him up three minutes longer he would have sent you a bill for fifty dollars for a stairway conference?" The final upshot was that I lost twenty thousand dollars of my original gain.

From: *We Were 49ers! Chilean Accounts of the California Gold Rush*, Edwin A. Beilharz and Carlos U. López (translators and editors) (Pasadena, CA: Ward Ritchie Press, 1976)

Justifying Stealing a Gold Claim, c. January 1850

Alfred T. Jackson

Jackson, a pioneer miner, wrote his diary during the days of the California Gold Rush in the mid-19th century. Specifically, the diary detailed his experiences from 1850 to 1852. Some fifty or so years after the diary was written, Chauncey L. Canfield came into possession of it and sought to have it published in San Francisco in 1906. A major natural calamity, the Great San Francisco Earthquake, postponed the publication of Jackson's diary until later in the year. In the following vignette, Jackson makes note of the taking of a prosperous gold digging site from its rightful owners.

Only worked three days this week and took out fifteen ounces and a half. Our claim is as rich as those over on Brush Creek, and that ground has been considered the best of any around this section. There are lots of miners tramping over the country from one locality to another and we hear stories of the big yield of gold everywhere in the foothills. I have talked with men from Mariposa and Tuolumne Counties who claim to have left ounce diggings because they had heard of better places North. It is strange what a restless, discontented lot of gold seekers roam around from one county to another. They can't make money fast enough at an ounce a day, but are prospecting for some spot where they can take out a bushel or more of gold in a week, and as there have been plenty of such strikes made it keeps them excited and continually on the tramp. I was chatting yesterday with a miner from Mariposa Country and he was telling me of the discovery at a camp called Bear Valley that had set the country wild. It seems there are a lot more Mexicans in that part of the State than here and they do a good deal of mining. It was noticed that for

115

a couple of weeks the "greasers" had been very flush, selling lots of dust at the store and playing "monte" for high stakes. Some of the miners put a watch on them and found them panning on a flat about a mile from the town, and they soon found out that the Mexicans had struck the biggest kind of a deposit. It made them mad to think that a lot of "greasers" were getting the benefit of it, so they organized a company and drove them away by threats and force and then worked the ground themselves. Out of a space forty feet square they took out two hundred and ten thousand dollars and that was the end of it; just a big pocket of gold mixed in the rocks, specimen gold he said, that is, jagged and rough and not rolled and water-worn as the dust is in the creeks and ravines. It was an outrage on the Mexicans, but the jumpers justified their action on the ground that California had been ceded to the United States, and that white men had superior rights to the mines. Anyway, they got away with the gold.

From: *The Diary of a Forty-Niner,* Chauncey L. Canfield (editor) (San Francisco: Morgan Shepard Company, 1908)

Captive Girls Brought into an Indian Village, March 21, 1851

Olive Oatman

Nine members of the Oatman family were traveling by wagon down the Old Santa Fé Trail en route to California when, seventy miles from Fort Yuma, they were set upon by Apaches who massacred six members of the family. A teen-aged boy, Lorenzo, was mistakenly left for dead. Two of his sisters, fourteen-year-old Olive and seven-year-old Mary Ann were taken captive. Although badly hurt, Lorenzo wandered around until he was found by friendly Indians who took him to other whites traveling the Trail. As soon as he could, Lorenzo began a search for his captive sisters. Mary Ann died of starvation in captivity. Olive was sold to other Indians but was finally reunited with Lorenzo after a five-year ordeal.

On the third day we came suddenly in sight of a cluster of low, thatched huts, each having an opening near the ground leading into them. It was soon visible from the flashing eyes and animated countenances of the Indians, that they were nearing some place of attraction, and to which anxious and interesting desire had been pointing. Two young girls, having traveled on foot two hundred miles in three days; with swollen feet and limbs, lame, exhausted, not yet four days remove from the loss of parents, brothers, and sisters, and torn from them, too, in the most brutal manner; away in the deeps of forests and mountains, upon the desolation of which the glad light or sound of civilization never yet broke; with no guides or protectors, rudely, inhumanly driven by untutored, untamed savages, the sight of the dwelling-places of man, however coarse or unseemly, was no very unwelcome scene. With all the dread possibilities, therefore, that might await them at any moment, nevertheless to get even into an Indian camp was home.

We were soon ushered into camp, amid shouts and song, wild dancing, and the crudest, most irregular music that ever ranter sung, or delighted the ear of an unrestrained superstition. They lifted us on the top of a pile of brush and bark, then formed a circle about us of men, women, and children of all ages and sizes, some naked, some dressed in blankets, some in skins, some in bark. Music then commenced, which consisted of pounding upon stones with clubs and horn, and the drawing of a small string like a fiddle-bow across distended bark. They ran, and jumped, and danced in the wildest and most furious manner about us, but keeping a regular circle.

Each, on coming to a certain point in the circle, marked by a removed piece of turf in the ground, would bend himself or herself nearly to the ground, uttering at the same time a most frightful yell, and making a violent gesticulation and stamping. Frequently on coming near us, as they would do in each evolution, they would spit in our face, throw dirt upon us, or slightly strike us with their hand, managing, by every possible means, to give us an early and thorough impression of their barbarity, cruelty, and obscenity. The little boys and girls, especially, would make the older ones merry by thus taunting us. It seemed during all this wild and disgusting performances, that their main ambition was to exhibit their superiority over us, and the low, earnest, intense hate they bore toward our race. And this they most effectually succeeded in accomplishing, together with a disgusting view of the obscenity, vulgarity, and grossness of their hearts, and the mean, despicable, revengeful dispositions that burn with hellish fury within their untamed bosoms.

From: *Captivity of the Oatman Girls* (Carlton & Porter, Publishers, 1857)

Olive Oatman—Showing Scarring of Her Captivity

Fighting Comanches on the Santa Fé Trail May 21, 1853

James M. Fugate

Little is known of James M. Fugate but his home region of LaFayette County, Missouri, had been a principle outfitting point for wagon trains bound for New Mexico and using the Old Santa Fé Trail. Later in life, Fugate wrote his memories of his early adventures and first printed in a small volume carrying the title, The Heart of the New Kansas. *In the narrative that follows, Fugate describes a desperate battle between him and his traveling companions and a larger force of Comanche warriors.*

In April 1853, young, vigorous, and never having seen as much of the world as generally fills the ambition of fellows in their early days of manhood, I engaged as teamster to drive through with a train of ox-wagons loaded with merchandise for the Santa Fe trade. We left LaFayette county, Missouri, the 24th day of April; our company comprised 45 men, armed with the old-fashioned long-range rifles, each a Colt's navy revolver and bowie knife. Our teams numbered 210 head of cattle, in all.

Kansas was one vast wild plain, over which roving bands of hostile Indians were constantly cutting off emigrant and freight trains on their way to New Mexico and the Californias.

After leaving the settlement some distance, we overtook twelve men with three wagons, who had discovered there was danger ahead and were awaiting reinforcements before venturing farther. This increased our fighting force to 57 robust, well-armed men.

Our first serious trouble began after reaching the Arkansas Valley, at a point near where Hutchinson now stands, and where we had gone into camp about noon of May 21st. While at dinner we were suddenly startled by the alarm cry, "Indians!"

Before we had got our teams and wagons fairly in corral, they were charging around us on their horses, yelling and firing like demons. Taken at such a dangerous disadvantage and surprise, we were just in that position which makes men fight with desperation, and instantaneously our rifles were pealing forth their notes of defiance and death to the dusky murderous foe.

We were completely encircled by the savages, who proved to be Comanches, swinging upon the opposite side of their ponies exposing but little of themselves to our aim by firing under their horses' necks. Their deadly missiles were soon playing havoc among our cattle. The poor creatures were madly surging and bellowing around, endangering us to a death beneath their feet, worse to be feared within the enclosure than the foe without. This new danger soon drove us outside the enclosures of wagons in full view of the Indians.

We had now fairly got our hands in, and were tumbling their ponies at a rapid rate. Few Indians after their ponies fell, escaped a rifle bullet. The Indians were narrowing their circle until twenty-five yards scarcely intervened between us. But the motion of their steeds unsteadied their aim until it was but random, while the closer they pressed us the more destructive became every shot we fired.

Such fighting could not last long. After the first few rounds the savages mostly substituted the gun with the bow and arrows. Finding themselves getting most terribly worsted in the combat, they made a dash to ride down and tomahawk us all in one death struggle. I tell you, then, we had no child's play. Outnumbered four or five to one in a hand-to-hand fight to the death is a serious thing. We were soon mingling together, but driven against the wagons, we could dodge or parry their blows with the tomahawk, while the rapid flashes from the celebrated "navy" in each man's hand, was not so easily avoided by the savage warriors. We made the ground too hot for them, and with yells of baffled rage, they broke and fled, carrying off all their killed and wounded but three, which they had to leave.

Now for the first time since the fight began we had time to take in our situation. One of the bravest and best of our comrades, young Gilbert, was shot through the heart while fighting the savages back with clubbed rifle, his revolver having missed fire. He lay as he fell, with his hand clenched around the stock of his gun as though he would take the weapon with his departed spirit to the other world where he might avenge his death upon the savages who had paid such a dear penalty for their last work. Many others of our company were wounded, two of them severely. The dead and dying ponies were scattered about on the prairie with the arms and accouterments of their savage owners about them; while several of our cattle were also dead and dying from wounds made by missiles aimed for us.

The remainder of the day was spent in burying our poor comrade on the spot made sacred by his life's blood (which we did as well as we could under the circumstances), caring for our wounded, and gathering up the spoils of the fight. We destroyed everything belonging to the Indians that we could not carry away, and along towards night-fall moved about a mile up the river, where we went into camp.

After the excitement consequent upon the fight began to subside, we had much to talk over about our chances of fighting our way with such a small force through the entire boundless plains before us to New Mexico. The future looked hopeless indeed, but J.W. Jones who commanded the outfit, swore he would go to Santa Fe, or go to _____. We dare not show the white feather, then.

Reprinted from *On the Santa Fé Trail* edited by Marc Simmons by permission of the University Press of Kansas.

Attending a Fandango, September 29, 1853

Baldwin Möllhausen

Born in Germany in 1825, Möllhausen sailed to America for the first time in 1849. After holding a few odd jobs, he heard about a scientific expedition headed by a fellow German that would go into the American Southwest. Möllhausen gained a place in the expedition and traveled for more than a year. In early-1853 he returned to Germany. The American government organized several expeditions to seek out the best route for a transcontinental railway. He joined one of the groups that was going west out of Fort Smith, Arkansas. By August 1854, Möllhausen's adventures in the American West were over and he again returned to Germany. There, he became a noted author of more than thirty-nine novels and other literary works. He died in 1905. The following narrative was taken from his book, Diary of a Journey from the Mississippi to the Coasts of the Pacific, *first published in 1858.*

The Alcalde presented himself as early as possible, in company with the most distinguished citizens of Anton Chico, to give our whole party a solemn invitation to a fandango, to be held in the evening; and it is needless to say the invitation was joyfully accepted.

We all set to work directly to rummage up the most elegant ball costumes that circumstances permitted; needles and thread were seen in brisk motion in all quarters, and chasms and openings in our well-worn garments, originating either in accident or in severe service on our long journey, disappeared as if by magic. An artificial black was, for the first time for many days, superinduced upon our *chaussure*; and the most gorgeous shirt collars and fronts were manufactured out of stiff drawing paper.

We were a comical-looking troop, nevertheless, when we set off in the evening to the festive scene, being summoned thereto by the church bells, which are obliged to accommodate themselves to the double duty of calling people to Divine Service and to the fandangos. Some of us, who wore a somewhat creased, but extremely fashionable, hunting coat on the upper part of our persons, terminated in leathern leggings and heavy boots. Others showed civilisation on their lower extremities, but a decided tendency towards savage life at the top. The majority boasted the paper linen I have mentioned, and there was even one pair of white kid gloves seen among us, though with considerable apertures at the seams, through which the sunburnt hands became visible. The wearing of arms at the ball was expressly forbidden, but one did, nevertheless, occasionally see the brown end of a revolver, or the bright blade of a bowie-knife gleaming out. In this picturesque attire we betook ourselves to the building erected for public purposes next to the church, and having obtained at the doors some very bad refreshments for very good payment, we entered a long narrow hall, where we were welcomed by the Alcalde and a crowd of Mexicans in laced *calcineros*, and of Mexican fair ones in thick veils or light shawls; and the various nations were soon mingled together, and doing their utmost to understand and be understood. Their efforts were not particularly successful, but the tongues went merrily, the black-eyed señoritas made delicate cigaritos, which they lighted and offered to their visitors, the whiskey-punch went briskly round and the orchestra, consisting of two guitars and a violin, soon summoned us to the waltz.

The dancing began, the pairs moving at first in a serious and deliberate manner; but the stately magistrate, in his shirt sleeves, gave the musicians a sign that accelerated the movements of their fingers, and of the feet of the dancers on the dusty clay floor. The bright-eyed señoritas were indefatigable, the degenerate descendants of the Spaniards looked with evident complacency at their own nimble limbs, and the wildest excitement gleamed from the bearded visages of the Americans. There was not a single dance in which they did not take part, and in defiance of all rules of art and fashion; but setting to work with a will, they maintained their places in the most complicated operations.

The Mexicans regarded with a kind of compassion the awkward movements of our fellows, and the confusion they created in the figures; but the laughing fair ones did not seem at all distressed by them, but during every pause rolled up little cigaritos, began to smoke them, and then presented them, with an amiable smile, to their partners, who could only accept them with a "Thank you," and "Ah, if I did but know a little Spanish!"

The impossibility of communication between the various nationalities did not seem at all to check our merriment. We danced, and sang, and laughed, and drank, and did not go home till morning, but then, happily, without the mirth having been interrupted by any quarrels, or broken heads, which was the more praiseworthy, as wagoner and soldiers (among the latter specimens from all the nations of Europe) had thought proper to join in the revels, and that moreover with unsteady feet and cloudy brains.

When the sun shed his first beams on our camp on the following morning he found everything perfectly still, and only a loud snoring, from the interior of the tents, announced that the members of the Expedition were enjoying a refreshing slumber after the bodily fatigues of the night and the spirituous indulgences that had fallen to their share.

Laziness seem to hold undisputed sway over the whole valley of Anton Chico. The cocks crowed in the little town, and the mules neighed in the distant ravines, but their tones struck no other ear than those of the sentinels, who, leaning on their muskets, were doubtless making sorrowful reflections on the hard fate that had debarred them from sharing in the delights of the last night's festivity.

From: *Diary of a Journey from the Mississippi to the Coasts of the Pacific* (New York: Johnson Reprint Corporation, 1969, reprinted from the original 1858 edition)

A Bride's Possessions, c. May 1854

Bethenia Owens-Adair

Bethenia Owens (1840–1912) was born in Virginia, but as a toddler she was a member of one of the first large caravans to travel the Oregon Trail. The Owens family settled in the Willamette Valley. Only fourteen years of age, Bethenia married a neighbor, Lagrande Henderson Hill, and gave birth to a child at sixteen. At age eighteen, Bethenia kicked the traces of convention and left her husband. When a family friend asked Bethenia why she left her husband, she replied that "he whipped my baby unmercifully, and struck and choked me,—and I was never made to be struck by mortal man!" She returned to her parents' home and learned to read and write. Highly valuing education, Bethenia continued her education until at age forty, she became the first woman physician in the West. She retired from the medical profession in 1906. The following story was extracted from her 1906 book, Gleanings from a Pioneer Woman Physician's Life.

Just prior to our marriage, Mr. Hill had bought a farm of 320 acres on credit, four miles from my father's home, for $600, to be paid for in two years. The improvements on it consisted of a small cabin, 12 × 14 in dimensions, made of round logs, with the bark on them, each notched deeply enough at its end to dovetail into its neighbors above and below it. The cracks still remaining after this rude fitting were filled with mixed mud and grass, but this cabin had never yet been "chinked." It was covered with "shakes" (thick, hand-made shingles three feet long) which were kept in place by poles, tied down at each end. The door was so low that a man had to stoop to go in and out, and it was fastened with the proverbial latch and string. The cabin had neither floor nor chimney, and the wide cracks admitted both drafts and vermin. Later I gathered grass

126

and fern, mixed them with mud, and filled these cracks, thus shutting out the snakes and lizards, which abounded in that region, and which had made me frequent and alarming visits. The window consisted of two panes of glass set in an opening made by sawing out a section of one of the logs for that purpose.

About twelve acres of land were fenced, and had been seeded to oats and wheat for one or two years. A rough, open shed sufficed to shelter six or eight head of stock, and surrounding it was a corral for milking cows, and a calf-pen adjoining it.

Our furniture consisted of a pioneer bed, made by boring three holes in the logs of the wall in one corner, in which to drive the rails. Thus the bedstead required but one leg. The table was a mere rough shelf, fastened to the wall, and supported by two legs. Three smaller shelves answered for a cupboard, and were amply sufficient for my slender supply of dishes, which comprised mostly tinware, which was kept scrupulously bright and shining. My sugar bowl, cream jug, steel knives and forks (two-tined) and one set of German silver teaspoons, I had bought with my own little savings before my marriage.

My cooking utensils were a pot, tea-kettle and bake-oven (all of iron), a frying-pan and coffee-pot, a churn, six milk pans, a wash tub and board, a large twenty or thirty-gallon iron pot for washing purposes, etc., and a water bucket and tin dipper. All these things, including a full supply of groceries, I got on my father's account, as he had told me to go to the store and purchase what I wanted. This I did in the afternoon of my wedding day, the ceremony having taken place at 10 a.m. He also gave me a fine riding mare, Queen (my saddle I had already earned long before), one fresh cow and a heifer calf, which I selected; also one cow which would be fresh in the early fall, and a wagon and harness. In addition, mother gave me a good feather bed, and pillows, a good straw bed, a pair of blankets and two extra quilts. My husband's possessions were a horse and saddle, a gun, and less than twenty dollars in money; but I considered this a most excellent start in life. I knew what my father and mother had done, and I then believed that my husband was the equal of any man.

From: *Gleanings from a Pioneer Woman Physician's Life* (Portland, OR: Mann & Beach, Printers, 1906)

"Day and Night Cannot Dwell Together," c. December 1854

Chief Seattle

Born about 1790 in the Puget Sound region in the present state of Washington, Noah Seattle became chief of an alliance of tribes called the Duwamish Confederacy. Converting to Christianity, Chief Seattle advocated a peaceful coexistence between his Indian brethren and the newcomers to the area, the white man. In addition to having a namesake city, Chief Seattle is also well known for a speech that he delivered when the newly-appointed U.S. Governor and Commissioner of Indian Affairs, Isaac Stevens, visited the Territory in 1854 to negotiate a treaty with Chief Seattle to purchase Indian land and move the Duwamish Confederacy to a reservation. Chief Seattle's speech was written from incomplete notes taken by Dr. Henry Smith and published more than thirty years later in a Seattle newspaper. Smith's rendition of the speech uses flowery prose common to Victorian society and was likely embellished by Smith. But Smith's version probably contains the gist of the message that Chief Seattle was imparting to his listening audience, although his wording may have been different—we will never know. Smith describes the day when Chief Seattle and Governor Stevens met when he wrote, "The Bay swarmed with canoes and the shore was lined with a living mass of swaying, writhing, dusky humanity, until old Chief Seattle's trumpet-toned voice rolled over the immense multitude like the startling reveille of a bass drum, when silence became as instantaneous and perfect as that which follows a clap of thunder from a clear sky." Smith further related that when Chief Seattle stood to make his speech, he "Plac[ed] one hand on the governor's head, and slowly pointing heavenward with the index finger of the other, he commenced his memorable address in solemn and impressive tones." The following is an edited version of Chief Seattle's speech.

Yonder sky that has wept tears of compassion on our fathers for centuries untold, and which, to us, looks eternal, may change. Today it is fair, tomorrow it may be overcast with clouds. My words are like the stars that never set. What Seattle says, the great chief . . . can rely upon, with as much certainty as our pale-face brothers can rely upon the return of the seasons.

The son of the white chief [a reference to Governor Stevens] says his father sends us greetings of friendship and good will. This is kind, for we know he has little need of our friendship in return, for his people are many. They are like the grass that covers the vast prairies, while my people are few, and resemble the scattering trees of a storm-swept plain.

The great, and I presume also good, white chief sends us word that he wants to buy our lands but is willing to allow us to reserve enough to live on comfortably. This indeed appears generous, for the red man no longer has rights that he need respect, and the offer may be wise, also, for we are no longer in need of a great country.

There was a time when our people covered the whole land, as the waves of a wind-ruffled sea cover its shell-paved floor. But that time has long since passed away with the greatness of tribes now almost forgotten. I will not mourn over our untimely decay, nor reproach my pale-face brothers for hastening it, for we, too, may have been somewhat to blame.

When our young men grow angry at some real or imaginary wrong, and disfigure their faces with black paint, their hearts, also, are disfigured and turn black, and then their cruelty is relentless and knows no bounds, and our old men are not able to restrain them.

But let us hope that hostilities between the red-man and his pale-face brothers may never return. We would have everything to lose and nothing to gain.

True it is, that revenge, with our young braves, is considered gain, even at the cost of their own lives, but old men who stay at home in times of war, and old women, who have sons to lose, know better. . . .

Your God loves your people and hates mine, he folds his strong arms lovingly around the white man and leads him as a father leads his infant son, but he has forsaken his red children, he makes your people wax strong every day, and soon they will fill the land; while my people are ebbing away like a fast-receding tide, that will never flow again. The white man's God cannot love his red children or he would protect them. They seem to be orphans who can look nowhere for help. How then can we become brothers? How can your father become our father and bring us prosperity and awaken in us dreams of returning greatness?

Your God seems to us to be partial. He came to the white man. We never saw Him; never even heard His voice. He gave the white man laws but He had no word for His red children whose teeming millions filled this vast continent as the stars fill the [heavens]. No, we are two distinct races and must remain ever so. There is little in common between us. The ashes of our ancestors are sacred and their final resting place is hallowed ground, while you wander away from the tombs of your fathers seemingly without regret.

Your religion was written on tablets of stone by the iron finger of an angry God, lest you might forget it. The red man could never remember nor comprehend it.

Our religion is the traditions of our ancestors, the dreams of our old men, given them by the great Spirit . . . and written in the hearts of our people. . . .

Day and night cannot dwell together. The red man has ever fled the approach of the white man, as the changing mists on the mountain side flee before the blazing morning sun.

However, your proposition seems a just one, and I think my folks will accept it and will retire to the reservation you offer them, and we will dwell apart and in peace, for the words of the great white chief seem to be the voice of nature speaking to my people out of the thick darkness that is fast gathering around them like a dense fog floating inward from a midnight sea.

It matters but little where we pass the remainder of our days.

They are not many.

The Indian's night promises to be dark. No bright star hovers above the horizon. Sad-voiced winds moan in the distance. Some grim Nemesis of our race is on the red man's trail, and wherever he goes he will still hear the sure approaching footsteps of the fell destroyer and prepare to meet his doom, as does the wounded doe that hears the approaching footsteps of the hunter. A few more moons, a few more winters, and not one of all the mighty hosts that once filled this broad land or that now roam in fragmentary bands through these vast solitudes will remain to weep over the tombs of a people once as powerful and as hopeful as your own.

But why should we repine? Why should I murmur at the fate of my people? Tribes are made up of individuals and are no better than they. Men come and go like the waves of a sea. . . . Even the white man, whose God walked and talked with him, as friend to friend, is not exempt from the common destiny. We *may* be brothers after all. We shall see. . . .

Even the rocks that seem to lie dumb as they swelter in the sun along the silent seashore in solemn grandeur thrill with memories of past events connected with the fate of my people, and the very dust under your feet responds more lovingly to our footsteps than to yours, because it is the ashes of our ancestors, and our bare feet are conscious of the sympathetic touch, for the soil is rich with the life of our kindred.

The sable braves, and fond mothers, and glad-hearted maidens, and the little children who lived and rejoiced here, and whose very names are now forgotten, still love these solitudes, and their deep fastnesses at eventide grow shadowy with the presence of dusky spirits. And when the last red man shall have perished from the earth and his memory among white men shall have become a myth, these shores shall swarm with the invisible dead of my tribe, and when your children's children shall think themselves alone in the field, the store, the shop, upon the highway or in the silence of the woods they will not be alone. In all the earth there is no place dedicated to solitude. At night, when the streets of your cities and villages shall be silent, and you think them deserted, they will throng with the returning hosts that once filled and still love this beautiful land. The white man will never be alone. Let him be just and deal kindly with my people. . . .

From: Smith, Henry. "Early Reminiscences Number 10, Scraps from a Diary" (*Seattle Sunday Star*, October 29, 1887)

Wanting to Minister to Another Woman, August 31, 1855

Mountain Charley

Mrs. Elsa Jane Guerin, also known as "Mountain Charley" published her auto-biography in 1861. Allegedly, she was born Elsa Jane Forest in Louisiana, but masqueraded as a man for several years in the mid-1800s and had trekked across the Southwest before participating in the Pikes Peak gold rush of 1859. In 1860, she supposedly married a Denver bartender, H. L. Guerin. Whether Mrs. Guerin, in the guise of Mountain Charley, was an impostor in men's clothing while traveling throughout the West cannot be determined. Several other women published accounts that they were the authentic Mountain Charley. While the true identity of Mountain Charley may never be known, the following story told by Mrs. E. J. Guerin is poignant. The reader will have to judge its veracity.

Our journey across this desert was not the most pleasant portion of our journey. Many of our cattle died on the way, and on every side we saw evidences that a similar fate had befallen not a few of those which had preceded us. In crossing we came to the Boiling Springs, of which there is nearly a hundred, one of which is almost or quite a hundred yards in diameter. The thermometer in the water, in some cases, indicated 160E. It was warm enough to make tolerable good coffee, and we were also enabled to "do up" some washing without the trouble of making a fire.

We saw many cases of destitution along the road, many of which were of the most heart-rending character. All along were the carcasses of cattle, and at intervals a rudely rounded hillock would show where slept some unfortunate whose search for wealth had ceased forever. One day I had ridden somewhat in advance of our train, when, in passing a rude tent my attention was attracted to it by a faint moaning. I rode up and dismounted when I was shocked to find within, a woman lying on some dirty blankets, and by her, two little children. All were emaciated to the last degree, and were most pitiable objects. The woman could scarcely find strength to inform me of her trouble, but she managed in the faintest of tones to tell me that several days before her husband had gone on to find feeding ground, and their team had died the day he left. He had intended to return in two or three days at farthest, and had left them provisions for only that time. He had now been gone a week and she had not tasted food in four days. As soon as our train came up we relieved them and took them in one of our wagons. Not many miles distant we came across the body of a man, who had evidently died from fatigue and inanition. The woman recognized it with a faint but agonizing shriek, for in the wasted form before her she saw her husband. My readers can but feebly imagine the terrible sorrow that seized upon her soul—a sorrow, it seems to me, heightened by every circumstance that could give it depth or strength. Thousands of miles from home—in the midst of a terrible desert—property all gone—a widow and two helpless children—the body of the husband and father lying lifeless upon the sands—what more fearful combination of circumstances could there be to give poignancy to her grief, or add horror to the event? I longed to disclose to her my sex, and minister to her in that manner in which only one woman can to another—yet I did not dare to, and I was forced to give her only that rough consolation which befitted my assumed character. Heaven preserve me from ever witnessing another scene so harrowing as that in which the poor woman recognized her dead husband.

Reprinted from *Mountain Charley, or the Adventures of Mrs. E. J. Guerin, Who Was Thirteen Years in Male Attire* edited by Fred W. Mazzulla by permission of the University of Oklahoma Press.

Wilderness First-Aid, c. 1855

Grizzly Adams

Born James Capen Adams (1812–1866) in Massachusetts, Adams was a shoe-maker in his youth. But the life of a cobbler bored Adams and he longed for ad-venture. The 1849 California gold rush provided him with an excuse to lead a more adventuresome life. Leaving his wife and children to fend for themselves, Adams joined the huge migration from the East to seek his fortune in the West. Like most Forty-niners, Adams did not reap riches from the goldfields and in dis-gust, left California for the Rocky Mountains. Living the life of a mountain man, Adams found that he could earn a living by collecting brown bears, grizzlies, wolves, elks, cougars, etc., and selling them to zookeepers and exhibitionists such as P. T. Barnun. It was from this occupation that Adams became known by his nickname, "Grizzly." In the following excerpt, Adams recounts a day when his hunting companion was mauled by a cougar.

Solon and I started out very early; and, coming to a spot where two ravines came together, he started up one and I the other. I had not gone more than a quarter of a mile before I heard Solon cry out for help. I bounded up the ridge which separated us, and, upon reaching the top, saw him lying under a large tree in the other ravine, and a panther on top of him, apparently gnawing into his neck. I shouted to him to lie still, and, drawing my rifle, fired at the beast; but, in my anxiety to shoot wide of my comrade, I did not strike the panther fair, and he bounded off into the bushes, and escaped.

In answer to my inquiries in relation to this singular adventure, Solon told me that as he was walking up the ravine, looking only forward, and paying no attention to the trees overhead, the beast suddenly leaped upon his back and struck him to the ground. In the same moment that he fell, he cried out for me, and pulled the cape of his buckskin coat over his neck—and this evidently saved his life. How he came to have such forethought was strange; some others might have done so, but most men would never have thought of it; I, for one, would have sooner drawn my knife and fought. I asked why he did not fight; he replied that he was afraid to move, supposing that it would only infuriate the animal. Such a caution, said I, would have been good in case of a bear; but the panther is made of different stuff. By nature a coward and a sneak, he has the cruelty of cowardice, daring the combat only when he has a sure advantage, and wreaking a bloodthirsty ferocity most upon an unresisting victim. A determined stroke with a knife, though it might not have killed, would have terrified and put him to flight.

In the meanwhile, I stripped the coat from Solon's back, and found his shoulders severely scratched by the panther's claws. His neck, also, was badly bitten, but not dangerously; for the buckskin had fortunately saved it. Still the wounds were serious enough to require the best of my surgical skill, and I at once placed them under treatment. I led the patient directly to a spring which was not far distant; and, making him bend over it, with a piece of hollowed bark I poured water over his wounds, until he complained bitterly of the cold. I then put on his shirt, saturated with water, and over that, his coat; and, drawing off my own coat, put that, also, upon him. This was an easy matter, as my shoulders were much broader than his, and besides, my clothing was always worn very loose, so as to give me perfect freedom of action.

A further article of prescription was, that he should drink as much water as possible; but he replied that he was not thirsty, and wished to know why he should do so. I explained the reason, by saying that he would soon become warm; the water would, more readily, induce perspiration, and that would ease his pains. He then followed the direction; and, as we returned to camp, though he started stiff, in a short time, by warming up and perspiring, he felt well, and traveled as comfortably as ever.

From: *The Adventures of James Capen Adams, Mountaineer and Grizzly Bear Hunter of California* (Boston: Theodore H. Hittle, 1861)

Report on the Mormon Handcart Company, November 2, 1856

George D. Grant

In the mid-1850s several thousand Mormon pioneers made the difficult and dangerous trek West by pushing or pulling small handcarts over a distance greater than 1,500 miles. Most other emigrants of this time used covered wagons but the Mormon handcart companies used this cheaper, but more onerous means of traveling. To many, pushing a handcart was a demonstration of faith and sacrifice. Simple in its design, a handcart was small, usually with a five feet long bed set on an axle between two narrow, lightweight wheels. From the bed of the cart were two long shafts connected by a cross-member that a pusher could lean his or her body into. The carts could carry approximately 400 to 500 pounds. For the emigrants who began their journey in mid-1856, the trek West became an ordeal of starvation, privation, and death as vividly summarized by the following letter from Grant to the Mormon leader, Brigham Young.

Devil's Gate

President Brigham Young:

Dear Brother:—Knowing the anxieties you feel for the companies still out, and especially for the Hand-cart Company, I have concluded to send in your son Joseph A. and br. Abel Garr on an express from this place.

We had no snow to contend with, until we got to the Sweet Water. On the 19th and 20th of October we encountered a very severe snow storm. We met br. Willie's company on the 21st; the snow was from six to ten inches deep where we met them. They were truly in a bad situation, but we rendered them all the assistance in our power. Br. William H. Kimball returned with them, also several other brethren. The particulars of the company you have doubtless learned before this time.

Previous to this time we had sent on an express to ascertain, if possible, the situation and whereabouts of the company yet back, and report to me. Not thinking it safe for them to go farther than Independence Rock, I advised them to wait there. When we overtook them they had heard nothing from the rear companies, and we had traveled through snow from 8 to 12 inches deep all the way from Willow creek to this place.

Not having much feed for our horses they were running down very fast, and not hearing anything from the companies, I did not know but what they had taken up quarters for the winter, consequently we sent on another express to the Platte bridge. When that express returned, to my surprise I learned that the companies were all on the Platte river, near the upper crossing, and had been encamped there nine days, waiting for the snow to go away, or, as they said, to recruit their cattle.

As quick as we learned this, we moved on to meet them. Met br. Martin's company at Greasewood creek, on the last day of October; br. Hodgett's company was a few miles behind. We dealt out to br. Martin's company the clothing, &c, that we had for them; and next morning, after stowing our wagons full of the sick, the children and the infirm, with a good amount of luggage, started homeward about noon. The snow began to fall very fast, and continued until late at night. It is now about 8 inches deep here, and the weather is very cold.

It is not of much use for me to attempt to give a description of the situation of these people, for this you will learn from your son Joseph A. and br. Garr, who are the bearers of this express; but you can imagine between five and six hundred men, women and children, worn down by drawing hand carts through snow and mud; fainting by the wayside; falling, chilled by the cold; children crying, their limbs stiffened by cold, their feet bleeding and some of them bare to snow and frost. The sight is almost too much for the stoutest of us; but we go on doing all we can, not doubting nor despairing.

Our company is too small to help much, it is only a drop to a bucket, as it were, in comparison to what is needed. I think that not over one-third of br. Martin's company is able to walk. This you may think is extravagant, but it is nevertheless true. Some of them have good courage and are in good spirits; but a great many are like children and do not help themselves much more, nor realize what is before them.

I never felt so much interest in any mission that I have been sent on, and all the brethren who came out with me feel the same. We have prayed without ceasing, and the blessing of God has been with us.

Br. Charles Decker has now traveled this road the 49th time, and he says he has never before seen so much snow on the Sweet Water at any season of the year.

I am sorry to inform you of the death of br. Tennant, among those who have fallen by the way side.

Br. Hunt's company are two or three days back of us, yet br. Wheelock will be with them to counsel them, also some of the other brethren who came out.

We will move every day toward the valley, if we shovel snow to do it, the Lord helping us.

I have never seen such energy and faith among the "boys," nor so good a spirit as is among those who came out with me. We realize that we have your prayers for us continually, also those of all the Saints in the Valley. I pray that the blessings of God may be with you and all those who seek to build up the kingdom of God on the earth.

GEORGE D. GRANT

From: "Captain Grant's Report from Devil's Gate," printed in the *Deseret News*, November 19, 1856

Mormon Handcart Company at Western Campsite

Provisions for Crossing the Plains, c. 1859

Randolph B. Marcy

A United States Army officer and Western explorer, Captain Marcy was born in Massachusetts in 1812. He spent most of his early career on the northwest frontier in Michigan and Wisconsin. He served in the Mexican War under General Zachary Taylor. In 1852 he was assigned the command of a seventy-man exploring expedition across the Great Plains in search of the source of the Red River. Afterward, Marcy published an account of his adventures in a report titled, Exploration of the Red River of Louisiana, In the Year 1852, *which became a classic. Marcy was assigned the duty of compiling a semi-official guidebook for the War Department. The result,* The Prairie Traveler, *published in 1859 became an important source for information for Western overland travelers. Marcy was eventually promoted to brigadier general. He retired from the army in 1881 and he died in 1887. The following advice for travelers across the Great Plains was taken from Marcy's 1859 book,* The Prairie Traveler.

Supplies for a march should be put up in the most secure, compact, and portable shape. Bacon should be packed in strong sacks of a hundred pounds to each; or, in very hot climates, put in boxes and surrounded with bran, which in a great measure prevents the fat from melting away.

If pork is used, in order to avoid transporting about forty percent of useless weight, it should be taken out of the barrels and packed like the bacon; then so placed in the bottom of the wagons as to keep it cool. The pork, if well cured, will keep several months in this way, but bacon is preferable.

Flour should be packed in stout double canvas sacks well sewed, a hundred pounds in each sack.

Butter may be preserved by boiling it thoroughly, and skimming off the scum as it rises to the top until it is quite clear like oil. It is then placed in tin canisters and soldered up. This mode of preserving butter has been adopted in the hot climate of southern Texas, and it is found to keep sweet for a great length of time, and its flavor is but little impaired by the process.

Sugar may be well secured in India rubber or gutta-percha sacks, or so placed in the wagon as not to risk getting wet.

Desiccated or dried vegetables are almost equal to the fresh, and are put up in such a compact and portable form as easily to be transported over the plains. They have been extensively used in the Crimean war, and by our own army in Utah, and have been very generally approved. They are prepared by cutting the fresh vegetables into think slices and subjecting them to a very powerful press, which removes the juice and leaves a solid cake, which, after having been thoroughly dried in an oven, becomes almost as hard as a rock. A small piece of this, about half the size of a man's hand, when boiled, swells up so as to fill a vegetable dish, and is sufficient for four men. It is believed that the antiscorbutic properties of vegetables are not impaired by desiccation, and they will keep for years if not exposed to dampness. Canned vegetables are very good for campaigning, but are not so portable as when put up in the other form. The desiccated vegetables used by our army have been prepared by Choillet and Co., 46 Rue Richer, Paris. There is an agency for them in New York. I regard these compressed vegetables as the best preparation for prairie traveling that has yet been discovered. A single ration weighs, before being boiled, only an ounce, and a cubic yard contains 16,000 rations. In making up their outfit for the plains, men are very prone to overload their teams with a great variety of useless articles. It is a good rule to carry nothing more than is absolutely necessary for use upon the journey. One cannot expect, with the limited allowance of transportation that emigrants usually have, to indulge in luxuries upon such expeditions, and articles for use in California can be purchased there at less cost than that of overland transport.

The most portable and simple preparation of subsistence that I know of, and which is used extensively by the Mexicans and Indians, is called "cold flour." It is made by parching corn, and pounding it in a mortar to the consistency of coarse meal; a little sugar and cinnamon added makes it quite palatable. When the traveler becomes hungry or thirsty, a little of the flour is mixed with water and drunk.

The allowance of provisions for each grown person, to make the journey from the Missouri River to California, should suffice for 110 days. The following is deemed requisite, viz.: 150 lbs. of flour, or its equivalent in hard bread; 25 lbs. of bacon or pork, and enough fresh beef to be driven on the hoof to make up the meat component of the rations; 15 lbs.

of coffee, and 25 lbs. of sugar; also a quantity of saleratus or yeast pow-
ders for making bread, and salt and pepper.

These are the chief articles of subsistence necessary for the trip, and
they should be used with economy, reserving a good portion for the western half of the journey. Heretofore many of the California emigrants have
improvidently exhausted their stocks of provisions before reaching their
journey's end, and have, in many cases, been obliged to pay the most ex-
orbitant prices in making up the deficiency.

From: *The Prairie Traveler: A Hand-Book for Overland Expedition, with Maps, Illustrations and Itineraries of the Principal Routes Between the Mississippi and the Pacific*
(Washington: Published by authority of the War Department, 1859)

Lonely Emigrant Train Westward-Bound

Overland by Stagecoach, October 10, 1858

Waterman L. Ormsby

John Butterfield was the initial guiding force of the Overland Mail Company. Through his leadership, overland stagecoach routes that had been established piecemeal were consolidated into an transcontinental route stretching from the Mississippi River to the Pacific Ocean. In 1858 Waterman L. Ormsby (1834–1908) became the first through passenger on the first west-bound stage of the Overland Mail Company. At the time, Ormsby was a special correspondent for the New York Herald. *He wrote a series of articles about his trip, and consolidating them, had them published in a book,* The Butterfield Overland Mail. *The following story was extracted from Ormsby's book and provides a interesting and vivid summary of his adventure.*

Safe and sound from all the threatened dangers of Indians, tropic suns, rattlesnakes, grizzly bears, stubborn mules, mustang horses, jerked beef, terrific mountain passes, fording rivers, and all the concomitants which envy, pedantry, and ignorance had predicted for all passengers by the overland mail route over which I have just passed, here am I in San Francisco, having made the passage from the St. Louis post office to the San Francisco post office in twenty-three days, twenty-three hours and a half, just one day and half an hour less than the time required by the Overland Mail Company's contract with the Post Office Department. The journey has been by no means as fatiguing to me as might be expected by a continuous ride of such duration, for I feel almost fresh enough to undertake it again.

The route is prolific in interest to the naturalist, the mineralogist, and all who love to contemplate nature in her wildest varieties, and throughout the whole 2,700 miles the interest in new objects is not allowed to flag. I have found the deserts teeming with curious plants and animal life, the mountain passes prolific in the grandest scenery, and the fruitful valleys suggestive of an earthly paradise; while, if this trip may be considered a criterion, the alleged danger from Indians is all a bugbear. . . .

The whole distance from St. Louis to San Francisco . . . is made to be 2,866 miles, comprising probably some of the most difficult roads in existence. Here are the tables:

Time Table of First Overland Mail—St. Louis to San Francisco

Place	Table Time for Leaving	Actual Time of Leaving	Miles from St. Louis
St. Louis, Mo., and Memphis, Tenn......	Sep. 16, 8 a.m.	Sep. 16, 8 a.m.	
P.R.R. terminus..........	Sep. 16, 6 a.m.	Sep. 16, 6:15 p.m.	160
Springfield, Mo..........	Sep. 18, 7:45 a.m.	Sep. 17, 4 p.m.	303
Fayetteville [Ark.]......	Sep. 19, 10:15 a.m.	Sep. 18, 12 p.m.	403
Fort Smith, Ark..........	Sep. 20, 3:30 a.m.	Sep. 19, 3:30 a.m.	468
Sherman, Texas..........	Sep. 22, 12:30 a.m.	Sep. 20, 4:40 p.m.	673
Fort Belknap, do........	Sep. 23, 9 a.m.	Sep. 22, 7 a.m.	819½
Ft. Chadbourne, do...	Sep. 24, 3:15 p.m.	Sep. 23, 7 p.m.	955
El Paso......................	Sep. 28, 11 a.m.	Sep. 30, 5:50 a.m.	1,369
Soldier's Farewell.......	Sep. 29, 8:30 p.m.	Oct. 1, 10:15 a.m.	1,519
Tucson, Arizona.........	Oct. 1, 1:30 p.m.	Oct. 2, 10 p.m.	1,703
Gila River, Ariz	Oct. 2, 9 p.m.	Oct. 5, 6:15 a.m.	1,811
Fort Yuma, Cal..........	Oct. 4, 3 a.m.	Oct. 5, 6:15 a.m.	1,979
Ft. Tejon via Los Angeles...........	Oct. 7, 7:30 a.m.	Oct. 8, 4:33 a.m.	2,494
Visalia, Cal................	Oct. 8, 11:30 a.m.	Oct. 8, 11:50 p.m.	2,621
Fireburg [Firebaugh's] Ferry......................	Oct. 9, 5:30 a.m.	Oct. 9, 11:50 a.m.	2,703
Arr. San. Fran.............	Oct. 10, 8:30 a.m.	Oct. 10, 7:30 a.m.	2,866

Thus you will perceive that we arrived here an hour before the time table time, which, being twenty-three hours and a half less than contract time, made our passage twenty-three days, twenty-three hours and a half, and, deducting the difference of time between St. Louis and San Francisco, our passage was made in twenty-three days and twenty-three hours and a half—a feat never yet equaled in overland travel, since, including detentions and stoppages, changing horses, meals, &c., our average speed was a fraction over five miles an hour. It may seem slow at first, but, when the quality of road . . . is considered, I think all will concede that it is remarkably quick time.

The following table shows very nearly the rate of speed of the stages over each division of the road, throwing off small fractions:

Rate of Speed from Point to Point

	Miles per hour
Pacific Railroad terminus to Fort Smith, Ark.............	5½
Fort Smith, Ark., to Sherman, Tex..............................	5½
Sherman, Tex., to Fort Chadbourne, Tex....................	3¾
Fort Chadbourne, Tex., to Franklin, Tex., opposite El Paso..	2⅔
El Paso to Tucson, Arizona...	9
Tucson, Arizona, to Los Angeles, Cal.........................	5
Los Angeles, Cal., to San Francisco, Cal....................	9

The low rate of speed between Chadbourne and El Paso is accounted for by the fact that that route comprises an entirely wild country across the great Staked Plain, seventy-five miles without water, and one hundred and thirteen miles up the sierras, where stations had not yet been established. In fact, there is not a human habitation, except the company stations, on this whole distance of over four hundred miles. Fortunately, the energy of Mr. Kinyon and his assistants on this end of the route made up the lost time of the others, and brought the mail in with flying colors. You will perceive by the table that from Franklin, opposite El Paso, the fastest time on the road was made.

From: "Overland to California," published by the *New York Herald*, Thursday, November 11, 1858, and reprinted in *The Butterfield Overland Mail*, Lyle H. Wright and Josephine M. Bynum (editors) (San Marino, CA: The Huntington Library, 1998)

Scalping Comanche Warriors, c. 1859

James Pike

James Pike (?–1867) lived in Ohio and Missouri as son of a newspaper editor. In 1859 he arrived in Texas and joined the Texas Rangers, taking part in a series of campaigns against Comanche Indians. In the beginning of the Civil War and after Texas seceded from the Union, Pike went north and joined the Fourth Ohio Cavalry. During the war, Pike served the Union as a spy, courier, and a scout. He was captured and imprisoned by Confederates, but later escaped. After the Civil War ended, Pike was commissioned as a lieutenant in the First U.S. Cavalry. In 1867, during an Indian attack, Pike became so frustrated because his rifle jammed that he slammed it onto a nearby boulder causing it to accidently discharge and killed him. Pike had previously written about his life as a Texas Ranger and as a soldier in the Civil War. The book was published in 1865 with the title, The Scout and Ranger: Being the Personal Adventures of Corporal Pike of the Fourth Ohio Cavalry. *The following story was extracted from that book. The story refers to Texas Ranger action against a warring band of Comanche Indians. In the story, Pike is allied with Caddo Indians whose reservation was nearby to Fort Belnap, west of Fort Worth.*

We were all well concealed, behind bushes, rocks, and trees, lying down as closely to the ground as possible, to await the unsuspecting Comanches, who believed that they had but two men to contend with. Nor did we lie long idle. Soon the enemy, some forty in number, came scouring in, at full speed, closely following the trail we had made, as if by instinct. On they came, till they arrived within rifle range, when Casa Maria drew from his pouch a whistle made from the thigh bone of an eagle, and blew one long, low note, which was followed up by three short, quick, piercing ones; and instantly a volley from Caddoe rifles, greeting the flank of the over confident and unsuspecting Comanches, who broke in every direction—some flying from the field, not to return again. A portion of the savages, however, more resolute than the remainder, soon rallied, and seemed determined to hold us, till reinforcements arrived from the village; and they at once commenced a rapid and well directed fire. But they fought at a disadvantage, as we were thoroughly protected by our position, while they were compelled to stand out upon the open ground. They did not dismount, as is usual; but each warrior rode up within range, discharged his piece, and galloped off to a place of safety, where he reloaded, and returned to discharge it again.

A word of command from our Chief, almost instantly changed the whole aspect of the struggle. The men, on hearing it, bounded from their places of concealment, and with guns, pistols, bows, and lances, charged out upon the mounted Comanches. Arrows flew thick and fast for a brief interval; and rapidly we were nearing the foe, and a hand to hand encounter seemed imminent; but before our band had reached the spot where our enemies stood, they wheeled their animals, and fled from the field, utterly foiled and beaten.

Once masters of the field, the whistle of the Caddoe Chief was heard again, and instantly his men commenced disposing of the fallen Comanches. There were on the ground, seven killed, and nine wounded; and the dispatching of the latter was at once commenced. All were slain, and their scalps added to the trophies of victory.

Some of the wounded struggled fiercely with lance and bow, but all were either shot or tomahawked by the infuriated but exulting Caddoes. Some yielded up their lives with stoical firmness, chanting their own death song, though suffering the most intense agony, until the Caddoes would leap upon them, and, with a blow of the tomahawk, end their torture in a bloody death. Others begged piteously that their lives might be spared; but there was no mercy in the breast of the victor for the foe, though fallen and helpless.

As long as the fight lasted, I could shoot and yell with the best of them; but, the struggle over and the success complete, my heart sank within me, and I sickened at the bloody work in which my comrades appeared to take so great a delight. But there was no escape for me; I must stand by and witness it all, without a murmur or a remonstrance. To have interposed an objection would have but added to the magnitude of the tortures inflicted; and, perhaps, brought down upon my own head the vengeance of Casa Maria and his men. That I might, at least, turn away from the scene, I mounted my horse and rode a short distance, as if looking out for Comanches, till the work of slaughter had ended.

Scalping, barbarous as it is, is reduced to an art among the Indians. The victor cuts a clean circle around the top of the head, so that the crown may form the center, and the diameter of the scalp exceed six inches; then, winding his fingers in the hair, he puts one foot on the neck of the prostrate foe, and with a vigorous pull tears the reeking scalp from the skull. To the dead, this, of course, would not be absolute cruelty; but it is too frequently the case that the process is performed and the scalp severed while yet the mangled victim lives; and there are instances where parties have recovered, and long survived this barbarous mutilation. Occasionally, a warrior is not satisfied with the part of the scalp usually taken, but bares the skull entirely, and carries away in triumph even the ears of his victim.

The scalping concluded and the trophies gathered up and secured, another shrill whistle brought the victors into their saddles, and we began a precipitate retreat to our own village. For several miles we marched in solid column; but an order from the Chief scattered the crowd, and every man took the direction which best suited his fancy.

From: *The Scout and Ranger: Being the Personal Adventures of Corporal Pike of the Fourth Ohio Cavalry as a Texas Ranger, in the Indian Wars, Delineating Western Adventure; Afterward a Scout and Spy, in Tennessee, Alabama, Georgia, and the Carolinas, Under Generals Mitchell, Rosecrans, Stanley, Sheridan, Lytle, Thomas, Crook, and Sherman* (New York: J. R. Hawley & Co., 1865)

Burial at Mountain Meadows, May 6, 1859

Charles Breiver

The large influx of emigrant wagon trains passing through Utah caused enormous tensions with the Mormom population because most of the emigrants looked down on the Mormon religion and considered the Church's acceptance of plural marriages as sacrilegious to the teachings of Christianity. Further, the emigrant train of thirty to forty wagons, containing about 140 people, that was entering the area of southwest Utah called Mountain Meadows, near Cedar City, in September 1857, were at the wrong place at the wrong time. About this time the Mormon government was having difficulty with the United States. Tragically for the emigrant train, two or more regiments of U.S. troops had been ordered to Utah to ensure that the laws of the U.S. were properly enforced. The Mormons saw this as a heavy-handed action by "Gentiles" (non-Mormons) and as discriminatory treatment. The emigrants on the ill-fated train were mainly from Arkansas, and were considered as the "most obnoxious kind of Gentiles." These and other perceptions were used as justification of the slaughter of all of the 120 men, women, and children of the emigrant train by the Mormons and their Indian allies. About sixty Mormons, painted and disguised as Indians, along with a larger number of Indians from the Paiute tribe launched a surprise dawn attack on the wagon train. After the attack began, the emigrants put up a strong defense that lasted for several days. Because it looked like the emigrants might hold out for a longer time, the Mormons and their Indian allies concocted a plan of deception. The Mormons got one of their leaders, John D. Lee, to enter the emigrant camp and declare that he and his fellow Mormons had driven the Indians away, and that they would accompany the emigrants to Cedar City and safety if the

150

emigrants would give up their weapons. Convinced that Lee's party was their salvation, the emigrants gave up their arms and followed Lee away from their defensive position. Hiding behind a hill, the Mormons and Indians attacked and killed every person on the emigrant train, save for a few children who were thought to be so young that they would not remember what had taken place. More than a year and a half after the slaughter, Charles Breiver wrote a report on his findings at the site.

Utah Territory May 6ᵗʰ 1859
Camp at Mountain Meadows

Captain [R. P. Campbell, 2d Dragoons],

I have the honor to report that this morning accompanied by the Detachment of men furnished by your order, I proceeded to inter the remains of the men women and children of the Arkansas emigrant train, massacred by the Mormons at the Mountain Meadows, Utah Territory, in the month of September, eighteen hundred and fifty seven.

At the Scene of the first attack, in the immediate vicinity of our present camp, marked by: a small defensive trench made by the emigrants, a number of human skulls and bones, and hair were found scattered about, bearing the appearance of never having been buried, also remnants of bedding and wearing apparel.

On examining the trenches or excavations which appear to have been within the corral and within which it was supposed some written account of the massacre might have been concealed, some few human bones, human hair, and what seemed to be the feathers of bedding, only were discerned.

Proceeding twenty five hundred yards in a direction N 15 W. I reached a ravine fifty yards distant from the road bordered by a few bushes of Scrub oak in which I found portions of the skeletons of many bodies, skulls, bones and matted hair most of which on examination, I concluded to be those of men.

Three hundred and fifty yards further on, and in the same direction, another assembly of human remains were found, which by all appearances had been left to decay upon the surface—Skull and bones most of which I believe to be those of women, some also of children probably ranging from six to twelve years of age. There too were found masses of womens hair, childrens bonnets such as are generally used upon the plains, and pieces of lace, muslin, calicoes and other material, part of women's and children's apparel. I have buried thirteen skulls and many more scattered fragments.

Some of the remains above referred to were found upon the surface of the ground with a little earth partially covering them, and at the place where the men were massacred some lightly buried, but the majority were scattered about upon the plain. Many of the skulls bore marks of violence, being pierced with bullet holes, or shattered by heavy blows, or cleft with some sharp edged instrument. The bones were bleached and worn by long exposure to the elements and bore the impress[ion] of the teeth of wolves or other wild animals.

The number of skulls found upon the ground near the spring or position of first attack, and adjoining our camp, were eight in number. These with the other remains there found were buried under my supervision at the base of the hill upon the hill side of the Valley.

At a place twenty five hundred yards distance from the spring, the relative positions and general appearance of the remains, seemed to indicate that the men were there taken by surprise and massacred. Some of the skulls showed that fire arms had been discharged close to the head. I here buried eighteen skulls and parts of many more skeletons found scattered over the space of a mile towards the lines, in which directions they were no doubt dragged by the wolves.

No names were found upon any article of apparel or any peculiarity in the remains, with the exception of one bone, the upper jaw, in which the teeth were very closely crowded and which contained one front tooth more, than is generally found.

Under my direction, the above mentioned remains were all properly buried, the respective locality being marked with mounds of stone.

Very respectfully, Your Obedt. Servt.
(seg) Chs. Breiver,
Asst. Surgn U.S. Army

Reprinted from *Mountain Meadows Witness: The Life and Times of Bishop Philip Klingensmith* by Anna Jean Backus, by permission of The Arthur H. Clark Company. Copyright © 1995 The Arthur H. Clark Company.

A New Home at Gold Hill, c. July 1860

Mollie Dorsey Sanford

One of the dominating and frustrating facts of the Old West was the huge short-age of women. For example, when the first California census was taken in 1850, men outnumbered women by twelve to one. In many mining camps there were no women at all. Men of the Old West often held white women up as sainted figures and couldn't do enough for them. For example, in 1850 the wife of a Forty-niner wrote in her diary: "I am afraid I should have had a very mistaken impression of my own importance if I had lived long among [these men]. At every stopping-place they made little fires in their frying pans and set them around me, to keep off the mosquitoes while I took my meal. As the columns of smoke rose about me I felt like a heathen goddess to whom incense was being offered." The following story was excerpted from Mollie Sanford's (1838–1915) diary and tells of her ex-periences living in a small mining camp named Gold Hill, northwest of present-day Boulder, Colorado. Her diary was published with the title, Mollie: The Jour-nal of Mollie Dorsey Sanford in Nebraska and Colorado Territories, 1857–1866.

We left Denver Sat. 28th, afternoon. Traveled 4 miles and camped. Reached Boulder Sunday afternoon, a distance of 30 miles. Our road was very rough, full of boulders. Here there is an extensive valley and some farms, fenced in. Boulder is composed of perhaps a dozen cab-ins. Boulder Creek is a fast rushing stream, clear as crystal, and full of small trout. Under the shadow of immense mountains this little spot is sheltered, a picturesque place for habitation. On Monday morning we began ascending the mountains. We would go up such steep places that I thought the wagon would fall back on me. I would yell to get out, but found my breath too short to climb far. Our driver assured me the cattle were sure-footed and it was safer to ride, so I would climb back and rest. But I could but be charmed with the surroundings. The rocks are grand! the hills covered with evergreens of spruce and pine, flowers are growing everywhere, peeping here and there from the crevices of the rocks, bright cold springs start out here and there, and silvery cascades come leaping down the mountainsides. Altho we seemed so high, there were peaks that rose hundreds of feet above us. There are a number of cabins on Gold Hill occupied by miners, the largest owned by Holly and Holt, who are putting up a stamp mill. We are in the gulch below, where McKnight is putting up his mill. By [Mollie's husband] is to do the blacksmithing for the company, and as was arranged I am to cook for the men. My heart sinks within me when I see there are 18 or 20, and no conveniences at all. There is a rough log cabin, neither chinked nor daubed, as they call it, no floor, and only a hole cut out for a door and window. A "bunk" is made in one corner. This is covered with pine boughs, and on this are spread our comforts and blankets. We have no mattress—can't even get straw or hay to fill a bed tick. I have to cook out of doors by a fire, but have mustered my small cook stove into service, but that will only hold one loaf of bread, or one pie at a time. All I have furnished to cook is bread, meat, and coffee. The cups and plates are of tin. A long table is made in a shed made of the pine boughs outside the cabin. No table linen is supplied. I fear I shall sink under this burden. It is not what my fancy painted it.

By has been helping me until I get started, but he does all sorts of awkward things. If this does not take the romance out of me, then I'm proof against *anything*. McKnight is a rough sort of man and don't seem to know that a woman needs more to do with than men. Mr. Holly comes down to see us often and looks as if he pitied me. There are some very nice boys here. They are nice to me in every way. They sing of evenings and that helps while the time away. They sang "Home Sweet Home" last night and I softly cried myself to sleep.

August 7th, Sabbath evening

I snatch a moment to write tonight. The week has been spent in monotonous routine. Cook, cook, bake, bake! The fire to cook by is built in a pile of rocks. They get so hot that it almost burns my face to a blister. The boys voted they would get their own dinner today, so Judge Holly, By, and I took a long walk up where we had a lovely view of the snowy range, and also of the plains, that stretched out like a map. We can see Denver 40 miles away. Called at a cabin and had a sight of a new little baby a week old. I should call her "Treasure" if she were mine. There are only 5 ladies on this Hill.

.... I feel that—
> It was for him I left my happy home.
> With him 'mid all life's cares to roam.
> To him I gave my maiden heart,
> And bade all other loves depart.

Reprinted from *Mollie: The Journal of Mollie Dorsey Sanford in Nebraska and Colorado Territories, 1857–1866* by permission of the University of Nebraska Press. Copyright 1959 by the University of Nebraska Press.

A Mysterious Corpse, c. 1860

William F. Drannan

Little is known of William F. Drannan except through his two books, Thirty-One Years on the Plains and in the Mountains, *published in 1899 and its sequel published in 1910 with the title,* William F. Drannan, Chief of Scouts as Pilot to Emigrant and Government Trains, Across the Plains of the Wild West of Fifty Years Ago. *Drannan claimed that he was an early explorer and scout who was befriended by and traveled with the likes of well-known trailblazers such as Kit Carson and John C. Fremont. The following vignette was taken from Drannan's 1910 book and tells the story of a man who died a lonely death accompanied only by his faithful companion.*

Everything went smoothly with Jim and me which brought us to Honney Lake. The night we reached Honney Lake, we camped in a little grove of timber near a pearling stream of cool, sparkling water about a half a mile south of the trail.

We had eaten our supper, and were about to spread our blankets and turn in for the night, when we heard a dog bark close to our camp, but it was too dark to see him. Jim said, "Don't that beat any thing you ever heard?"

We listened a moment and then it was a howl, and then in a moment he barked again. Jim said, "You stay in camp, Will and I will take my gun and see what is the matter."

In a moment Jim called, "I see him." I waited about an hour before Jim came back and was beginning to feel anxious about him. When I heard his footsteps he said, "I followed that dog nearly a mile and then I found the cause of his howling and what do you think it was?"

I answered, "Jim, I have no idea," to which he said, "Well, I will tell you. I found the body of a dead man laying on his blanket just as if he was laying down to rest. I did not get near the dog, until I had discovered the body, and then he was very friendly with me, and came and whined, and wagged his tail, as if he knew me. I looked all around, but I could find nothing but the body lying on the blanket. I could not see that there had been a fire, and I saw no signs of a horse or anything else, and the strange part of it is that, although the dog was so friendly with me I could not coax him away from the body which I suppose was his master."

I asked Jim, what he thought it was best to do. He answered, "What can we do, Will? We have no tools to dig a grave with, and the body is laying among the rocks, and I expect that dog will stay beside it and starve to death."

"Wouldn't it be a good idea to go to the place in the morning and pile rocks on the body, to keep the wolves and other wild animals from eating it up?" Jim said, "Yes, we will do that, and we will shoot some jackrabbits and leave them with the dog, so he can have something to eat for a few days anyhow."

On the way over to the place where the body lay we killed three rabbits and threw them to the dog, and he ate them as if he was nearly starved, and I have always thought that his master died of starvation, as he had no gun or pistol with which to kill anything to eat, and Jim thought that he must have got lost from some emigrant train and wandered around until he was too weak to go farther and lay down and died with no one but his faithful dog to watch over him in his last moments.

We covered him up with stones and brush, the best we could and left him and the poor dog together although we tried every way we could to tempt the animal away. The faithful dog would not leave his master's body. After trying persuasion until we saw it was no use, Jim said, "Let's put a rope around his neck and lead him off." I answered, "No, Jim, if he will not be coaxed away, it would not be right to force him to leave his dead master." Jim said, "It seems too bad to leave him to starve, but you are right, Will," and so we left him, and we never saw him again.

From: *William F. Drannan, Chief of Scouts as Pilot to Emigrant and Government Trains, Across the Plains of the Wild West of Fifty Years Ago* (Chicago: Thos. W. Jackson Publishing Company, 1910)

Suspicious Shooting of an Officer, c. October 1860

James E. Farmer

Having run away from home as a teenager, most of Farmer's life was associated with the U.S. Army in one way or another. Farmer was part of the Union forces that defeated the Confederates at the battle of Glorieta in New Mexico. Later, he worked as a sutler at Fort Sumner, New Mexico, and served as an Indian agent at Fort Sill, Oklahoma. He wrote a manuscript of his memoirs in an attempt to stave off lying in a pauper's grave because he had not saved any money for his retirement. It is suspected that his memoirs may not have greatly altered his retirement income.

The Captain held up his hand, the Company halted. The Indians told the Captain about some Navajos near. He had his men dismount, intending to use them as Infantry. Each fourth man holding horses. We moved very carefully. Lying down in skirmish line order, and after some time the men were motioned to crawl forward, the Captain well in advance.

We found ourselves looking into a valley and saw 10 to 11 Indians sitting near two fires against a bluff, which formed a half circle. After a few moments the Captain motioned the men back to their horses. After giving some instructions to the Indian guides we started on. After going about 500 yards we turned to our left sharply and found that we were closing the outlet, the guides reached the other side of the amphitheater at the same time. We charging promptly without any command being given. In a very short time there were no Indians left; as the Company charged, the scouts opened fire directly across our line.

I stayed close to the Captain. He pulled up and deliberately dismounted and as he reached the ground he fell. I was at his side in a moment, asking what was the matter. I then realized that he was dead. I rode up to Sergeant McGraw who was having the bugler blow the assembly and told him that the Captain was dead. He immediately ordered inspection of arms, as the Company was not using the rifles; on inspection of arms it was found that none of them had been discharged. Discipline was very severe in those days and I heard many of the enlisted men say that if opportunity offered itself they would spare one shot for some of the officers, for whom they had a grievance. Knowing these things was the reason McGraw ordered an inspection. The cross fire of the Indian scouts was what killed Captain McLane, a very brave man, and a kind and generous gentleman.

Reprinted from *My Life with the Army in the West*, Dale F. Giese (editor) (Santa Fe, NM: Stagecoach Press, 1993) by permission of Dale F. Giese.

Dissolution of a Partnership, c. Winter 1860

William J. McConnell

This story deals with two miners who joined as partners in a placer gold mining venture in California. The word "placer" is derived from the Spanish word for sand bank or stream eddy. Gold in placer sites was usually eroded out of rock and the resulting grains were transported by water and deposited in ancient streambeds. The work of placer mining carried with it a tremendous set of hardships and challenges. In order to find gold-bearing gravel, miners had to sink shafts next to existing creeks down to older streambeds that had been covered up by ten to twenty feet of muck, dirt, and rocks. The major tools for digging was the shovel and the pick-axe and the work was back-breaking and often earned very little money for the miners. Faced with such uncertainty and to spread the risk, many miners formed partnerships. This is the story of such a partnership. Its author, William John McConnell (1839–1925), was born in Michigan but moved to California in 1860 to seek his fortune in mining, the cattle business, merchandising, and banking. He then resided in Oregon where he was a deputy U.S. marshal (1865–1867) and later became the president of the Oregon State senate. Then, he moved to Idaho and ran for, and was elected to the U.S. Senate. Thereafter, he was elected Governor of Idaho and served from 1892-1896. This story was extracted from McConnell's 1926 book, Frontier Law: A Story of Vigilante Days.

I first became interested with a placer miner named Cox in a placer claim on American Ridge, about one mile below Mormon Island. I acquired one-half interest in a placer property, which consisted of the ground included in two placer claims, and a miner's cabin sufficiently large to house two men. The furnishings of the cabin were of the simplest and most primitive kind—two narrow bunks, two homemade stools, one small table, and a number seven cook stove, together with a homemade cupboard built against one side of the wall.

The man Cox with whom I had associated myself as a mining partner was of the usual type of American placer miners, a few of whom may yet be found in all placer mining camps along the Pacific Coast. Usually they are ripe in experience—typical "old bachelors," and good cooks of the kind of food to which they have been accustomed. They may not be lazy, but most of them have acquired a tired feeling, which uncharitable persons may mistake for laziness. Mormon Island had for its foremost citizens a coterie of this class of miners.

I was young, physically vigorous, and had not yet acquired the tired feeling. My partner was congenial and a good teacher of mining, but upon me soon fell most of the hard work. However, I was being taught to mine, and did not object, especially as my partner did not appear to be a physically strong man. He proved, however, to be a neat and cleanly housekeeper. After supper every night he would wash and put away the dishes, and then usually suggest that we go to town.

The general resort was the Forty Drops. There we would usually find the old bachelor miners, all of whom preferred assembling at the Forty Drops to spend their evenings rather than to remain in their lonely, and generally poorly ventilated cabins. Here in the old saloon, shorn of the glory and hilarity of earlier days, night after night and usually every afternoon, were seated a silent group of persons engaged in a game they called "draw." My partner Cox appeared to enjoy playing this game. As I became acquainted with the men who frequented that end of the Forty Drops, the reason dawned upon me why he and others of his class of miners were always broke. They did not drink to excess, but they simply contributed their money to professional gamblers who paid periodical visits to our camp to collect from their willing victims.

I noticed eventually that the other type of visiting miners at the Forty Drops seldom or never came back to the rear of the saloon where cards were being played. They came in to the bar, usually bought a drink or a cigar, and after paying for their purchase walked out again. Those who patronized the card tables were almost invariably American born, and when not engaged in playing some game of cards indulged in telling stories, or discussing politics. They were men of varied experience, most of whom had been born and reared in some of the towns on the banks of the Mississippi River or its tributaries. Their number included men of the learned professions as well as artisans. As may be imagined, the experiences they related were, many of them, of a character to startle and horrify a tenderfoot like myself.

To the credit of these hardened old timers I must say that they never tried to induce me to join them in their social glass, or in their card games.

The probable reason for their not asking me to take part in their card games was that they all knew that I had traded my watch and revolver, and paid my last dollar for my interest in our placer claim. My partner Cox was the general manager and treasurer; therefore it was known to every person in the camp that I had no money. The very good reason was that our mine did not yield enough revenue to leave a surplus after Cox's losings at the gaming tables and our modest grocery bills had been paid.

I had not, up to early in December, asked Cox for a statement of our finances. Then he smilingly and in the best humor possible advised me that we had been playing in bad luck; that he had lost in almost every sitting in the game during November, and that we owed the grocer and the butcher for our last month's bills. However, he thought by cleaning up our string of sluices and tail race we would be able to square our debts. The next morning we accordingly cleaned up everything, and fortunately as he had predicted, we found enough gold dust to settle all our debts. He then proposed to me that we sever our mining partnership; or rather that he would quit and turn over the claim, cabin, tools, and mining outfit to me. I accepted his proposition.

From: *Frontier Law: A Story of Vigilante Days* (Chicago: World Book Company, 1923)

The Longest Pony Express Ride, c. May 1861

Robert Haslam

For a short period the Pony Express offered the fastest mail delivery between St. Joseph, Missouri, and Sacramento, California. The Pony Express operated from April, 1860 to October 1861 when it was superseded by the telegraph. During that time 183 men are known to have ridden for the Pony Express and Robert "Pony Bob" Haslam (1840–1912) was one of them. Haslam answered an ad for Pony Express riders similar to one appearing in a California newspaper which read: "Wanted. Young, skinny, wiry fellows. Not over eighteen. Must be expert riders. Willing to risk death daily. Orphans preferred." The job paid $100 a month. In one ride, Haslam carried the news of Lincoln's election as President, riding 130 miles, in 8 hours, 10 minutes using 13 relays of horses. He was ambushed by Indians, shot with flint-head arrows through the lower jaw, fracturing it on both sides and knocking out five teeth. The following story was published in 1908 and details Haslam's account of the longest round-trip ride of the Pony Express.

About eight months after the Pony Express was established, the Pi-Ute War commenced in Nevada. Virginia City, then the principal point of interest, and hourly expecting an attack from the hostile Indians, was only in its infancy. A stone hotel on C Street was in course of construction and had reached an elevation of two stories. This was hastily transformed into a fort for the protection of the women and children. From the city the signal fires of the Indians could be seen on every mountain peak, and all available men and horses were pressed into service to repel the impending assault of the savages.

When I reached Reed's Station, on the Carson River, I found no change of horses, as all those at the station had been seized by the whites to take part in the approaching battle. I fed the animal that I rode, and started for the next station, called Bucklands, afterward known as Fort Churchill, fifteen miles farther down the river. It was to have been the termination of my journey, as I had changed my old route to this one, in which I had had many narrow escapes, and been twice wounded by the Indians.

I had already ridden seventy-five miles; but, to my great astonishment, the other rider refused to go on. The superintendent, W. C. Marley, was at the station, but all his persuasion could not prevail on the rider, Johnson Richardson, to take the road. Turning then to me, Marley said: "Bob, I will give you $50 if you make this ride." I replied, "I will go at once."

Within ten minutes, when I had adjusted my Spencer rifle, which was a seven-shooter and my Colt's revolver, with two cylinders ready for use in case of emergency, I started. From the station onward it was a lonely and dangerous ride of thirty-five miles, without a change, to the Sink of the Carson. I arrived there all right, however, and pushed on to Sand Springs, through an alkali bottom and sand hills, thirty miles farther, without a drop of water all along the route. At Sand Springs I changed horses and continued on to Cold Springs, a distance of thirty-seven miles. Another change and a ride of thirty more miles brought me to Smiths Creek. Here I was relieved by J. G. Kelley. I had ridden 190 miles, stopping only to eat and change horses. . . .

After remaining at Smith's Creek about nine hours, I started to retrace my journey with the return express. When I arrived at Cold Springs to my horror I found that the station had been attacked by Indians, the keeper killed, and all the horses taken away. I decided in a moment what course to pursue—I would go on. I watered my horse, having ridden him thirty miles on time, he was pretty tired, and started for Sand Springs, thirty-seven miles away. It was growing dark, and my road lay through heavy sage brush, high enough in some places to conceal a horse. I kept a bright lookout and closely watched every motion of my poor pony's ears, which is a signal for danger in an Indian country. I was prepared for a fight, but the stillness of the night and the howling of the wolves and coyotes made cold chills run through me at times; but I reached Sand Springs in safety and reported what had happened. Before leaving, I advised the station keeper to come with me to the Sink of the Carson, for I was sure the Indians would be upon him the next day. He took my advice, and so probably saved his life, for the following morning Smith's Creek was attacked. The whites, however, were well protected in the shelter of a stone house, from which they fought the savages for four days. At the end of that time they were relived by the appearance of about fifty volunteers from Cold Springs. These men reported that they had buried John Williams, the brave keeper of that station, but not before he had been nearly devoured by the wolves.

When I arrived at the Sink of the Carson, I found the station men badly frightened, for they had seen some fifty warriors decked out in their war-paint and reconnoitering. There were fifteen white men here, well armed and ready for a fight. The station was built of adobe, and was large enough for the men and ten or fifteen horses, with a fine spring of water within a few feet of it. I rested here an hour, and after dark started for Buckland's, where I arrived without a mishap and only three and a half hours behind schedule time. I found Mr. Marley at Buckland's and when I related to him the story of the Cold Springs tragedy and my success, he raised his previous offer of $50 for my ride to $100. I was rather tired, but the excitement of the trip had braced me up to withstand the fatigue of the journey. After a rest of one and a half hours, I proceeded over my own route from Bucklands to Fridays Station, crossing the Sierra Nevada. I had traveled 380 miles within a few hours of schedule time, and was surrounded by perils on every hand.

From: William Lightfoot Visscher, *A Thrilling and Truthful History of the Pony Express or Blazing the Westward Way and other Sketches and Incidents of Those Stirring Times* (Chicago: Rand, McNall & Co., 1908)

"Everything Went Off Quietly," December 24, 1862

Isaac Heard

In August 1862 the Great Sioux Uprising began on the Minnesota frontier. It led to the wholesale massacre of hundreds of white settlers of all ages and both sexes. When news of the outbreak reached Minnesota Governor Alexander Ramsey, he asked General Henry H. Sibley to assume command of troops to suppress the uprising. In late September, with the Battle of Wood Lake, many warriors surrendered and others were captured. Sibley appointed a five-member military commission to try the Indians accused of participating in the affair. The commission gave the death sentence to 303 Indians. President Abraham Lincoln was the final authority, however, and he commuted the sentences of all but 38 Indians. Sibley commuted the sentence of one Indian. On December 27, 1862, Sibley telegraphed the President that "the 38 Indians and half-breeds ordered by you for execution were hung yesterday at 10 A.M. Everything went off quietly."

On Wednesday [December 24, 1862] each Indian set apart for execution was permitted to send for two or three of his relatives or friends confined in the same prison for the purpose of bidding them a final adieu, and to carry such messages to absent relatives as each person might be disposed to send. . . .

There is a ruling passion with many Indians, and Tazoo could not refrain from its enjoyment even in this sad hour Ta-ti-mi-ma was sending word to his relatives not to mourn for his loss. He said he was old, and could not hope to live long under any circumstances, and his execution would not shorten his days a great deal, and dying as he did, innocent of any white man's blood, he hoped would give him a better chance to be saved; therefore he hoped his friends would consider his death but as a removal from this to a better world. . . .

In shaking hands with Red Iron and Akipa, Tazoo said: "Friends, last summer you were opposed to us. You were living in continual apprehension of an attack from those who were determined to exterminate the whites. Yourselves and families were subjected to many taunts, insults, and threats. Still you stood firm in our friendship for the whites and continually counseled the Indians to abandon their raid against the whites. Your course was condemned at the time, but now you see your wisdom. You were right when you said the whites could not be exterminated, and the attempt indicated folly; you and your families were prisoners, and the lives of all in danger. Today you are here at liberty, assisting in feeding and guarding us, and thirty nine men will die in two days because they did not follow your example and advice."

Several of the prisoners were completely overcome during the leave-taking, and were compelled to abandon conversation. Others again (and Tazoo was one) affected to disregard the dangers of their position, and laughed and joked apparently as unconcerned as if they were sitting around a camp-fire in perfect freedom.

On Thursday, the women who were employed as cooks for the prisoners, all of whom had relations among the condemned, were admitted to the prison. This interview was less sad, but still interesting. Locks of hair, blankets, coats, and almost every other article in possession of the prisoners, were given in trust for some relative or friend who had been forgotten or overlooked during the interview of the previous day. . . .

Late on Thursday night, in company with Lieutenant Colonel Marshall, the reporter visited the building occupied by the doomed Indians. . . .

They were all fastened to the floor by chains, two by two. Some were sitting up, smoking and conversing while others reclining, covered with blankets and apparently asleep. The three half-breeds and one or two others, only, were dressed in citizens' clothes. The rest all wore the breechclout, leggins, and blankets, and not a few were adorned with paint. The majority of them were young men, though several were quite old and gray-headed, ranging perhaps toward seventy. One was quite a youth, not over sixteen. They all appeared cheerful and contented, and scarcely to reflect on the certain doom which awaited them. To the gazers, the recollection of how short a time since they had been engaged in the diabolical work of murdering indiscriminately both old and young sparing neither sex nor condition, sent a thrill of horror through the veins. Now they were perfectly harmless, and looked as innocent as children. They smiled at your entrance, and held out their hands to be shaken, which yet appeared to be gory with the blood of babes.

At half past seven all persons were excluded from the room except those necessary to help prepare the prisoners for their doom. Under the superintendence of Major Brown and Captain Redfield, their irons were knocked off, and one by one were tied by cords, their elbows being pinioned behind and the wrists in front, but about six inches apart. This operation occupied till about nine-o'clock. In the mean time the scene was much enlivened by their songs and conversation, keeping up the most cheerful appearance. As they were being pinioned, they went round the room shaking hands with the soldiers and reporters, bidding the 'good-by,' etc. White Dog requested not to be tied, and said that he could keep his hands down; but of course his request could not be complied with . . . After all were properly fastened, they stood up in a row around the room, and another exciting death song was sung.

At precisely ten o'clock the condemned were marshaled in a procession and, headed by Captain Redfield, marched out into the street, and directly across through files of soldiers to the scaffold, which had been erected in front, and ere delivered to the officer of the day, Captain Burt. They went eagerly and cheerfully, even crowding and jostling each other to be ahead, just like a lot of hungry boarders rushing to dinner in a hotel. . . .

As they commenced the ascent of the scaffold the death song was again started, and when they had all got up, the noise they made was truly hideous. It seemed as if Pandemonium had broken loose. It had a wonderful effect in keeping up their courage. One young fellow, who had been given a cigar by one of the reporters just before marching from their quarters, was smoking it on the stand, puffing away very coolly during the intervals of the hideous 'Hi-yi-yi,' 'Hi-yi-yi,' and even after the cap was drawn over his face he managed to get it up over his mouth and smoke. Another was smoking his pipe. The noose having been promptly adjusted over the necks of each by Captain Libby, all was ready for the fatal signal.

The solemnity of the scene was here disturbed by an incident which, if it were not intensely disgusting, might be cited as a remarkable evidence of the contempt of death which is the traditional characteristic of the Indian. One of the Indians, in the rhapsody of his death song, conceived an insult to the spectators which it required an Indian to conceive, and a dirty dog of an Indian to execute.

The refrain of his song was to the effect that if a body was found near New Ulm with his head cut off, and place in a certain indelicate part of the body, he did it. 'It is I,' he sung, 'it is I;' and suited the action to the word by an indecent exposure of his person, in hideous mockery of the triumph of that justice whose sword was already falling on his head.

Three slow, measured, and distinct beats on the drum by Major Brown, who had been announced as signal officer, and the rope was cut by Mr. Duly (the same who killed Lean Bear, and whose family were attacked)—the scaffold fell, and thirty-seven lifeless bodies were left dangling between heaven and earth. One of the ropes was broken, as but little signs of life were observed; but he was immediately hung up again. While the signal-beat was being given, numbers were seen to clasp the hands of their neighbors, which in several instances continued to be clasped till the bodies were cut down.

As the platform fell, there was one, not loud, but prolonged cheer from the soldiery and citizens who were spectators, and then all were quiet and earnest witnesses of the scene. For so many, there was but little suffering; the necks of all, or nearly all, were evident dislocated by the fall, and the after struggling was slight. The scaffold fell at quarter past ten o'clock, and in twenty minutes the bodies had all been examined by Surgeons Le Boutillier, Sheardown Finch, Clark, and others, and life pronounced extinct.

From: *History of the Sioux War and Massacre* (St. Paul, MN: St. Paul Press, December 24, 1863)

Scene of the Execution of Thirty-Eight Sioux Indians

Beans, Anyone? c. 1863

Daniel Ellis Conner

Traveling the frontier of the Old West was tough, tiring, and dirty work—up before dawn, in the saddle all day or bullwhacking an oxen-drawn wagon, and, hopefully, having a hot meal before bedding down at night exposed to the elements. Usually at least one person was assigned the responsibility for preparing the meals. Oftentimes, that meant that others would assist in the preparation of meals by gathering firewood, carrying water and hunting game. The ingenuity, perseverance, and sheer stubbornness required to prepare food under these circumstances surely matches the determination, courage and independence of the settlers, ranchers, and townsfolk who followed in the frontier cooks' footsteps. The author of the following narrative, Conner, was a member of the Joseph Walker party of gold seekers whose circuitous route raised the suspicions of General James H. Carleton, commander of Union forces in the Southwest. The Walker party had first gone across northern Arizona to Colorado. Then they went through New Mexico and the Chiricahua Apache strongholds to Tucson, a known hotbed of Confederate sympathizers. Finally, they traveled up the Hassayampa River and discovered gold near today's Prescott, Arizona. Conner's experiences prospecting in the West and traveling with the Walker party are detailed in the book, A Confederate in the Colorado Gold Fields.*

We passed the dilapidated remains of Bent's old fort. There was nothing left of it but a portion of the adobe walls, the highest part of which were not probably more than seven feet. Some parts of those old weather-beaten walls were crumbled quite to the foundation. We guess its locality at about forty miles above the present site of Fort Lyon, on the

Arkansas River. Early one morning attention was drawn by the interesting remark that the long-sought Rocky Mountains were in sight.

Cooking and all other camp duties were quickly suspended amidst the
stirring about after good positions to look for the mountains. "Where are
they?" and "I don't see them" and so on were heard impatiently expressed all about the camp. But the dim outlines of Pike's Peak, like a
cloud so much higher than expected at that distance was plainly visible
and equally deceptive. I saw a supposed cloud, but failed to notice it until I was told to look at the cloud. Then I believed that it was a cloud until time enough had transpired for a cloud to change its shape at least
enough to detect.

But it proved indeed to be a cloud that never changed. As the sun arose
gradually, the fixed and dim outlines of this grand old sentinel of the
Rocky Mountains also gradually went out before we left the camp. Nor
did we see it again during that day, nor did its outlines after a day's travel
toward it appear more plainly marked on the following morning than
when we first saw it. And indeed could we see it only in the early morning for many days' travel after its first appearance.

The distance to this peak was estimated at 170 miles. But whatever may
have been its true distance it was evidently a long way off, plainly evidenced by the little change that a week's travel made in its appearance.
The whole body or outline of the Rocky Mountains came in sight slowly
and as gradually as did the peak. My impatience gradually subsided, as I
became accustomed to the elephant, long before reaching it.

We drove up near the riverbank just after a long dry stretch and determined to refresh the stock while near the water and therefore pitched
camp at noon. Nearly all of the party wandered off from the camp except
the herders who took the stock across the river to graze, because of the
grass being burned on our side, and except also one of each men, who are
supposed to attend camp duty in the absence of those who chose to go in
quest of fresh meat for the replenishing of the common larder.

I refused to go hunting for game and therefore represented my mess.
Being ordered by our steward before he left to cook a kettle of beans for
supper, I proceeded to work off the task as soon as the hunters departed.
It was my first attempt at cooking of any kind, for I had always exchanged
my cooking services until this effort. I proceeded to fill a four-gallon
sheet-iron camp kettle with those small, dry, white navy beans, which are
always used on the plains by the army, and by the way a splendid prairie
dish when properly seasoned. After the kettle was filled and a sufficiency
of water poured on to cover them, they were hung on the camp hooks
over the fire, and I considered my work done. I therefore laid down on a
blanket to read. It was not long, however, before the kettle began to over-
flow. Yes, I discovered that I had put a little too many beans in the kettle

and therefore dipped out a quart tin-cup full and again settled myself on the blanket. Pretty soon the kettle overflowed again. I took out another quart cup full. It ran over again and I obtained a larger vessel and filled it. I soon discovered that all the vessels in our branch of this department would fail in point of capacity, and I crawled into the wagon and searched for and finally found a prospecting pan, brought it out, and filled it. And still the original kettle was full and on the increase. I here stepped over to the campfires and proposed to furnish the respective messes with beans partially cooked, as it would save fuel. No, they didn't want any, as their kettles were as full as they would hold and quite sufficient for supper and breakfast, and they had no way of carrying them in a soft state. They appeared ignorant of the dilemma, but when the "boys" came in at night, these cooks knew more about my bean-cooking than I did.

Although we were a long distance from a supply depot and couldn't afford waste, I went back to my kettle and dipped beans out of that kettle and sowed them broadcast on the prairie, and continued the process until I finally got the bulk of the beans to conform to the capacity of the kettle. But I had one consolation: that there was plenty for the whole mess. I was thenceforth excused from the culinary department, but it was a long while before I heard the last of that miserable pot of beans. One of the members of the party who was particularly complimentary of my thoughtfulness in cooking the beans to different degrees—from half raw to well-done, in order to suit the different tastes—began to get loud, and from thence loudest, on the subject of cooking beans.

But revenge came at last, as it always does. He was in the wagon a short time after this incident, throughout the whole day, while we were on a long dusty and dry stretch without water. Toward evening, he awoke from his stupor very hungry. For the want of something to do he reached for a sack of dried apples upon which he munched until arriving in camp at night. He stupidly crawled out of the wagon and instead of going at this camp duties he took a seat, complaining that he didn't feel well. Pretty soon supper was ready, but our friend couldn't eat his supper, but concluded to take a cup of coffee and retire for the night. His complaints increased rapidly. It was now evident to him that hot coffee and dried apples either agreed too well together, or didn't agree at all. Each member of the party were alternately engaged during the night, to keep him from either choking or bursting. He recovered, however, but was still weak when morning came. He was still in his blankets after daylight, and I went close to him and ventured to say to him that it was a pretty day, and that Pike's Peak appeared so close that the snow on it was plainly visible. He remarked, "D——n Pike's Peak. I am not well yet." I further ventured to ask how he would have his beans cooked. He quickly replied that "D——n ruffians would rather annoy a sick man than a well one."

I now asked him how he would have his dried apples for breakfast, with or without coffee. I was already fixed to leave after this question, and didn't wait a moment after he reached for his belt of six-shooters, to see what he would do. After he got entirely well, he never seemed as pleasant as he had been before this circumstance, nor did he ever say "beans" to me again.

Reprinted from *A Confederate in the Colorado Gold Fields* edited by Donald J. Berthrong and Odessa Davenport by permission of the University of Oklahoma Press.

The Greatest of Wrongs, c. 1863

Geronimo

Born in Arizona in 1829 into the Southern Chiricahua Apache tribe, Geronimo was the grandson of the tribal chief, Maco. As a youth the Chiricahua's major enemy was the Mexicans but later the tribe's most dangerous opponent was the United States Army. While forced to live on a reservation in Indian Territory, Geronimo told the story of his life in 1905–1906 to Asa Daklugie, the son of a chief who had fought with Geronimo. Daklugie had received some education from the whites and was able to translate Geronimo's story to S. M. Barrett who was then superintendent of education in nearby Lawton, Oklahoma. Barrett had the book entitled, Geronimo: His Own Story, *published in 1906. Geronimo died in 1909 at a military hospital at Fort Sill, still a prisoner of war.*

Perhaps the greatest wrong ever done to the Indians was the treatment received by our tribe from the United States troops about 1863. The chief of our tribe, Mangus-Colorado, went to make a treaty of peace for our people with the white settlement at Apache Tejo, New Mexico. It had been reported to us that the white men in this settlement were more friendly and more reliable than those in Arizona, that they would live up to their treaties and would not wrong the Indians.

Mangus-Colorado, with three other warriors, went to Apache Tejo and held a council with these citizens and soldiers. They told him that if he would come with his tribe and live near them, they would issue to him, from the Government, blankets, flour, provisions, beef, and all manner of supplies. Our chief promised to return to Apache Tejo within two weeks. When he came back to our settlement he assembled the whole tribe in council. I did not believe that the people at Apache Tejo would do as they

175

said and therefore I opposed the plan, but it was decided that with part of the tribe Mangus-Colorado should return to Apache Tejo and receive an issue of rations and supplies. If they were as represented, and if these white men would keep the treaty faithfully, the remainder of the tribe would join him and we would make our permanent home at Apache Tejo. I was to remain in charge of that portion of the tribe which stayed in Arizona. We gave almost all of our arms and ammunition to the party going to Apache Tejo, so that in case there should be treachery they would be prepared for any surprise. Mangus-Colorado and about half of our people went to New Mexico, happy that now they had found white men who would be kind to them, and with whom they could live in peace and plenty.

No word ever came to us from them. From other sources, however, we heard that they had been treacherously captured and slain. In this dilemma we did not know just exactly what to do, but fearing that the troops who had captured them would attack us, we retreated into the mountains near Apache Pass.

During the weeks that followed the departure of our people we had been in suspense, and failing to provide more supplies, had exhausted all of our store of provisions. This was another reason for moving camp. On this retreat, while passing through the mountains, we discovered four men with a herd of cattle. Two of the men were in front in a buggy and two were behind on horseback. We killed all four, but did not scalp them; they were not warriors. We drove the cattle back into the mountains, made a camp, and began to kill the cattle and pack the meat.

Before we had finished this work we were surprised and attacked by United States troops, who killed in all seven Indians—one warrior, three women, and three children. The Government troops were mounted and so were we, but we were poorly armed, having given most of our weapons to the division of our tribe that had gone to Apache Tejo, so we fought mainly with spears, bows, and arrows. At first I had a spear, a bow, and a few arrows; but in a short time my spear and all my arrows were gone. Once I was surrounded, but by dodging from side to side on my horse as he ran I escaped. It was necessary during this fight for many of the warriors to leave their horses and escape on foot. But my horse was trained to come at call, and as soon as I reached a safe place, if not too closely pursued, I would call him to me. During this fight we scattered in all directions and two days later reassembled at our appointed place of rendezvous, about fifty miles from the scene of this battle.

About ten days later the same United States troops attacked our new camp at sunrise. The fight lasted all day, but our arrows and spears were all gone before ten o'clock, and for the remainder of the day we had only rocks and clubs with which to fight. We could do little damage with these weapons, and at night we moved our camp about four miles back into the mountains where it would be hard for the cavalry to follow us. The next day our scouts, who had been left behind to observe the movements of the soldiers, returned, saying that the troops had gone back toward San Carlos Reservation.

A few days after this we were again attacked by another company of United States troops. Just before this fight we had been joined by a band of Chokonen Indians under Cochise, who took command of both divisions. We were repulsed, and decided to disband.

After we had disbanded our tribe the Bedonkohe Apaches reassembled near their old camp vainly waiting for the return of Mangus-Colorado and our kinsmen. No tidings came save that they had all been treacherously slain. Then a council was held, and as it was believed that Mangus-Colorado was dead, I was elected Tribal Chief.

For a long time we had no trouble with anyone. It was more than a year after I had been made Tribal Chief that United States troops surprise and attacked our camp. They killed seven children, five women, and four warriors, captured all our supplies, blankets, horses, and clothing, and destroyed our tepees. We had nothing left; winter was beginning, and it was the coldest winter I ever knew. After the soldiers withdrew I took three warriors and trailed them. Their trail led back toward San Carlos.

From: *Geronimo's Story of His Life* (New York: Duffield Publishers, 1906)

Geronimo

Inflation Comes to the Frontier, c. May 1863

Edwin Ruthven Purple

Heading toward California as a gold-rushing forty-niner, Edwin Purple changed course and lit out for present-day Montana after he heard of a gold strike there. Settling near the Bannack City goldfields, Purple prospected and peddled merchandise to other miners. During this time he witnessed crimes and vigilante justice, Indian attacks on the miners and depredations by miners on the Indians. An independent observer, Purple chronicled his adventures, and in the following vignette he explains the reality of frontier economics.

Gold miners as a class are in no way credulous of reports which they hear about the discovery of new diggins. They believe in them implicitly, and the more marvellous the account is of their extent and richness, the more easily are they convinced of the truth of the story. The day after Fairweather & his party reached Bannack City, the report they brought had spread like wild fire among the Miners, and it lost nothing of its original brilliancy as it circulated from mouth to mouth.

Fairweather and his party remained in town for two or three days, making their purchases of tools, provisions, &c., during which time large numbers of the Bannackites were making their preparations to accompany them. These were the busiest and liveliest times I ever saw in the town. The few goods were rapidly bought up by the Miners. Pack and riding saddles. Horses and Mules were in great demand and brought extravagant prices. Dick Hamilton, who had come in on the 30th of April with a stock of goods, was kept up half the night, with John Sharp and myself as Assistants in his store, waiting on the men who flocked to it, to purchase their supplies. The fluctuation of the Gold Market in New York was nothing compared to the fluctuation of prices for merchandize in Bannack at this time.

One morning Dick Hamilton commenced selling Rope for packing at $1 per pound. At 10 o'clock the price was advanced to $1.50, by noon it was $2.00, and by 4 o'clock the demand was so great that a further advance was put upon it of 50 cents per pound, and continuing to sell rapidly, Dick put up the price to $3.00 per pound, at which rate it continued till the close of business at night; when the next day it was offered and sold out at $3.50 per pound.

Reprinted from *Perilous Passage: A Narrative of the Montana Gold Rush, 1862–1863* edited by Kenneth N. Owens by permission of the Montana Historical Society Press.

The Vigilante Committee
Takes Care of Slade,
c. January 1864

X. Beidler

Because of lawlessness believed to be caused by an organized band of criminals led by the Sheriff, William Plummer, some activist men of Virginia City met in late-1863 and formed a Vigilante Committee. The rationale for the Committee was it believed that only by executing every suspected member of the band could law be restored to Virginia City. The Committee adopted bylaws and an oath of allegiance was required of its membership. The oath was taken by twenty-four citizens and X. Beidler was among them. During January and February of 1864 the Committee executed twenty-one men by hanging with a few more in the months following. Not one of the executed men had a trial, nor an appeal, and usually not even a chance to set his affairs in order before being hung. X. Beidler was born in Pennsylvania in 1831 and died in Montana in 1890. This incident is taken from his reminiscences as dictated in 1880 but was not published until 1957 as, X. Beidler Vigilante.

The theater was crowded with men with their wives and daughters, who had come to see the acting. In the play, Kate Harper came out on the stage dressed as a Ballet girl to give a dance and as she commenced Slade ordered her in a loud and vulgar voice to take off the balance of her dress, which disgusted the audience and they commenced leaving. Men with their wives and daughters could not stay. The show ended right there and I avoided Slade that evening as well as I could and I did not see him after the theater.

Next morning Slade was still running wild and run a milk wagon off the grade and spilled all the milk and then went and whipped Dan Harding and Charley Edwards, his own men, then came uptown and run it for all it was worth. Merchants closed their stores to avoid trouble and Slade held the Fort. I went to Jerry Sullivan . . . and asked him if he couldn't get Slade to go home. Jerry said he couldn't touch him. I went to Kiscadden and asked him if he could get Slade home. Just at this time Slade came into the store and said: "X, I guess the Vigilante Committee is played out."

I said: "It looks so but you will change your mind in three hours."

He looked at me very enquiringly with those eyes of his and asked how I knew. I told him he would see, and I again asked Kiscadden to try to coax him to go, and Slade said he would if Kiscadden would give him his Derringer, which he did and I then told Slade to get on his favorite horse, old "Copperbottom" and cross the hill, which he did. He rode a short distance, and got off "Copperbottom," at Pfouts' store and insulted him in a very disgusting manner.

While he was hard at work doing this dirty work, over two hundred honest, determined miners headed by Capt. Williams were just turning the corner and getting in sight, and came up to Pfouts' store. Capt. Williams stepped up and arrested Slade while he was holding up Pfouts, Fox, and Davis with a Derringer in each hand. Capt. Williams was backed by two hundred miners, each one of which could have shook out two or three dollars of pay dirt out of the rims of their hats, and who had rifles and revolvers in abundance. Slade looked around and said: "My God!"

He was informed he had one hour to live and if he had any business to attend to he had better do it. I was well aware of the approach of the Committee and was informed long before that the boys' rifles and revolvers were being cleaned and loaded fresh, which meant business. I had begged Slade to go home but I knew when he got off his horse, and I made the remark to Kiscadden, that it was his last ride. If Slade had gone off when he was told, the Committee would not have hung him at that time.

Slade was taken into the back room of the store to settle up his business and begged all the time most piteously for his life.

A party was sent to arrange a place for the execution. They went down the Gulch and found an empty beef scaffold, made the noose and fixed everything for the hanging, and when the hour given by the Committee to Slade had expired Slade expired with it.

The town was very excited, people running to and fro and not knowing the result of the Committee's business—if Slade was King, or if the Vigilantes had won. But very little talk was going on. Each man of the Committee kept place with determination and his mouth shut but the determination on their lips soon let the people know that Slade was hung.

While Slade was standing on the boxes, under the scaffold, with the rope around his neck, he asked for Col. W. F. Sanders, and the boys around were afraid to do much shouting and I said: "Boys, pass the word along for Sanders," which was done, but he could not be found and Slade then asked for Aleck Davis, who came up and talked with the doomed man.

Slade asked Davis to plead with the crowd for his life and Davis said: "Mr. Slade I can only repeat your words, I have no influence but would gladly do so if I had."

The two hundred miners were getting impatient and shouted: "Time's up!" These men were running mines on their own account and wanted to get back and clean up and attend to their business as they did not come on any child's play. . . .

Capt. Williams, when he heard how impatient the miners were getting, said: "Men do your duty." And Slade died. . . .

Mrs. Slade had been sent for and was expected every minute and she was known to be a very desperate woman and the Committee had wisely ordered some parties to intercept her if she came before the hanging. Jim Kiscadden came to me and said: "X, can't I get men enough to cut Slade down before Mrs. Slade gets here?"

I got some friends of mine and I cut him down and we packed him to the Virginia City Hotel and took the ropes off his legs, arms and feet, and just as I was through, someone said: "Mrs. Slade is coming!"

I threw a blanket over the things to hide them from her and she rushed into the room and threw herself on the body of her dead husband. I went down stairs. The miners returned to their work and the town quieted down and peace reigned. Slade was neatly dressed and prepared for burial and taken across the hill and buried . . . Mr. Kiscadden afterwards married Mrs. Slade. . . .

Reprinted from *X. Beidler Vigilante* edited by Helen Fitzgerald Sanders and William H. Bertsche, Jr. by permission of the University of Oklahoma Press.

Hand-to-Hand Fighting an Apache Brave, c. August 1864

John C. Cremony

Cremony spent most of his life in the Old West. He served as an interpreter to the U.S. Boundary Commission for three years, 1849–51. He was a Major of California Volunteer Cavalry, operating in Arizona, New Mexico, Texas and Western Arkansas. He wrote Life among the Apaches *in 1868.*

No one expected an attack in so open, exposed and unsheltered a place, yet it was the very one selected for such a purpose. The wily savages knew that we would be upon our guard in passing a defile, a thick wood, or a rocky cañon; and also judged that we might be careless while crossing an open plain. They were well acquainted with the dusty character of the road, and relying on it to conceal their presence, had secreted themselves close to its southern edge, awaiting our approach.

At a certain spot, where a dozen or two yucca trees elevated their sharp-pointed leaves about four feet above ground, and while we were shrouded in a cloud of dust, a sharp, rattling volley was poured into us from a distance of less than twenty yards. It has always been a matter of astonishment to me that none of our party were either killed or wounded; but we lost two mules and three horses by that fire. The dense dust prevented the Apaches from taking aim, and they fired a little too low. It was no time for hesitation, and the order was at once given to dismount and fight on foot. We could distinguish little or nothing; shot after shot was expended in the direction of the savages; now and then a dark body would be seen and made a target of as soon as seen. Each man threw himself flat upon the ground; but scarcely any could tell where his companions were. It was pre-eminently a fight in which each man was on "his own hook."

While we laid prostrate the dust settled somewhat, and we were about to obtain a good sight of the enemy, when John Wollaston cried out—"Up boys, they are making a rush." Each man rose at the word, and a hand to hand contest ensured which beggars all description. It was at this juncture that our revolvers did the work, as was afterward shown. Again the dust rose in blinding clouds, hurried up by the tramping feet of contending men. We stood as much chance to be shot by each other as by the savages. The quick rattling of pistols was heard on all sides, but the actors in this work of death were invisible. The last charge of my second pistol had been exhausted; my large knife lost in the thick dust on the road, and the only weapon left me was a small double-edged, but sharp and keen, dagger, with a black whalebone hilt, and about four inches long on the blade. I was just reloading a six-shooter, when a robust and athletic Apache, much heavier than myself, stood before me, not more than three feet off. He was naked with the single exception of a breach cloth, and his person was oiled from head to foot. I was clothed in a green hunting frock, edged with black, a pair of green pants, trimmed with black welts, and a green, broad-brimmed felt hat. The instant we met, he advanced upon me with a long and keen knife, with which he made a plunge at my breast. This attack was met by stopping his right wrist with my left hand, and at the same moment I lunged my small dagger full at his abdomen. He caught my right wrist in his left hand, and for a couple of seconds—a long time under such circumstances—we stood regarding each other, my left hand holding his right above my head, and his left retaining my right on a level with his body. Feeling that he was greased, and that I had no certain hold, I tripped him with a sudden and violent pass of the right foot, which brought him to the ground, but in falling he seized and carried me down with him. In a moment the desperate savage gained the ascendant, and planted himself firmly on my person, with his right knee on my left arm, confining it closely, and his left arm pinioning my right to the ground, while his right arm was free. I was completely at his mercy. His personal strength and weight were greater than mine. His triumph and delight glared from his glittering black eyes, and he resolved to lose nothing of his savage enjoyment. Holding me down with the grasp of a giant, against which all my struggles were wholly vain, he raised aloft his long, sharp knife, and said—Pindah lickoyee das-ay-go, dee-dah tatsan," which means, "the white-eyed man, you will be soon dead." I thought as he did, and in that frightful moment made a hasty commendation of my soul to the Benevolent, but I am afraid that it was mingled with some scheme to get out of my predicament, if possible.

To express the sensations I underwent at that moment is not within the province of language. My erratic and useless life passed in review before me in less than an instant of time. I lived more in that minute or two of our deadly struggle than I had ever done in years, and, as I was wholly powerless, I gave myself up for lost—another victim to Apache ferocity. His bloodshot eyes gleamed upon me with intense delight, and he seemed to delay the death-stroke for the purpose of gladdening his heart upon my fears and inexpressible torture. All this transpired in less than half a minute, but to me it seemed hours. Suddenly he raised his right arm for the final stroke. I saw the descending blow of the deadly weapon, and knew the force with which it was driven.

The love of life is a strong feeling at any time; but to be killed like a pig, by an Apache, seemed pre-eminently dreadful and contumelious. Down came the murderous knife, aimed full at my throat, for his position on my body made that the most prominent part of attack. Instantly I twisted my head and neck one side to avoid the blow and prolong life as much as possible. The keen blade passed in dangerous, proximity to my throat, and buried itself deeply in the soft soil, penetrating my black silk cravat, while his right thumb came within reach of my mouth, and was as quickly seized between my teeth. His struggles to free himself were fearful, but my life depended on holding fast. Finding his efforts vain, he released his grasp of my right arm and seized his knife with his left hand, but the change, effected under extreme pain, reversed the whole state of affairs. Before my antagonist could extricate his deeply-buried weapon with his left hand, and while his right was held fast between my teeth, I circled his body and plunged my sharp and faithful dagger twice between his ribs, just under his left arm, at the same time making another convulsive effort to throw off his weight. In this I succeeded, and in a few moments had the satisfaction of seeing my enemy gasping his last under my repeated thrusts. Language would fail to convey anything like my sensations during that deadly contest, and I will not attempt the task.

From: *Life among the Apaches: Interpreter to the U.S. Boundary Commission, Under the Hon. John R. Bartlett, in 1849, '50 and '51, and Late Major of California Volunteer Cavalry, Operating in Arizona, New Mexico, Texas and Western Arkansas* (San Francisco: A. Roman and Company, 1868)

Life Is Cheap on the Yellowstone, October 1, 1864

Fanny Kelly

Born in Canada in 1845, Fanny Wiggins married Josiah Kelly when she was a teenager. In May 1864, she and her husband and her adopted seven-year-old daughter, Mary, joined a small number of others who were heading to Idaho to start a new life. On July 12th the small group of wagons were attacked in Wyoming by a large band of raiding Oglala Sioux warriors. Most of the men were killed and Kelly and her daughter were taken captive. Kelly tried to secret Mary from their captors by slipping her off her horse during a ride on their first night in captivity and telling Mary to hide until all the Indians had passed and then to walk back from where they came. Kelly was to later learn that little Mary was caught and killed by the Indians. After several months of captivity, Kelly was ransomed and released to the U.S. Army.

While the savages lingered in camp about the banks of the Yellowstone River, apparently fearing, yet almost inviting attack by their closeness to the soldiers, a large Mackinaw, or flatboat, was seen coming down the river. From their hiding places they watched its progress like the tiger waiting for his prey.

At sundown, the unsuspecting travelers pushed their boat toward the shore to camp for the night.

The party consisted of about twenty men, women, and children. Suspecting no danger, they left their arms in the boat.

With a vicious yell, the savages set upon them, dealing death and destruction in rapid strokes.

The defenseless emigrants made an attempt to rush to the boat for arms, but were cut off, and their bleeding bodies dashed into the river as fast as they were slain. Then followed the torture of the women and children.

Horrible thought! from which all will turn with sickened soul and shuddering cry to Heaven, "How long, O Lord! how long shall such inhuman atrocities go unpunished?"

Not a soul was left alive when that black day's work was complete; and the unconscious river bore away the warm tide of human blood and sinking human forms.

When the warriors returned to our camp, they held high their frightful trophies of bloodstained clothes and ghastly scalps.

My heartsick eyes beheld the dreadful fruits of carnage; and, among the lot, I saw a woman's scalp with heavy chestnut hair, a golden brown, and four feet in length, which had been secured for its beauty. The tempting treasure lost the poor girl her life, which might have been spared; but her glorious locks were needed to hang on the chief's belt.

During that season nearly all the flatboats coming from the mining regions that floated down the Yellowstone River to the Missouri were attacked, and in some instances one or more of the occupants killed. The approach of this boat was unknown, and the Indians had ample time to plan their attack so that not a soul should escape.

That night the whole camp of braves assembled to celebrate the fearful scalp dance; and from the door of my tent I witnessed the savage spectacle, for I was ill, and, to my great relief, was not forced to join the horrid ceremony.

A number of squaws occupied the center of the ring they formed, and the pitiless wretches held up the fresh scalps that day reaped from the harvest of death.

Around them circled the frantic braves, flourishing torches and brandishing weapons, and screaming the most ferocious barks and yells, and wild distortions of countenance.

Some repeatedly boasted of bravery and prowess while others lost their own identify in mocking their dying victims in their agony.

Leaping first on one foot, then on the other, accompanying every movement with wild whoops of excitement, they presented a scene which would be never forgotten.

The young brave who bore the beautiful locks as his trophy did not join in the dance. He sat alone, looking sad.

I approached and questioned him, and he replied that he regretted his dead victim. He brought a bloodstained dress from his lodge, and told me it was worn by the girl with the lovely hair, whose eyes haunted him and made him sorry.

After being cognizant of this frightful massacre, I shrank more than ever from my savage companions, and pursued my tasks in hopeless despondence of ever being rescued or restored to civilized life.

From: *Narrative of My Captivity among the Sioux Indians* (Hartford, CT: Mutual Publishing Company, 1871)

Fanny Kelly

Testimony on the Sand Creek Massacre, March 14, 1865

John S. Smith

On November 29, 1864, about five hundred men of the 1ˢᵗ Colorado Cavalry under the command of Colonel John M. Chivington attacked a camp of Cheyenne and Arapaho Indians in southeastern Colorado on the Big Sandy Creek (also known as Sand Creek). The result of this attack was one of the largest massacres of Indians, especially of women and children, in the history of the Old West. The attack was made at sunrise, without warning, and about five or six hundred Indians were killed with a loss to the cavalry of seven killed, forty-seven wounded, with one missing. Virtually all of the Cheyenne chiefs were killed, including Black Kettle, White Antelope, Little Robe, Left Hand, Knock Knee and One Eye. The person giving testimony in the following narrative, John S. Smith, was a United States Indian interpreter and special Indian Agent.

Question: How many Indians were there? *Answer: There were 100 families of Cheyennes, and some six or eight lodges of Arapahoes.*

Question: How many persons in all, should you say?

Answer: About 500 we estimate them at five to a lodge.

Question: 500 men, women and children?

Answer: Yes, sir.

Question: Had there been, to your knowledge, any hostile act or demonstration on the part of these Indians or any of them?

Answer: Not in this band. But the northern band known by the name of Dog soldiers of Cheyennes, had committed many depredations on the Platte.

Question: Do you know whether or not Colonel Chivington knew the friendly character of these Indians before he made the attack upon them?

Answer: It is my opinion that he did.

Question: Did you tell Colonel Chivington the character and disposition of these Indians at any time during your interviews on this day?

Answer: Yes, sir.

Question: What did he say in reply?

Answer: He said he could not help it; that his orders were positive to attack the Indians.

Question: From whom did he receive these orders?

Answer: I do not know; I presume from General Curtis.

Question: Did he tell you?

Answer: Not to my recollection.

Question: Were the women and children slaughtered indiscriminately, or only so far as they were with the warriors?

Answer: Indiscriminately.

Question: Were there any acts of barbarity perpetrated there that came under your own observations?

Answer: Yes, sir; I saw the bodies of those lying there cut all to pieces, worse mutilated than any I ever saw before; the women cut all to pieces.

Question: How cut?

Answer: With knives; scalped; their brains knocked out; children two or three months old; all ages lying there; from sucking infants up to warriors.

Question: Did you see it done?

Answer: Yes, sir; I saw them fall.

Question: Fall when they were killed?

Answer: Yes, sir.

Question: Did you see them when they were mutilated?

Answer: Yes, sir.

Question: By whom were they mutilated?

Answer: By the United States troops.

Question: Were there any other barbarities or atrocities committed there other than those you have mentioned, that you saw?

Answer: Yes, sir; I had a half-breed son there, who gave himself up. He started at the time the Indians fled; being a half-breed he had but little hope of being spared, and seeing them fire at me, he ran away with the Indians for the distance of about a mile. During the fight up there he walked back to my camp and went into the lodge. It was surrounded by soldiers at the time. He came in quietly and sat down; he remained there that day, that night, and the next day in the afternoon; about four o'clock in the evening, as I was sitting beside the camp, a soldier came up outside of the lodge and called me by name. I got up and went out; he took me by the arm and walked towards Colonel Chivington's camp, which was about sixty yards from my camp. Said he, "I am sorry to tell you, but they are going to kill your son Jack." I knew the feelings towards the whole camp of Indians, and that there was no use to make any resistance. I said, "I can't help it." I then walked on towards where Colonel Chivington was standing by his camp-fire when I had got within a few feet of him I heard a gun fired, and saw a crowd run to my lodge, and they told me that Jack was dead.

From: *Congressional Testimony of Mr. John S. Smith* (Washington: U.S. Government Printing Office, March 14, 1865)

Scene of the Sand Creek Massacre

Assault on a Prairie Dog Town, c. Fall 1866

Silas Seymour

Published in 1867 under the heady title, Incidents of a Trip Through the Great Platte Valley, to the Rocky Mountains and Laramie Plains, in the Fall of 1866, With a Synoptical Statement of the Various Pacific Railroads, and an Account of the Great Union Pacific Railroad Excursion to the One Hundredth Meridian of Longitude, *Seymour's (1817–1890) book gives modern readers a vivid account of what an early train trip through the Old West was like. In the following excerpt Seymour describes one of the favorite pastimes of the Old West rail traveler, killing all living things within the range of the gun—in this case, prairie dogs.*

The train halted for nearly two hours, for the purpose of enabling the excursionists to pay their respects to the inhabitants of by far the largest town through which they had passed since leaving Chicago. This pleasing duty had been in contemplation as the train passed westward two days previously, and was prevented only by the lateness of the hour.

This town occupies an area of about twenty-five square miles, and the railroad track passes through its center. The visit was evidently a surprise to the vast number of its quiet and peaceful inhabitants, and no preparations had therefore been made . . . for their distinguished guests.

Their native politeness and curiosity, however, induced many of them, soon after the arrival of the train, to peep out of their doors and chatter an incoherent welcome; but the salutation which awaited them was not of a kind calculated to encourage a protracted acquaintance of even this unsatisfactory nature, and all civilities were therefore soon at an end.

The *huntists* of the party soon spread themselves over several acres of the town, in the hope of securing a few specimens as mere matter of curiosity. Several hundred shots were fired; and, if the accounts of our brave *huntists* may be credited, at least one half that number had been killed; but by some strange fatality or illusion, on arriving at the spot where the ball was seen to strike them, they were not there. Only one was brought to the train, and he, after being subjected to the critical examination of all the excursionists, was turned over to the cook; and the last that was seen of him, he was rapidly disappearing before the steady gaze of Professor Ayer, who protested meantime that, "it had come to a pretty pass, if this grand excursion was reduced to such a strait that its guests were obliged to subsist on *prairie-dog*."

These prairie-dog cities are a great curiosity in their way. They generally occupy the most dry and elevated table lands of the Plains. The Union Pacific Railroad passes through or near many of them.

The harmless little animals are somewhat the nature, and about one-half the size of the common ground hog or woodchuck. They burrow in the ground, and evidently subsist, without water, upon grass and roots in the near vicinity of their town, as they are never seen far away from it.

From: *Incidents of a Trip Through the Great Platte Valley, to the Rocky Mountains and Laramie Plains, in the Fall of 1866, With a Synoptical Statement of the Various Pacific Railroads, and an Account of the Great Union Pacific Railroad Excursion to the One Hundredth Meridian of Longitude* (New York: D. Van Nostrand, 1867)

A Cowboy Wedding, Winter 1866

John S. Collins

Women were in short supply in the Old West, especially young unmarried women. Although the odds were stacked in their favor because men hugely outnumbered them, finding suitable marriage partners was a real challenge for these women and was made more difficult if they lived in out-of-the-way places. But the hormonal urge is strong and throughout the ages young men and young women have overcome obstacles in their paths and find and marry one another. The following story about a young love that leads to marriage was recorded by John S. Collins (1839–1910). Collins was among the small number of men that recorded some of his adventures and observations and had them published.

If any romance can be attached to incidents of mountain life with one to five feet of snow on the ground, and the mercury thirty degrees below zero, the following is deserving of a place among romances.

Charles A. Pollard and I owned a ranch on Labonte Creek, in Wyoming, beginning at its mouth where it empties into the Platte River, and extending south up the valley nearly five miles. Mr. Pollard had two sons, one named Percy E. All his life had been spent on the Laramie River and on Labonte Creek. Taking naturally to cattle and cowboy life, he became an expert horseman, and one of the very best cattle men. He knew every brand on the range for a hundred miles around, as well as he knew his own name, and was always in demand by cattle owners as one of the experts in handling both cattle and horses, and attended all the round-ups of the season—and yet a mere boy.

At the head of Horseshoe Creek, up near Laramie Peak, was a little saw mill, which supplied lumber to settlers building ranch houses in the vicinity. In the course of time the "P.C." ranch built a frame house at the crossing of the stream, and Percy, with one of the ranch hands, made frequent trips up to the mill in the mountains for lumber and logs. The mill owner, a Mr. Austin, with his family lived there summer and winter among the pine trees. The weather was always severe in winter, but the winter's snow in many ways facilitated his getting out logs and hauling them to the mill to keep it running in summer.

The daughter of the owner of the mill, Miss Austin, was a comely mountain girl, endowed with industrious habits, good sense, and her share of good looks—honest and loyal to the core. It was not long until Percy's frequent trips to the mill became of so much interest to him that rain or shine he was always ready to "pull for the mountains." The trip could be made from the ranch in a day, with good roads and pleasant weather. Coming down with a load of logs or lumber, the wagon would not stand up under the load without the brake and rough locking the wheels. It took nearly two days to come down with a load. Percy was counted a number one hand with a team, and a resourceful ingenuity enabled him to get out of all sorts of scrapes which log hauling occasionally brought him.

When snow came in the mountains, and an occasional thaw on the Labonte, the roads were icy, and even rough-locking the wagon wheels would not prevent the wagon slipping on side hills. At such times the cowboy would stay in the mountain saw mill camp over night, awaiting more favorable roads and weather. As the days shortened, Percy thought that four days was about right for a trip, and he so planned that his layovers were at the house of the sawyer. Winter was now on in earnest and it was impossible to haul logs through deep snow. There was work to be done at the ranch—fences to fix, wood to chop, cattle to feed. Six days was a long week. Every Sunday Percy had a new bronco to break, and this took him over the old road to the saw mill. Monday morning, however, always found him home at the ranch for breakfast. He was known by all the cowboys and men of the country and was well liked, always lending a hand to every one he found in trouble with cattle, horses, etc., and the boys were as ready to do him a turn.

One morning he got out of bed and found a level foot of snow on the ground, and the snow still falling, and not a shod horse on the place.

"Carrie, let me ride your bay mare to Douglas—I'll be back tonight. She don't ball up or stumble like the broncos," Percy called to his sister in the next room.

"Not going to town in this storm, are you?"

"Yep," Percy answered, and with Carrie's consent he was off to saddle the mare. Before closing the door, he called back, "If I bring that preacher back with me, can we keep him a couple of days?" And he did not wait for an answer. His sister watched him swing open and close the big gate without getting down, and heard the clatter of hoofs as he crossed over the bridge. Then she began wondering what the boy had on his mind.

Late at night he came stamping into the house, having fed and bedded the mare down. Then they all began firing questions at him until they came too close to the "main chance," and he unrolled his bed down on the floor near the big wood stove and turned in. As a last answer he said, "I went after the preacher and some of the boys to help me pack him up to the saw mill." People in the vicinity remember that at the time all the roads were blocked with snow drifts, and the ravines filled in places fifty feet deep, but Percy had important business on hand and a few snow drifts would not stop him. The preacher didn't come with Percy, but would come to the ranch the following Thursday, if it stopped snowing and the trail was open to the ranch.

The next two or three days were busy times with the boy. He visited five or six ranches and got several cowboys to agree to go with him on Wednesday and to bring some lead horses to beat a trail through the drifts to the saw mill. Two or three pack horses carried rolls of bedding; some had no packs, but Sister Carrie's bay mare had an empty cowboy saddle and carried no load.

Wednesday they all started for the mountains, Percy having left word at home to keep the preacher there until he came back—"and have a big supper and some cake." It was hard work walking back and forth through the snow-drifts, leading and riding the trail until it was made passable.

As the home of the Austins, the young woman and her mother had a table well filled with such things to eat as could be found in a house in the mountains which had been snowed in for over two weeks. The meal consisted of bacon, bread, and canned goods, prepared in the very best way. The cowboys unrolled their beds and bunked on the floor after supper. The next morning the horses were brought up, bundles of bedding packed on with a few extra bundles the horses had not carried up to the mill. Then Percy told the young lady, "That preacher is a tenderfoot, and we could not get him up here, but if he had come I would have lashed him on a horse, so we are going to pack you down to mother's and be married there, if the preacher don't go back on us." It was thirty degrees below zero on the mountains. A sharp wind kept the snow flying. Everybody was in the saddle. Ropes were fastened from the bits to horses' tails to keep them in line. The caravan started, Percy bringing up the rear, leading behind him the bay mare that carried his bride-to-be.

They all reached the ranch safely, but nearly frozen. The preacher had arrived, and the marriage ceremony was performed. Then came a square meal. The preacher and the boys bunked around on the floor for the night.

The next morning all pulled out for home, the preacher going on horse-back to Douglas, ten dollars richer than when he came.

From: *My Experiences in the West* (Chicago: The Lakeside Press, R. R. Donnelley & Sons Company, 1970, reprinted from the 1904 Edition, *Across the Plains in '64 . . .*)

The Problem with Disobeying Orders, December 21, 1866

Margaret Irvin Carrington

Born in 1831, Margaret Irvin Carrington was the first wife of Colonel Henry B. Carrington, the defensive-minded commander of Fort Phil Kearney. The fort was built by Colonel Carrington on the Bozeman Trail in present-day Wyoming. Determined to teach the United States a lesson after it took the sacred Black Hills, Chief Red Cloud and Crazy Horse of the Oglala Sioux coaxed eighty-one troopers and civilians, led by Captain (brevet Lieutenant Colonel) William Judd Fetterman, out of the defenses of the fort resulting in a massacre of the entire column. Using decoys, the Indians led Fetterman's troops away from the fort and over Lodge Trail Ridge although Colonel Carrington had ordered Fetterman not to pursue the Indians over the ridge. Margaret Carrington died in 1870 and her husband, the colonel, remarried Frances Grummond, the wife of one of the officers who died in the Fetterman massacre.

Though snow covered the mountains, and there was every indication of the return of severe weather, the morning was quite pleasant. Men only wore blouses at their work, and the train, although much later than usual, went to the Pinery with a strong guard, so that the teamsters, choppers, and escort, all armed, numbered not far from ninety men.

The children ran in about 11 o'clock, shouting "Indians!" and the pickets on Pilot Hill could be distinctly seen giving the signal of "Indians," on the line of the wood road; and news was also furnished that the train was in corral only a short distance from the garrison.

The officers and all the ladies were soon watching for other usual demonstrations, while a detail was being organized to relieve the train.

Brevet Lieutenant-Colonel Fetterman, then walking back and forth before his quarters, near where the colonel was giving his instructions, asked and obtained permission to go with the detachment.

Lieutenant Grummond, also at his own request, took a part of Company C, 2d United States Cavalry,–making the whole force just seventy-eight officers and men. Captain Brown, unknown to the officers of the garrison, as well as citizens Wheatley and Fisher, both experienced frontiersmen and good shots, also joined the party. . . .

The orders were given in front of Lieutenant Grummond's house, next the colonel's, and those who were present heard them repeated with distinctness and special urgency. Lieutenant Wands was also instructed to repeat them. As if peculiarly impressed with some anticipations of rashness in the movement, the colonel, just after the command left, went across the parade-ground to a sentry platform, halted the mounted party, and gave additional orders, understood in the garrison, and by those who heard them, to be the substantial repetition of the former.

The health of Mrs. Grummond was such that Lieutenant Wands and other friends urged him [Lieutenant Grummond], for his family's sake, to be prudent, and avoid all rash movements and any pursuit that would draw them over Lodge Trail Ridge, and to report to Brevet Lieutenant-Colonel Fetterman the orders he had received. These orders were, in so many words, "to relieve the train, and under no circumstances to cross the ridge." Everybody knew why special emphasis was given to these orders.

Only two days before, Brevet Major Powell had been sent out to relieve a train, and obeyed his orders literally, although, as he afterward said, he was sorely tempted to pursue, but became afterward convinced that certain destruction would have been the result. . . .

Before Captain Fetterman left, a few Indian pickets were seen on Lodge Trail Ridge, and a few were below the fort at the road crossing. Two or three case shot, dropped near them, dismounted one and brought nearly thirty out of the brush. These at once disappeared. After the detachment had been gone a short time, finding that Captain Fetterman had left without a surgeon, the colonel sent Dr. Hines, with one of his own orderlies, to join the train and report to Captain Fetterman; Doctor Hines started, but soon returned with the news that the train had safely pursued its route to the woods; that Captain Fetterman was on the ridge to the north, out of view, and that there was so many Indians in sight that he could not join the party. It was about noon, and a man rushed in to say that firing was renewed. Every shot could be heard, and there was little doubt that a desperate fight was going on in the valley of Peno Creek beyond the ridge. The presence of Lieutenant Grummond with the party gave us new anxiety, and many heartfelt prayers were offered that he might return in safety. The colonel was on the "lookout," on headquarters building, and gave his orders before coming down.

It seemed long, but was hardly twelve minutes before Captain Ten Eyck, Lieutenant Matson, Dr. Hines, and Dr. Ould, with a relieving party, were moving, on the run, for the scene of action. We had all watched Captain Fetterman until the curve of Sullivant Hills shut him off, and then he was on the southern slope of the ridge, apparently intending to cut off the retreat of the Indians from the train. Wagons and ambulances were hurried up; the whole garrison was on the alert; extra ammunition for both parties was started, and even the prisoners were put on duty to give the guard and all available men their perfect freedom for whatever might transpire. Couriers were sent to the woods to bring back the train and its guard, to secure its support, as well as from the fear that the diversion of Captain Fetterman from his orders might still involve its destruction; and shortly Captain Arnold came to report that the whole force of armed men left at the post, including guard and everything, was but one hundred and nineteen men.

Until the wagons galloped out of the gate, we could see a solitary Indian on the highest part of Lodge Trail Ridge; but he soon disappeared. All this time firing was increasing in intensity, and in little more than thirty minutes,—after one or two quick volleys, the rattle of file-firing, and a few scattering shots, —a perfect silence ensued. There were then many anxious hearts, and *waiting* was perfectly terrible! The movements of Captain Ten Eyck were watched with intensest interest. The pickets could give no information, and a messenger sent upon Sullivant Hills could see neither Indians nor troops. It was just before Captain Ten Eyck's party reached the top of the hill across the Piney, north of the Virginia City road, that all firing ceased. Soon orderly Sample was seen to break away from the command and make for the fort, with his horse, on the run. He brought the message that the valleys were full of Indians, and that several hundred were on the road below, yelling and challenging them to come down; but nothing could be seen of Fetterman. As was afterward learned, this party was on the very field of carnage, and doubtless they were completing their robbery and butchery. It was after dark when Captain Ten Eyck returned, with forty-nine of the bodies, and made the terrible announcement that all were killed.

To a woman whose house and heart received the widow as a sister, and whose office it was to advise her of the facts, the recital of the scenes of that day, even at this later period, is full of pain; but at the time, the Christian fortitude and holy calmness with which Mrs. Grummond looked upward to her Heavenly Father for wisdom and strength, inspired all with something of her same patience to know the worst and meet its issues.

The body of Lieutenant Grummond had not been rescued, and there was some faint hope that stragglers might yet come in and break the absolute gloom of the tragedy by some explanatory and redeeming feature.

At last the wood train came in, having seen nothing of Fetterman, not even having heard the firing, or suspected any additional danger after repulsing their own immediate assailants. Imagination only can suggest how wide-sweeping would have been the massacre had any considerable portion of the hostile bands renewed the attack upon the train after the successful decoy of the others to inevitable destruction.

With the next morning came a meeting of officers, with universal disinclination, generally expressed, to venture a search for the remaining dead. The safety of any small party seemed doubtful, and the post itself might be imperiled by a large draft upon the garrison. But the colonel had made up his mind, and freely expressed his purpose "not to let the Indians have the conviction that the dead could not be rescued;" and besides this, the very men who had passed through the war without blanching began to form ideas of the numbers and barbarity of the Indians, which threatened to take away one-half their real strength. So the colonel informed Mrs. Grummond that he should go in person, and would bring home her husband. Captain Ten Eyck, Lieutenant Matson, and Dr. Ould went with the party. Long after they left, and they left with the cheerful Godspeed of every woman and soldier of the garrison, on a holy mission, the pickets, which were distributed on the line of march, indicated their progress, and showed that neither the fort nor the detachment could be threatened without such connection of signals as would advise both and secure co-operation whatever might ensue.

Long after dark, the wagons and command returned with the remaining dead, slowly passing to the hospital and other buildings made ready for their reception. . . .

From: *Ab-sa-ra-ka: Home of the Crows* (Philadelphia: J. B. Lippincott and Company, Publishers, 1868)

Chief Red Cloud—Nemesis of Fort Phil Kearney

The Battle Scene of the Fetterman Massacre, December 22, 1866

Henry B. Carrington

Henry Beebee Carrington (1824–1912) was born in Connecticut and educated at Yale College. He pursued a military career and in the early days of the Civil War, he was appointed Colonel of the 18th U.S. Infantry. At war's end he was a Brigadier General and was assigned the duty to open a wagon route to Montana through Wyoming. The route was known as the Bozeman Trail, a shortcut from the main overland trail. The Bozeman Trail overlaid earlier Indian, trader, and exploration routes. It went directly through the last and best of the Sioux and Cheyenne hunting grounds and the Indians watched as their centuries-old lifestyle, their freedom, and very existence were threatened. It was along the Trail that Carrington built Fort Phil Kearney and fought off attacks by area Sioux, led by Chief Red Cloud. It was at this U.S. Army outpost that one of the most chilling defeats in the history of the Old West was inflicted on the U.S. Army. In the following report, Carrington describes the battlefield of the so-called "Fetterman Massacre." The story was taken from the official report contemporaneously rendered by Carrington and reprinted in his book, The Indian Question, *first published in 1884.*

Headquarters Post, Fort Philip Kearney,
Dakota Territory

I respectfully state the facts of fight with Indians on the twenty-first ultimo. . . . The following day . . . I took eighty men and went to the scene of action, leaving a picket to advise me of any movement in the rear, and to keep signal communication with the garrison.

The scene of action told its own story.

The road, on the little ridge where the final stand took place, was strewn with arrows, arrow-heads, scalp-poles, and broken shafts of spears. The arrows that were spent harmlessly, from all directions, show that the command was suddenly overwhelmed, surrounded, and cut off, while in retreat. Not an officer or man survived! A few bodies were found at the north end of the divide, over which the road runs, just beyond Lodge Trail Ridge.

Nearly all were heaped near four rocks, at the point nearest the fort, these rocks, enclosing a space about six feet square, having been the last refuge for defense. Here were also a few unexpended rounds of Spencer cartridge.

Fetterman and Brown had each a revolver-shot in the left temple. As Brown always declared that he would reserve a shot for himself, as a last resort, so I am convinced that these two brave men fell, each by the other's hand, rather than undergo the slow torture inflicted upon others.

Lieutenant Grummond's body was on the road, between the two extremes, with a few others. This was not far from five miles from the fort, and nearly as far from the wood-train. Neither its own guard nor the detachment could, but any possibility, have helped each other, and the train was incidentally saved by the fierceness of the fight, in the brave but rash impulse of pursuit.

The officers who fell believed that no Indian force could overwhelm that number of troops well held in hand.

Their terrible massacre bore marks of great valor, and has demonstrated the force and character of the foe; but no valor could have saved them.

Pools of blood on the road and sloping sides of the narrow divide showed where Indians bled fatally; but their bodies were carried off. I counted sixty-five such pools in the space of an acre, and three within ten feet of Lieutenant Grummond's body. Eleven American horses and nine Indian ponies were on the road, or near the line of bodies; others, crippled, were in the valleys.

At the northwest or farther point, between two rocks, and apparently where the command first fell back from the valley, realizing their danger, I found citizens James S. Wheatley and Isaac Fisher, of Blue Springs, Nebraska, who, with "Henry Rifles," felt invincible, but fell, one having one hundred and five arrows in his naked body. The widow and family of Wheatley are here.

The cartridge shells about them told how well they fought. Before closing this report, I wish to say that every man, officer, soldier, or citizen, who fell, received burial, with such record as to identify each.

Fetterman, Brown, and Grummond lie in one grave; the remainder also share one tomb, buried, as they fought, together; but the cases in which they were laid are duly placed and numbered. . . .

I give some of the facts as to my men, whose bodies I found just at dark, resolved to bring all in namely:—

Eyes torn out and laid on the rocks.

Noses cut off.

Ears cut off.

Chins hewn off.

Teeth chopped out.

Joints of fingers cut off.

Brains taken out and placed on rocks, with members of the body.

Entrails taken out and exposed.

Hands cut off.

Feet cut off.

Arms taken out from socket.

Private parts severed, and indecently placed on the person.

Eyes, ears, mouth, and arms penetrated with spear-heads, sticks, and arrows.

Punctures upon every sensitive part of the body, even to the soles of the feet and palms of the hand.

All this does not approximate the whole truth. . . . I have said enough. It is a hard but absolute duty. . . .

> I am, very respectfully,
> Your obedient servant,
> Henry B. Carrington,
> Colonel 18th U.S. Infantry
> Commanding Post.

From: *The Indian Question* (Mattituck, NY: J. M. Carroll & Company, 1909)

Martial Law on the Plains, June 16, 1867

Henry Morton Stanley

Born in Wales in 1841, Stanley is best-known for uttering the words, "Dr. Livingstone, I presume?" A well known British explorer, Stanley fought in the American Civil War, served in the merchant marine and as a journalist in the American West. After receiving fame for his chronicles of Africa and his dealings with primitive African tribes, Stanley credited this ability to his earlier experiences with the Indians of the American West. In the following vignette, Stanley makes note of the dour punishments meted out for infractions committed by soldiers or civilians under military rule while he was on a tour of U.S. Army forts in the West. Stanley died in England in 1904.

Flogging appears to be revived in the army on the plains, and citizens are shocked at some un-American scenes which have been witnessed here, and it is said that we are drifting to the time-hallowed institutions of Russia and Egypt, where the lash, the knout, the bastinado are still in vogue. On or about the 12th instant, within the limits of the military reservation of Fort Sedgwick, and within one mile of the fort, a soldier received twenty-five lashes for stealing a gun, the property of one Mart Code, a trader living at Julesburg. In the same week a soldier of the 30th Infantry, by orders, was laid out on the ground under a hot broiling sun, and a stake fastened at each limb, to which he was firmly bound, thus laying him out according to a mode well known to military officers, and which is entitled "spread-eagle fashion." He was left in that position for two hours; in the meantime the buffalo gnats covered his face by thousands, causing intense suffering to the unfortunate fellow. "For two hours he screamed, cried, begged, entreated for the love of God to be let loose. For

209

two hours he roared; I couldn't stand it any longer; I tell you, sir, his face was perfectly bunged up." Such were the words of his lieutenant to a group of officers, who expressed deep commiseration for the man's sufferings.

While visiting headquarters on the morning of the 15th we heard that a white citizen was to receive one hundred lashes some time during the day, for giving a bottle of whisky to soldiers. There was neither trial nor court-martial, merely a summary dismissal after the manner of a Pasha. "Let him have one hundred lashes." What a fuss is kicked up all over the country if a child is switched by its teacher or parent; but here is an instance of a citizen, who, while sick of a disease which, like a cancer, had eaten up his very features, was stripped and flogged before two hundred soldiers.

Some days ago . . . a stranger, giving his name as Hendriks, made his appearance at Pole Creek in the vicinity of Wilson's Ranch. He was incapacitated by illness from performing manual labour. He loitered around the ranch until the night of the 14th, when he was accosted by two men dressed in citizen's garb, who politely requested him to buy them some whisky, at the same time furnishing him with the requisite funds. He willingly acceded to the request, and in a few moments delivered to them the bottle of whisky. In about an hour afterward he was arrested and brought into the guard-house of the 30th Infantry. At 9 A.M. of the 15th his case was reported by Lieutenant Lantz of Company F, 30th Infantry. About twelve o-clock the offender was brought forth escorted by two soldiers. Complete preparations had already been made for the punishment. A scantling with a board nailed transversely was planted in the ground. About two hundred soldiers and a small squad of citizens gathered to witness the proceedings. Two soldiers with plaited thongs in their hands stood on the right and left of the cross. On the soldiers, with their instruments of torture, and the cross, the unfortunate fellow gazed in dismay. Lieutenant Lantz informed the sergeant that he did not order his punishment, but that he "would like to see him flogged." On hearing this, the orderly sergeant of Company F, assisted by the two soldiers, divested him of almost every article of clothing. They then bound him to the cross, and when all was ready the sergeant gave the signal to proceed. The men detailed to strike raised their arms aloft, and, swinging the ropes over their shoulders, the one on the right brought the hissing lash full on the naked hips of the man, who sprang convulsively upwards as if shot.

Before sixteen strokes had been administered blood was welling in streams down his legs and pouring into his shoes. Blood was splashed over some of the spectators. After the fiftieth stroke the body assumed a livid colour, and the skin hung in strips and flakes. Men stopped their ears, and turned away from the horrid sight. A respectable citizen, named

F.L. Seward . . . turned to Lieutenant Lantz, and said, "For God's sake, stop that; you will kill him." Lantz, supposing the bleeding wretch had received enough, motioned the executioners to desist. After the flogging had ceased the poor fellow was ordered by Lantz from the reservation. He managed with some difficulty to put on his nether garments, sighing and groaning deeply. After being dressed he turned to the lieutenant, and said: "I did not sell the whisky to soldiers, nor did I know they were soldiers, as they wore civilian clothes." Having uttered this, he turned from the camp, dragging his mangled limbs painfully along toward the sand bluffs. We have heard since that he hailed from the State of New York. Some soldiers state that they counted one hundred and eight strokes, but the sergeant states eighty two to have been the number delivered.

From: *My Early Travels and Adventures* (New York: Scribner's, 1895)

The Wagon Box Fight, August 1, 1867

R. J. Smyth

As a member of the Carrington Powder River Expedition of 1866, R. J. Smyth took part in one of the most lop-sided victories in the Plains Indian Wars fought near Fort Phil Kearney. A few miles from the fort, civilian contractor woodcutters and their infantry guards were attacked by a force of mounted Sioux warriors that outnumbered them about a hundred to one. The wagons used to transport the cut cordwood had their boxes removed and deposited in an oval in a large clearing and were to be used as defensive shelters in case of an Indian attack. On the first of August 1867 thirty-two woodcutters and soldiers sought shelter in fourteen wagon bodies. Instead of the Springfield muzzle-loading musket, the defenders were armed with the new breech-loading rifle that could be reloaded rapidly. It has been estimated that more than 1,100 Indians were killed or wounded while the defenders lost two killed with two others severely wounded. In this narrative Smyth describes the fight.

On the day of the wagon box fight, accompanied by my partner, I left the fort before daylight. We went to the foot-hills to get some deer. A short time after daylight we discovered a lot of Indian smoke signals on the hills, and decided that we had better get back to the fort. In making our way back we followed the Little Piney down for some distance, and found that the country was full of Indians. We then struck out for the wood train. The Indians had got between us and it. We then went to the wagon-box corral, and got there none too soon.

The wagon boxes were of the ordinary government boxes. They were set off from the wagons, as the wagons were in corral. The intervals between were packed with logs, bales of blankets, clothing, sacks of corn,

212

etc. The wagon box that I was detailed to fight in had gunny sacks of corn placed on edge two deep on the inside of the box, with a two inch auger hole at the point where the four sacks came together. This made good protection for the body when lying down.

There was a surplus of ammunition and guns. I had two Spencer carbines, and two revolvers (six-shot army Colt's). During the first charge I emptied the carbines and the revolvers less two shots (reserved for myself in case of a show down). The balance of our men must have fired as many shots as I did. The soldier that was in the box with me had a needle gun and a Spencer; also one or two revolvers. And he kept them busy while he lived. This man was an infantry soldier—do not remember his company. He was shot through the head, dying in about two hours after being shot.

Lieutenant Jenness had just cautioned me not to expose my person, and to hold my fire until I was sure of getting an Indian at each shot. He had moved a few feet from my box when he was shot through the head. I think he died instantly. He was a grand, good man, and a fearless officer. I told him to keep under cover. He stated he was compelled to expose himself in order to look after his men.

I got a slight wound in my left hand; a bullet came in through my porthole, which I thought was close shooting for a Sioux.

This fight lasted about four hours, and was very hot from the start. I had been in several Indian fights prior to this time, but never saw the Indians make such a determined effort to clean us up before. They should have killed the entire party. They certainly had force enough to ride over us, but our fire was so steady and severe that they could not stand the punishment.

Our men stood the strain well, held their fire until the bullets would count. In fact, shooting into such a mass of Indians as charged on us the first time, it would be nearly impossible for many bullets to go astray. In all my experience in fighting Indians prior to this time, I never saw them stand punishment so well as they did at this time; they certainly brought all their sand with them. In charging on our little corral they rode up very close to the wagon boxes, and here is where they failed. Had they pushed home on the first charge, the fight would not have lasted ten minutes after they got over the corral.

Many dead and wounded Indians lay within a few feet of the wagon boxes. The wounded Indians didn't live long after the charge was over. They would watch and try to get a bullet in on some of our men. We had to kill them for self-protection. Anyway, it was evening up the Fetterman deal. They never showed mercy to a wounded white man, and should not expect any different treatment. I had a canteen of water when the fight commenced, and used most of it to cool my guns.

I do not try to estimate the number of Indians, but, as my partner said, "The woods were full of them." This was the largest gathering of Indians that I ever saw, and the hardest fighting for that I ever encountered.

When the reinforcements came in sight we took on a new lease of life, and when they dropped a shell over the Indians we knew that the fight was won. Indians will not stand artillery fire. They call it the "wagon gun." The reinforcements came just in time. One hour more of such fighting would have exhausted our men and ammunition.

Reprinted from Cyrus Townsend Brady's 1904 *Indian Fights and Fighters* by permission of the University of Nebraska Press.

Chief Red Cloud During the Wagon Box Fight

Diary of a Horse Trader, c. 1867

Evans S. McComas

The diary of Evans S. McComas passed to his daughter who then passed it to a niece, Mrs. Elma T. Havemann. Mrs. Havemann put the diary into the library of the University of Oregon. It was published in 1954 with the title, A Journal of Travel. *The diary begins by its chronicles of the overland journey that McComas made on the Oregon Trail as he traveled from Iowa City to Oregon in 1862. Afterward, the diary's entries record McComas' experiences in the West as a storekeeper, horse trader, ditch digger, hotelier, and a miner. In 1868 McComas finally found his occupational calling—newspaper editing. He and a printer, John E. Jeffrey, founded the* Mountain Sentinel. *In 1881 McComas sold his interest in the newspaper. He became involved in a hodge-podge of other activities but returned to the publishing business in 1890 when he founded the* Grande Ronde Chronicle *and in 1895 the* North Pacific Mining Review. *McComas died in Oregon in 1911. The following diary entries give the reader a look at the wheeling and dealing of a horse trader of the Old West.*

Aug. 12th. Bought a pony of an Indian for $18. Took a ride & sold him for $20. Bought a horse of Steinheiser & Co. (Jews) for $30. Traded him for a gray pony, gave five dollars to boot.

Sund. 19th. Traded my gray pony for another white one and got $25 to boot. Got a wild one this time. Gave a Dutchman $2.50 to ride it. He got throwed five times but finally "won." Monday sold my wild pony for $25. Thursday bought a mare saddle and bridle for $30 in greenbacks. Sold the saddle for five and traded the pony for a saddle and agreed to play the "first ten" at Seven Up to see whether I should get five or ten dollars to boot. "Won." Bought a pony for $25 traded him off in less than five minutes even for the Steinheiser horse. Sold the horse the next morning for $30. Have established the reputation of being a regular dealer in cayuse horse flesh.

30th. Bought two saddles for $28 one a ladies saddle which I sold for $15.

31st. Traded a riding saddle for a roan mare and gave $22.50 to boot. Bought a white pony for $60 and traded for an iron gray mare and gave ten dollars to boot in order to own the nicest riding pony in La Grande. Sold the roan mare for $40.

Sept. 8th. Bought the white pony (which I owned once before and traded for my fancy riding pony) for $40.

Sept. 11th. Sold the white pony for $45. Traded my iron gray mare for a large fine sorrel Spanish mare and gave $25 to boot. She proved to be hard to ride being the very devil to "buck." Traded her for a bay horse and got $50 to boot.

24th. A man came to prove my bay horse away from me. I was going to send the constable after my mare and the fellow when traded for her but he happened to come to town so I made him "potlatch" $65.00 for the bay horse to give him to the owner. First snow fell on the mountains last night while I was in Union Town where I had gone to buy a race mare but she being sold I did not get her.

Sept. 28th. Bought an iron gray Spanish horse at auction for $39.50 also one cream colored mare for $25 and an iron gray mare for $15.50.

Sept. 30th. Burned all my old letters from home amounting to some 125, which had afforded me many a cheerful perusal.

Oct. 1st. Attended a Democratic mass meeting 15 miles from La Grande and witnessed a sad accident. An old friend of mine Wm. I. Macaulay, a young man far from home and friends met an untimely death by being throwed from the sorrel mare that I once owned. While riding a race he was thrown against a fence and only lived about ten hours. Poor "Bill" a true friend and generous companion. It is to be hoped that he is better off than any of us who witnessed his violent and untimely death. Traded the iron gray mare for a watch, got $7.50 to boot. Sold the cream colored mare at auction, got $21.00. Traded the iron gray horse for 45 bush. Oats. Sold them for $45.

From: *A Journal of Travel edited by* Martin Schmitt (Portland, OR: Champoeg Press, 1954)

Letter to a Bereaved Father, August 23, 1867

George Armstrong Custer

On July 2, 1867, twenty-five-year-old Lieutenant Lyman Kidder, an Indian guide, and ten soldiers were killed near Fort Wallace. Kidder had served the Union in the Civil War as a first lieutenant. At the end of the war, Kidder went to Dakota Territory where his father was a Justice of the Supreme Court. Although he was expected to follow a legal career, young Kidder opted for a career in the Army. Consequently, President Andrew Johnson gave Kidder an appointment as a second lieutenant and he was assigned to Fort Sedgwick in the Colorado Territory. In the following letter, penned by General Custer, not only is Lieutenant Kidder's death outlined, but the grave dangers of travel in Indian country in the 1860s is underscored.

Yours of the 18th inst. is just received. In reply I will endeavor to state all the facts and circumstances connected with the finding of your son's remains. He, with ten men, one an Indian guide belonging to the Pawnees, was sent as bearer of dispatches from Fort Sedgwick to the forks of the Republican River, where I was supposed to be encamped with my command. This point is distant from Sedgwick about 90 miles in a southeasterly direction. The dispatches of which your son was the bearer were important orders by telegraph from General Sherman.

Unfortunately, upon the evening of the day of the departure of Lieut. Kidder from Fort Sedgwick, I broke camp and set out on a lengthened march westward, leaving the main southern trail which led to Fort Wallace, and over which a considerable force had passed twenty-four hours previous.

I am thus minute in detail, as it was at this point that your son left my trail and followed the large trail toward Wallace. In returning from my

218

scout, I marched for Wallace, striking the trail above referred to but a few miles south of the point at which I had left it.

I at once discovered the trail of Lieut. Kidder and party, going toward Wallace, and knowing the dangerous country through which he must pass, and the probabilities of encountering an overwhelming force of savages, I became at once solicitous regarding his fate.

The second day after striking the trail, we reached Beaver Creek at a point about forty miles northeast from Fort Wallace. Here we discovered evidence of a conflict. Two horses which had been slain recently excited my suspicions.

At the discovery of the two slain horses, I halted my command and grazed for a few hours, in the meantime sending out parties in different directions to discover further evidences of the engagement which had apparently taken place.

The horrible truth of the massacre of your son and his entire party, was soon rendered evident. Upon being informed that a number of bodies had been discovered nearby, I, in company with several of my officers, at once visited the spot.

There were eleven bodies discovered, this being the number of your son's party. I, as well as all the officers with me, endeavored to discover or distinguish the body of your son from those of his men. The Indians, however, had carried off everything which might indicate his rank, and our efforts were fruitless.

I regretted this particularly, knowing what a satisfaction it would have been to his friends to have had it in their power to remove his remains at some future time. I caused a grave to be prepared on the spot where the lives of this little band had been given up, and consigned their remains to one common grave.

From the large number of arrows picked up on the ground, and from other indications to be observed, it was evident that a desperate struggle had ensued before the Indians were successful in over-powering their victims.

It is satisfactorily believed that the party which attacked your son was Roman Nose and his tribe of Cheyenne warriors. The ground near which the bodies of your son and his party lay, was thickly strewn with exploded metallic cartridges, showing conclusively that they had defended themselves a long time, and most gallantly, too, against their murderous enemies.

Another proof of the determined gallantry exhibited by your lamented son and his little party, was the fact that the bodies, which were probably found as they fell, were lying near each other, thus proving that none had endeavored to flee or escape after being surrounded, but all had died nobly fighting to the last. No historian will ever chronicle the heroism which was probably here displayed. We can picture what determination, what bravery, what heroism must have inspired this devoted little band of martyrs when surrounded and assailed by a vastly overwhelming force of bloodthirsty, merciless and unrestrained barbarians, and that they manfully struggled to the last, equally devoid of hope or fear.

Believe me, sir, although a stranger to you, and unknown to your son, I deeply sympathize with you and yours in this most sad and lamentable bereavement; and gladly would I tender to the wounds of your affliction such healing consolation as lies in the power of mortals to give; but I know how weak and futile must my efforts prove, and that in great bereavement like that to which you are now subjected, there is but one power, one source, to which we may hopefully look for that consolation you so much require.

Very truly yours,
G. A. Custer, Bvt. Maj.-Gen.

Reprinted from E. A. Brininstool, *Troopers With Custer: Historic Incidents of the Battle of the Little Big Horn* (Lincoln, NE: University of Nebraska Press, 1989) by permission from Stackpole Books.

The Fight at Beecher Island, September 17, 1868

George A. Forsyth

Born in Pennsylvania in 1837, Forsyth's family had military roots. His great-grandfather had fought in the Revolutionary War but was killed in an Indian raid in 1788. His grandfather was wounded in the War of 1812. An uncle died defending the Alamo in 1836. When the Civil War broke out, Forsyth had just finished his bar examinations, but he joined the United States Army and served honorably. Following the end of the Civil War, Forsyth remained in the Army and was assigned to duty in the West and against the Plains Indians. Indian raids in Kansas in 1868 led Forsyth to the fight at Beecher Island, located in eastern Colorado. Forsyth's description of the fight was first published by Harper's New Monthly Magazine *in an article titled, "A Frontier Fight."*

At early dawn, as I was standing by a sentry near one of the outposts, closely scanning the sky-line between ourselves and the rising ground to our right which lay furthest up the stream, I suddenly caught sight of an object moving stealthily between us and the horizon. At the same moment the sentry saw it, and simultaneously cocking our rifles, we stood alert, with straining eyes and listening ears. An instant later the soft thud of un-shod horses' hoofs upon the turf came to our ears, and peering just above the crest of the rising ground between us and the horizon, we caught sight of waving feathers crowning the scalp-locks of three mounted warriors. The sharp crack of our rifles rang out almost simultaneously, and, with the cry of "Indians! Turn out! Indians!" we ran backward towards our camp, firing as we ran at a group of mounted warriors which instantly surrounded the hill, where, pausing for a few seconds, evidently for reinforcements, they broke into a gallop and came rushing down on our camp,

221

shouting, and beating Indian drums, and rattling dried hides, in an endeavor to stampede our horses; but by this time nearly every man was standing with his horse's lariat wrapped around his left arm, and ready for a shot at the stampeding party as they bore down upon us. A scattering volley from the scouts dropped one of their number from his saddle, and they sheered off, carrying with them two of our four mules, and two horses that had not been securely picketed, in violation of orders. The attempted stampede had proved a failure. "Saddle up quickly, men!" was my next order, and in an incredibly short time the command was saddled and bridled, and in another moment every man was fully and completely equipped. The two men whose horses were stampeded, owing to their own negligence, started on a run towards where they had disappeared, evidently thinking that there was a possibility of their recovery. Ordering them back with a few sharp words, I told the men to stand to horse, having already made up my mind what course to pursue in case I was heavily outnumbered. It had begun to be light enough by this time to see dimly surrounding objects within a few hundred yards, when suddenly Grover, who stood by my side, placed his hand on my shoulder and said, "Oh, heavens, general, look at the Indians!"

Well might he say "look at the Indians!" The ground seemed to grow them. They appeared to start out of the very earth. On foot and on horseback, from over the hills, out of the thickets, from the bed of the stream, from the north, south, and west, along the opposite bank, and out of the long grass on every side of us, with wild cries of exultation, they pressed towards us. A few sharp volleys from the command, who stood coolly to horse, each man having his bridle thrown over his left arm, staggered them for a moment, and then they hastily fell back out of range. It was scarcely so much of a surprise party as they had planned, and they were somewhat astonished to find an active and responsive reception committee promptly on hand and ready to accord them a warm and enthusiastic welcome on their very first appearance.

I now saw clearly that there was but one course to take. So completely were we surrounded, and so greatly outnumbered, that our only hope lay in a successful defense, and I determined, in any event, that they should pay dearly for the lives of my scouts before ornamenting the ridge-poles of their lodges with our reeking scalps.

The command was ordered to lead their horses to the little island just in front of us, to form a circle facing outward, securely tie their horses to the bushes just outside of the circle so formed, throw themselves on the ground, and intrench themselves as rapidly as possible, two men working together, protecting each other in turn as they alternatively threw up the earth to cover themselves. As we moved in almost a solid front to the little island, leading our horses, a few of our best shots, under Beecher,

Grover, and McCall, kept up a rapid and steady fire from our flanks to cover the movement, which seemed for a few moments to puzzle the Indians, for they had apparently left the way open on the east, down the stream, and, I think, looked to see us mount and attempt a retreat that way; but I knew enough of Indian craft to be certain that the little gorge just around the bend of the steam in that direction would be lined with warriors, and I knew, furthermore, that once established on the island, there was no direction from which they could take us unawares during daylight.

Three of our best men remained temporarily in the long grass on the bank of the river, covering the north end of the island, thereby holding in check any unusually adventurous warriors who might be inclined to attempt to crawl up that way through the river-bottom. Scarcely were the horses tied in a circle when the men threw themselves on the ground and began firing from beneath the animals, when it suddenly seemed to dawn upon the savages that they had been outgeneraled, for as we started towards the island, judging by their actions in signaling their comrades on the opposite bank, they fully expected that we would cross the stream. Now they saw their error, and also realized, too late, the mistake they had made in not occupying the island themselves.

Apparently infuriated at their blunder, and almost instantly comprehending the advantage we would have should we fortify ourselves, they made a desperate onslaught upon us, their various chiefs riding rapidly around just outside of rifle range, and impetuously urging their dismounted warriors to close in upon us on all sides. Many of the mounted Indians sprang from their horses also, and running forward they lined both banks of the river, and from the reeds and long grass poured in a steady and galling fire upon us. A few of our men had been hit, one killed, and several more badly wounded; our horses were being shot down on all sides, the poor animals plunging and rearing at their tethers, and adding their cries to the wild shouts of the savages and the steady crack of the rifles on every side. At the height of this crisis—for to us it was the crisis of the day—one of them shouted:

"Don't let's stay here and be shot down like dogs! Will any man try for the opposite bank with me?"

"I will," answered some one from the opposite side of the circle.

"Stay where you are, men. It's our only chance," I shouted, as I stood in the centre of the command, revolver in hand. "I'll shoot down any man who attempts to leave the island."

"And so will I," shouted McCall.

"You addle-headed fools, have you no sense?" called out Beecher, whose every shot was as carefully and coolly aimed as though he was shooting at a target.

"Steady, men! Steady, now! Aim low. Don't throw away a shot," was my oft-repeated command, in which I was seconded by Beecher, McCall, and Grover. "Get down to your work, men. Don't shoot unless you can see something to hit. Don't throw away your ammunition, for our lives may depend upon how we husband it."

This was my constantly iterated and reiterated command for the first twenty minutes of the attack. And now discipline began to tell. Many an Indian had fallen to the rear badly wounded, and some had been borne back dead, judging from the wild wails of the women and children, who could now be seen covering the bluffs back of the valley on the north side of the stream; and so hot had the scouts made it for the Indians close in on the river's bank that they had crawled back out of short range, evidently satisfied that it was safer, as far as they were concerned, to send their bullets from a longer distance. During this comparative lull in the fight the men were not idle, and with their butcher-knives to cut the sod, and their tin plates to throw up the sand, most of them had already scooped out a hold the length of their body, from eighteen inches to two feet in depth, and piling up the sand on the side facing the enemy, had an ample cover against rifle bullets. I still stood upright, walking from man to man, but from every side came appeals for me to lie down. As we were now in fairly good shape, and the men cool and determined, I did so. Scarcely had I lain down when I received a shot in the fore part of the right thigh, the bullet ranging upward; and notwithstanding it remained embedded in the flesh, it was by far the most painful wound I have ever received. For a moment I could not speak, so intense was the agony. Several of the men, knowing I was hit, called out to know if I still lived, but it was at least a full minute before I could command my voice and assure them I was not mortally hurt. In the meantime one or two Indians had crawled up on the lower end of the island, and, hidden by a few bushes, were annoying us very much. However, the elder Farley, who, with Harrington, Gantt, and Burke, had temporarily taken position close upon the bank of the river, saw the flash of one of their rifles from the centre of a little bush, and the next instant a bullet from his rifle went through the very middle of the bush and crashed into the brave's brain, and a wild half-smothered shriek told us there was one less of our enemies to encounter. As we heard nothing more from the other one, I concluded that he dare not again risk exposing his position by using his rifle.

As I was now about the only man of the command unprotected by a rifle-pit, Doctor Mooers (who had been doing splendid service with his rifle, as he was a capital shot) suggested the enlarging of his pit to accommodate us both. Several of the men promptly went to his assistance in enlarging and deepening it; but while they were doing so, in leaning over to caution one of the men, who I thought was firing a little too fast for really good shooting, I was obliged, in order to ease my wounded thigh, to draw up my left leg as I lay prone on the earth, and, unfortunately for me, one of the Indians sent a bullet through it, breaking and shattering the bone badly about mid-way between the knee and ankle.

In my present condition, with my left leg broken, and a bullet in my right thigh, I was, save for the fact that I still retained command, something of a spectator. Gradually working myself to one end of the pit on my elbows, dragging my body along with no inconsiderable pain, I was able to partially sit up, and, by resting my elbows against and upon the fresh earth, crane my head forward so as to obtain a clear view of the field.

Nearly all of our horses lay dead around us; a few of them, badly wounded, still plunged and moaned and strained at their lariats as bullet after bullet entered their bodies, and had I been certain that I could spare the ammunition, I would have directed my own men to put the poor beasts out of their misery. Meanwhile the dead bodies of their companions stopped many a bullet intended for us. It must have been nearly or quite eight o'clock in the morning. The cover of any kind that commanded our island, such as reeds, long grass, trees, turf, plum thickets, and in some places small piles of stones and sand thrown up hastily by themselves, was all fully occupied by the Indian riflemen.

Riding around just out of range of our rifles were several hundred mounted warriors, charging here and there, shouting, gesticulating, waving their rifles over their heads, and apparently half frenzied at the thought of the blunder they had made in permitting us to obtain possession of the island. Riding up and down their line was a warrior, evidently chief in command, of almost gigantic stature. I was almost certain who it must be, so calling out to Grover, I asked the question, "Is not the large warrior Roman Nose?"

"None other," was the reply. "There is not such another Indian on the plains."

"Then these are the northern Cheyenne?"

"Yes, and the Ogallalah and Brulé-Sioux, and the dog soldiers, as well. There are more than a thousand warriors here."

"I doubt that," was my reply.

"General, there are nearly five hundred of the northern Cheyenne alone here in the fight with Roman Nose," said Grover. I would not allow myself to believe his statement, and, furthermore, I did not wish the command to be disheartened, so I shouted back: "Nonsense! Grover. There are not more than five hundred warriors here altogether, if so many. You must be taking in some of the women and children," for just back of the mounted warriors the bluffs were covered with women and children watching the progress of the fight. A muttered reply from Grover, which I did not catch, convinced me that he still held to his first expressed opinion, while the men around me estimated the number far greater than either of us. I now know that Grover's estimate was very nearly correct.

Leaning too far forward to get a better view of the mounted warriors, who seemed to be moving towards the cañon below us, from where we had on the preceding day debouched into the little valley we were now besieged in, I rather rashly exposed my head, and some one of the Indian riflemen promptly sent an excellent line shot towards it. The bullet struck me just on the top of my soft felt hat, which, having a high crown, was fortunately doubled down, so it glanced off, cutting through several thicknesses of felt, but nevertheless knocked me almost senseless to the bottom of my rifle-pit. It was seconds ere I could completely recover myself and crawl back to my sitting position.

About this time several of the mounted Indians, for some cause that I was not able to determine, dashed up within rifle range, and from their horses took a sort of pot-shot at us. Doctor Mooers, who had been closely watching their approach as they careened around the island, gradually lessening their distance, watched his opportunity and shot one of them through the head. As the brave fell dead from his horse he remarked, "That rascally redskin will not trouble us again." Almost immediately afterwards I heard the peculiar thud that tells the breaking of bone by a bullet. Turning to the doctor, I saw him put his hand to his head, saying, "I'm hit," his head at the same time falling forward on the sand. Crawling to him, I pulled his body down into the pit and turned him upon his back, but I saw at once that there was no hope. A bullet had entered his forehead just over the eye, and the wound was mortal.

Once more placing my back against the side of the rifle-pit, and again raising myself upon my elbows, I peered over the little earthwork with rather more caution than before. On looking towards the opposite bank, and down the stream, I saw most of the mounted warriors had disappeared, and those who remained were slowly trotting towards the little gorge I have before mentioned, and again I distinctly hear the clear notes of an artillery bugle. Others of the mounted warriors now moved towards the gorge, and it flashed upon me that Roman Nose was forming his warriors for a charge just around the bend of the river, out of sight, and beyond rifle range.

We had not long to wait. A peal of the artillery bugle, and at a slow trot the mounted warriors came partially into view in an apparently solid mass at the foot of the valley, halting just by the mouth of the cañon on the opposite side of the river from which we had emerged the preceding day. Closely watching the mounted warriors, I saw their chief facing his command, and, by his gestures, evidently addressing them in a few impassioned words. Then waving his hand in our direction, he turned his horse's head towards us, and at the word of command they broke at once into full gallop, heading straight for the foot of the island. I was right in my surmise; we were to be annihilated by being shot down as they rode over us. As Roman Nose dashed gallantly forward, and swept into the open at the head of his superb command, he was the very beau ideal of an Indian chief.

He was a man over six feet and three inches in height, beautifully formed, and, save for the crimson silk sash knotted around his waist, and his moccasins on his feet, perfectly naked. His face was hideously painted in alternate lines of red and black, and his head crowned with a magnificent war-bonnet, from which, just above his temples and curving slightly forward, stood up two short black buffalo horns, while its ample length of eagles' feathers and herons' plumes trailed wildly on the wind behind him; and as he came swiftly on at the head of his charging warriors, in all his barbaric strength and grandeur, he proudly rode that day the most perfect type of a savage warrior it has been my lot to see. Turning his face for an instant towards the women and children of the united tribes, who literally by thousands were watching the fight from the crest of the low bluffs back from the river's bank, he raised his right arm and waved his hand with a royal gesture in answer to their wild cries of rage and encouragement as he and his command swept down upon us; and again facing squarely towards where we lay, he drew his body to its full height and shook his clinched fist defiantly at us; then throwing back his head and glancing skywards, he suddenly struck the palm of his hand across his mouth and gave tongue to a war-cry that I have never yet hard equaled in power and intensity.

No sooner were the charging warriors fairly under way than a withering fire was suddenly poured in upon us by those of the Indians who lay in ambush around us intently watching our every movement, in the vain hope that they might sufficiently cow us to protect their charging column against our rifles. I had expected this action, but I well knew that once their horsemen came within a certain radium their fire must cease.

Sitting upright in my pit as well as I was able, and leaning backward on my elbows, I shouted, "Now!" and "Now!" was echoed by Beecher, McCall, and Grover. Instantly the scouts were on their knees, with their rifles at their shoulders. A quick flash of their eyes along the barrels, and forty good men and true sent their first of seven successive volleys into the ranks of the charging warriors.

Crash!

On they come, answering back the first volley with a ringing warwhoop.

Crash!

And now I begin to see falling warriors, ay, and horses too; but still they sweep forward with yet wilder yells.

Crash!

They seem to be fairly falling over each other; both men and horses are down in heaps, and wild shrieks from the women and children on the hills proclaim that they too see the slaughter of their braves; but still they come.

Crash!

They have ceased to yell, but yet come bravely on. What? No! Yes, down goes their medicine-man; but Roman Nose still recklessly leads the column. But now I can see great gaps in their ranks, showing that our bullets have told heavily among them.

Crash!

Can I believe my eyes? Roman Nose is down! He and his horse lie dead together on the sand, and for an instant the column shakes; but a hundred yards more and they are upon us!

Crash!

They stagger! They half draw rein! They hesitate! They are breaking!

Crash!

And like an angry wave that hurls itself upon a mighty rock and breaks upon its rugged front, the Indians divide each side of the little breastwork, throw themselves almost beneath the off side of their chargers, and with hoarse cries of rage and anguish break for either bank of the river, and scatter wildly in every direction, as the scouts, springing to their feet with a ringing cheer, pour in volley after volley from their revolvers almost in the very faces of their now demoralized and retreating foe.

But now, to me, came the hardest blow of the whole day. Lieutenant Beecher rose from his rifle-pit, and, leaning on his rifle, half staggered, half dragged himself to where I lay, and calmly lying down by my side, with his face turned downward on his arm, said, quietly and simply: "I have my death-wound, General. I am shot in the side, and dying."

"Oh no, Beecher—no! It can't be as bad as that!"

"Yes. Good-night." And then he immediately sank into half-unconsciousness. In a few moments I heard him murmur, "My poor mother;" and then he soon grew slightly delirious, and at times I could hear him talking in a semi-unconscious manner about the fight; and at sunset his life went out. And thus perished one of the best and bravest officers in the United States Army.

Turning towards where my guide Grover lay, I somewhat anxiously put the question," Can they do better than that, Grover?"

"I have been on the plains, man and boy, General, for more than thirty years, and I never saw anything like that before. I think they have done their level best," was his reply.

From: *Thrilling Days in Army Life* (New York: Harper and Brothers, 1900)

A Desperate Moment in the Fight at Beecher Island

Why I Don't Mingle in Society, September 22, 1868

James Chisholm

Born in Scotland in 1838, Chisholm emigrated to America near the end of the Civil War. After gold was discovered in southwestern Wyoming in 1867 and with the memories of the California Gold Rush still vivid, the Chicago Tribune *sent out a correspondent in order to have a man on the spot to capture the essence of the discovery and its aftermath. Chisholm, who had worked for the rival* Chicago Times, *was hired by the* Tribune *to be its reporter. In March 1868 Chisholm was on his way to the newly-discovered gold fields and he returned to Chicago the following December. In this vignette, Chisholm describes female society in the small mining town of Miner's Delight which was located approximately ten miles due east of South Pass City, Wyoming.*

Society in the city of Miner's Delight consists of three females. The first is a plump, dumpling-faced woman built very much in the shape of a bale of cotton drawn together in the middle, and with a big coal scuttle on the top. She has one white haired little darling and she dotes right onto it. The second is a shadowy secluded kind of a being whose profile I have had a few passing glimpses of while passing her cabin door. I don't know who or what she dotes onto. The third I will call Dalilah. She is an adventuress. She dotes onto Jack Holbrook. Jack is interested in the Miner's Delight and she is interested in Jack.

Dalilah is not beautiful. She is not handsome. Her face is lean and spotty and unhealthy looking, and the upper part of her form is like an old whale bone umbrella not properly folded. She was not a respectable person when she first struck the camp, but she is not studying virtue under Jack. The miners used to address her familiarly as "Candy," but now she puts on airs and they call her Mrs. Holbrook. When any of the old hands call her by her old name and ask impertinent questions, she tosses her head and tells them to go along. So Jack is left in undisturbed possession and she is the mistress of his mud covered cabin.

Therefore I don't mingle in society.

Reprinted from *South Pass 1868* courtesy of the University of Nebraska Press.

Just Desserts for
a Mule, c. 1868

William F. Cody

Iowa-born in 1845, Cody's father was a state legislator but moved his family into unsettled territory in Kansas in 1852. At age twenty-two he became known as "Buffalo Bill" as he was responsible for supplying the Union Pacific Railway workers with meat. He was a trapper, a bullwhacker, Pony Express rider, wagon master, stagecoach driver, Civil War soldier and organizer and owner of Buffalo Bill's Wild West Show. He used his fame and public attention as a soapbox for Western causes and derided the U.S. government into keeping its pledges to the Indians. Buffalo Bill died in 1917 and is buried in Colorado.

The commanding officer at Fort Dodge was anxious to send some dispatches to Fort Larned, but the scouts, like those at Fort Hays, were rather backward about volunteering, as it was considered a very dangerous undertaking to make the trip. As Fort Larned was my post, and as I wanted to go there anyhow, I said to Austin that I would carry the dispatches, and if any of the boys wished to go along, I would like to have them for company's sake. Austin reported my offer to the commanding officer, who sent for me and said he would be happy to have me take his dispatches, if I could stand the trip on top of all that I had already done.

"All I want is a good fresh horse, sir," said I.

"I am sorry to say that we haven't a decent horse here, but we have a reliable and honest government mule, if that will do you," said the officer.

"Trot out your mule," said I, "that's good enough for me. I am ready at any time, sir."

The mule was forthcoming, and at dark I pulled out for Fort Larned, and proceeded uninterruptedly to Coon Creek, thirty miles out from

Dodge. I had left the main wagon road some distance to the south, and had traveled parallel with it, thinking this to be a safer course, as the Indians might be lying in wait on the main road for dispatch bearers and scouts.

At Coon Creek I dismounted and led the mule by the bridle down to the water, where I took a drink, using my hat for a dipper. While I was engaged in getting the water, the mule jerked loose and struck out down the creek. I followed him in hopes that he would catch his foot in the bridle rein and stop, but this he seemed to have no idea of doing. He was making straight for the wagon road, and I did not know what minute he might run into a band of Indians. He finally got on the road, but instead of going back toward Fort Dodge, as I naturally expected he would do, he turned eastward toward Fort Larned, and kept up a little jog trot just ahead of me, but would not let me come up to him, although I tried it again and again. I had my gun in my hand, and several times I was strongly tempted to shoot him, and would probably have done so had it not been for fear of bringing Indians down upon me, and besides he was carrying the saddle for me. So I trudged on after the obstinate "critter," and if there ever was a government mule that deserved and received a good round cursing it was that one. I had neglected the precaution of tying one end of my lariat to his bit and the other to my belt, as I had done a few nights before, and I blamed myself for this gross piece of negligence.

Mile after mile I kept on after that mule, and every once in a while I indulged in strong language respecting the whole mule fraternity. From Coon Creek to Fort Larned it was thirty-five miles, and I finally concluded that my prospects were good for "hoofing" the whole distance. We—that is to say, the confounded mule and myself—were making pretty good time. There was nothing to hold the mule, and I was all the time trying to catch him—which urged him on. I made every step count, for I wanted to reach Fort Larned before daylight, in order to avoid if possible the Indians, to whom it would have been "pie" to have caught me there on foot.

The mule stuck to the road and kept on for Larned, and I did the same thing. Just as day was beginning to break, we—that is the mule and myself—found ourselves on a hill looking down into the valley of the Pawnee Fork, in which Fort Larned was located, only four miles away; and when the morning sun belched forth we were within half a mile of the post.

"Now," said I, "Mr. Mule, it is my turn," and raising my gun to my shoulder, in "dead earnest" this time, I blazed away, hitting the animal in the hip. Throwing a second cartridge into the gun, I let him have another shot, and I continued to pour the lead into him until I had him completely laid out. Like the great majority of government mules, he was a tough one to kill, and he clung to life with all the tenaciousness of his obstinate nature. He was, without doubt, the toughest and meanest mule I ever saw, and he died hard.

The troops, hearing the reports of the gun, came rushing out to see what was the matter. They found that the mule had passed in his chips, and when they learned the cause they all agreed that I had served him just right. Taking the saddle and bridle from the dead body, I proceeded into the post and over to Dick Curtis' house, which was headquarters for the scouts, and there put in several hours of solid sleep.

From: *Buffalo Bill's Own Story of His Life and Deeds* (Chicago: Homewood Press, 1917)

While grading track — and hunting buffalo — for the Kansas Pacific Railroad, after the Civil War, 21-year-old William Cody allegedly received the nickname "Buffalo Bill" after bringing down 11 of the beasts with 12 shots.

Buffalo Bill

The Death of Innocents, c. November 1868

George Armstrong Custer

Although he graduated last in his class at West Point, just two years later when he was only twenty-three years old, Custer had become the youngest general in the U.S. Army in the Civil War. Considered one of the best calvary commanders that America has ever produced, Custer is perhaps best-known for his disastrous defeat beside the Little Bighorn in 1876. Before that, however, Custer was widely criticized for his 1868 winter campaign that led to the battle of the Washita in which countless Indian women and children were massacred. This narrative is taken from Custer's account of the incident in that fight.

One party of troopers came upon a squaw endeavoring to make her escape, leading by the hand a little white boy, a prisoner in the hands of the Indians, and who doubtless had been captured by some of their war parties during a raid upon the settlements. Who or where his parents were, or whether still alive or murdered by the Indians, will never be known, as the squaw, finding herself and prisoner about to be surrounded by the troops and her escape cut off, determined, with savage malignity, that the triumph of the latter should not embrace the rescue of the white boy. Casting her eyes quickly in all directions to convince herself that escape was impossible, she drew from beneath her blanket a huge knife and plunged it into the almost naked body of her captive. The next moment retributive justice reached her in the shape of a well-directed bullet from one of the troopers' carbines. Before the men could reach them life was extinct in the bodies of both the squaw and her unknown captive.

From: *My Life on the Plains, or Personal Experiences with Indians* (New York: Heldon & Company, 1874)

A Rose among Thorns, c. November 1868

Frances Anne Mullen Boyd

The number of women traveling or living in the West was small. Although few in number, of those were the wives of soldiers being stationed at one fort or another. Such was the case of Frances Boyd whose husband, Orsemus Boyd, was assigned duties at some of the most remote frontier posts in Nevada, New Mexico and Texas. Lieutenant Boyd graduated from West Point and the couple married in 1867. After nearly eighteen years of marriage and following her husband from post to post, Orsemus Boyd became seriously ill on a scout against the Apaches and died in 1885.

The almost chivalrous kindness of frontiersmen has become proverbial with women who have traveled alone in the far West, where the presence of any member of the sex is so rare the sight of one seems to remind each man that he once had a mother, and no attention which can be shown is ever too great. . . .

It seemed indeed odd on this and succeeding nights to see huge, stalwart men preparing food, baking the inevitable biscuits in Dutch ovens over the coals in open fireplaces, and being so well pleased if we seemed to enjoy what was placed before us. . . .

On arriving at the cabin . . . we found it occupied by fifteen men. As usual, we were ensconced in the only bed. I tried to feel doubly protected, instead of embarrassed, by the vicinity of so many men; nor did I consider it necessary to peer about in an effort to learn how they disposed of themselves. I well knew it was too cold to admit of any sleeping outside. Being startled by some noise in the night, I drew back the curtains, and looked on a scene not soon to be forgotten. Not only were the men ranged in rows before us, but the number of sleepers had been augmented by at least six dogs, which had crept in for shelter from a severe snow-storm, that covered the ground to the depth of ten inches or more.

From: *Cavalry Life in Tent and Field* (New York: J. S. Tait, 1894)

The Golden Spike Is Driven, May 10, 1869

Alexander Toponce

At 12:47 p.m. an ordinary iron spike was driven into a regular tie. The single word "done" was tapped out by telegraph operators signaling the transcontinental joining of a railway line, running from the East Coast to the West Coast. Toponce was born in France in 1839 and soon afterward his family emigrated to America and settled in New York. Destined for adventure, fifteen-year-old Toponce headed West. He worked as a bullwhacker, drove a stagecoach, rode for the pony express, worked for the U.S. Army, and dabbled in entrepreneurial schemes. Toponce died in 1923.

I saw the Gold Spike driven at Promontory, Utah. I had a beef contract to furnish meat to the construction camps of Benson and West. This West was my good friend, Bishop Chauncey W. West of Ogden. They had a grading contract with the Central Pacific and their camp was near Blue Creek. I also furnished beef for some of the Union Pacific contractors.

The Golden Spike could have been driven a couple of weeks earlier than it was. But the two companies had settled on Promontory as the meeting place some days prior to the actual meeting.

The Central Pacific had been planning to make the junction at Ogden as to be in touch with Salt Lake City and the settlements in Utah. But the Union Pacific planned to lay their iron as far west as Humboldt Wells, in Nevada, and had most of their grade completed that far west.

If the Union Pacific had crowded their work as hard as the Central Pacific did in the last two weeks the Golden Spike would have been driven a good many miles to the west. The Union Pacific employed white labor, largely Irish, and the Central Pacific had Chinese labor. The Irish and Chinese met on promontory Hill. . . .

On the last day only about 100 feet were laid and everybody tried to have a hand in the work. I took a shovel from an Irishman and threw a shovel full of dirt on the ties just to tell about it afterward.

A special train from the west brought Governor Leland Stanford of California and C.P. Huntington, Crocker, Hopkins and lots of California wine.

Another special train from the east brought Sidney Dillon, General Dodge, T.C. Durant, John R. Duff, S.A. Seymour, a lot of newspaper men, and plenty of the best brands of champagne.

Another train made up at Ogden carried the band from Fort Douglas, the leading men of Utah Territory, and a small, but efficient supply, of Valley Tan.

It was a very hilarious occasion, everybody had all they wanted to drink all the time. Some of the participants got "sloppy" and these were not all Irish and Chinese, by any means.

California furnished the Golden Spike. Governor Tuttle of Nevada furnished one of silver. General Stanford presented one of gold, silver and iron from Arizona. The last tie was of California laurel.

When they came to drive the last spike, Governor Stanford, president of the Central Pacific, took the sledge and the first time he struck he missed the spike and hit the rail.

What a howl went up! Irish, Chinese, Mexicans, and everybody yelled with delight. Everybody slapped everybody else on the back and yelled "He missed it. Yee." The engineers blew the whistles and rang their bells. Then Stanford tried it again and tapped the spike and the telegraph operators had fixed their instruments so that the tap was reported in all the offices, east and west, and set bells to tapping in hundreds of towns and cities.

Then Vice President T.C. Durant of the Union Pacific took up the sledge and he missed the spike the first time. Then everybody slapped everybody else again and yelled, "He missed it too, yow!"

It was a great occasion, everyone carried off souvenirs and there are enough splinters of the last tie in museums to make a good bonfire. When the connection was finally made the U.P. and the C.P. engineers ran their engines up until their pilots touched. Then the engineers shook hands and had their pictures taken and each broke a bottle of champagne on the pilot of the other's engine and had their pictures taken again. . . .

Both before and after the spike driving ceremony there were speeches, which were cheered heartily. I do not remember what any of the speakers said now, but I do remember that there was a great abundance of champagne.

From: *Reminiscences of Alexander Toponce* (Salt Lake City, UT: Katie Toponce, Century Printing, 1923)

Paying Attention to a Good Pony, c. 1869

Frank Grouard

Brought to the New World by Spaniards in the 1500s, the horse was to become the chief means of transportation and gave an Indian hunter an important edge in securing game and fighting his enemies. Nothing could be as important to an Indian warrior as a good, swift pony. Grouard was a one-of-a-kind plainsman. Born in 1850 in Polynesia of a Mormon missionary and a Polynesian woman, he was brought to Utah by a Mormon foster mother when he was eight. At sixteen he ran away to Montana and worked a series of jobs. In 1875 he showed up at the Red Cloud Indian Agency in Nebraska saying that he had been living among the Sioux for six years. Grouard claimed that he was captured by renegade Sioux and his life was spared by Sitting Bull. Because of his intimate knowledge of the Sioux language, their habits and land, he was hired as an army scout by General Crook. In the following narrative, Grouard tells a story about the life-savings importance of paying attention to the antics of a pony.

Among the Indians no sport or excitement could equal the buffalo hunt. There was considerable danger in it but nothing to compare with the excitement. Every brave kept a trained pony for the buffalo chase—one that was used for nothing else—and the intelligence of some of those animals was wonderful. I really believe the ponies enjoyed a buffalo hunt as keenly as did their masters. When I became possessed of my first buffalo pony, the Indian from whom I got it told me of all its good qualities and laid particular stress upon the fact that the animal always gave warning of approaching danger. I paid little attention to the buck's talk at the time, but it was very distinctly recalled on an occasion I am about to speak of.

241

The Bark Creek country along the Yellowstone River was a great feeding ground for the buffalo, and one season we moved our camp down there. Our supply of meat had got very light, and we also wanted robes with which to make lodges. We killed a great many buffalo during our stay in that locality and were about ready to move. It was decided to have one more hunt before leaving, and preparations were made accordingly. The buffalo had drifted some distance from our camping ground, and the Indians were in the habit of moving camp from day to day as the chase progressed. When we started off in the last hunt, the entire camp went along, and as soon as the herd of buffalo was sighted, the bucks jumped upon their ponies and began the chase.

On this particular occasion I became so intent upon running the buffalo that I got a long way in advance of the other hunters. I killed a couple of buffalo and got off my horse to skin them, fastening my pony to the carcass of one of the dead animals. While I was at work, my pony began to act strangely. It would run around in a half-circle, then back again, and seemed to be trying to attract my attention. I paid no particular heed to the actions of the pony until I recalled what its former owner had told me about its giving warning of danger; then I untied it, jumped upon its back, and rode up on a hill to see if anything unusual was occurring. Seeing nothing, I returned to my work. The pony began to caper about worse than ever, and I finally became so nervous and frightened that I left the two buffalo and started back to where we had left the pack animals. I had not gone over two miles before I heard shooting, and glancing over my shoulder in the direction from which I had come, I saw a large party of Crow warriors charging down onto our people. I gave the alarm as quickly as I could, but before the Sioux braves could get together, the enemy had killed nineteen of them and departed. My pony had sniffed the danger while I was skinning the buffalo, but I failed to find the least sign of the attacking party and supposed my animal was restless at being separated from the rest of the pony herd. If it had not been for the actions of the pony, I would have been caught in a nice trap and lost my life.

From: DeBarthe, Joe. *Life and Adventures of Frank Grouard* (St. Joseph, MO: published by Joe DeBarthe, 1894)

Floating the Grand Canyon, August 14, 1869

John Wesley Powell

On May 24, 1869, New York-born John Wesley Powell (1834–1892) and nine men headed down the Green River in Wyoming down through the Grand Canyon, a daring nine-hundred mile journey in four boats. Less than a month later one of the adventurers left the group saying, "I have had more excitement than a man deserves in a lifetime. I am leaving." Continuing down the Green River where it merges into the Colorado and enters the Grand Canyon, three others approached Powell after spending weeks on the tumultuous river and announced that they were leaving the expedition because they feared for their lives. Only two days later Powell and his remaining six men entered into the calm waters outside of the Grand Canyon and safety. The three men who had left the expedition only two days earlier met their deaths at the hands of the Shivwits Indians as they trekked outside the canyon area. Powell repeated much of the journey again in 1871 and 1872 to make a more thorough study of the Green and Colorado Rivers.

At daybreak we walk down the bank of the river, on a little sandy beach, to take a view of a new feature in the canyon. Heretofore, hard rocks have given us bad river; smooth water; and a series of rocks harder than any we have experience in. The river enters the granite!

We can see but a little way into the granite gorge, but it looks threatening.

After breakfast we enter on the waves. At the very introduction, it inspires awe. The canyon is narrower than we have ever before seen it; the water is swifter; there are but few broken rocks in the channel; but the walls are set, on either side, with pinnacles and crags; and sharp, angular buttresses, bristling with wind and wave-polished spires, extend far out into the river.

Ledges of rocks jut into the stream, their tops sometimes just below the surface, sometimes rising few or many feet above; and island ledges, and island pinnacles, and island towers break the swift course of the stream into chutes, and eddies, and whirlpools. We soon reach a place where a creek comes in from the left, and just below, the channel is choked with boulders, which have washed down this lateral canyon and formed a dam, over which there is a fall of thirty or forty feet; but on the boulders we can get foothold, and we make a portage.

Three more such dams are found. Over one we make a portage; at the other two we find chutes, through which we can run.

As we proceed, the granite rises higher, until nearly a thousand feet of the lower part of the walls are composed of this rock.

About eleven o'clock we hear a great roar ahead, and approach it very cautiously. The sound grows louder and louder as we run, and at last we find ourselves above a long, broken fall, with ledges and pinnacles of rock obstructing the river. There is a descent of, perhaps, seventy-five or eighty feet in a third of a mile, and the rushing waters break into great waves on the rocks, and lash themselves into a made, white foam. We can land just above, but there is not foothold on either side by which we can make a portage. It is nearly a thousand feet to the top of the granite, so it will be impossible to carry our boats around, though we can climb to the summit up a side gulch, and, passing along a mile or two, can descend to the river. This we find on examination; but such a portage would be impracticable for us, and we must run the rapid, or abandon the river. There is no hesitation. We step into our boats, push off and away we go, first on smooth but swift water, then we strike a glassy wave, and ride to its top, down again into the trough, up again on a higher wave, and down and up on waves higher and still higher, until we strike one just as it curls back, and a breaker rolls over our little boat. Still, on we speed, shooting past projecting rocks, till the little boat is caught in a whirlpool, and spun around several times. At last we pull out again into the stream, and now the other boats have passed us. The open compartment of the "Emma Dean" is filled with water, and every breaker rolls over us. Hurled back from a rock, now on this side, now on that, we are carried into an eddy, in which we struggle for a few minutes, and are then out again, the breakers still rolling over us. Our boat is unmanageable, but she cannot sink, and we drift down another hundred yards, through breakers; how, we scarcely know. We find the other boats have turned into an eddy at the foot of the fall, and are waiting to catch us as we come, for the men have seen that our boat is swamped.

They push out as we come near, and pull us in against the wall. We bail our boat, and on we go again.

From: *Exploration of the Colorado River of the West and Its Tributaries. Explored in 1869, 1870, 1871, and 1872, under the Direction of the Secretary of the Smithsonian Institution* (Washington: Smithsonian Institution, 1875)

Being Fast on the Draw, c. January 1870

John Wesley Hardin

The son of a Methodist minister, but having killed his first man at the age of fifteen, Hardin became one of the most notorious gunslingers in the Old West. Considered cool as a cucumber, Hardin was known to be quick on the draw and used his guns with skill. The result: Hardin had killed more than twenty men before he was captured and imprisoned. In 1895, as he was whiling away his time at the Acme Saloon in El Paso, Hardin was killed by a shot in the back of his head fired by constable, John Selman. After his death a manuscript of his autobiography was found among his personal papers. It was first published in 1896 with the title, The Life of John Wesley Hardin, as Written by Himself.

About 25 miles from Pisga a circus was going on at a place called Horn Hill. One of the circus men had had a row with some of the citizens, resulting in some men being shot. We knew nothing about this and upon getting to town went to a hotel to get a bed. The circus people had all of the beds engaged, so we could not get a one. About 10 p.m. we went out to the circus campfires. It was quite cold and while we were all standing round the fire I accidentally struck the hand of a circus man who was lighting his pipe with a fagot from the fire. I begged his pardon at once and assured him it was pure accident. He, however, just roared and bellowed and swore he would "smash my nose." I told him to smash and be damned, that I was a kind of a smasher myself. He said: "You are, are you?" struck me on the nose, and started to pull his gun. I pulled mine and fired. He fell with a .45 ball through his head. Barrickman covered the crowd until we could make a truce. I saddled our horses and we rode off, apparently to the north, but soon changed our course south. We

246

met nobody who knew us, so after Barrickman had ridden with me about sixteen miles, he returned to Pisga and I went on to Brenham by way of Kosse, Calvert, and Bryant. I was young then and loved every pretty girl I met, and at Kosse I met one and we got along famously together. I made an engagement to call on her that night and did so. I had not been there long when someone made a row at the door of the house. She got scared and told me it was her sweetheart, and about this time the fellow came in and told me he would kill me if I did not give him $100. I told him to go slow, and not to be in such a hurry; that I only had about $50 or $60 in my pocket, but if he would go with me to the stable I would give him more as I had the money in my saddle pockets. He said he would go, and I, pretending to be scared, started for the stable. He said, "Give me what you have got first." I told him all right, and in so doing, dropped some of it on the floor. He stooped down to pick it up and as he was straightening up I pulled my pistol and fired. The ball struck him between the eyes and he fell over, a dead robber.

From: *The Life of John Wesley Hardin, from the Original Manuscript as Written by Himself* (Seguin, TX: Smith & Moore, Publishers, 1896)

A Frontier House Beautiful,
April 11, 1871

Emma Thompson Just

In 1854, Emma's family emigrated from England to Utah, after having joined the Mormon Church. Soon after arriving in America, fifteen-year-old Emma married a soldier and a fellow British émigré, George Bennett. After taking his young wife to different locations throughout the West, Bennett decided to return to England. To begin their journey back to England, Bennett took Emma to Montana to catch an east-bound Missouri River steamboat. Upon reaching Montana, Bennett decided not to return to England and would not permit Emma to return either. George thereafter abandoned Emma in Montana. She was then five months pregnant. Without home, hearth or husband, Emma renewed her acquaintance with Nels Just, a young Danish Mormon who she had befriended when she first arrived in America. After a short courtship, Emma and Nels married and moved to Idaho. There she lived a hard but rewarding life with Nels and her children. Emma's reminiscences of her life on the Blackfoot River in Idaho were published in 1923 under the title, Letters of Long Ago.*

Blackfoot River, Idaho Territory

My dear Father:

Our first winter has been a very pleasant one. Very little snow and an early "breaking up." I rather feared a winter like the one we spent in Soda Springs and had that been the case I could not have had your letter for several weeks yet, as we have to go twenty miles for even the possibility of a letter and it often ends in just a possibility, for the service is very uncertain. The mail is carried by the stage drivers and left at the station that seems most convenient.

Our first "house" is not one that would be likely to lure Queen Victoria from her throne, but it is ours, because we have made it with the simple materials that God left strewn around here for us. It is only a hole in the ground, it differs from the habitations of the lesser animals, however, in the flatness of its walls and the squareness of its corners. It has no windows, but is lighted by a tallow dip and the cheerful fire on the hearth. We feel very wealthy because of our cook stove. You and I, father, lived and laughed in the days of the open fire. So with the stove to furnish us heat and a splendid heavy buffalo skin to keep the cold from coming in the opening that we use for a door, we have kept comfortable.

For furniture, well, first we have a wonderful bedstead that Nels has made. Four legs made from a pine pole, with holes bored in them to put in side pieces, which are also made of pine poles. Then down the sides are many holes bored and through them run strips of cowhide, laced back and forth, making springs. For mattress we have a tick filled with cured bunch-grass, that was cut with a scythe while the weather was warm. We have one chair, only one that I brought with me from Montana, and a table of rough pine boards that was given to us by a man at Fort Hall. We each had bedding and our dishes are so few I hate to enumerate.

Things will be better, though, even in another year, for we have many plans for building and improving, but there is no work that will bring in anything. Last year it was different, there was work for everyone while they were building the fort eleven miles from here. Aunt and I made good money. I baked bread for thirty-five men, which meant thirty-five loaves, in a little number seven stove. That alone was quite a day's work, but they paid me either five cents a loaf or pound for pound of flour. That is, when I used a pound of flour for soldier bread I put a pound aside for ourselves and in the course of the summer it grew into a mighty pile. Besides this, Aunt and I together cooked for six of the mechanics, milked twenty cows and sold butter and milk to the soldiers, did washing and anything that would bring in money. I used to be dreadfully tired, but it was not so bad, and how I wish now that we had some of the work and some of the pay, it would help so much in the building of another house. . . .

We shall plant a small garden, very small though, for the problem of irrigation is the next one. We have the land and we have the water, but the next thing is to bring them together. This year the garden will be a hand-made affair, watered with a bucket.

The spring has brought some activities of the kind peculiar to frontier localities. An occasional trapper drops in on us on his way to a summer job or to market the furs from his winter's catch. How we welcome such company! Some of these fellows have good educations and have drifted here from the states, where everything is civilized. We listen to them eagerly, beg them to remain longer to share our primitive hospitalities and sigh when they pass on.

Freddie sends you a big hug and wishes you would come and see us. I join in the wish, but I know that you will enjoy being quiet for a few years after the travel and hardship of the past.

With my best love,
Emma

From: *Letters of Long Ago* (Caldwell, ID: Caxton Publishers, 1923)

Concerns of an Officer's Wife, c. Autumn 1872

Frances M. A. Roe

Frances Marie Antoinette Mack was born in New York and was educated at a private school. She met Fayette Washington Roe, a Virginian who graduated from West Point in 1871. Immediately upon his graduation and commissioning, Fayette and Frances were married. Thereafter, they left for his first assignment at Fort Lyon, Colorado Territory. It was at this post where Frances began writing her narratives about her life as an Army wife. Beginning in 1871 and continuing through 1888, Frances wrote lively and mainly pleasurable accounts of the hardscrabble life of an Army wife on the frontier. Her experiences were many as she and Fayette were transferred from Western post to post, including assignments in Colorado Territory, Indian Territory, and Montana Territory. Her reminiscences of Army life were first published in 1909. Frances died in 1920 and is buried in Arlington National Cemetery.

This place is becoming more dreadful each day, and every one of the awful things I feared might happen here seems to be coming to pass. Night before last the post was actually attacked by Indians! It was about one o'clock when the entire garrison was awakened by rifle shots and cries of "Indians! Indians!" There was pandemonium at once. The "long roll" was beaten on the infantry drums, and "boots and saddles" sounded by the cavalry bugles, and these are calls that startle all who hear them, and strike terror to the heart of every army woman. They mean that something is wrong—very wrong—and demand the immediate report for duty at their respective companies of every officer and man in the garrison.

Faye jumped into his uniform, and saying a hasty good-by, ran to his company, as did all the other officers, and very soon we could hear the shouting of orders from every direction.

251

Our house is at the extreme end of the officers' line and very isolated, therefore Mrs. Hunt and I were left in a most deplorable condition, with three little children—one a mere baby—to take care of. We put them all in one bed and covered them as well as we could without a light, which we did not dare have, of course. Then we saw that all the doors and windows were fastened on both sides. We decided that it would be quite impossible for us to remain shut up inside the house, so we dressed our feet, put on long waterproof coats over our nightgowns as quickly and silently as possible, and then we sat down on the steps of the front door to await— we knew not what. I had firm hold of a revolver, and felt exceedingly grateful all the time that I had been taught so carefully how to use it, not that I had any hope of being able to do more with it than kill myself, if I fell in the hands of a fiendish Indian. I believe that Mrs. Hunt, however, was almost as much afraid of the pistol as she was of the Indians.

Ten minutes after the shots were fired there was perfect silence throughout the garrison, and we knew absolutely nothing of what was taking place around us. Not one word did we dare even whisper to each other, our only means of communication being through our hands. The night was intensely dark and the air was close—almost suffocating.

In this way we sat for two terrible hours, ever on the alert, ever listening for the stealthy tread of a moccasined foot at a corner of the house. And then, just before dawn, when we were almost exhausted by the great strain on our strength and nerves, our husbands came. They told us that a company of infantry had been quite near us all the time, and that a troop of cavalry had been constantly patrolling around the post. I cannot understand how such perfect silence was maintained by the troops, particularly the cavalry. Horses usually manage to sneeze at such times.

There is always a sentry at our corner of the garrison, and it was this sentinel who was attacked, and it is the general belief among the officers that the Indians came to this corner hoping to get the troops concentrated farthest from the stables, and thus give them a chance to steal some, if not all, of the cavalry horses. But Mr. Red Man's strategy is not quite equal to that of the Great Father's soldiers, or he would have known that troops would be sent at once to protect the horses.

There were a great many pony tracks to be seen in the sand the next morning, and there was a mounted [Indian] sentinel on a hill a mile or so away. It was amusing to watch him through a powerful field glass, and we wished that he could know just how his every movement could be seen. He sat there on his pony for hours, both Indian and horse apparently perfectly motionless, but with his face always turned toward the post, ready to signal to his people the slightest movement of the troops.

Faye says that the colored troops were real soldiers that night, alert and plucky. I can readily believe that some of them can be alert, and possibly good soldiers, and that they can be good thieves too, for last Saturday night they stole from us the commissary stores we had expected to last us one week—everything, in fact, except coffee, sugar, and such things that we keep in the kitchen, where it is dry.

The commissary is open Saturday mornings only, at which time we are requested to purchase all supplies, we will need from there for the following week, and as we have no fresh vegetables whatever, and no meat except beef, we are very dependent upon the canned goods and other things in the commissary.

Last Saturday Mrs. Hunt and I sent over as usual, and most of the supplies were put in a little dugout cellar in the yard that we use together— she having one side, I the other. On Sunday morning Farrar happened to be the first cook to go out for things for breakfast, and he found that the door had been broken open and the shelves as bare as Mother Hubbard's. Everything had been carried off except a few candles on Mrs. Hunt's side, and a few cakes of laundry soap on mine! The candles they had no use for, and the thieves were probably of a class that had no use for soap, either.

From: *Army Letters from an Officer's Wife, 1871–1888* (New York: D. Appleton, Publishers, 1909)

Exchanging Courtesies,
c. Autumn 1872

Cyrus Townsend Brady

Born in Pennsylvania, Brady (1861–1920) graduated from the U.S. Naval Academy at Annapolis in 1883. Seeking another life, Brady resigned his commission in 1886 and moved west to Nebraska. There he joined the Episcopal church and soon after, studied for its priesthood. He was ordained and served the church as a missionary in Colorado, Kansas and Missouri. In the 1890s Brady found that he had a literary bent and tried his hand at writing. He found a publisher and began publishing a number of novels including, For Love of Country, When Blades Are Out and Love's Afield, A Little Traitor to the South, *and several others. His books became popular and due to the increasing demands on his time, Brady resigned from the priesthood and focused on writing, balancing his literary efforts between historical nonfiction works and novels. It was during this time that Brady's most popular book was published,* Indian Fights and Fighters. *The following vignette was contained in his 1900 book entitled,* Recollections of a Missionary in the Great West.

In one of the border towns we had services in an abandoned saloon. The building was not in a very good location for a saloon; that's why it was abandoned. But it would do very well for a church,—any old place would do for that, you know,—so we cleaned it out and fixed it up nicely. The town had been a very wild one, and the saloon had been one of the worst there, which is saying a good deal. Men had been killed within its walls, and some grim, ominous stains under the chancel carpet, which, like Rizzio's blood, could not be washed out, told the story; but one of the best missions I ever served was located just there.

Services were held on one week-day, afternoon and night, every six weeks or so, as I could get to them, and were so popular that nearly the whole town attended them. A wandering and somewhat dilapidated amusement company—a concert troupe, I think it was—once drifted into the town and made arrangements to give a performance on the night appointed for the services. Very few tickets were sold, and when they inquired the reason they found out that almost everybody was going to church. They came to us then with a pitiful tale, which their appearance bore out, of hard times, bad luck, and small houses, and wanted to know if we could not help them in some way. They said that if I would appoint the hour of service for seven o'clock they would postpone their performance until half-past eight. Besides, they would give me a free ticket, and all hands come to my "show" if I would go to theirs.

I accepted their offer, of course. They were all interested attendants at the service, and I believe they reaped a fair reward by their compromise from their own performance afterwards. That is the only instance on record, so far as my knowledge goes, where a theatrical company postponed its performance for Church services.

From: *Recollections of a Missionary in the Great West* (New York: Charles Scribner's Sons, 1900)

A Visit to Denver, c. October 1873

Isabella L. Bird

An Englishwoman born in 1831, Bird took an excursion into the American West in 1873 and called it, "no region for tourists and women." The reminiscent of her journey was published in 1878 in a serial format for the English weekly, Leisure Hour, *under the title, "Letters from the Rocky Mountains." Her description of the people inhabiting Denver paints a vivid picture and is probably representative of similar characters in other regions in Old West.*

It is a busy place, the . . . distributing point for an immense district, with good shops, some factories, fair hotels, and the usual deformities and refinements of civilization. Peltry shops abound, and sportsman, hunter, miner, teamster, emigrant, can be completely rigged out at fifty different stores. At Denver, people who come from the East to try the "camp cure" now so fashionable, get their outfit of wagon, driver, horses, tent, bedding, and stove, and start for the mountains. Asthmatic people are there in such numbers as to warrant the holding of an "asthmatic convention" of patients cured and benefitted. Numbers of invalids who cannot bear the rough life of the mountains fill its hotels and boarding-houses, and others who have been partially restored by a summer of camping out, go into the city in the winter to complete the cure. It stands at a height of 5,000 feet, on an enormous plain, and has a most glorious view of the Rocky Range. . . . The number of "saloons" in the streets impresses one, and everywhere one meets the characteristic loafers of a frontier town, who find it hard even for a few days or hours to submit to the restraints of civilization, as hard as I did to ride sidewise . . . Denver men go to spend the savings of months of hard work in the maddest dissipation, and there are such characters as "Comanche Bill," "Buffalo Bill," "Wild Bill," and "Mountain Jim."

A large number of Indians added to the harlequin appearance of the Denver streets . . . They belonged to the Ute tribe, through which I had to pass . . . The Indian stores and fur stores and fur depôts interested me most. The crowds in the streets, perhaps owning to the snow on the ground, were almost solely masculine. I only saw five women . . . There were men in every rig: hunters and trappers in buckskin clothing; men of the Plains with belts and revolvers, in great blue cloaks, relics of the war; teamsters in leathern suits; horsemen in fur coats and caps and buffalo-hide boots with the hair outside, and camping blankets behind their huge Mexican saddles; Broadway dandies in light kid gloves; rich English sporting tourists, clean, comely, and supercilious looking; and hundreds of Indians on their small ponies, the men wearing buckskin suits sewn with beads, and red blankets, with faces painted vermilion and hair hanging lank and straight, and squaws much bundled up, riding astride with furs over their saddles.

Town tired and confused . . . I was glad when a man brought Birdie at nine yesterday morning. He said she was a little demon, she had done nothing but buck, and had bucked him off on the bridge! I found that he had put a curb on her, and whenever she dislikes anything she resents it by bucking. I rode sidewise till I was well through the town, long enough to produce a severe pain in my spine, which was not relieved for some time even after I had changed my position. It was a lovely Indian summer day, so warm that the snow on the ground looked an incongruity. I rode over the Plains for some time, then gradually reached the rolling country along the base of the mountains, and a stream with cotton-woods along it. . . .

From: *A Lady's Life in the Rocky Mountains* (New York: G. P. Putnam's Sons, Publishers, 1881)

Double Perils of Frontier Women, c. 1873

Elizabeth B. Custer

Elizabeth ("Libbie") Bacon (1842–1933) was born and reared in Monroe, Michigan. She met George Armstrong Custer when he had been sent from his native Ohio to Monroe to live with his half sister, Lydia Reed. After graduating from West Point in the early days of the Civil War, Custer returned to Michigan where he met Libbie in the spring of 1864. George distinguished himself during the War and at age twenty-three, was promoted from captain to brigadier general. After suffering a war wound, George returned to Monroe to recuperate. During that time, he and Libbie were married. After their marriage, Libbie and George became almost inseparable as Libbie followed her new husband on most of his military posts. Later, during his assignments to the Western garrisons, George was court-martialed and suspended from the U.S. Army for a year for leaving his military unit and paying an unauthorized visit to Libbie. After Custer's 1876 death in the valley of the Little Big Horn River, Libbie did what she could to further his reputation. She wrote laudatory accounts of his life that portrayed him as both a military genius and a cultivated and budding statesman. The following story was extracted from her 1885 book, Boots and Saddles: Or Life in Dakota with General Custer. *The event in the story took place when Libbie and George were en route to a new military post in Dakota Territory.*

My husband and I kept up our little detours by ourselves as we neared the hour for camping each day. One day one of the officers accompanied us. We left the higher ground to go down by the water and have the luxury of wandering through the cottonwood trees that sometimes fringed the river for several miles. As usual, we had a number of dogs leaping and racing around us. Two of them startled a deer, and the general bounded after them, encouraging the others with his voice to follow. He had left his friend with me, and we rode leisurely along to see that the younger dogs did not get lost. Without the least warning, in the dead stillness of that desolate spot, we suddenly came upon a group of young Indian warriors seated in their motionless way in the underbrush. I became perfectly cold and numb with terror.

My danger in connection with the Indians was two-fold. I was in peril from death or capture by the savages, and liable to be killed by my own friends to prevent my capture. During the five years I had been with the regiment in Kansas I had marched many hundred miles. Sometimes I had to join my husband going across a dangerous country, and the exposure from Indians all those years had been constant. I had been a subject of conversation among the officers, being the only woman who, as a rule, followed the regiment, and, without discussing it much in my presence, the universal understanding was that anyone having me in charge in an emergency where there was imminent danger of my capture should shoot me instantly. While I knew that I was defended by strong hands and brave hearts, the thought of the double danger always flashed into my mind when we were in jeopardy.

If time could have been measured by sensations, a cycle seemed to have passed in those few seconds. The Indians snatched up their guns, leaped upon their ponies, and prepared for attack. The officer with me was perfectly calm, spoke to them coolly without a change of voice, and rode quickly beside me, telling me to advance. My horse reared violently at first sight of the Indians, and started to run. Gladly would I have put him to his mettle then, except for the instinct of obedience, which anyone following a regiment acquires in all that pertains to military directions. The general was just visible ascending a bluff beyond. To avoid showing fear when every nerve is strung to its utmost, and your heart leaps into your throat, requires superhuman effort. I managed to check my horse and did not scream. No amount of telling over to myself what I had been told, that all the tribes on this side were peaceable and that only those on the other side of the river were warlike, could quell the throbbing of my pulse. Indians were Indians to me, and I knew well that it was a matter of no time to cross and recross on their little tublike boats that shoot madly down the tide.

What made me sure that these warriors whom we had just met were from the fighting bands was the recollection of some significant signs we had come upon in the road a few days previous. Stakes had been set in the ground, with bits of red flannel peculiarly fastened on them. This, the guide explained, meant warnings from the tribes at war to frighten us from any further advance into their country. Whether because of the coolness of the officer, or because the warriors knew of the size of the advancing column, we were allowed to proceed unharmed. How inter-minable the distance seemed to where the general awaited us, uncon-scious of what we had encountered! I was lifted out of the saddle a very limp and unconscious thing.

From: *Boots and Saddles: Or Life in Dakota With General Custer* (New York: Harper Publishing Co., 1885)

A Buffalo Hunter Calculates His Earnings, c. 1874

Frank H. Mayer

Born in Louisiana in 1850, Mayer was a surveyor, a rancher, an editor, and a buffalo hunter. Buffalo hunters like Mayer almost drove the American bison into extinction. Estimates as high as forty million buffalo roamed the Great Plains. American Indians hunted them for food and other necessities. In the 1860s, new army posts were established on the Plains. The army contracted local hunters to supply buffalo meat to feed the troops. In the 1870s, railroad companies did the same to feed their construction crews. When tracks were laid and large buffalo herds began to delay the railroads, the railway companies capitalized on this and solved their problem of buffalo on the tracks by advertising hunting buffalo by rail—shooting from the rail cars and leaving the animals dead near the tracks. In the following vignette, Mayer relates that he found the life of a buffalo hunter hard and the pay small. Mayer died in Fairplay, Colorado, in 1954.

When I went into the business, I sat down and figured that I was indeed one of fortune's children. Just think! There were 20,000,000 buffalo, each worth at least $3–$60,000,000. At the very outside cartridges cost 25 cents each, so every time I fired one I got my investment back twelve time over. I could kill a hundred a day, $300 gross, or counting everything, $200 net profit a day. And $200 times thirty, would be, let me see, $200 times thirty—that would be $6,000 a month—or three times what was paid, it seems to me, the President of the United States, and a hundred times what a man with a good job in the 1870's could be expected to earn. Was I not lucky that I discovered this quick and easy way to fortune? I thought I was. I had dreams of opulence in a short time, and what if the life was hard, the hazards present all the time? The end was worth whatever it cost. I would buy a big house, wear a silk stovepipe hat, marry a beautiful girl, and rear a large family of stalwart sons, not one of whom would ever have to touch a rifle or drink out of a polluted buffalo wallow.

Oh, those were fine dreams! But they never did seem to materialize exactly. Always something coming up, some damned thing that took all the profit away. One time, because of a long rainy spell, about a fourth of the hides would spoil while drying. Or I would go into a new country and find it completely shot out, as frequently happened. Now and then, in spite of my care and skill as a stalker, the buff would spook mysteriously, and all I would get for my pains was a horseback ride back to camp. And sometimes . . . well, there was always something.

I suppose hunters have to be like gold prospectors, though, always thinking that tomorrow would be better. But always there was that dream that next season, yes, next season in an entirely new place, I'd recoup my losses, and make that fickle jade Fortune stand and deliver what I had coming to me.

Not that I actually lost money, you understand; just that I didn't make what I thought I should make . . . The hell of it was that presently— within a year or a year and a-half after I got into the business—we hit what I now know is called diminishing returns. We called it a scarcity of buff. It was. The more he was hunted and hounded the wilder the buffalo became, and with, say, 5,000 rifles a day leveled at him, it wasn't long until there was very little of him, or her, left to shoot. So we had to spend more and more time in the wagons exploring one range after another . . . We did it the hard way, riding miles and miles and miles in a stiff Mexican saddle over the uncharted plains, looking into every gully and prowling around every stream bed, on the off chance that we would find a "sleeper" herd—this is to say, a herd that some other runner had overlooked.

All of this took time, days of time, and expenses went on, even if the barrel of my rifle was cold for weeks on end. And my dreams of fortune— they grew dimmer and dimmer as the months went by. But I stuck. I was no quitter. But I was fast becoming a bankrupt, I'll tell you.

My first two years (1872–1873) I did right well, considering the value of the dollar in those days. My account books show that my share for the two years—that is to say, the net—was right around $6,000. I didn't make as much the first year ($2,900) as the second, when I turned in a profit of $3,100. This was on hides alone. My third year, however (1874), was my big year on the range; after that I slid down to nothingness. By that time I had gone into the smoked tongue, specimen bull heads, and meat business as side issues. I know exactly what I grossed and netted this year, and the account looks as follows:

Hides	$3,020.00
Meat	1,260.00
Tongues	905.00
Heads	250.00
Total	$5,435.00

This, mind you, was my gross; my net came to $3,124—and that was my big year on the buffalo ranges. Let some other men tell you about earning $50,000, $60,000 a year—I am telling the truth.

So you see our running was not all cream. I wouldn't do the same amount of hard work, take the same chances again for any man's $50,000. I couldn't if I wanted to—and I don't want to. On my first two years, deducting interest on investment, overhead, and so forth, I barely came out even; I think my net for the two years was around $2,800. And a little over $100 a month is mighty poor pay for the financial and physical output, not counting liability for disease and violent death!

I am quite confident that I was among the highest rewarded five men on the range. I have since talked to a dozen of the runners I knew and one and all remarked, "Well, you got more out of it than any feller I know of."

So I am quite safe in my surmise that a good high average of all the runners engaged was less than $1,000 per year net. All fantastic tales of "enormous" profits in the game were simply the distorted visions of some magazine writer who wouldn't know buffler meat from domesticated bull rump.

It is only fair to say that had I been able to save and sell all the meat of the animals killed in 1874, I would have netted about $5,000 more than I actually did. But much meat spoiled unavoidably and the market wasn't as active as it should have been. Beside, it entailed too much time as well as work in preparing the meat and in hauling it into the railroad. In my last full year on the range, I sold less than $2,000 worth of hides, but realized over $4,000 for meat alone. But overhead was so great that I could not find my heart any longer in the game, so I quit.

From: *The Buffalo Harvest* (Denver: Sage Books, 1958)

Slaughtering Buffalo for Sport

"Doctoring" in the Seventh Cavalry, July 21, 1874

Theodore Ewert

Born in Prussia, Ewert (1847–1906) was fourteen-and-a-half-years-old when he first joined the United States Army in 1861 as a private. He lived in Chicago at the time of his enlistment under the name of August C. Ewert. By 1864 he had been promoted to the officer ranks but was dismissed from the army after he was convicted by a court-martial in 1864 for being drunk on duty and gambling. In 1867 Ewert enlisted as a private in the 7th U.S. Cavalry but was soon promoted to sergeant. Before he enlisted in the 7th Cavalry, Ewert changed his name to Theodore Ewert. In 1883, Ewert was promoted to captain, and in 1902 was listed as a colonel of the Illinois Adjutant General Corps. The narrative that follows was taken from Ewert's diary during the 7th Cavalry's expedition into the Black Hills during the summer of 1874.

Having made fourteen miles we encamped on a small tributary [on the] Red River. Being on duty as Orderly Trumpeter made it imperative for me to remain around headquarters, and as one of the men of my company, John Cunningham, was lying ill in one of the ambulances, I went to him to see if any assistance or help could be rendered. On coming to the ambulance I found Cunningham lying on his back, his person exposed to every passerby, and dying. Jumping on the wheel I covered him decently and inquired of Private Keller of "K" Company, who was also ill at the same ambulance, when the doctor had been to see them and found that neither one of these had been near them since the previous evening. Cunningham was taken with acute dysentery about the 13th, and went on the sick report. The doctor? (A civilian contract doctor???) Marked him for duty. The disease becoming worse, he went on again on the 17th, when

"Butcher" Allen (as the men afterwards called him) marked him for duty again. The 18th, on the line of march, Cunningham, through weakness and loss of blood, fainted and fell off his horse, when Sergeant Connelley, by directions of Colonel Benteen, took him to the ambulance [in] spite of these pattern doctors who were guardians of the health of a thousand men, and now this man lay in the broiling rays of a July sun, dying, crazy through the neglect of men who were paid high salaries to recruit the broken-down health of the soldiers of the United States. My first step was to the tent of the Chief Medical Officer, Dr. Williams. I found him lying on his bed in a drunken sleep. I called on him and shook him, but he would not wake up. Then seeing the Adjutant General, Lieutenant Calhoun, I rode up to his tent. I went to him and begged him to get the doctor to come over and see Cunningham. While talking to him the tears came into my eyes as I described to him Cunningham's condition and he, seeing how earnest I took the matter to heart, went immediately and with great effort awoke Dr. Williams. This gent?, after rubbing his eyes and thinking over the matter for fifteen minutes, finally staggered over to the ambulance, with some trouble raised himself on the steps attached to the rear of the ambulance, looked at the dying man for a moment with a drunken stare, then staggered back to his tent, fell on his bed and slept. I now sent word over to our company that Cunningham was dying and in a very few moments a dozen or more of the boys were with me, and we were discussing the propriety of reporting the doctor to Gen'l Custer when Professor Donaldson stepped up to the crowd and asked us the cause of the excitement, which we told him. He gave us an order on the Sutler for anything that we might need for our poor, dying comrade, then went to Gen'l Custer and reported our case to him. The General sent for Dr. Williams, but finding him under the influence of the flowing bowl, sent him back to his tent, then called for Dr. Allen. This "drunken specimen of Doctorism" came and claimed that Cunningham was not dying. He prescribed a few opium pills and left. That evening, four of us volunteered to set up with him. At 11:25, poor Cunningham paid the debt of Nature and died, purely through the neglect of the men claiming to be doctors, men who were paid by the Government to look after the health of its soldiers and who only managed to drink the brandy furnished by the same Government for the use of its sick soldiers.

A large hospital tent was brought along and stretched every day for the use of Gen'l Custer and staff as a dining room. Whether it was intended for this use by the Government, or whether it was issued for the accommodation of the sick is left to the judgment of the reader. This much, however, every man with us knows, that up to date, no sick man saw the inside of that or any other tent, but they were left to lay in the rickety old ambulance, in sun or rain, hot or cold, and death now claimed one victim, the result of such usage. In civil life a man will take compassion on a dog in inclement weather. In the army it is far different; sick or dying, he instills no compassion except, perhaps, in the breast of his comrade, and he is powerless to help him. The men in "H" Company were justly indignant at the death of our comrade, but what could they do but keep quiet? Murmur they did, but at that it remained.

From: *Private Theodore Ewert's Diary of the Black Hills Expedition of 1874*, John M. Carroll and Lawrence A. Frost (editors) (Piscataway, NJ: Consultant Resources Incorporated, 1976)

Capturing Wild Mustangs, c. September 1875

Nat Love

Born into slavery in Tennessee in 1854, Nat Love learned how to take care of himself as his father was "sort of foreman of the slaves on the plantation," and his mother "presided over the kitchen at the big house." Freed from slavery by the defeat of the South in the Civil War, Love's family tried to sharecrop for their former slave master. Love, however, wanted to see the world and the desire "to go grew on [him] from day to day." Love's luck took a turn for the better when he won $100 in a lottery. With that money, Love struck out for the West going to Dodge City. From then on, Love made a name for himself in the West. He was nicknamed "Deadwood Dick" and he counted among his friends and acquaintances well-known Westerners such as Bat Masterson, Jesse and Frank James, Billy the Kid, Buffalo Bill Cody and many others. Love's memoirs were first published in 1907 under the heady title, The Life and Adventures of Nat Love, Better Known in Cattle Country as "Deadwood Dick"; A True Story of Slaver Days, Life on the Great Cattle Ranges and on the Plains of the "Wild and Woolly" West, Based on Facts and Personal Experiences of the Author. *In the selection that follows, Love and his cowboy companions seek to capture a herd of wild mustangs.*

It was a bright clear morning in September as we were all gathered at the old home ranch, prepared to start on the great mustang hunt. There was one of the best men from each of the big cattle ranges in the panhandle and Arizona country, making twenty of the best range riders ever assembled together for a single purpose, while we were mounted on the best and fastest horses the Texas and Arizona cattle country could produce, while a horse rustler had left four days before with twenty more equally as good horses, giving each of us two horses apiece. We carried with us four days' rations, containing dried beef, crackers, potatoes, coffee—we had no sugar. The mess wagon well stocked with provisions for a two months' trip had also left four days before for a place in the wild horse district, where we knew the mustangs were to be found.

Many of the cattle men of Texas and Arizona were present to see us off, and the boss gave us a little talk on what was expected of us, and said, among other things, we were twenty of the best and gamest cowboys who ever roamed the western plains, and that he knew we would make good on hearing these words—we one and all resolved to do our best.

And swinging into the saddle we emptied our guns as a parting salutation and started on a dead run across the plains towards the scene of our duty. After a hard ride of ten days we sighted a band of about seventy-five mustangs. We at once proceeded to run them down. It was decided that twenty of us should surround the herd in a large circle, ten or fifteen miles across, which would leave a space of several miles between each rider, but not of a greater distance than he could easily cover when he saw the band coming his way or heard our signals.

The horse rustler was to keep the extra horses at a place where they would be safe and at the same time handy to the riders. Our plans completed, each rider made preparations to start for his station. But here another difficulty arose. We had not yet seen anything of our cook and mess wagon. It had not arrived at the place agreed upon, although it has had ample time to do so. Our provisions which we carried were quite low, so after waiting as long as we could, and the mess wagon failing to show up, we decided to start the hunt and take our chances on grub from what we could knock over with our guns.

Accordingly the boys all started out for their several stations. After waiting a reasonable length of time to give them an opportunity to reach their positions, we made for the herd, which as near as we could judge contained about seventy-five of the prettiest horses it was ever my pleasure to see. The magnificent stallion who happened to be on guard had no sooner seen us than he gave the danger signal to the herd, who were off like the wind, led by a beautiful snow white stallion. To get them going was our only duty at present, and we well knew the importance of saving our saddle horses for the more serious work before us. Therefore we only walked our horses, or went on a dog trot, keeping a sharp lookout for the herd's return.

The band of wild horses would run ten or fifteen miles across the prairie, where they would catch sight of the other boys, then off they would go in another direction, only to repeat the performance, as they struck the other side of the circle. In this way they would make from fifty to sixty miles to our ten, and we were slowly working them down. We kept them going this way day and night, not giving them a moment's rest or time to eat. After keeping them on the go this way for ten days we were able to get within a mile of them and could see some of the stallions taking turns at leading the herd, while other stallions would be in the rear fighting them on. In a few days more we were near enough to begin shooting the stallions out of the herd. Then we could handle them a great deal better. At this time our want of grub began to tell on us. Our cook and mess wagon had not showed up, so we had long since given them up as lost. We believed they had been captured by the Indians and future events proved we were right.

Our only food consisted of buffalo meat of which we were able to secure plenty, but buffalo meat for breakfast, dinner and supper every day without bread or salt is not the most palatable bill of fare, especially when it is all we had day after day, without any prospect of a change until we got home. But we were game and resolved to stay with our work until it was finished, especially as we only had twenty men and everyone was badly needed in the work ahead of us, so we did not think we could spare a man to return home after grub. So we swallowed our buffalo meat day after day and kept the horses moving.

They were now pretty well worked down, and we proceeded to work them toward a place where we could begin to rope them. There were now only a few stallions left in the herd as we had shot nearly all of them, and the others were too tired to cause us any trouble. We had now been out of grub over three weeks except buffalo meat and such other game as we could bring down with our guns. Our fears that the cook and mess wagon had been captured by the Indians proved well founded, as we about this time met an outfit who had seen the place where the cook was killed. They said the surroundings indicated that quite a large band had surprised the cook and driver, but that they had put up a brave fight as evidenced by the large number of empty rifle and revolver shells scattered around. Our first impulse after hearing this was to start in pursuit of the red skins and get revenge, but calmer judgment showed that such a course would be useless, because the Indians had a couple of weeks start on us and we did not know what tribe had committed the offense as there were so many Indians in that part of the country and in the Indian territory, and besides our horses were in no shape to chase Indians, so much to our regret our comrades had to go unrevenged at least for the present, but we all swore to make the Indians pay dearly, especially the guilty ones, if it were possible to discover who they were. We continued to work the mustangs back and forth, and in thirty days from the time we started out we had about sixty head hemmed up in Yellow Fox Canyon and were roping and riding them. They were not hard to handle as they were so poor some of them could hardly walk. This was not to be wondered at, as we had kept them on the go for the past thirty days, never once giving them a moment's rest day or night, and in that time they had very little to eat and no sleep. After roping and riding them all we got them together and headed for home.

Arriving at the ranch the mustangs were allowed to eat all they wanted and were roped and ridden until they were fairly well broken, when they were turned out with the other ranch horses. They proved good saddle horses, but as soon as they were turned out with the ranch horses they would start for their old feeding grounds, leading the other horses with them. We found it impossible to thoroughly domesticate them, so for that reason we gave them up as a bad proposition, and did not attempt to capture any more, though at that time thousands of wild mustangs were on the plains of Texas, Arizona, Wyoming and in fact all over the West. They were large, fine and as pretty a lot of horses as one could wish to see. They were seldom molested, though once in a while the Indians would make a campaign against them and capture a few, but not often, as they were so hard to capture. It was not worth the trouble, as it was almost impossible to approach them nearer than two miles, and there was always some stallions on the lookout while the others grazed over the plains, so it was out of the question to surprise them. At the first sign of danger the stallion sentinel would give his shrill neigh of warning and the herd were off like the wind.

We received unstinted praise from our employers for bringing to a successful conclusion the errand on which we were sent under such trying circumstances. But now that we were where grub was plentiful we looked on our experience as nothing to make a fuss over.

From: *A Tue History of Slavery Days, Life on the Great Cattle Ranges and On the Plains of the 'Wild and Woolly' West, Based on Facts, and Personal Experiences of the Author* (Los Angeles: Wayside Press, 1907)

Nat Love (a.k.a. "Deadwood Dick")

Searching for "Stone Bones,"
c. Autumn 1875

James Henry Cook

Born in Michigan, James Cook (1858–1942) moved to the Old West before he reached his teens. During his early life, Cook worked at many occupations that were associated with a young man's life in that place and at that time: being a ranch cowboy, trapping, Indian mediator, exploring and serving as a military scout, and supplying meat to railway workers as a market-hunter. Cook married Kate Graham and soon thereafter obtained a ranch on the Niobrara River in present Sioux County, Nebraska, founded earlier by his father-in-law. Under Cook's management the 13,000 acre ranch prospered and became a resting place for Red Cloud's band of Oglala Sioux. Soon after the area was settled by white emigrants, paleontologists like Othniel C. Marsh made expeditions to the Cook's Agate Springs Ranch where Cook had found a number of "stone bones," mammal fossils from the more than nineteen million year-old Miocene epoch. Today, the ranch site is the home of the Agate Fossil Beds National Monument, from whose quarries many museums have received their fossils. In the following story, Cook tells of his first introduction to paleontology.

I first learned of the bones of strange creatures which had once lived in the land of the Sioux–bones now turned to stone. I was shown some of the petrifactions. A piece of gigantic jawbone containing a molar three inches in diameter was shown to me. American Horse explained that it had belonged to a "thunder horse" which had lived a long time ago, and that the creature would sometimes come down upon the earth in a thunderstorm and chase the buffalo, striking and killing some of them with his great hoofs. Once when the Sioux people were near starvation, this big horse had driven a herd of buffalo into their camp in the midst of a violent thunderstorm, and the Sioux had killed a great many of them with their arrows and lances. This occurred "way back," when the Indians had no horses.

While I was the guest of Red Cloud on this occasion, Professor O.C. Marsh, of the Smithsonian Institution and Yale College, came over from Fort Laramie with a government escort. He wanted permission from the Sioux to hunt for fossils in their country. The Sioux, however, did not take kindly to this proposition, thinking that it was really gold and not "stone bones" that the white chief wanted to find. I heard a great deal of the Indian side regarding bone-hunting in the Sioux hunting grounds. I met Professor Marsh and talked with him. Then I went to Red Cloud's lodge and talked the matter over with him. I told him that Professor Marsh was a friend of the Great Father at Washington; that, if he were allowed to hunt for stone bones, I thought he would be a good friend to the Sioux people; and that I was sure he was not hunting for yellow lead (gold).

Red Cloud said that if Professor Marsh were a good man, he would help him and his people get rid of the agent who was then in charge of them, and whom they cordially disliked and openly accused of dishonesty. When this was brought to the attention of Professor Marsh, he took the matter in hand, and an investigation of affairs took place at Red Cloud Agency. Records of the U.S. Indian Department show that the result of this investigation was most pleasing to Red Cloud and his people, if not to some of their white brothers. Professor Marsh was given a Sioux name, Man-That-Picks-Up-Bones (Wiscasa Pahi Huhu) and was allowed to come with his field parties and prospect for fossils without molestation. The Professor and Red Cloud became such fast friends that the Chief was entertained by Professor Marsh at his home in New Haven, Connecticut, and there the two were photographed with clasped hands and the peace pipe between them.

From: *Fifty Years on the Old Frontier as Cowboy, Hunter, Guide, Scout, and Ranchman* (New Haven, CT: Yale University Press, 1923)

The Fight on the Little Bighorn, June 25, 1876

Black Elk

During the waning period of the American Civil War, General George Armstrong Custer was the youngest general officer of the U.S. Army. He was known as a dashing daredevil who would go to nearly any length to subdue his foresworn enemies. Remaining in military service after the close of the Civil War, Custer was assigned to several posts on the Western plains. At the time of this narrative, Custer was in command of the 7th U.S. Calvary. The Seventh was Custer's pride and joy. He had great faith in its ability to subjugate the Indian tribes of the Great Plains. Custer was proud to argue that under his leadership the Seventh Calvary could whip any body of Indians that he was to encounter, regardless of their size. Just a few days before America began the celebration of its first centennial, Custer had his chance to prove the fighting worth of the Seventh Calvary against a large body of Indians. At the time of this event, Black Elk (1863–1950) was a thirteen-year-old Oglala Sioux boy who, along with several thousand Plains Indians from diverse tribes, were camped along the snaking Little Bighorn River in southern Montana Territory. His account of the events on June 25, 1876, were extracted from the book, Black Elk Speaks: Being the Life Story of a Holy Man of the Oglala Sioux, *as told through John G. Neihardt and first published in 1932.*

Several of us boys watched our horses together until the sun was straight above and it was getting very hot. Then we thought we would go swimming, and my cousin said he would stay with our horses till we got back. When I was greasing myself, I did not feel well; I felt queer. It seemed that something terrible was going to happen. But I went with the boys anyway. Many people were in the water now and many of the women were out west of the village digging turnips. We had been in the water quite a while when my cousin came down there with the horses to give them a drink, for it was very hot now.

Just then we heard the crier shouting in the Hunkpapa camp, which was not very far from us, "The chargers are coming! They are charging! The chargers are coming!" Then the crier of the Oglalas shouted the same words; and we could hear the cry going from camp to camp northward clear to the Santees and Yanktonais.

Everybody was running now to catch the horses. We were lucky to have ours right there just at that time. My older brother had a sorrel, and he rode away fast toward the Hunkpapas. I had a buckskin. My father came running and said: "Your brother has gone to the Hunkpapas without his gun. Catch him and give it to him. Then come right back to me." He had my six-shooter too—the one my aunt gave me. I took the guns, jumped on my pony and caught my brother. I could see a big dust rising just beyond the Hunkpapa camp and all the Hunkpapas were running around and yelling, and many were running wet from the river. Then out of the dust came the soldiers on their big horses. They looked big and strong and tall and they were all shooting. My brother took his gun and yelled for me to go back. There was brushy timber just on the other side of the Hunkpapas, and some warriors were gathering there. He made for that place, and I followed him. By now women and children were running in a crowd downstream. I looked back and saw them all running and scattering up a hillside down yonder.

When we got into the timber, a good many Hunkpapas were there already and the soldiers were shooting above us so that leaves were falling from the trees where the bullets struck. By now I could not see what was happening in the village below. It was all dust and cries and thunder; for the women and children were running there, and the warriors were coming on their ponies.

Among us in the brush and out in the Hunkpapa camp a cry went up: "Take courage! Don't be a woman! The helpless are out of breath!" I think this was when Gall stopped the Hunkpapas, who had been running away, and turned them back.

I stayed there in the woods a little while and thought of my vision. It made me feel stronger, and it seemed that my people were all thunder-beings and that the soldiers would be rubbed out.

Then another great cry went up out in the dust: "Crazy Horse is coming! Crazy Horse is coming!" Off toward the west and north they were yelling "Hoka hey!" like a big wind roaring, and making the tremolo; and you could hear eagle bone whistles screaming.

The valley went darker with dust and smoke, and there were only shadows and a big noise of many cries and hoofs and guns. On the left of where I was I could hear the shod hoofs of the soldiers' horses going back into the brush and there was shooting everywhere. Then the hoofs came out of the brush, and I came out and was in among men and horses weaving in and out and going upstream, and everybody was yelling, "Hurry! Hurry!" The soldiers were running upstream and we were all mixed there in the twilight and the great noise. I did not see much; but once I saw a Lakota charge a soldier who stayed behind and fought and was a very brave man. The Lakota took the soldier's horse by the bridle, but the soldier killed him with a six-shooter. I was small and could not crowd in to where the soldiers were, so I did not kill anybody. There were so many ahead of me, and it was all dark and mixed up.

Soon the soldiers were all crowded into the river, and many Lakotas too; and I was in the water awhile. Men and horses were all mixed up and fighting in the water, and it was like hail falling in the river. Then we were out of the river, and people were stripping dead soldiers and putting the clothes on themselves. There was a soldier on the ground and he was still kicking. A Lakota rode up and said to me: "Boy, get off and scalp him." I got off and started to do it. He had short hair and my knife was not very sharp. He ground his teeth. Then I shot him in the forehead and got his scalp.

Many of our warriors were following the soldiers up a hill on the other side of the river. Everybody else was turning back down stream, and on a hill away down yonder above the Santee camp there was a big dust, and our warriors whirling around in and out of it just like swallows, and many guns were going off.

I thought I would show my mother my scalp, so I rode over toward the hill where there was a crowd of women and children. On the way down there I saw a very pretty young woman among a band of warriors about to go up to the battle on the hill, and she was singing like this:

"Brothers, now your friends have come!
Be brave! Be brave!
Would you see me taken captive?"

When I rode through the Oglala camp I saw Rattling Hawk sitting up in his tepee with a gun in his hands, and he was all alone there singing a song of regret that went like this:

"Brothers, what are you doing that I can not do?"

When I got to the women on the hill they were all singing and making the tremolo to cheer the men fighting across the river in the dust on the hill. My mother gave a big tremolo just for me when she saw my first scalp.

I stayed there awhile with my mother and watched the big dust whirling on the hill across the river, and horses were coming out of it with empty saddles.

After I showed my mother my first scalp, I stayed with the women awhile and they were all singing and making the tremolo. We could not see much of the battle for the big dust, but we knew there would be no soldiers left. There were many other boys about my age and younger up there with their mothers and sisters, and they asked me to go over to the battle with them. So we got on our ponies and started. While we were riding down hill toward the river we saw gray horses with empty saddles stampeding toward the water. We rode over across the Greasy Grass to the mouth of a gulch that led up through the bluff to where the fighting was.

Before we got there, the Wasichus [white men] were all down, and most of them were dead, but some of them were still alive and kicking. Many other little boys had come up by this time, and we rode around shooting arrows in the Wasichus. There was one who was squirming around with arrows sticking in him, and I started to take his coat, but a man pushed me away and took the coat for himself. Then I saw something bright hanging on this soldier's belt, and I pulled it out. It was round and bright and yellow and very beautiful and I put it on me for a necklace. At first it ticked inside, and then it did not any more. I wore it around my neck a long time before I found out what it was and how to make it tick again.

Then the women all came over and we went to the top of the hill. Gray horses were lying dead there, and some of them were on top of dead Wasichus and dead Wasichus were on top of them. There were not many of our own dead there, because they had been picked up already; but many of our men were killed and wounded. They shot each other in the dust. I did not see Pahuska, and I think nobody knew which one he was. There was a soldier who was raising his arms and groaning. I shot an arrow into his forehead, and his arms and legs quivered. I saw some Lakotas holding another Lakota up. I went over there, and it was Chase-in-the-Morning's brother, who was called Black Wasichu. He had been shot through the right shoulder downward, and the bullet stopped in his left hip, because he was hanging onto the side of his horse when he was hit. They were trying to give him some medicine. He was my cousin, and his father and my father were so angry about this, that they went and butchered a Wasichu and cut him open. The Wasichu was fat, and his meat looked good to eat, but we did not eat any.

There was a little boy, younger than I was, who asked me to scalp a soldier for him. I did, and he ran to show the scalp to his mother. While we were there, most of the warriors chased the other soldiers back to the hill where they had their pack mules. After awhile I got tired looking around. I could smell nothing but blood, and I got sick of it. So I went back home with some others. I was not sorry at all. I was a happy boy. Those Wasichus had come to kill our mothers and fathers and us, and it was our country. When I was in the brush up there by the Hunkpapas, and the first soldiers were shooting, I knew this would happen. I thought that my people were relatives to the thunder beings of my vision, and that the soldiers were very foolish to do this.

General George Armstrong Custer

The Spoils of War,
June 26, 1876

Wooden Leg

When George Armstrong Custer led his Seventh Cavalry into the valley of the Little Bighorn, he found himself confronted by one of the largest hostile Indian villages ever seen on the Plains. Approximately sixteen hundred of these Indians were Cheyennes but they were dwarfed by a larger number of Sioux. A physician, and long-time resident of Montana, Thomas B. Marquis, became interested in the Battle of the Little Bighorn and sought out an Indian participant who could describe the view of the battle through Indian eyes. Marquis found an aging Cheyenne named Wooden Leg who provided him with an oral autobiography. Acting as his interpreter, Marquis wrote down the stories related to him by Wooden Leg and had them published in 1931 with the title, Wooden Leg: A Warrior Who Fought Custer. *The below story was extracted from that book.*

I slept late that next morning after the great battle. The sun had been up an hour before I awoke. I went to the willow lodge of my father and mother. When I had eaten the breakfast given to me by my mother I got myself ready again to risk death in an effort to kill other white men who had come to kill us. I combed and braided my hair. My braids . . . were full and long, reaching down my breast beyond the waist belt. I painted anew the black circle around my face and the red and yellow space enclosed within the circle. I was in doubt about which clothing to wear, but my father said the soldier clothing looked the best, even though the coat sleeves ended far above my wrists and the legs of the breeches left long bare spots between them and the tops of my moccasins. I put on my big white hat captured at the Rosebud fight. My sister Crooked Nose got my horse for me. Soon afterward I was on my way up and across the valley and on through the river to the hill where the first soldiers were staying [troops under the command of Major Marcus Reno].

I had both my rifle and six shooter. I still was without my medicine shield and my other medicine protectors that had been lost on Powder river. Most of the other Cheyennes and Sioux had theirs. The shields all were of specially shrunken and toughened buffalo skin covered with buckskin fringed and painted, each with his own choice of designs, for the medicine influence. I went with the other young men to the higher hills around the soldiers. I stayed at a distance from them and shot bullets from my new rifle. I did not shoot many times, as it appeared I was too far away, and I did not want to waste any of my cartridges. So I went down and hid in a gulch near the river.

Some soldiers came to get water from the river, just as our old men had said they likely would do. The white men crept down a deep gulch and then ran across an open space to the water. Each one had a bucket, and each would dip his bucket for water and run back into the gulch. I put myself, with others, where we could watch for these men. I shot at one of them just as he straightened up after having dipped his bucket into the water. He pitched forward into the edge of the river. He went wallowing along the stream, trying to swim, but having a hard time at it. I jumped out from my hiding place and ran toward him. Two Sioux warriors got ahead of me. One of them waded after the man and struck him with a rifle barrel. Finally he grabbed the man, hit him again, and then dragged him dead to the shore, quite a distance down the river. I kept after them, following down the east bank. Some other Sioux warriors came. I was the only Cheyenne there. The Sioux agreed that my bullet had been the first blow upon the white soldier, so they allowed me to choose whatever I might want of his belongings.

I searched into the man's pockets. In one I found a folding knife and a plug of chewing tobacco that was soaked and spoiled. In another pocket was a wad of the same kind of green paper taken from the soldiers the day before. It too was wet through. I threw it aside. In this same pocket were four white metal pieces of money. I knew they were of value in trading, but I did not know how much was their value. In later times I have learned they were four silver dollars. A young Cheyenne there said: "Give the money to me." I did not care for it, so I gave it to him. He thanked me and said: "I shall use it to buy for myself a gun." I do not remember now his name, but he was a son of One Horn. A Sioux picked up the wad of green paper I had thrown upon the ground. It was almost falling to pieces, but he began to spread out some of the wet sheets that still held together. Pretty soon he said:

"This is money. This is what white men use to buy things from the traders."

I had seen much other paper like it during the afternoon before. Wolf Medicine had offered to give me a handful of it. But I did not take it. I already had thrown away some of it I had found. But even after I was told it could be used for buying things from the traders, I did not want it. I was thinking then it would be a long time before I should see or care to see any white man trader.

I went riding over the ground where we had fought the first soldiers during the morning of the day before. I saw by the river, on the west side, a dead black man. He was a big man. All of his clothing was gone when I saw him, but he had not been scalped nor cut up like the white men had been. Some Sioux told me he belonged to their people but was with the soldiers.

As some of us were looking at the body of an Indian who had been with the soldiers, an old Sioux said:

"This is a Corn Indian [Arikara], not a Crow nor Shoshone."

He showed us the differences in appearance, especially the earrings and the hair dressing. The Crow men wore their hair cut off above the forehead and roached up. The Shoshones had almost the same way of placing this foretop. The Corn Indians kept their hair in braids, parted like that of the Sioux and Cheyennes, but the Corn Indian parting was not in the middle of the top, as ours was. I examined again the one I had helped in beating to death. I learned he also was a Corn Indian. I found yet a third one. We who had killed them were young men, and there was great excitement at the time, so we had not observed their tribal connection. We had supposed them to be the same Crows and Shoshones we had fought on the upper Rosebud creek a few days before. Now there began to be talk that maybe these soldiers were not the same ones we had fought there. Or, perhaps they had added the Corn Indians to their forces since that time. There were different opinions on the matter.

Some Sioux caught a mule that wandered out from the place where the soldiers were together on the hilltop. The animal was going down toward the river when the Indians got it. They tried to lead it toward their sheltered place behind a knoll, but it would not go. It appeared to be wanting a drink of water. One Sioux got behind it and whipped it, while a companion pulled at the leading strap. But the mule just stood there, would not move. On its back were packs of cartridges. The Sioux took these and let the mule go.

I went with other Cheyennes along the hills northward to the ground where we had killed all of the soldiers. Lots of women and boys were there. The boys were going about making coups by stabbing or shooting arrows into the dead men. Some of the bodies had many arrows sticking in them. Many hands and feet had been cut off, and the limbs and bodies and heads had many stabs and slashes. Some of this had been done by the warriors, during and immediately after the battle. More was added, though, by enraged and weeping women relatives of the Sioux and Cheyennes who had been killed. The women used sheathknives and hatchets.

A dog was following one of the Sioux women among the dead soldiers. I did not see any other dog there, neither on that day nor on the day before, when the fight was on. There were some Indian dogs tangling among the feet of the horses at the time of the fighting of the first soldiers, on the valley above the camps. But even here most of them were called away by the women and old people going to the western hilltops.

Three different soldiers, among all of the dead in both places of battle, attracted special notice from the Indians. The first was the man wearing the buckskin suit and who had the colored writing and pictures on his breast and arms. Another was the black man killed among the first soldiers on the valley. The third was one having gold among his teeth. We did not understand how this metal got there, nor why it was there.

Paper boxes of ammunition were in the leather bags carried on the saddles of the soldiers. Besides, in all of the belts taken from the dead men there were cartridges. Some belts had only a few left in them. In others the loops still contained many, and occasionally one almost full. I did not see nor hear of any belt entirely emptied of its cartridges.

All during that forenoon, as well as during the afternoon and night before, both in the camps and on the battle grounds, Indians were saying to each other: "I got some tobacco." "I got coffee." "I got two horses." "I got a soldier saddle." "I got a good gun." Some got things they did not understand.

One young Cheyenne took something from a dead soldier just after all of them had been killed. He was puzzled by it. Some other looked at it. I was with them. It was made of white metal and had glass on one side. On this side were marks of some kind. While the Cheyenne was looking at it he got it up toward his ear. Then he put it up close.

"It is alive!" he said.

Others put it to their ears and listened. I put it up to mine.

"Tick-tick-tick-tick-tick-tick," it was saying.

We talked about its use. We agreed generally it was that soldier's special medicine. Many Indians came and wondered about it. The young man decided to keep it for his own medicine.

When I was getting ready the next morning to go and fight again the soldiers staying on the hilltop, the Cheyenne young man had a crowd around him again examining his strange white man medicine. They were listening, but it made no sound. After different ones had studied it, he finally threw it away as far as he could throw it.

"It is not good medicine for me," he said. "It is dead."

I saw another soldier medicine thing something like this one, but the other one was larger and it did not make the ticking noise. It acted, though, like it was alive. When it was held with the glass side up a little arrow fluttered around. When it was held quiet for a while the arrow gradually stopped fluttering. Every time it stopped the point of the arrow was toward the north, down the valley. There was talk then of other soldiers coming from that direction, so it was decided this medicine object was useful for finding out at any time where might be soldiers. Little Shield had it when I saw it. He gave it to High Walking. Another Cheyenne got a pair of field glasses. We understood them. This was a big pair.

Cleaners for the rifles puzzled us a while. They were in joints and were carried in a long hole in the end of the wooden stock. Pretty soon we learned what was their use. I saw one rifle that had a shell of cartridge in its barrel. A Sioux had it. He could not put into the gun any other cartridge, so he threw it into the river.

Yellow Weasel, a Cheyenne, got a bugle. He tried to make a noise with it, but he could not. Others tried. Different ones puffed and blowed at it. But nobody could make it sound out. After a while we heard a bugle making a big noise somewhere among the Sioux. The Cheyennes said: "The Sioux got a good one. This one Yellow Weasel has is not good. He might as well throw it away." But he kept it, and it was not long until he was making it sound.

One Cheyenne got a flag. There were several others among the Sioux. I do not know just how many they got, but I believe I saw nine of them.

Bridle bits were thrown away, but the leather parts were kept. I got two sets of bridle reins, but no other parts of the bridles. A Cheyenne gave them to me. All of the soldier boots were taken from them. But they were not worn by the Indians. The bottoms were cut off and discarded. Only the tops were used. These made good leather pouches, or the leather was cut up to make something else. Old men were allowed to have all of the saddles. But only a few of the Cheyenne old men got them. I saw lots of Sioux old men riding around on soldier saddles, either on the soldier horses or the Indian horses. . . .

During the afternoon it was learned that yet another band of white men were coming up the Little Bighorn valley. All of the young men wanted to fight them. A council of chiefs was held. They decided we should continue in our same course—not fight any soldiers if we could get away without doing so. All of the Indians then got ready to move.

Late in the afternoon the procession of tribes was in movement. Again, as at all other times, the Cheyennes went ahead and the Uncpapas came last. Several parties of young men went aside to go across the river and shoot again among the soldiers camped on the high hill. A few stayed there until darkness came.

Reprinted from *Wooden Leg: A Warrior Who Fought Custer* courtesy of the University of Nebraska Press, Bison Book edition reprinted from the Midwest Company 1931 edition.

Little Big Horn Battlefield in 1901

The Murder of Wild Bill Hickok, August 2, 1876

Black Hills Pioneer

James Butler Hickok was born in Illinois in 1837. He left Illinois at age eighteen to begin his life in the West. Hickok served as a scout and as a sharpshooter in the Union Army during the Civil War. After the war, Hickok served as a guide for General William T. Sherman's tour of the West. In 1869 he was elected sheriff of Hays City, Kansas. Later, he was appointed marshal of Abilene, Kansas, where he tried to control the behavior of Texas cowboys. In 1871, the city council of Abilene decided it no longer needed Hickok's services and discharged him. Buffalo Bill Cody enticed Hickok to join his Wild West Show in 1873 and he toured with Cody for five months before returning to the West. Hickok went to Deadwood, South Dakota, in 1876 and it was there that a vagrant, Jack McCall, murdered Hickok while he played poker. His poker hand at the time of his death included a pair of aces and a pair of eights, which has since that time become known as a "dead man's hand." McCall was first tried by a miner's court in Deadwood and found not guilty. Later, he was tried by a court of the Dakota Territory, found guilty, and was hanged in 1877. The first newspaper report of Hickok's murder was published in the Black Hills Pioneer *on August 5, 1876.*

On Wednesday about 3 o'clock the report stated that J.B. Hickok (Wild Bill) was killed. On repairing to the hall of Nuttall and Mann, it was ascertained that the report was too true. We found the remains of Wild Bill lying on the floor. The murderer, Jack McCall, was captured after a lively chase by many of the citizens, and taken to a building at the lower end of the city, and a guard placed over him. As soon as this was accomplished, a coroner's jury was summoned, with C.H. Sheldon as foreman, who after hearing all the evidence, which was the effect that, while Wild Bill and others were at a table playing cards, Jack McCall walked in and around directly back of his victim, and when within three feet of him raised his revolver, and exclaiming, "damn you, take that," fired; the ball entering at the back of the head, and coming out at the centre of the right cheek causing instant death.

From: *Black Hills Pioneer.* "Assassination of Wild Bill . . . " (Black Hills, SD, August 5, 1876)

The Great Northfield Raid, September 7, 1876

Cole Younger

Eighteen seventy-six was a notable year in the Old West as that was the year that George Armstrong Custer met his comeuppance in the valley of the Little Big Horn, Wild Bill Hickok was shot dead at a poker table in Deadwood, South Dakota, and the James Gang found a hot reception during a bank-robbing adventure that turned sour in Northfield, Minnesota. The attempted robbery at Northfield was masterminded by Jesse James, the leader of the James Gang. Also participating in the raid was Jesse's brother, Frank James, and Cole Younger and his brothers, Bob and Jim, along with Charley Pitts, Clell Miller and Bill Chadwell, the latter who was a native Minnesotan and familiar with Northfield. When the fancy-dressed gang members rode into Northfield, they stood out among the mostly Swedish-descent farmers and immediately raised suspicions. After a town citizen raised the alarm of a bank robbery in progress, other citizens came pouring out onto the street with shotguns, rifles and pistols blazing. Although Jesse and Frank James eluded capture, the three Younger brothers were quickly captured in a neighboring town to Northfield. They were tried and convicted and sentenced to life imprisonment. Robert died in prison in 1889, but Cole and James were paroled in 1901. James committed suicide in 1902, but Cole returned to his native Missouri, where he lectured, traveled with a wild West show, and authored books on his life. In the following vignette, Cole Younger (1844–1916) relates the James Gang's raid on Northfield as he saw it. The story was extracted from his book, The Story of Cole Younger, *first published in 1903.*

While Pitts and I were waiting for Bob and Chadwell we scouted about, going to Madelia and as far as the eastern part of Cottonwood county, to familiarize ourselves with the country. Finally, a few days later, the boys joined us, having bought their horses at Mankato.

We then divided into two parties and started for Northfield by somewhat different routes. Monday night, Sept. 4, our party were at Le Sueur Center, and court being in session, we had to sleep on the floor. The hotel was full of lawyers, and they, with the judge and other court attendants, had a high old time that night. Tuesday night we were at Cordova, a little village in Le Sueur county, and Wednesday night in Millersburgh, eleven miles west of Northfield. Bob and his party were then at Cannon City, to the south of Northfield. We reunited Thursday morning, Sept. 7, a little outside of Northfield, west of the Cannon River.

We took a trip into town that forenoon, and I looked over the bank. We had dinner at various places and then returned to the camp. While we were planning the raid it was intended that I should be one of the party to go into the bank. I urged on the boys that whatever happened we should not shoot any one.

"What if they begin shooting at us?" some one suggested.

"Well," said Bob, "if Cap is so particular about the shooting, suppose we let him stay outside and take his chances."

So at the last minute our plans were changed, and when we started for town Bob, Pitts and Howard went in front, the plan being for them to await us in the square and enter the bank when the second detachment came up with them. Miller and I went second to stand guard at the bank, while the rest of the party were to wait at the bridge for the signal—a pistol shot—in the event they were needed. There were no saddle horses in evidence, and we calculated that we would have a considerable advantage. Wrecking the telegraph office as we left, we would get a good start, and by night would be safe beyond Shieldsville, and the next day could ride south across the Iowa line and be in comparative safety.

But between the time we broke camp and the time they reached the bridge the three who went ahead drank a quart of whisky, and there was the initial blunder at Northfield. I never knew Bob to drink before, and I did not know he was drinking that day till after it was all over.

When Miller and I crossed the bridge the three were on some dry goods boxes at the corner near the bank, and as soon as they saw us went right into the bank, instead of waiting for us to get there.

When we came up I told Miller to shut the bank door, which they had left open in their hurry. I dismounted in the street, pretending to tighten my saddle girth. J.S. Allen, whose hardware store was near, tried to go into the bank, but Miller ordered him away, and he ran around the corner, shouting:

"Get your guns, boys; they're robbing the bank."

Dr. H.M. Wheeler, who had been standing on the east side of Division street, near the Dampier house, shouted "Robbery! Robbery!" and I called to him to get inside, at the same time firing a pistol shot in the air as a signal to the three boys at the bridge that we had been discovered. Almost at this instant I heard a pistol shot in the bank. Chadwell, Woods and Jim rode up and joined us, shouting to people in the street to get inside, and firing their pistols to emphasize their commands. I do not believe they killed any one, however, I have always believed that the man Nicholas Gustafson, who was shot in the street, and who, it was said, did not go inside because he did not understand English, was hit by a glancing shot from Manning's or Wheeler's rifle. If any of our party shot him it must have been Woods.

A man named Elias Stacy, armed with a shot-gun, fired at Miller just as he was mounting his horse, filling Clell's face full of bird shot. Manning took a shot at Pitts' horse, killing it, which crippled us badly. Meantime the street was getting uncomfortably hot. Every time I saw any one with a bead on me I would drop off my horse and try to drive the shooter inside, but I could not see in every direction. I called to the boys in the bank to come out, for I could not imagine what was keeping them so long. With his second shot Manning wounded me in the thigh, and with his third he shot Chadwell through the heart. Bill fell from the saddle dead. Dr. Wheeler, who had gone upstairs in the hotel, shot Miller, and he lay dying in the street.

At last the boys who had been in the bank came out. Bob ran down the street toward Manning, who hurried into Lee & Hitchcock's store, hoping in that way to get a shot at Bob from behind. Bob, however, did not see Wheeler, who was upstairs in the hotel behind him, and Wheeler's third shot shattered Bob's right elbow as he stood beneath the stairs. Changing his pistol to his left hand, Bob ran out and mounted Miller's mare. Howard and Pitts had at last come out of the bank. Miller was lying in the street, but we thought him still alive. I told Pitts to put him up with me, and I would pack him out, but when we lifted him I saw he was dead, and I told Pitts to lay him down again. Pitts' horse had been killed, and I told him I would hold the crowd back while he got out on foot. I stayed there pointing my pistol at any one who showed his head until Pittts had gone perhaps 30 or 40 yards, and then, putting spurs to my horse, I galloped to where he was and took him up behind me.

"What kept you so long?" I asked Pitts.

Then he told me they had been drinking and had made a botch of it inside the bank. Instead of carrying out the plan originally formed, seizing the cashier at his window and getting to the safe without interruption, they leaped right over the counter and scared Heywood at the very start. As to the rest of the affair inside the bank I take the account of a Northfield narrator:

With a flourish of his revolver one of the robbers pointed to Joseph L. Heywood, head bookkeeper, who was acting as cashier in the absence of that official, and asked:

"Are you the cashier?"

"No," replied Heywood, and the same question was put to A.E. Bunker, teller, and Frank J. Wilcox, assistant bookkeeper, each of whom made the same reply.

"You are the cashier," said the robber, turning upon Heywood, who was sitting at the cashier's desk. "Open that safe—quick or I'll blow your head off."

Pitts then ran to the vault and stepped inside, whereupon Heywood followed him and tried to shut him in.

One of the robbers seized him and said:

"Open that safe now or you haven't but a minute to live."

"There's a time lock on," Heywood answered, "and it can't be opened now."

Howard drew a knife from his pocket and made a feint to cut Heywood's throat, as he lay on the floor where he had been thrown in the scuffle, and Pitts told me afterward that Howard fired a pistol near Heywood's head to scare him.

Bunker tried to get a pistol that lay near him, but Pitts saw his movement and beat him to it. It was found on Charley when he was killed, so much more evidence to identify us as the men who were in Northfield.

"Where's the money outside the safe?" Bob asked.

Bunker showed him a box of small change on the counter, and while Bob was putting the money in a grain sack Bunker took advantage of the opportunity to dash out of the rear window. The shutters were closed, and this caused Bunker an instant's delay that was almost fatal. Pitts chased him with a bullet. The first one missed him, but the second went through his right shoulder.

As the men left the bank Heywood clambered to his feet and Pitts, in his liquor, shot him through the head, inflicting the wound that killed him.

We had no time to wreck the telegraph office, and the alarm was soon sent throughout the country.

From: *The Story of Cole Younger* (Chicago, The Henneberry Press, 1903)

Cole Younger

Two Hundred Shots in Four Minutes, c. October 1876

N. A. Jennings

Philadelphia-born Napoleon Augustus Jennings (1856–1919) spent much of his youth at a private school in New Hampshire. But he longed for adventure and at age eighteen, Texas became his new home and service as a Texas Ranger became his new occupation. Upon the death of his father, Jennings returned to Pennsylvania. But, used to the open range of the West, Jennings again headed in that direction where he worked at a number of occupations including: cowboy, miner, and stage driver. With enough Western adventure under his belt, Jennings finally returned to Philadelphia and served out the remaining years of his life in the newspaper business. The following story was selected from Jennings' book, A Texas Ranger, first published in 1899.

It was raining the morning we left camp, twenty-five strong, and started by an old, unused trail up the Nueces River. All day long the rain poured down in torrents, wetting us to the skin. I remember how, after emptying the water out of my pistol holster two or three times, I cut the end of the holster off, so that it would not hold water.

When we camped that night it was hard work to start the camp-fires, for everything in the way of fuel was soaked. Our plan under such circumstances was to get a piece of dead wood and split it so as to get the dry core. This we cut up fine and so started a little blaze which had to be carefully nursed until, by gradually adding larger and larger pieces, enough of a fire was under way to receive wet sticks and dry them.

I lay in two or three inches of water that night, on the ground, and protected my face with my hat to keep the cold rain-drops from hitting it. My clothes and blankets were wringing wet, but so were those of every man in the party. The next day the rain continued as hard as ever, and so it was for the ten days we were on the march up the Nueces. There was not a minute that it cleared off. The river, which ordinarily was a small enough stream, was so swollen that it was three or four miles wide in places. Every night we lay in the rain and every morning we started out again to ride in it.

In any other country, the sick-list would doubtless have been a large one under such conditions, but the Rangers suffered no ill effects from the continuous drenching. Horace Rowe, who was inclined to be consumptive, improved wonderfully in health on the trip and gained in weight. The spirits of the men never lagged for a moment. . . .

All the way up the Nueces we took every man prisoner we met and made him fall in with us. By the time we reached Carrizo Springs we had over a score of these prisoners, but we effectually prevented the news of our advance upon Fisher's stronghold from becoming known, for it was his gang of desperadoes we were after.

On the night of October 1st, we reached a point near Fisher's house, and succeeded in capturing one Noley Key, a member of his gang. I know not what threats Armstrong used to Key, but he at the last willingly acted as our guide. He told Armstrong that Fisher and his men were away from home. We surrounded the settlement and closed in on it, only to find that Key told the truth and that no one was there but the women and children.

But Armstrong did not give up. He took Key aside and drew from him the information that a band of horse-thieves were in camp on the banks of Lake Espintosa, six or seven miles distant. Key told Armstrong that seven men were in the band, and that they had forty or fifty stolen horses which they were going to drive farther north in a few days.

Armstrong immediately divided his men, sending eighteen of the Rangers down to another desperado settlement and taking six with him to go to the lake. The six were Devin, Durham, Evans, Boyd, Parrott, and myself. Key acted as our guide and we started off. The rain had ceased during the afternoon and a full moon was riding high in the heavens.

We rode slowly for about an hour and then turned off into some woods, where we dismounted. Key pointed out the location of the thieves' camp and then was told to remain where he was, with Evans and Devine who were left in the woods in charge of the horses.

"Boys," said Armstrong to the four men who were left with him, "we are going to capture those thieves or kill them. The reason I did not bring more men along was because I was afraid these fellows wouldn't resist us if we were so many. Key tells me that they stood off the Sheriff and his posse a few nights ago, and so they'll be looking for officers and be prepared to fight. That's just what we want. If they will only fire at us, we can rush in on them and kill the last one of them. Nothing but that will break up this gang. I only hope they'll show fight. Now, come along and don't make any noise."

We advanced slowly and cautiously through the brush, and soon came to a wide, open space, near the lake. We looked across the open space and saw the camp-fire of the horse-thieves' camp, but could see no one stirring. Very cautiously, bending down and moving as swiftly as we could in that position, we approached the fire. We were within twenty-five yards of it, when suddenly a figure rose and a yell split the silence.

"Here they come, boys! Here they come!" shouted the man who had arisen. In an instant the seven men at the camp were up and the one who had shouted fired at us.

I heard Armstrong cry, "Damn you, you'll shoot at an officer, will you?" and then the firing grew furious on both sides. We rushed in on them and there was a continual blaze from the firearms.

Just in front of me was a man emptying his six-shooter at me and I raised my carbine and fired at him. The moment before I fired he had his mouth open, yelling curses at me; but with my shot he dropped like a dog. I thought I had killed him and turned my attention to the others, but, except for one man with whom Boyd was having a fierce hand-to-hand fight with knives, all were either dead or had jumped into the lake.

Over and over rolled Boyd and the desperado, but in the end Boyd jerked himself loose, his knife dripping with the thief's heart-blood.

The fight lasted not more than three or four minutes, but in that time fully two hundred shots were fired. We turned over the bodies of the dead men. They were all well-known desperadoes—John Martin, alias "One-eyed John;" "Jim" Roberts, and George Mullen. The man whom I shot was named McAlister. I was bending over and looking at his face, when I saw his eyes move.

"Hello!" I cried; "this man isn't dead."

McAlister looked straight at me and began to beg for his life.

"For God's sake, gentlemen, don't kill me," he begged piteously. "For God's sake don't kill me!"

"No one wants to kill you," I said. "We are not murderers. Would you like some water?"

He murmured that he would, and I took a tin cup from beside the camp-fire and went down to the lake and dipped it full of water. When I returned to him, I put it to his lips and he drank. He told me he was wounded in the leg and a part of his jaw was also shot away. I thought he would surely die, but we promised to send a wagon for him and made him as comfortable as we could before we left him. Then we returned to where we had left our horses with Devine and Evans.

As I was walking silently along in the woods with the rest of the boys, I heard suddenly, close in front of me, the sharp click of a gun being cocked, and the quick demand:

"Halt!"

I stopped so quickly that I nearly fell over backward. It was Devine who gave the command, and in a moment we told who we were. Evans stood close to Devine.

"Where's Noley Key?" asked Armstrong.

"Dead," said Devine.

"Dead?"

"Yes. When he heard the firing, he jumped up and started to run, and we fired at him. One of us killed him, for there's a bullet-hole in is back." We went over and looked at Key where he lay, face downward. I felt badly about him, for on the way to the camp he had been talking in a pleasant way to me and I had given him some tobacco. He was no great loss to the community, however, for he was a well-known horse-thief.

From: *A Texas Ranger* (New York: Charles Scriber's Sons, 1899)

A Walk before Breakfast, c. 1877

Joseph H. Pickett

Someone once said that "freedom and beauty dwell in the mountains." This certainly seems so when one sees the Rocky Mountains for the first time, especially the area around Silverton, Colorado. At that place it seems that Mother Nature pulled out all the stops. Natural beauty abounds. While always lovely, autumn is special. The locals call this time of the year, "Colorfest." It is then that, as if by magic, the lush green of the mountain sides is transformed into gold, red, bronze, and deep shades of purple. The aspen trees, located at the highest elevations, are the first to make the break from green as they put on their golden colors and when their leaves are caught in a breeze, they shimmer like the purest gold. The aspens are followed by the cottonwoods, located along the rivers and creeks. They, too, adorn themselves in gold. Ohio-born in 1832, Joseph H. Pickett loved the mountains of the West. He lived in Colorado as a missionary for the American Home Missionary Society after graduating from Yale College in 1858 and the Theological Seminary at Andover, Massachusetts. Pickett enjoyed nature walks in the mountains and forests. His vivid description of an early morning walk was extracted from his book, Memoirs of Joseph W. Pickett, *published in 1880.*

Come with me in my walk before breakfast up Anvil Mountain. Right back of the house, we are up a hundred feet. It was steep! Stop on this plateau. Look into what was once Baker's Park, now Silverton, at our feet; and on the other side, half a mile away, the Animas. Beyond rise abruptly the majestic mountains. A little way up is timber line, and then awful ruggedness, snow and rock. How the morning sun pours into this side-hill! Look at the aspens, —see their fresh leaves. In ten minutes, we can walk up to where they are just budding. See the delicate flowers, —here a little fern, and there a strawberry in full bloom; yes, a number of them among these rough rocks. Look at those chipmunks, such as we used to see in childhood in Ohio. How they play amid the rocks! A dozen are in plain sight. And the robins,—we thank God that they are here to make it so home-like. How sweetly they fill this sparkling air with melody! But up we go, and pause beneath the dark pine. Here we stop at this city, for the gamblers, for all; then, from these lofty heights, I pray for my field, for . . . our nation and the world, that Christ's kingdom may come. But the great heights still tower far above us, and we must go down.

From: *Memoirs of Joseph W. Pickett, Missionary Superintendent in Southern Iowa and in the Rocky Mountains for the American Home Missionary Society* (Boston: Congregational Publishing Society, 1880)

The Death of Crazy Horse, c. September 1877

Thomas American Horse

As a young warrior, Crazy Horse was recognized as a leader of his people, the Oglala Lakotas. He earned his reputation not only by his skill and daring in battle, but also by his fierce determination to preserve the Lakota way of life and by fighting white incursions onto Lakota land. Crazy Horse was the epitome of resistance to the whites, refusing to back up a single step from white encroachments. He helped defeat the U.S. Army at Fort Phil Kearney by destroying William J. Fetterman's brigade in 1867. Under his leadership, Crazy Horse turned back General George Crook when he tried to advance up the Rosebud Creek to join with George A. Custer at the Little Bighorn. Joining forces with Sitting Bull on June 25, 1876, Crazy Horse helped to flank Custer's Seventh Cavalry and thus, destroyed them to a man. Crazy Horse was starved into surrendering to the U.S. Army in May, 1877, when the decline of the buffalo population almost decimated his followers during the winter of 1876–77. Thomas American Horse was age ninety-six when he described the killing of Crazy Horse in the following story.

I will now tell here what I know about Chief Crazy Horse. From north where Crazy Horse was staying he was brought back by another Indian with the understanding that he is to meet some officials in Fort Robinson. As Crazy Horse and his companion Fast Thunder entered the military post Crazy Horse was taken into custody unknowingly by him. And as he was taken to the guardhouse, he noticed the bars on the door. One Indian companion called to his attention and said they are going to put you in prison so you must do something and he was walking with Fast Thunder, but he walked ahead a few steps and Fast Thunder's wife walking behind them. And when Crazy Horse heard what the other Indian said he attempted to break loose from the guards but another guard carried a rifle with a bayonet attached stabbed him in one kidney. And Crazy Horse said leave me alone, you have killed me. So as they let him loose he fell face down on the ground and died soon afterwards. And as he lie there Fast Thunder's wife took her blanket and covered him up. And soon after that American Horse went back to the camp and brought with him an Indian blanket and spread it on the ground and put the body on the blanket and wrapped him up. Of course, when Crazy Horse's father heard the sad news he went to the fort with a travois and demanded that he be permitted to take his son's body, which the request was granted. So he took the body away.

Reprinted from *To Kill an Eagle: Indian Views on the Last Days of Crazy Horse* edited by Edward Kadlecek and Mabell Kadlecek by permission of Johnson Books.

"I Will Fight No More Forever," October 5, 1877

Chief Joseph

Born in Oregon in 1840, Joseph was given the name Thunder-Rolling-Down-the-Mountain. His father was one of the first Nez Perce converted to Christianity and supported peace with whites. In 1855 a reservation was established for the Nez Perce, stretching from Oregon to Idaho. But after the discovery of gold in Nez Perce territory, the U.S. government took back some six million acres and told the tribe to remove itself to a much smaller reservation in Idaho. Angry young warriors staged a raid on a white settlement killing several whites. In reprisal, the United States Army pursued the fleeing Nez Perce. For over three months more than 2,000 U.S. soldiers fought numerous battles and skirmishes with the Nez Perce band that numbered about 700 with fewer than 200 of them considered warriors. Finally, Chief Joseph capitulated. The commander of the U.S. troops pursuing the Nez Perce, General Oliver Otis Howard, had appointed a young officer as his adjutant, Lt. Charles Erskine Scott Wood. On the late-afternoon of October 5, 1877, Lt. Wood recorded in his diary, "About an hour or so before sunset there came from the ravine below, up to the knoll on which we were standing, a picturesque and pathetic little group. Joseph was the only one mounted, and he sat, his rifle across his knees at each side of his horse talking earnestly. Slowly they mounted to where we stood at the top. General Howard and Colonel Miles were grouped together, and a little retired, myself, Lieutenant Howard, Lieutenant Long, and further back an orderly and Arthur Chapman, the interpreter. . . . When the Indians reached the summit those on foot stopped and went back a little, as if all was over. Then, nothing but silence. Joseph threw himself off his horse, draped his blanket about him, and carrying his rifle in the hollow of one arm, changed from the stooped attitude in which he had been listening, held himself very erect, and with a quiet pride, not exactly defiance, advanced toward

General Howard and held out his rifle in token of submission. General Howard smiled at him, but waved him over to Colonel Miles, who was standing beside him. Joseph quickly made a slight turn and offered the rifle to Miles, who took it. Then Joseph stepped back a little, and Arthur Chapman stepped forward so as to be between Joseph and the group of two—Howard and Miles. I was standing very close to Howard, with a pencil and a paper pad which I always carried at such times, ready for any dictation that might be given. Joseph again addressed himself to General Howard, as was natural." (From: Wood, Charles Erskine Scott. The Pursuit and Capture of Chief Joseph*). In 1904 Joseph died of what was characterized as a "broken heart."*

Tell General Howard I know his heart. What he told me before—I have it in my heart. I am tired of fighting. Too-hul-hul-sit is dead. Looking Glass is dead. He-who-led-the-young-men-in-battle is dead. The chiefs are all dead. It is the young men now who say 'yes' or 'no.' My little daughter has run away upon the prairie. I do not know where to find her—perhaps I shall find her too among the dead. It is cold and we have no fire; no blankets. Our little children are crying for food but we have none to give. Hear me, my chiefs. From where the sun now stands, Joseph will fight no more forever."

From: Howard, Oliver Otis. "Supplementary Report: Non-Treating Nez Perce Campaign," December 26, 1877, *In Report of the Secretary of War*, 1877)

Surrender of Chief Joseph of the Nez Perce

Geronimo Makes Demands,
c. Spring 1878

Tom Horn

Al Sieber was chief of scouts for the Sixth Cavalry and Tom Horn was his inter-
preter. At the time of the following event Sieber had been sent out of Fort Whip-
ple to track down the Apache band led by Geronimo and see if they could be
coaxed back onto the San Carlos Reservation in New Mexico. Twice before,
Geronimo had lived on the reservation but only for a short time. Now, the U.S.
Department Commander, General Wilcox, accused the renegade Apaches of "rob-
bing and raiding and killing" and although he considered the Sixth Cavalry one
of the best regiments in the U.S. Army, he felt like they were unable to track down
and corner Geronimo. The scouting force headed up by Sieber was tasked by
Wilcox to find Geronimo and reason him back onto the reservation. In 1904, Tom
Horn was hanged in Cheyenne, Wyoming, for the murder of a fourteen-year-old
boy. Horn maintained his innocence.

Certainly a grand-looking war chief he was that morning as he stood there talking to Sieber; six feet high and magnificently proportioned, and his motions as easy and graceful as a panther's. He had an intelligent-looking face, but when he turned and looked at a person, his eyes were so sharp and piercing that they seemed fairly to stick into him. Anyhow, that was how they looked to me; but I was a little shaky, anyhow.

"How are you, young man?" said he to me in Apache.

I told him I was all right. I might as well have told him I was a little shaky, for he knew it anyhow. He asked us to come over into the center of the circle, where we had the talk, and then he said to Sieber: "Who will interpret for you?" Sieber told him I would do it.

While Sieber could talk Apache very well and understand it very well, still he could not talk anyways near well enough to take in all that a man like Geronimo said. Geronimo then said to me: "I speak very fast, some-time. Can you undertake to interpret as fast as I talk?"

I told him he had but one mouth and tongue, that I could see, and for him to let loose. "Well spoken!" said he; and then he asked Sieber what he had come down there for, and Sieber said to hear what he (Geronimo) had to say. "I want to hear you talk," said Sieber.

Well, the big talk was on; and how that old renegade did talk! Of the wrongs done him by the agent, and by the soldiers, and by the White Mountain Apaches, and by the Mexicans and settlers, and he had more grievances than a railroad switchman, and he wanted to go back to live on the Reservation. He wanted to be allowed to have a couple of Mexicans to make mescal for him, and he wanted the government to give him new guns and all the ammunition he could use. He wanted calico for the women, and shoes for the children when there was snow on the ground, and any and everything he ever saw or heard of he wanted. Geronimo was the biggest chief, the best talker, and the biggest liar in the world, I guess, and no one knew this better than Sieber.

Geronimo must have talked an hour or two, and Sieber never said a word in reply. At last Geronimo stopped talking, for he had asked for everything he could think of, and he was a natural born genius at thinking of things.

Sieber sat perfectly still for some time, and then arose and looked around him, and it was sure a beautiful spot where we were camped, and Sieber looked around as though he was admiring the view and the camp.

"Tom, tell Geronimo just what I say, no more and no less," said he. "You have asked for everything that I know anything about," continued Sieber, "except to have these mountains moved up into the American country for you to live in, and I will give you till sundown to talk to your people and see if you don't want these mountains moved up there to live in. If you are entitled, by your former conduct, to what you have asked for, then you should have these mountains too." That was all. Sieber turned and walked out of the council.

Not an Indian stirred nor spoke for a long time, and then Geronimo arose and said: "Anybody's business that is in that man's hands will be handled as he says, or it won't be handled at all. We will meet here again at sundown."

Everybody then went his own way. I went back to our camp and Sieber was lying down on his back on his blankets looking up at the sky, and he did not move for a long time. At last he got up and said to me: "Tom, did you ever know of another such a man as Geronimo?" Of course I never did, and I told him so.

From: *Life of Tom Horn, Government Scout and Interpreter, Written by Himself: A Vindication* (Denver: Louthan Book Company, 1904)

Girl-Stealing, c. Summer 1878

James Willard Schultz

James Willard Schultz (1859–1947) lived in and wrote about the northwestern portion of Montana now included with the Blackfeet Reservation and Glacier National Park. In 1877, at the age of eighteen, he traveled from his birthplace in New York to the Montana Territory. He became interested in the Piegan Blackfeet tribe, and lived for many years among them as an accepted member of their nation. Soon after he married a Blackfoot woman, Nat-ah'-ki, and settled down to live the life of an Indian. Schultz was able to put his rich experiences into a career as an author. His most successful book was published in 1907 with the title, My Life as an Indian. *The following story was extracted from that book and describes the desperate attempt of a young Blackfoot to marry the girl of his dreams, but her father will have none of it. The story will likely have a familiar ring to it for many readers.*

Sorrel Horse's brother-in-law, Liś-sis-tsi (Woverine) and I became great friends, I soon learned to use the sign language, and he helped me in my studies of the Blackfoot language.

Part of that summer we passed at the foot of the Belt Mountains, and part on Warm Spring Creek and the Judith River. I joined in the buffalo runs, and on my swift and well-trained horse managed to kill my share of the animals. I hunted antelope, elk, deer, bighorn, and bear with Wolverine.

There were days when Wolverine went about with a long face and a preoccuped air, never speaking except to answer some question. One day in August when he was in this mood I asked him what was troubling him.

"There is nothing troubling me," he replied. Then after a long silence; "I lied; I am in great trouble. I love Piks-ah'-ki and she loves me, but I

308

cannot have her; her father will not give her to me. Her father is a Gros Ventre, but her mother is Piegan. Long ago my people protected the Gros Ventres, fought their battles, helped them to hold their country against all enemies. And then the two tribes quarreled, and for many years were at war with each other. This last winter they made peace. It was then I first saw Piks-ah'-ki. She is very beautiful; tall, long hair, eyes like an antelope, small hands and feet. I went much to her father's lodge, and we would look at each other when the others there were not noticing. One night I was standing by the doorway of the lodge when she came out for an armful of wood from the big pile lying there. I took hold of her and kissed her, and she put her arms around my neck and kissed me back. That is how I know she loves me. Do you think that she would have done that if she did not love me?"

"No, I do not think she would."

His face brightened as he continued: "At that time I had only twelve horses, but I sent them to her father with a message that I would marry his daughter. He sent the horses back and these words: "'My daughter shall not marry a poor man!'"

"I wen with a war party against the Crows and drove home eight head of their best horses. I traded for others until I had thirty-two in all. I sent a friend with them to the Gros Ventre camp to ask once more for this girl; he returned, driving back the horses. This is what her father said: 'My daughter shall never marry Wolverine, for the Piegans killed my son and my brother.' He looked at me hesitatingly two or three time and finally said: "The Gros Ventres are encamped on the Missouri, at the mouth of this little (Judith) river. I am going to steal the girl from her people, will you go with me?"

"Yes," I quickly replied. . . ."

We left camp at dusk, for it was not safe to ride over the plains in the daytime; too many war parties of various tribes were abroad, seeking glory and wealth in the scalps and chattels of unwary travelers. We rode out of the Judith valley eastward on to the plain, and when we were far enough out to avoid the deep coulées running into it, turned and paralleled the course of the river. Wolverine led a lively but gentle pony on which we had packed some bedding and a large bundle done up in a fine buffalo robe and bound with many a thong. These things he had taken out of camp the night before and hidden in the brush. There was a glorious full moon, and we were able to trot and lope along at a good pace. . . .

On Wolverine went, urging his horse and never looking back, and I kept close and said nothing, although I thought the pace too fast. When at last day began to break we found ourselves in a country of high pine-clad buttes and ridges, and two or three miles from the Judith valley. Wolverine stopped and looked around. . . .

We unsaddled in a grove of cottonwoods and willows and led our horses to water. On a wet sand bar where we came to the steam there were a number of human footprints so recently made that they seemed to be as fresh as our own tracks. . . .

"Crees, or men from across the mountains," said Wolverine, again examining the tracks. "No matter which; they are all our enemies."

"How could you know," I asked, "that those whose tracks we saw are not Crows, or Sioux, or other people of the plains?"

"The footprints were wide, rounding; even the prints of their toes could be seen; because they wore soft-bottom moccasins. Only these people use such footwear; all those of the plains here wear moccasins with hard parfleche soles."

"I will go around the inner edge of the grove and have a look at the country."

Presently Wolverine returned. "The war party passed through the grove," he said, "and went on down the valley. About two nights from now, they will be trying to steal the Gros Ventre horses."

[Wolverine] undid the buffalo robe bundle and spread out a number of articles; heavy red and blue cloth, enough for two dresses. The stuff was made in England and the traders sold it for about $10 a yard. Then there were strings of beads, brass rings, silk handerkerchiefs, Chinese vermilion, needles, thread, earrings—an assortment of things dear to the Indian women.

"For her," he said, laying them carefully aside. . . .

Up to this time Wolverine had made no definite plan to get the girl away. Sometimes he would say that he would steal into the camp and to her lodge at night, but that was certainly risky, for if he did succeed in getting to the lodge without being taken for an enemy come to steal horses he might awaken the wrong woman and then there would be a terrible outcry. On the other hand, if he boldly went into the camp on a friendly visit, no doubt old Bull's Head, the girl's father, would suspect his purpose and closely watch her.

"I knew that my medicine would not desert me," he suddenly said that afternoon. "We will ride boldy into camp, to the lodge of the great chief, Three Bears. I will say that our chief sent me to warn him of a war party working this way. I will say that we ourselves have seen their tracks along the bars of the river. Then the Gros Ventres will guard their horses; they will ambush the enemy; there will be a big fight, big excitement. All the men will rush to the fight, and that will be my time. I will call Piks-ah'-ki, we will ride out fast."

Again we rode hard all night, and at daylight came in sight of the wide dark gash in the great plain which marked the course of the Missiouri. We had crossed the Judith the evening before, and were now on a broad trail worn in deep furrows by the travois and lodge poles of many a camp of Piegans and Gros Ventres, traveling between the great river and the mountains to the south. The sun was not high when at last we came to the pine-clad rim of the valley and looked down into the wide, long bottom at the mouth of the Judith; there, gleaming against the dark foliage of a cottonwood grove, were the lodges of the Gros Ventres. . . .

We rode into the camp stared at by all as we passed along. The chief's lodge was pointed out to us. We dismounted at the doorway, a youth took charge of our horses and we entered. Three or four guests were enjoying an early feast and smoke. The chief motioned us to the seat of honor on his own couch at the back of the lodge. . . .

The pipe was passed and we smoked a few whiffs from it in our turn. A guest was telling a story, when he finished it the chief turned to us, and asked, in good Blackfoot, whence we had come. Nearly all the older Gros Ventres spoke Blackfoot fluently, but the Blackfoot never could speak Gros Ventre; it was too difficult for anyone not born and reared with them to learn.

"We come," Wolverine replied, "from up the Yellow (Judith) river, above the mouth of the Warm Spring. My chief, the Big Lake, gives you this"—producing and handing him a long coil of rope tobacco—"and asks you to smoke with him in friendship."

"Ah!" said Three Bears, smiling, and laying the tobacco to one side. "Big Lake is my good friend."

"My chief also sends word with me that you are to keep close watch of your horses, for some of our hunters have found signs of a war party traveling this way. We ourselves, this white man and I, we also have come across their trail. We saw it yesterday morning up the river. There are twenty, maybe thirty of them, and they are on foot. Perhaps tonight, surely by tomorrow night, they will raid your herd."

It was thought that the expected enemy would possibly arrive that night; so as soon as it was dark nearly all the men of the camp picked up their weapons and crept out through the sage brush to the foot of the hills, stringing out far above and below and back of their feeding herds. Wolverine and I had our horses up and saddled, and he told the chief that in case a fight began we would ride out and join his men. My comrade went out early in the evening, I sat up for an hour or more, and as he did not return, I lay down, covered myself with a blanket and was soon asleep, not waking until morning.

Wolverine was just getting up. After breakfast he told me that he had found a chance to whisper to Piks-ah'-ki the night before, when she had come outside for wood, and that she had agreed to go with him whenever the time came. He was in great spirits, and as we strolled along the shore of the river could not help breaking out in the war songs which the Blackfeet always sing when they are happy.

Along near noon, after we had returned to the lodge, among other visitors a tall, heavy, evil-featured man came in; by the nudge Wolverine gave me as he sat down opposite and scowled at us I knew that he was Bull's Head. He had a heavy growth of hair which he coiled on his head like a pyramid. He talked for some time with Three Bears and the other guests, and then, to my surprise, began to address them in Blackfoot, talking at us, and there was real and undisguised hatred in his tone.

"This story of an approaching war party," he said, "is all a lie. The Big Lake sends word that his people have seen their trail; now, I know that the Piegans are cowards; still, where there are so many of them they would be sure to follow such a trail and attack the enemy. No, they never saw any such trail, never sent any such word; but I believe an enemy has come, and is in our camp now, not after our herds but our women. Last night I was a fool. I went out and watched for horse stealers; I watched all night, but none came. Tonight I shall stay in my lodge and watch for women stealers, and my gun will be loaded. I advise you all to do the same."

And having had his say, he got up and strode out of the lodge, muttering, undoubtedly cursing all the Piegans, and one in particular. . . .

Again at dusk we saddled our horses and picketed them close to the lodge. . . . He told me that Piks-ah'-ki had been under guard of her father's Gros Ventre wives all day; the old man not trusting her Piegan mother to accompany her after wood and water for the lodge. I again went to sleep early, my companion going out as usual.

This time I was awakened by the firing of guns out on the flat, and a great commotion in camp, men shouting and running toward the scene of the fight, women calling and talking excitedly, children shrieking. I hurried out to where our horses were picketed, carrying my own rifle and Wolverine's. As soon as he had left the lodge Wolverine, who was lying nearby in the sage brush, ran to it and called his sweetheart's name. Out she came, followed by her mother, carrying several little bags. A minute later they came to where I stood, both women crying. Wolverine and I unfastened the horses.

"Hurry," he cried, "hurry."

He gently took the girl from where she was crying in the embrace of her mother and lifted her into the saddle, handing her the bridle reins.

"Listen," said the mother, "you will be good to her; I call the Sun to treat you as you do her."

"I love her, and I will be good to her," Wolverine answered, and then to us: "Follow me, hurry."

Away we went over the flat, straight for the trail upon which we had entered the valley, and straight toward the fight raging at the foot of the hill. We could hear the shots and shouts; see the flash of the guns. This was more than I had bargained for; I was sorry I had started out on this girl-stealing trip; I didn't want to charge in where the bullets of a fight that didn't interest me were flying. But Wolverine was leading, his sweetheart riding close behind him, and there was nothing for me to do but follow them. As we neared the scene my comrade began to shout: "Where is the enemy? Kill all the horse thieves. Where are they? Where do they hide?"

I saw his point. He didn't intend that the Gros Ventres should mistake us for some of the raiders.

The firing had ceased and the shouting; but we knew that there in the moonlit sage brush both parties were lying, the one trying to sneak away, the other trying, without too much risk, to get sight of them. We had put a hundred yards or more now between us and the foot of the hill, and I was thinking that we were past the danger point when, with a sputter of fire from the pan and a burst of flame from the muzzle, a flint-lock gun crashed right in front of Wolverine. Down went his horse and he with it. Our own animals suddenly stopped. The girl cried out: "They have killed him! Help, white man, they have killed him!"

But before we could dismount we saw Wolverine extricate himself from the fallen animal, spring to his feet and shoot at something concealed in the sage brush. We heard a deep groan, a rustling, and then Wolverine bounded to the place and struck something three or four hard blows with the barrel of his rifle. Stooping over, he picked up the gun which had been fired at him.

"I count a coup," he laughed, and running over to me and fastening the old fuke in the gun sling on the horn of my saddle, said, "Carry it until we get out of the valley."

I was about to tell him that I thought he was foolish to delay us for an old fuke, when right beside of us, old Bull's Head appeared, seeming to have sprung all at once out of the brush, and with a torrent of angry words he grasped the girl's horse by the bridle and attempted to drag her from the saddle. She shrieked and held on firmly, and then Wolverine sprang upon the old man, hurled him to the ground, wrenched his gun from him, and flung it far; then he leaped lightly up behind Piks-ah'-ki, dug his heels into the pony's flanks, and we were off once more, the irate father running after us and shouting for assistance to stop the runaways. We saw other Gros Ventres approaching, but they did not seem to be hurrying, nor did they attempt in any way to stop us. We went on as fast as we could up the steep, long hill.

We were four nights getting back to the Piegan camp, Wolverine riding part of the time behind me and part of the time behind the girl. We picked up, en route, the precious bundle which Wolverine had cached, and it was good to see the girl's delight when she opened it and saw what it contained. That day while we rested she made herself a dress from the red cloth, and I can truthfully say that when she had arrayed herself in it, and put on her beads and rings and earrings, she certainly looked fine. She was, as I afterward learned, as good as she was handsome. She made Wolverine a faithful and loving wife.

From: *My Life as an Indian* (New York: Doubleday, 1907)

Christmastime at Fort Dodge, December 24, 1878

Mary Leefe Laurence

The life of a child of a soldier of the Old West could have been a lonely life because mobility and being away from one's greater family was a way of life. But military parents tried their best to instill in their children the idea that a military post was, in itself, a large family. To many of these children their home was anywhere, their friends everywhere, and they grew up with the knowledge that home is where the heart is and where the family is, with no dependence on the dwelling or its location. Mary Leefe's father, John George Leefe, was born in England and immigrated to New York as a toddler. He joined the Union Army during the Civil War and thus, began his army career which was to span until 1901. Mary Leefe (1872–1945) accompanied her family from one military post to another from 1874 through 1898. She married her cousin, Frederick Sturgis Laurence, in 1911, at age 39. When she was in her seventies, Mary wrote her memoirs which focused on her life from age six to twenty-six and titled, Daughter of the Regiment, Memoirs of a Childhood in the Frontier Army, 1878–1898. *The following story of her memories of a Christmas Eve at Fort Dodge, Kansas, was excerpted from that book.*

The inner life of a post is something the public never sees. It sees, from the outside, post police details forcibly herding back men who "have had too much" in some red-light district, or some man carried, kicking, to the guardhouse, or groups of prisoners under armed guard cutting grass and cleaning up roads. From this they may conclude that living among such men cannot be pleasant. But we who dwelt among them knew the gold in human character to be found among them under human failings and, with this outlook, could dwell among them happily.

Especially at Christmastime was this family feeling evident, thrown together as we were, alone, in that far-off plains post. Christmas was the
outstanding event of the year. In our family it was, first and foremost, the
birthday of our Lord, Jesus Christ.

Weeks before the event our household was in a great state of excitement. Mysterious packages coming from a distance were stored away in
a closet by Grandma Pinckney and Daddy went about the house with a
smile and a subtle twinkle in his eye. When the great night arrived we
were all grouped about the piano to sing the old sweet chorals, ending
with "Silent Night," a reverent hush following. The entire house was lit
up with candles in every window. Excitement knew no bounds when the
hour arrived for the garrison Christmas tree party in the administration
building. This was an occasion when the entire garrison, excepting officers and men on guard or other outside duty, gathered with the members
of their families in the large hall where the tree had been erected.

The preliminaries to be gone through in our case whetted impatient anticipation. The boys were washed "behind the ears" and told to sit down
with a book to keep them off the floor. My sister dressed in all white with
a blue sash having a big bow in the back. I too was in white, but with pink
ribbons and sash. My father wore a tight fitting uniform and a pair of
black boots we had never seen before and which later came to be detected
on Santa Claus. The two boys were in black velvet suits and white collars.

Our parlor had tambour lace curtains, wine-colored velvet drapes, a
rug to match, and the white mantel with a vase or two on it, and, of
course, the piano. So would our Christmas Eve begin. Then, for safety, the
candles in the windows were extinguished and we all repaired to the administration building. The great tree, brilliantly lit with real candles and
carefully watched by two enlisted men, stood upon the stage at one end.
It seemed to our young eyes at least fifteen feet tall. The hall was painted
white and lit by many kerosene lamps on brackets and central fixtures. It
was festooned with garlands of evergreen and filled with the odor of
burning wax candles. An orchestra of enlisted men furnished the music
for dancing which was to follow the distribution of gifts. These were
grouped about the tree and along the walls of the stage. There were dolls,
Noah's arks, animals, and every conceivable kind of toy for the kids,
brought from afar on orders placed weeks before. But many of the toys
were made by women of the fort such as dolls in complete costume, even
to coats and hats. They had been made from dainty bits in the clothing of
officers' and soldiers' wives. . . .

What excitement when Santa Claus came in from a side door on the
stage to distribute the gifts! I was so overcome with awe that I ran and hid
behind the big bass viol. One of the musicians bid me not to be afraid and
go up and get my gifts. I edged timidly up to Santa Claus. There was

something funny about his eyes, they looked just like my daddy's. I was no longer afraid.

When the presents had all been distributed and Santa had retired, chorals were sung and the floor cleared for dancing. I ran to my mother with my presents and looked round for my daddy. He was nowhere to be seen, but shortly came out the side door through which Santa had disappeared. The children sat along the walls and watched the dancing begun by their elders. First, the commanding officer and his lady, then the other officers present, in order of rank, with their partners, followed by the non-commissioned officers in the same order down to and including the many private soldiers present, till the floor was filled. The children had their chance in an interlude, during which they were also treated to refreshments—popcorn, cake, and ice cream.

We were bundled up to be taken home. Those among the elders who had no children and who so desired remained to pursue the dancing to a later hour. Outside all was still and the stars shone as they only can on a clear winter night on the plains. Someone struck up "Silent Night" and the various groups diverging on the paths leading to the officers' and married soldiers' quarters joined in, filling the stillness of the night with this sweet melody.

Enforcement of Civil Rights Laws, c. 1879

Baylis John Fletcher

By signing the Emancipation Proclamation during the Civil War, President Lincoln freed American slaves. It was Congressional legislation, however, that specified those privileges, immunities, and protections to all persons in the United States. After the conclusion of the Civil War, Congress passed The Civil Rights Act of 1866 which gave all Americans "the same right . . . for the security of their persons and property as is enjoyed by white citizens." Soon thereafter, the Congress passed The Civil Rights Act of 1870 which provided that "All citizens of the United States shall have the same right, in every State and Territory, as is enjoyed by white citizens." And, the Congress further enacted The Civil Rights Act of 1871 which provided that "Every person . . . of any State or Territory, subjects, or causes to be subjected to the deprivation of any rights, privileges . . . by the Constitution and laws, shall be liable . . . in an action at law." Thus, while Baylis John Fletcher (1859–1912) witnessed his employer assault a black man, he learned that such an action was against the law and that the lawmen of Cheyenne, Wyoming Territory, fulfilled their duty to uphold said laws. He also learned that Texas cowboys and their employers were not exempt from the liability imposed by the Civil Rights legislation.

Cheyenne was a frontier town of perhaps 15,000 people. The capital of Wyoming Territory, it had two railroads, one leading south to Denver and the Union Pacific running east and west from Ogden, Utah, to Omaha, Nebraska. After five months of rough life on the trail, we Texas cowboys, deprived as we had been of all the conveniences and comforts of civilization, were a picturesque squad as we rode into Cheyenne. Our neglected and dilapidated clothes were worn and patched, our hair was uncut, and our faces unshaven. We presented no particularly novel sight to the natives, however, as they were accustomed to the arrival of travel-worn cowboys.

At Cheyenne we delivered the oxen to some freighters who were running a trail of wagons from Cheyenne to Deadwood, Dakota, and other remote places. The wagonmaster who received the oxen took them at once to a blacksmith shop to be shod. To see shoes put on oxen was a novel sight to us Texans. First each animal was hogged down and two plates of steel were nailed to each foot. Then each toe of the animal had to have a separate plate or shoe.

We had not drawn anything on our wages during the entire trip. After we reached the city, we went to a bank where Mr. Arnett procured the cash to pay us off. Now we must buy clothes and assume the appearance of civilians. Almost the first man I met in the street was Landrum Poole, a neighbor from Liberty Hill. Landy, as he was called, had preceded us with another herd, and, having been several days in Cheyenne, he knew where to get just what we wanted in clothing. Under his guidance we bought complete outfits. We next repaired to barber shops, where we were trimmed before cleaning up and donning our new clothes. After undergoing such changes that we did not recognize one another, we again appeared on the street. Our next task was to find a place to stay.

A number of us went with Mr. Arnett to the Metropolitan Hotel. Our abode at that hostelry was short-lived, however. The next morning at breakfast a big Negro came in the dining room and took the chair next to Mr. Arnett as he sat at breakfast. It had been only fourteen years since the close of the Civil War, and race prejudice was still strong. Mr. Arnett, unfortunately, did not take time to protest. He merely arose and smashed his chair over the head of the Negro. The latter uttered a great outcry, which soon brought a policeman. He arrested Mr. Arnett and took him off to court, where he was heavily fined for the assault. The proprietor told us that he was unable to discriminate against Negro guests, as the Civil Rights bill had recently been enacted by Congress and the Territory of Wyoming was directly under federal control.

Reprinted from *Up the Trail in '79* edited by Wayne Gard by permission of the University of Oklahoma Press.

A Navaho Grandmother's Medicine, c. 1879

Left Handed

As a research fellow, Walter Dyk traveled to a Navaho reservation in the South-west to gather information on a study he was doing on clans and kinships in Navaho society. Although he learned much about Navaho spiritualism and other valuable anecdotes of the dramatic events in the lives of the Navaho, he felt that he was missing important information about their day-to-day existence. Then he met Left Handed and asked him to relate the events that shaped his life and to not leave out what may seem trivial. Left Handed did not know English and Dyk was not versed in the Navaho tongue, so Left Handed's stories were told through an interpreter with Dyk writing them down. The resulting stories were published by Dyk in 1938 with the title, Son of Old Man Hat.

There were two horses just as tame as they could be. I got one and put the rope around his neck and tied it around his jaw. Then I led him into a little arroyo and got on. I thought I'd chase the other one back to the boy, so we could both ride. I got a little way chasing that horse when, all at once, he kicked up and struck me right on the knee. As soon as he struck me I fell to the ground, and the horse I was riding walked away. I was crawling around, crying, and it was getting worse and worse every minute, hurting me so badly. Soon I couldn't move any more. I just lay there crying for a long time. After a while I crawled over to a stick that was lying close beside me and raised myself up. I had a hard time. The horse was walking around eating grass, and I went over where he was and led him into the arroyo again and got on him. It took me a long time. Then I started back to where the boy was herding. I said to him, "The horse kicked me. I can't walk, and it's hurting me so badly I've got to go back home."

When I got home and told my grandmother the horse had kicked me she got mad. That's the way she used to be, always getting mad over any little thing. "Why do you want to get after the horses? You know very well they'll kick, even though they're tame. There's nothing wrong with you. Get off that horse. I don't see that there's anything wrong with you. Get off the horse, I tell you." I said, "I can't move, grandmother, it hurts me so." She got up and said, "What's the matter with you? I don't see anything wrong with you." She came up to me and stood right by the horse and said, "Put your other leg over the horse towards me and put your arm around my shoulders." I put my leg over the horse and grabbed her about the neck, and as I got down off the horse I hit her again with that same knee. It sure hurt.

She let me down on the ground close to the hogan, and my leg got stiff, as it got cold, I guess. It hurt awfully. I couldn't stand on it. I began crawling to the hogan, and I was crying because it hurt me so. She was running around, talking to herself. I don't know what she was talking about, and there I was, suffering and sitting against the hogan. She gathered some wood and built a fire and put in some rocks, and then she went off up on the cliff. She was gone quite a while.

When she returned she had a great many different weeds. She said, "These are all medicine, different kinds of medicine." She dug a small hole, the rocks were good and hot, and she put them in and covered the hole with all these weeds. She chewed up some and spit that all around my knee. Then she said, "Put your leg over the hole, right on top of the weeds." I lay there, with my leg over the weeds, and she covered me with a blanket. Soon I felt the heat, and it was fine. After a while she said, "Lay your leg the other way." So I rolled over. Both sides of my leg were pretty well cooked. When it cooled down she took the blanket off me, and the pain was gone. But my leg was stiff. I couldn't move it, and it was swollen. It hurt a little bit, but there was no feeling to it. When I touched it it felt like nothing, as though it were dead.

I lay in bed all day. Every now and then, she asked me "How are you feeling?" and I'd reply, "I'm feeling all right." At times I never answered her. I hated her because she kept on talking to me. Then she'd get mad at me every once in a while. "I know you did it on purpose, because you don't want to herd. You don't want to do anything, you just want to lie in bed. That's why you let the horse kick you. I know you're glad to be doing nothing. I know you're glad to be lying in bed, and I bet that's not hurting at all." I was mad at her, but I could not say anything.

The next day I never said a word to her. I was mad because she'd spoken roughly to me. When she talked to me in the morning I just didn't answer her. After a while she began to speak to me in the kindest way. She said, "How are you, my little boy? I'm sorry you're suffering. I'd better do something more for you now." She built a fire and put in five rocks. The first time she put in three. Then she went out and brought in more weeds. "This time," she said, "I got some medicine to put on your knee. That's red-medicine." She had a bunch of it with roots and leaves. She pounded that up with a rock until it was just like adobe. Then she plastered my knee with it and bound it up with a rag. She dug another hole, a bigger one this time, and put in the five rocks and covered it with weeds. She said, "Lie on your belly." I laid my leg over the weeds, and she put something under my foot. It hurt as I lay there on my belly with my leg over the weeds, and I was crying. When the heat struck my knee it sure hurt. I couldn't stand it any longer. Still I just lay there, and all at once there was no feeling left. I quieted down then and lay for a long time. I began to like it. My leg felt fine as long as I held it over the hot rocks.

After a while she took off the cover, and I was all sweat. She took the rag off my knee and took away the medicine, and the swelling was gone. It was down, and the skin around my knee was all soaked up. She said, "Lie on your back this time." She poured some medicine down into the hole on to the hot rocks, and the steam felt fine. She covered my leg, and I lay there again for quite a while. When she took the covers off I rolled to my bed, and there she washed my knee with medicine, and after that she put some more all over it. This time she wrapped it up as tightly as she could. That felt fine too. She put a rag around it and then there was no more feeling to it.

Late in the afternoon she asked me, "How are you feeling?" I said, "I don't feel any pain. It hurts a little, but the pain is gone." She said, "Try to stand on it. Try to walk on it." She handed me a stick—she'd made me a cane—and I stood up. I walked a little way towards the door and back to me bed, and it felt all right. It hurt a little, but the pain was gone.

Night Tranquility at Fort Elliott, c. 1879

Henry O. Flipper

Fort Elliott was a U.S. Army outpost in the eastern Texas Panhandle from 1875 to 1890. Troopers from Fort Elliott patrolled the borders of Indian Territory to the east, policed cattle drives headed north to Kansas railroad depots, and in other ways protected and encouraged settlement of the region. The author of the story of a peaceful night at Fort Elliott, Henry O. Flipper (1856–1940), was born into a Georgia slave family. He learned to read at age eight with the help of a literate slave as his teacher and found that education could be an equalizing tool in a white-dominated society. Flipper continued his education with a zeal and in 1877, became the first African-American to graduate from West Point. He was assigned to posts in Texas and Oklahoma. Soon after being assigned as the Commissary Officer in Fort Davis in west Texas, Flipper was court-martialed for embezzlement and for making a false statement to his Commanding Officer. He was acquitted of the first charge but convicted of the second. Throughout the affair, Flipper maintained his innocence, but was dismissed from the service. Afterwards, Flipper became a surveyor and engineer and acted as a field representative of American petroleum companies in Latin America. Flipper and his supporters always maintained that his military dismissal was caused by racial animosity. In 1976, nearly a century after his dismissal, the army cleared Flipper's name and issued an honorable discharge certificate to his descendants. The following description of a tranquil Texas night was excerpted from Flipper's book, Black Frontiersman: The Memoirs of Henry O. Flipper.

I had a most peculiar experience one night at Elliott. I was Officer of the Day and, as I had to inspect the guard at least once between midnight and day light, I retired early. Early in the night I was awakened by what I thought, what I knew, was the fire call which the bugler was sounding. Wide awake, I jumped out of bed, dressed rapidly, buckled on my saber and rushed out on the front porch. There I stopped awe-struck. It was the most beautiful moonlight night I ever saw any where. There wasn't a light any where, not a person astir, not a sound any where. If a pin had dropped out in the grass on the parade ground, I would have heard it. I was impressed with the profound calmness, tranquility, beauty, and peacefulness of the night. I stood there many moments and enjoyed it. Of course, the fire call had not sounded. Probably dreaming, my subconscious mind took in the notes of taps, the call to extinguish lights, sounded every night in military garrisons. I had gone to bed before the time for taps and when it sounded was doubtless dreaming and confounded the two calls. Taps and fire call are very much alike. I surely enjoyed the impression made on me, in which the dominant feature was Peace.

Reprinted from *Black Frontiersman: The Memoirs of Henry O. Flipper* edited by Theodore D. Harris by permission of Texas Christian University Press.

2d Lieutenant Henry O. Flipper, c. 1878

"Burro Punching" in the San Juans, c. 1879

George M. Darley

Captain Charles Baker was the first miner to lead a party into the San Juan Mountains, near present-day Silverton, Colorado, in 1860. After finding a considerable deposit of silver, in 1861 a party of 300 miners came into the area. The coming of the Civil War put the claims on hold until war's end. In 1868, the Ute Indians signed a treaty opening the San Luis Valley to settlement and created new interest in the San Juan region's mineral resources. Prospectors made their way back into the Silverton area. A flood of miners entered the area and in 1873 alone, between 1,000 and 1,500 claims were staked. By 1875 more than 100 buildings had been constructed. The importance of "burros" (small donkeys) was indicated in the May 6, 1876 issue of the La Plata Miner *which gave the following report: "Last Tuesday afternoon our little community was thrown into a state of intense excitement by the arrival of jacks (donkeys), as they came into sight about a mile about town . . . It was a glad sight, after six long weary winter months of imprisonment to see the harbingers of better days, to see these messengers of trade and business, showing that once more the road was open to the outside world." Darley, the author of the following vignette, was a preacher who published his memoirs in 1899 under the title,* Pioneering in the San Juan.

Burro punching . . . means to walk behind a pack train punching the patient, sure-footed and valuable, although greatly abused little animal.

Often have I walked behind a burro when going to preach the Gospel in the "regions beyond." The term "burro-puncher" became so common during the early days of the "Great San Juan Excitement" that all who had anything to do with the little animal were called "burro-punchers." Some who are not counted among the "leading lights" in Colorado were glad to have a burro carry their "grub" and blankets when first they went into the San Juans. This was a safe way of traveling, considering the roughness of the trails. . . .

As a personal and particular friend of the faithful beast that has done so much to help develop Colorado, I regret that many believe the burro has cultivated the swearer as much as he has the state. Those who abuse the burro and swear at him like a pirate, curse everything; not because they are provoked, but because they are habitual swearers. When men have excused themselves for cursing on the ground that the burro is a "stubborn animal," I have answered: "Treat you as a burro is treated and you will become as stubborn as he."

The general belief among packers seems to be that a burro has no feelings, knows neither job nor pain and expects to be mistreated. Burros suffer terribly, and if men are to be punished for cruelty to animals (I sincerely hope they may be), some men will discover that none of God's creatures can be tortured and the culprit go free. "A righteous man regardeth the life of his beast," but the average "burro-puncher" seems to think that burros never die. They "just dry up and blow away." I admit they are hard to kill. A "baby burro" fell from the top of a cliff sixty feet in height, into the Gunnison River, and was not injured. On Bear Creek Trail, about five miles above Ouray, one packed with flour fell two hundred feet; the weight of the flour turned the burro heels up, and, striking in the snow, his life was saved. Yet the animal can be killed and it sometimes dies a natural death. While crossing deep streams, unless their ears are tied, they will drown; but by tying them up they can be pulled across without danger.

After a rope is tied to the burro's neck he is pushed into the stream. The men on the opposite bank begin pulling and, although the burro may go under repeatedly, he is landed all right. As soon as his ears are untied his voice is loosened and breaks forth in trumpet tones of rejoicing, loud enough to be heard far and near.

Those who are unacquainted with the trails in new mining-regions, and the way men travel through mining-regions, and the way men travel through Indian countries where there are no houses, bridges or wagon roads, have no idea of the difficulties that must be faced. In the winter of '79 a man brought a burro from Mineral Point, at the head of the Uncompahgre River, over Engineer Mountain, to the head of Henson Creek, on snow-shoes. He made the shoes of sole leather and taught the burro to use them. It was slow work, yet he succeeded in getting his "jack" across the range. This may sound "fishy," but it is true. Where a burro and a "burro-puncher" cannot go, no other creature need try.

From: *Pioneering in the San Juan: Personal Reminiscences of Work Done in Southwestern Colorado During the "Great San Juan Excitement"* (Chicago: Fleming H. Revell Company, Publishers, 1899)

Racing with Silvertips, c. 1880

James A. McKenna

The first edition of James A. McKenna's Black Range Tales *was published in 1936 as a Rio Grande Classic. According to a friend of McKenna's, he was born in Pennsylvania in 1851. He died in 1941 at the age of ninety. McKenna took a job on a steamboat running between Pittsburgh and St. Louis. In St. Louis he got work on the steamboat, Far West, that ferried supplies to army outposts on the Missouri River. McKenna got off at Kansas City and joined up with a wagon train heading toward Colorado and New Mexico. Eventually, he found himself in south central New Mexico in the area known as the "Black Range." When he became elderly, McKenna took sick and was taken to a Deming, New Mexico, sanatorium run by the Sisters of the Holy Cross. In the sanatorium, a Sister Foley listened to McKenna's stories and typed them up for him. The first edition of* Black Range Tales *was published soon after.*

At the head of the Mancos River in Colorado, where our luck at prospecting had dropped to the zero mark, Jim Wetherall and myself took a contract to furnish hay to Fort Lewis, a post on the La Platte River. The immense mesa where we cut this hay lay between Bear Mountain and Chicken Creek. For several weeks we were busy cutting and stacking the hay, but at last the job was done. We loaded the mules with mowers and hay rakes and sent them down to the settlement. Wetherall and myself stayed a day or two longer to measure the hay and hide a few tools we forgot to pack on the mules.

McGrew's dairy farm, the nearest ranch, was about fifteen miles across the mesa, on Chicken Creek. McGrew sold most of his dairy products in Silverton and Rico at a fine profit, sometimes getting over a dollar a pound for butter. To protect his milk cows from grizzlies, he had built extra strong corrals of rock. He also kept some fine shepherd dogs which were not afraid to drive off prowling bears. One of the dogs would run forward and nip the bear's feet, and when he snapped back, a second dog would nip his nose, and so between them the dogs worried the bears until they trotted off in disgust. In time the silvertips gave up hunting beef in the vicinity of McGrew's corrals.

When our work was done we headed for the ranch, where we expected to rest up for a few days. It was about four in the afternoon when we struck the trail. We had not gone far when the sun dropped behind Bear Mountain. In the thick dusk we plodded on, wishing that we had our guns along, for the bears had been bad that summer, and several men had been killed in that section. Our object was to get out of the meadows as soon as we could, for we felt there was less danger in the willow brakes along the river, but we were still in the open when the full moon rose in the east, whitening the meadow like snow.

We had not gone more than five miles when we both got the hunch we were being followed. At the next rise we looked back. No wonder we felt uneasy! About three hundred yards to our rear an immense grizzly was lumbering along the trail. We were in for it and we knew it. Away we went without stopping till we reached the next rise. We now sighted a second grizzly loping along about a hundred yards behind the first, which had gained quite a little in this strange race. Knowing that a sudden run would quickly wear us out and bring on the bears with a rush, we kept the same pace. Before heading into the willow brakes at Chicken Creek we halted once more to take stock of our enemy. Four grizzlies were now in plain sight standing out in the moon light on rises in the meadow.

The first one was within a hundred and fifty yards of us, just half as far from us as when we first sighted him. And we had virtually three more miles to cover before getting to McGrew's ranch! We began to shout, hoping that our cries for help would carry to the ears of the shepherd dogs. This roused the bears to a faster gait. At every turn or rise we took note that they had gained a few more yards.

About a mile from the ranch we heard the dogs barking, and they soon dashed by looking for the bears. The silvertips slowed up for a spell and then came on faster than ever, as if they had come to the conclusion not to give p. I still have it in mind that those silvertips knew we had no guns. But the dogs were giving them a song and a dance, to judge by the uproar, and we made a final spurt to reach the corrals.

By this time we had stumbled out of the brakes on to the mesa where the ranch lay. The bears roared, the dogs yelped, and we yelled, and McGrew told us afterwards, it sounded as if all hell had broken loose in the valley. The dogs could only head off one bear at a time, and the second bear soon passed the first. McGrew stood in the corral gate with his gun raised. With the nearest bear not more than twenty-five feet away we rushed through the gate, and McGrew slammed it shut just in the nick of time. Once inside the gate Jim and myself fell in a heap, too fagged out to move. McGrew fired towards the bears, being careful not to hit any of them, as he was afraid they would tear down his corrals if they got stirred up by wounds. The dogs kept after the silvertips till they finally shambled off, the losers in the most exciting race I ever took part in.

Reprinted from *Black Range Tales* by permission of the Rio Grande Press, Inc., copyright © 1936.

An "Almost Hung" Cowboy Is Jittery, c. Summer 1880

Ed Lemmon

Born in Bountiful, Utah, in 1857, Lemmon was raised at Liberty Farm Station on the Little Blue, near to present-day Hastings, Nebraska. In his years on the American Great Plains, Lemmon was a cowhand, trail rider, wagon boss and a ranch manager. He managed the largest fenced pasture in the world, comprising an area larger than the State of Rhode Island and having more than a million cattle on the spread. In 1946 Lemmon died in the town in South Dakota that carries his name. His reminiscences were published in 1969 with the title, Boss Cowman: The Recollections of Ed Lemmon 1857–1946.

When the roundup was working up the Niobrara, near the town of Cody, Nebraska, a man rode up on a very tall sorrel horse. The horse was branded U.S.I.C., meaning "inspected and condemned by the U.S. government." The fellow was riding an old U.S. McClellan saddle, and across the front of it he carried an old army Sharps rifle. He also had a Colt's six-shooter and a beltful of cartridges, mixed for use in both guns. He was wearing a slouch hat that had gone to seed, with a long lock of his hair sticking out of a hole in its crown. He had about a four-months' growth of hair and beard on his head and face, and a wild, hunted look in his eyes. He bore no resemblance to a cowboy, and we wondered if he was a detective in disguise, looking for some of the outlaws and absconders that worked with roundups.

When the fellow asked for the Seth Mabry outfit, we pointed out Johnson, the manager of Mabry's crew, and he rode up and said, "Crawford, don't you know me?"

The manager said, "No, and I don't think I want to." That set the man laughing. Then he went ahead and told Johnson (whose right name was Crawford) a story about some boyhood prank they had been mixed up in, down in Texas. At that, Johnson recognized the shabby traveler as an old friend, Billy Carter. Johnson told Carter to go to camp and get the wrangler to cut his hair and give him a shave, and when he came in for dinner he would fix him up with a better-looking outfit. When Billy rode out to the meeting place for the afternoon circle, I don't think a one of us could tell he was the same fellow that rode in on the U.S.I.C. horse.

We soon found out why he had looked so wild and dilapidated. It was not that he was in disguise, but because of isolation and exposure while on a long and roundabout ride from Rawlins Springs, all the while dodging pursuit. He had left Rawlins in a hurry, and under pressing circumstances. It seemed that a Chinese laundryman had been robbed by the rounders of the town. When he resisted, they beat him so bad he died. Billy had been hanging around with that bunch, so he was rounded up with them. The citizens' mob that undertook to deal with the gang picked out Billy and three others and marched them to a patch of timber where there were trees big enough to be used as ready-made scaffolds.

But there happened to be quite a few in the crowd that weren't in sympathy with hanging Billy. They tried to talk the rest of the mob out of it, and in so doing crowded the hangmen so close they did not take time to bind his hands before hustling him under a tree and putting a rope around his neck and over a limb. Just as Billy's feet cleared the ground the rope holders, slackened up a bit so they could give a harder pull. And Billy, bracing his toes and jumping into the air, grabbed the rope as high up as he could, then slipped the noose off his neck and ran. At the same time some of his sympathizers managed to make a sort of a path through the crowd into the timber, where a girl was waiting with a gun for him. And so he got away. He said he traveled by night and laid up by day, and all the time he could still feel that ticklish sawgrass rope around his neck, so it was no wonder he looked so wild when he showed up at our camp.

A few days later, while we were rounding up the Si Funk place on the north branch of the Niobrara, the first circlers came in and started a monte game on a spread blanket in the hay yard north of the stables. Billy had several bets down when someone hollered that a dozen cavalrymen were coming down the road. Billy grabbed the money roll in front of him, jumped on his horse, and was off for the sandhills to the south. He didn't even slow up for the river, which was about twenty feet wide, and his horse took it in one jump and didn't even break his stride. When the sergeant rode up with his troop, he said, "That fellow must think he is escaping from us, but he needn't worry, for no trooper ever sat on a horse like that. Anyway, I'm not looking for Texas outlaws, but for U.S. army deserters."

The Kid Died with His Boots *Off*, July 13, 1881

Pat Garrett

In the 1870s and into the early-1880s, the Territory of New Mexico experienced considerable lawlessness. William H. Bonney (a.k.a. "Billy the Kid") was among the most notable of the lawless breed. Born in New York in 1859, after several moves, Billy's mother took him and his siblings to Silver City, New Mexico. As a youngster, Billy was caught up in wrong-doings, but in 1877 his surly behavior took a more serious turn when Billy shot a blacksmith at Camp Grant, Arizona. Thereafter, Billy was on the run from the law and in late-1875 wandered into Lincoln County, New Mexico. Billy went to work for John Tunstall, a cultured father figure to Billy. In 1878 Tunstall was murdered by a gunslinger hired by a competitor rancher. Tunstall's murder infuriated Billy and other Tunstall followers and the result was the Lincoln County War. In 1880 Pat Garrett was made sheriff of Lincoln County. He had known Billy well—they spent time together during their off-work times and became fast friends. Garrett was ordered by New Mexico Governor Wallace to capture the Kid at all costs. The actual number of men that the Kid killed is conjectural, but contemporaneous stories alleged that the Kid killed five Apache braves, a blacksmith, three cardsharps and six to eight others during the Lincoln County War. Garrett was praised, for the most part, for killing the Kid in the beginning, but was later charged with murder. He was subsequently acquitted by a coroner's jury who ruled the killing of the Kid as justifiable homicide.

I concluded to go and have a talk with Peter Maxwell, Esq., in whom I felt sure I could rely. We had ridden to within a short distance of Maxwell's grounds when we found a man in camp and stopped. To Poe's great surprise, he recognized in the camper an old friend and former partner, in

Texas, named Jacobs. We unsaddled here, got some coffee, and, on foot, entered an orchard which runs from this point down to a row of old buildings, some of them occupied by Mexicans, not more than sixty yards from Maxwell's house. We approached these houses cautiously, and when within ear shot, heard the sound of voices conversing in Spanish. We concealed ourselves quickly and listened; but the distance was too great to hear words, or even distinguish voices. Soon a man arose from the ground, in full view, but too far away to recognize. He wore a broad-brimmed hat, a dark vest and pants, and was in his shirt sleeves. With a few words, which fell like a murmur on our ears, he went to the fence, jumped it, and waled down towards Maxwell's house.

Little as we then suspected it, this man was the Kid. We learned, subsequently, that, when he left his companions that night, he went to the house of a Mexican friend, pulled off his hat and boots, threw himself on a bed, and commenced reading a newspaper. He soon, however, hailed his friend, who was sleeping in the room, told him to get up and make some coffee, adding:—"Give me a butcher knife and I will go over to Pete's and get some beef; I'm hungry." The Mexican arose, handed him the knife, and the Kid, hatless and in his stocking-feet, started to Maxwell['s], which was but a few steps distant.

When the Kid, by me unrecognized, left the orchard, I motioned to my companions, and we cautiously retreated a short distance, and, to avoid the persons whom we had heard at the houses, took another route, approaching Maxwell's house from the opposite direction. When we reached the porch in front of the building, I left Poe and McKinney at the end of the porch, about twenty feet from the door of Pete's room, and went in. It was near midnight and Pete was in bed. I walked to the head of the bed and sat down on it, beside him, near the pillow. I asked him as to the whereabouts of the Kid. He said that the Kid had certainly been about, but he did not know whether he had left or not. At that moment a man sprang quickly into the door, looking back, and called twice in Spanish, "Who comes there?" No one replied and he came on in. He was bareheaded. From his step I could perceive he was either barefooted or in his stocking-feet, and held a revolver in his right hand and butcher knife in his left.

He came directly towards me. Before he reached the bed, I whispered: "Who is it, Pete?" but received no reply for a moment. It struck me that it might be Pete's brother-in-law, Manuel Abreu, who had seen Poe and McKinney, and wanted to know their business. The intruder came close to me, leaned both hands on the bed, his right hand almost touching my knee, and asked, in a low tone:—"Who are they Pete?"—at the same instant Maxwell whispered to me. "That's him!" Simultaneously the Kid must have seen, or felt, the presence of a third person at the head of the bed. He raised quickly his pistol, a self cocker, within a foot of my breast. Retreating rapidly across the room he cried: "Quien es? Quien es?" ("Who's that? Who's that?") All this occurred in a moment. Quick as possible I drew my revolver and fired, threw my body aside, and fired again. The second shot was useless; the Kid fell dead. He never spoke. A struggle or two, a little strangling sound as he gasped for breath, and the Kid was with his many victims.

Maxwell had plunged over the foot of the bed on the floor, dragging the bed-clothes with him. I went to the door and met Poe and McKinney there. Maxwell rushed past me, out on the porch; they threw their guns down on him, when he cried: "Don't shoot, don't shoot," I told my companions I had got the Kid. They asked me if I had not shot the wrong man. I told them I had made no blunder, that I knew the Kid's voice too well to be mistaken. The Kid was entirely unknown to either of them. They had seen him pass in, and, as he stepped on the porch, McKinney, who was sitting, rose to his feet, on of his spurs caught under the boards, and nearly threw him. The Kid laughed, but probably, saw their guns, as he drew his revolver and sprang into the doorway, as he hailed: "Who comes there?" Seeing a bareheaded, barefooted man, in his shirt-sleeves, with a butcher knife in his hand, and hearing his hail in excellent Spanish, they naturally supposed him to be a Mexican and an attaché of the establishment, hence their suspicion that I had shot the wrong man.

We now entered the room and examined the body. The ball struck him just above the heart, and must have cut through the ventricles. Poe asked me how many shots I fired; I told him two, but that I had no idea where the second one went. Both Poe and McKinney said the Kid must have fired then, as there were surely three shots fired. I told them that he had fired one shot, between my two. Maxwell said that the Kid fired; yet, when we came to look for bullet marks, none from his pistol could be found. We searched long and faithfully—found both my bullet marks and none other; so, against the impression and senses of four men, we had to conclude that the Kid did not fire at all. We examined his pistol—a self-cocker, caliber 41. It had five cartridges and one shell in the chambers, the hammer resting on the shell, but this proves nothing, as many carry their revolvers in this way for safety; beside this shell looked as though it had been shot some time before.

It will never be known whether the Kid recognized me or not. If he did, it was the first time, during all his life of peril, that he ever lost his presence of mind, or failed to shoot first and hesitate afterwards. He knew that a meeting with me meant surrender or fight. He told several persons about Sumner that he bore no animosity against me, and had no desire to do me injury. He also said that he knew, should we meet, he would have to surrender, kill me, or get killed himself. So, he declared his intention, should we ever meet, to commence shooting on sight.

On the following morning, the alcalde, Alejandro Segura, held an inquest on the body. Hon. M. Rudolph, of Sunnyside, was foreman of the coroner's jury. They found a verdict that William H. Bonney came to his death from a gun-shot wound, the weapon in the hands of Pat F. Garrett, that the fatal wound was inflicted by the said Garrett in the discharge of his official duty as sheriff, and that the homicide was justified.

The body was neatly and properly dressed and buried in the military cemetery at Fort Sumner, July 15, 1881. His exact age, on the day of his death, was 21 years, 7 months, and 21 days.

From: *The Authentic Life of Billy, the Kid* (Santa Fe, NM: New Mexican Printing and Publishing Company, 1882)

The Death of Billy the Kid—Shot by Sheriff Pat Garrett

Making Headlines at the O.K. Corral, October 26, 1881

John Clum

John Clum led an interesting and full life in the Southwest. He was an Indian agent and an Indian fighter who took Geronimo prisoner. Later, he became a newspaperman when he bought Tucson's Arizona Citizen in 1877 but sold it in 1880 after he had visited Tombstone and figured that the mining boom-town—it had become the largest town in Arizona Territory—needed its own newspaper. Clum founded The Epitaph *and had to move and refit the paper three times within a year just to keep pace with the rapid growth of the community. Shortly thereafter Clum was elected Tombstone's mayor but retained his journalistic duties. It was during this time that he witnessed the gunfight at the O.K. Corral.*

News was scarce for my next issue of "The Epitaph," so I wandered up-town in search of a human-interest story. Ike Clanton was leaning against an adobe wall at the corner of Fremont and Fourth streets holding a Winchester rifle in his arms much after the fashion of a mother holding her child, and fondling it accordingly. The Clanton family had lived in the Gila valley, not far from the eastern boundary of the Indian reservation, during the time I was in charge of the Apaches in San Carlos. I formed a casual acquaintance with several members of the Clanton clan at that time and had been on speaking terms with Ike ever since. In '79 the Clantons moved to a ranch west from Tombstone in the San Pedro valley and made it headquarters for outlaws in that section, a clearinghouse for cattle stolen in Mexico by the rustlers and smuggled across the line. Ike had been warned to keep out of Tombstone, and it was against the town law to carry firearms. My nose for news told me there was a good story in

339

the making, my conscience as mayor told me that Ike should be arrested and my story ruined.

"Good morning, Ike," I said, "Any new war on today?"

"Nothin' particular," replied Ike, turning on his cowboy heel and ambling down Fourth Street. That convinced me that Ike had something sinister on his mind, because usually he was more talkative, less taciturn. While I was debating what to do, I saw our chief of police, Virgil Earp, sauntering down the street toward Ike.

"Hello, Ike," said Virgil. "What are you doing in town?"

"Nothin' particular," replied Ike.

"Why the Winchester?"

"Oh, just happened to have it with me," said Ike, edging away.

"Wait a minute, Ike," said Virgil, taking hold of Ike's arm. "Let's you and I go over and call on Judge Wallace. You can tell him why you brought that cannon into town with you." All of which meant, of course, that Ike was arrested.

They walked down the street, Virgil still holding Ike's arm. Suddenly Ike made a break, tried to wrench away from Virgil's grip. But Virgil was on the job, pulled his six-shooter, and cracked Ike over the head with the butt end of it. Ike stretched his length on the sidewalk. Wyatt and Morgan Earp happened along about that time. The Earp brothers had an uncanny habit of happening along when trouble was brewing. Virgil, Wyatt, and Morgan disarmed Ike, revived him, and took him to the court where Judge Wallace fined him $25 and retained his weapons.

Ike did not like that a bit. "Wait till I get another gun," he yelled. "I'll kill every damn one of you Earps." Whereupon Morgan Earp pulled his own six-shooter out of its holster and offered it to Ike, handle first. Ike tried to grab it, but one of the deputy sheriffs pushed Ike back and told Morgan to put his gun away and get out of the court room. The three Earps walked out together, Ike tagging on behind still raving about how he was going to kill all of the Earps on sight.

Standing just outside the doorway was Tom McLowery, one of Ike Clanton's buddies and as tough an outlaw as was raised in those parts. A mean looking six-gun was sticking out from Tom's belt. "You Earps are a lot of —s," swore Tom. "I'll shoot it out with you anytime, anywhere."

"All right, Tom," said Wyatt Earp, "now's a good time and this is a good place, right here in front of the courtroom." As Wyatt spoke he slapped McLowery's face with his left hand and pulled his six-gun with his right hand. McLowery made no move. Cowardice makes a brave man mad. Wyatt flared up. "Pull your gun and fight, you yellow-livered skunk," roared Wyatt, "or I'll break this six-shooter over your head." Still McLowery made no move. That was the last straw. Down came Wyatt's gun on Tom's head and Tom passed out, temporarily. The three Earps walked down the street.

Busy forenoon, much conversation, but not a shot fired. I hurried back to the "Epitaph" office to write the story. It was a rattling good story, too, because for over a year the Clanton-McLowery gang of outlaws had been threatening to clean up Tombstone and the Earps. Virgil Earp was chief of police and a good one. Wyatt Earp was marshal. So the Earps represented the law and I was back of them 100 percent, both as mayor and an editor. Enforcing the law in Tombstone in 1880 and 1881 was not child's play; it was serious work for he-men.

Ike Clanton picked Tom McLowery up out of the gutter. Billy Clanton and Frank McLowery had been consuming a little liquor at the Oriental. They heard the news and went to the help of their respective brothers. Billy Claiborne, buddy of the Clantons, went along. All five went to the gunsmith's, evidently to add to their arsenal and ammunition supply. Then they repaired to the O.K. Corral for further conference. The O.K. Corral was on Fremont Street, directly opposite the office of the "Epitaph."

When the three Earps walked away from the prostrate form of Tom McLowery, they were joined by Doc Holliday and went into the Can-Can for lunch. About half past two there was a commotion in the O.K. Corral. Sheriff Behan was having an argument with the five members of the Clanton-McLowery gang. Somebody had told the Earps that the Clanton-McLowerys were organizing for a fight to the death. The Earps, always obliging in such matters, were on their way to the O.K. Corral to see about it. The sheriff had tried to disarm and arrest the Clanton gang but had failed both ways. He then went to intercept the Earps. But the Earps pushed him to one side and came marching on, Virgil and Wyatt in front, Morgan and Doc Holliday behind. Sheriff Behan brought up the rear, demanding peace in the name of the law.

The Clanton crowd was huddled close to the gate of the corral. The Earps walked up to within five feet of the Clantons. "Ike," said Virgil, "there has been a lot of loose talk around town by you and your gang of cutthroats. Throw up your hands, all of you!" The answer came instantly from two six-shooters. Then more six-shooters blazed so quickly they sounded like echoes of the first. Frank McLowery fell, shot through the abdomen. Tom McLowery ran to his nearby horse to get his rifle. Doc Holliday unlimbered his short-barrel shotgun and literally blew Tom into pieces. Morgan Earp drilled a hole clear through Billy Clanton's chest, but the game lad lay crumpled against the wall, calmly pouring lead at his adversaries.

Ike Clanton made a leap for Wyatt's gun arm, hoping to get Wyatt's gun out of commission. Wyatt could have killed Ike without even hesitating in the general warfare, but Wyatt was not that sort of fighter. He cracked Ike's knuckles with the barrel of his six-shooter, pushed Ike off, told him to run or fight and to be damn quick making up his mind. Ike beat it, to use a very modern expression. After the shooting stopped, Ike was discovered in the dark room of Fly's photograph gallery. So much for Ike.

Virgil Earp was prone on the ground, a bullet from Billy Clanton's gun having gone through his leg. But Virgil was still shooting. He clipped a piece out of Billy Clanton's ten-gallon hat. Billy shifted his position, took a potshot at Morgan Earp, and Morgan fell with a hole in his shoulder. John Behan, the sheriff, ran into the photograph gallery—bullets were flying too thick for Johnny. Frank McLowery, blood streaming from a gaping wound in his stomach, saw Morgan Earp fall. With heroic effort, Frank got to his feet and staggered toward Morgan, gun in hand. "Quick, Morg," yelled Wyatt, "get Frank McLowery!" Doc Holliday heard Wyatt's warning, turned quickly, and fired point blank at the tottering Frank. Morgan let loose at the same moment. Frank dropped in his tracks, dead. It is still a matter of dispute in Tombstone whether Doc or Morgan killed Frank McLowery. The important thing was that Frank was permanently out of the picture. Billy Clanton, with two holes through his middle, lay inert against the adobe wall.

Wyatt Earp, unscathed, looked over the field and reloaded his six-shooter. But the war was over. Of the five members of the Clanton gang, the two McLowerys and Billy Clanton were dead, Ike was hiding in the dark room, and Billy Claiborne had disappeared before the fight started. Virgil and Morgan Earp lay in the middle of Fremont Street, wounded but poised on elbows, guns ready to spit more death should any more of Ike's friends put in an appearance. Doc Holliday stood alongside Wyatt. Somebody's bullet had burned a nice little furrow along Doc's thigh, otherwise he had been untouched. The entire battle had lasted less than half a minute.

"Well, Doc," said Wyatt, "guess the show is over. Let's take Virg and Morg up to the doctor's."

"O.K.," agreed Doc. "They're not badly hurt." And the four of them started down Fremont Street. Sheriff Behan slipped out of his hiding place and approached the quartette.

"Wyatt," he said, "I think I will have to arrest you boys for murder." Wyatt pushed Johnny aside and said nothing. "I say, Wyatt . . ."

Wyatt stopped, looked at the Sheriff with those cold, steel-grey eyes of his. "Behan," he said, "you had your chance to do some arresting before the fight. If you had locked up that bunch of cutthroats when they came into town, there'd been no trouble. We haven't murdered anybody. We've only done our duty to Tombstone ourselves. Trot along now and and to forget it." And Johnny trotted.

Celebrating Reaching Womanhood on the Run, c. April 1882

Jason Betzinez

The Chiricahua Apaches had been camped beside the Gila River at the San Car-los Agency for more than two years. During that time smallpox decimated many of the camps and the Indians were terrified. Those who did not catch the disease moved their camps into the mountains to the north thinking that the higher ele-vation would be more healthy. Those who remained along the river took care of themselves as best that they could without any help from the agency. Fear of smallpox compounded the dislike the Indians had for San Carlos. The day came when, led by Geronimo, they broke out of camp and headed to Mexico. They were then considered hostile and were pursued by troops of the 4th Cavalry, com-manded by Lieutenant George A. Forsyth. When his memoirs were published in 1959, Betzinez was almost a hundred-years old.

Now a curious thing happened. One of the girls with us reached woman hood, so right away her parents arranged the traditional ceremony in her honor, even while the shooting was heard on the other side of the hill. Since this is one of the most important events in a woman's life the ceremony is never neglected, not even at a time such as this.

This girl was a member of the White Mountain Apaches, who with her parents had been living with us at San Carlos and who had been caught in this raid on the Netdahe. I think that her father had become a member of our band by marrying a Chihenne woman. The ceremony of reaching womanhood marks the time when a girl is ready for marriage. Of course all girls look forward to it eagerly even though if they look around them they should realize that all marriages do not turn out happily.

Before the ceremony begins the parents are very excited, trying to decide who should be the sponsor and who should conduct the ceremony. The sponsor is a close friend of the family, either a man or a woman, and to be selected as such is a mark of real affection. The person who conducts the ceremony is some respected old woman of the tribe who is experienced in such matters. To the sponsor the parents present any eagle feather, something all Indians value. The old woman who conducts the ceremony spreads out a rug or blanket on the ground, marks four footprints leading away from it toward a point about fifty yards away to the east, where the feather is placed on the ground in a dish or plate.

The girl who is the candidate is led forward, caused to stretch out on her face on the rug while the old woman performs some kind of incantation over her. Then the girl stands erect, steps successively in each of the footprints, runs to the feather, circles it, picks it up and brings it back to the starting point. Meanwhile all the crowd watches closely.

At the conclusion of this part of the ceremony the parents of the girl and the woman who is in charge of the ceremony exchange valuable gifts such as horses, saddles, or other worthwhile property. The second part of the ceremony is a great feast which lasts four days and nights. The food consists of barbecued cattle as well as wild fruit, berries, and roasted mescal plant. During this time you can hear the constant beat of the tom-tom making music for the fire dance. After the fire dance everyone joins in a circle facing the fire. The girl being honored takes a leading part all through these dances. On the last night of the feast and dance the men make presents to their dancing partners.

For the third phase of the ceremony a number of volunteers go out and cut four long poles each about eight inches in diameter and twenty feet or more in length. These are set in holes which have been dug at the corners of a square about five paces on the side. While the poles are being erected one of the elders of the tribe chants a song which keeps time for the men who are pulling the poles to an upright position. Now the poles are joined at the top with a number of limbs of trees, except that the east side of the square is left open. Thus a lodge is formed, in the center of which a small fire is built on the ground. Here the elder sings a special song meanwhile jingling a rattle made of the hoofs of a fawn. As he sings, the girl moves sideways, north and south, rising alternatively on her tows and heels. At the same time she holds up her arms with her hands even with her shoulders. Of course during this time she is well decorated from head to foot. Her dress is the finest kind of buckskin, covered with many small tin jingles as well as much beadwork.

Early on the morning of the fourth day a brief ceremony is held before pulling down the lodge at the end of which the elder orders the four poles to be pulled down. They are dragged eastward about a hundred feet and laid side by side with their tops pointed eastward. The tom-toms then cease beating and the ceremony is ended.

On the occasion of our flight to Mexico the ceremony was very much shortened because the warriors were in a hurry to start the night march.

Reprinted from *I Fought With Geronimo* with Wilbur Sturtevant Nye courtesy of the University of Nebraska Press.

The Killing of Jesse James, April 4, 1882

Kansas City Times

Jesse James, the son of a Baptist minister, was born in Missouri in 1847. At the age of fifteen, he joined a band of pro-Confederate guerrillas led by the infamous William Quantrill. After the war, Jesse formed a gang with his brother, Frank, and several others. They held up banks, stagecoaches, and trains until 1876, when the gang was decimated trying to rob a bank in Northfield, Minnesota. During that attempted robbery, citizens discovered the James Gang in the process of its robbery, and within minutes of organizing themselves, the citizens fired upon the gang as they exited the bank. All except Frank and Jesse were either killed, wounded or captured. With a $10,000 reward on his head, Jesse moved to St. Joseph, Missouri, with his family in the fall of 1881 to hide out. The reward proved appealing. Thus, while Jesse stood on a chair in the family home to dust and straighten a picture, Bob and Charlie Ford drew their guns. Bob Ford shot Jesse in the back of the head. The Ford brothers attempted to collect the reward, but found, instead, that they were charged with murder. They were sentenced to hang but were pardoned by the Missouri governor. Two years later, Charles Ford committed suicide and Bob Ford was killed in a bar room brawl in Creede, Colorado.

ST. JOSEPH, MO. April 4—About ten o'clock this morning a hurried report was made in this city that Jesse James had been shot and killed at his home in the south part of the this city, where he has been residing for the past six months, under the assumed name of Howard. In a few minutes an immense throng was on its way to the place designated, and on arrival there, found the report verified, and Jesse James dead, he having been assassinated by two members of the gang, Charles and Robert Ford, of Ray county, both of whom immediately surrendered themselves to the authorities.

The home where the great outlaw was killed is a frame building, a story and a half high, sitting in a little grove of fruit trees on one of the round ridges back of the World's hotel. It commands a view of the approaches for a long distance.

The wife of the outlaw first insisted that the name of the dead man was Howard, but later

MADE A FULL CONFESSION

of the whole affair, along with a history of the robberies in which her husband had been engaged. She said they resided last summer in Kansas City, but had removed to this city where Jesse hoped to reside in peace and earn an honest living. They brought with them two Ford boys who had since been living in their house. These boys are mere youths, apparently between 15 and 20 years of age. This morning after breakfast Robert Ford and Jesse went into the sitting room to some work about moving a stove, and Charles was assisting her in the kitchen washing dishes. After a little Charles also went into the room where the two men were; soon after she heard a shot and rushing in she found her husband laying on the floor shot to death, while on a chair lay his pistol, belt and cartridges, which he had removed while at work with the stove. The Ford boys both ran from the house, one jumping over the rear fence, the other running around by the front way. They both returned again and then started to the city to deliver themselves up and

CLAIM THE REWARD OFFERED

for Jesse James. They first came to the marshal's office, but finding him out, went direct to the sheriff and gave themselves into custody.

Soon after the shooting the reporters were informed by Coroner Heddens that a man had been shot and killed on thirteenth and Lafayette streets. Reaching the place indicated, and on approaching the door leading into the front room, a man was found lying on the floor cold in death, with blood oozing from his wounds. From the few who had gathered around the door, more from curiosity than anything else, it was inquired what was the cause of the shooting. None of them knew, but said we could find out from the man's wife, who was in the rear room. Walking into the room and passing around the dead man's body, we opened the door leading into the kitchen, where we found the

WIFE AND TWO LITTLE CHILDREN

a boy and a girl. When she discovered us with notebook in hand, she began to scream and said: Please do not put this in the paper! At first she refused to say anything about the shooting, but after some time she said the boys that had killed her husband had been living with them for some time, and that their names were Johnson, but no relation. Charles, she said was her nephew, but she had never seen Robert until he came home with her husband a few weeks ago. Robert was an old friend of her husband, and when he met him upon the street he invited him to come and see them. He came home with them that night and had remained ever since. When asked what her husband's name was she said it was Howard and that they had resided here about six months.

"Had your husband and the two Johnson boys ever had any difficulty?"

ON FRIENDLY TERMS

"Never. They have always been on friendly terms."

"Why, then did they do the deed?"

"That is more than I can tell. Oh, the rascals!" And at this she began to cry and ask God to protect her.

"Where were you when the shooting was done?"

"I was in the kitchen, and Charley had been helping me all morning with my work. He entered the first room, and in about three minutes I heard the report of a pistol; and upon opening the door I discovered my husband lying in his own blood upon the floor. I ran to the front door and Charles was getting over the fence, but Robert was standing in the front yard with a pistol in his right hand. I says: Oh you have killed him, and he answered: No, he didn't kill him, and turning around walked into the kitchen and then left with Charles, who was waiting for him outside the fence.

At this juncture the two Johnson boys made their appearance and gave themselves up to the officers, telling them the man they killed was

JESSE JAMES

and now they claim the reward. Those who were standing nearby drew their breaths in silence at the thought of being so near Jesse James, even if he was dead.

Marshal Craig said: My God, do you mean to tell me this is Jesse James?

Yes, answered the two boys in one breath. That man is Jesse James and we have killed him and don't deny it. We feel proud that we have killed a man who is known all over the world as the most notorious desperado that has ever lived.

THE WIFE'S FINAL CONFESSION

How are we to take your words for this? asked the marshal.

We do not ask you to take our words. There will be proof enough. The confession of the wife will be enough.

The marshal then took Mrs. Howard, as she called herself, into the room, and told her the name of her husband was not Howard, but James. She denied it at first, and when the marshal left her the reporter entered the room in company with three or four other gentlemen and one lady, who was present. Mrs. Howard, it is said your name is not Howard, but James, and you are the wife of Jesse James.

I can't help what they say. I have told the truth.

The boys who killed your husband have come back and given themselves up, and they say that he is Jesse James and your husband.

My God, can it be that they have come back? She was told that they were standing outside the house near the fence, and should see them with her own eyes. Walking through the room by her dead husband she caught sight of the ones who had killed her husband, and screaming at the top of her voice she called them cowards, and asked them why they had killed the one who had always befriended them. Then turning to the body of Jesse, she prayed that she and her children might be in death's cold embrace by his side. She then left the room, followed by the reporters, who told her that the boys were not mistaken, that it certainly must be Jesse. She uttered not a word, but the little 7 year old boy who stood by her side said God Almighty may strike me down if it is not pa.

The boys said their names are Ford and not Johnson as you said, continued the reporter,

Do they say so, and what else do they say?

That they killed him to get the reward.

Holding her dear little children closer to her bosom, she said:

I can't shield them long. Even after they had shot my husband, who has been trying to live a peaceable life, I protected them and withheld their names, but it is all true. My husband is Jesse James, and a kinder hearted, truer man to his family never lived.

This confession from the wife of the most notorious outlaw known to the annals of crime history created a profound sensation. The thought that

Jesse James has lived among us for the past six months, and walked our streets daily, causes one to shudder with fear. When the wife had made her confession, we asked her to tell about Jesse, Frank, and the Ford boys who had killed him. She said she would, but begged us to do all for her we could to keep them from dragging her husband's body all over the country. We promised to do this and also told her that she and her children should be taken care of.

MRS. JAMES STORY

Well, she said, the deed is done, and why should I keep quiet any longer? I will tell you the truth. Charles and Robert Ford are brothers, and reside in Ray country, near Richmond. They have been here some time with her husband, and little did I think they would ever kill him.

Were either one of the boys engaged in the Blue Cut robbery? asked the reporter.

Yes, Charlie was there, and was the one that hit the expressman in the head.

Where was Robert?

He was not at the Blue Cut robbery, but was at the Winston robbery.

Was Jesse at either robbery?

Yes, he was at the Blue Cut robbery, but not at the Winston. Jesse has been accused of being engaged in nearly all the robberies committed in the United States, but he was not half as bad a man as his enemies reported him. He has endeavored to live an honorable and peaceful life, but wherever he went he was hunted down by a lot of scoundrels who were not better than himself. We lived in Kansas City last summer, and Jesse was not discovered by anyone.

Where is Frank now?

I do not know. I have not seen or heard of Frank for a long time.

While the officers were searching for his pistols, guns and jewelry, Mrs. James said: I wish they would quit prowling around my house. They have no business with my dead husband's outfit.

THE BOYS AND THE WIDOW

The reporter then went out and interviewed the two Ford boys. They were both young, the older one not being more than 21 years of age. When asked why they killed Jesse, they said they wanted the reward.

You are young, but gritty.

We are all grit, said Charley. You never expected to see Jesse James' dead body in St. Joseph, but we thought we would create a sensation and put him out of the way.

The boys had upon their persons two revolvers each. Charley had a large forty-four caliber Smith & Wesson and a forty-four caliber Remington. Robert had one forty-five caliber Colt's and one forty-one caliber of the same make, but double action.

Jesse's arms consisted of one forty caliber Smith & Wesson and one forty-five caliber Colt's revolver, one breech loading shotgun, a Winchester rifle and two belts full of cartridges. The reporter visited Mrs. James in her room after interviewing Charley and Robert. She was very calm, her greatest trouble being to know what would become of herself and children. In speaking of the shooting she said: Dick Little has betrayed Jesse; in fact he has been a traitor for some time. Had it not been for this

JESSE WOULD STILL BE ALIVE.

Thus ended the life of a man who was feared and hated by more men than any one person who has ever committed a crime in the history of the republic. The house where the tragedy occurred is situated on the corner of thirteenth and Lafayette streets in the rear of a pretty steep bluff. The house is a plain, unassuming frame of seven rooms, one story high and painted white. It is a most unpretentious place and one that would not attract the attention of a passerby, as it has no marked or attractive features. It was formerly occupied by Alderman Aylesbury. The house was erected some two years ago, and about a year ago Aylesbury moved out, and last November those parties giving their name as Howard, rented it. The shooting occurred in the front room near the center of the floor. It occupies a very large lot, being some ninety feet front by 140 wide, and surrounded by a plain board fence with pickets in front. This house will now go to ornament the pages of history when the chronicles of this great and mighty country are written and handed down to posterity, as one of the few places of interest, it will be an object of curiosity to the people of this great country.

JESSE AND HIS FAMILY

Jesse James was about five feet eight inches in height, of a rather solid, firm and compact build, yet rather on the slender side. His hair was black, not overly long; blue eyes well shaded with dark lashes, and the entire lower portion of the face was covered by a full growth of dark brown or sun browned whiskers, which are not long and shaggy, but are trimmed and bear evidence of careful attention. His complexion was fair, and he was not sun burned to any considerable extent . . . He was neatly clad in a business suit of cashmere, of a dark brown substance, which fit him very neatly. He wore a short of spotless whiteness, with collar and cravat, and looked more the picture of a staid and substantial business man than the outlaw and robber that he was. The woman, his wife, is a neat and rather prepossessing lady, and bears the stamp of having been well brought up and surrounded by influences of a better and holier character than the reader would at first suppose. She is rather slender, fair of face, light hair, blue eyes with high forehead and marks of intelligence very strikingly apparent. She was clad in a neat fitting calico and at the time of the shooting was attending to her household duties in the kitchen. The two children, a little boy and girl, aged 4 and 7 years, were brought, neat and intelligent and seemed to grieve much over the deed which had in one short moment, deprived them of a father's love and protection. . . .

THE EXCITEMENT IN THE CITY

When the first rumors of the killing of Jesse James, the most notorious bandit, bank robber, and outlaw in American, became street talk, the residents of St. Joseph could hardly believe them, and not until the fact was finally admitted by the wife of the dead man, would they accept them as facts. It was too startling, that the man upon whose head a reward of $10,000 had been set, should for months have lived in this midst unknown, and thousands visited the little house, about half a mile from the public square for a glimpse of the dead man, whose name for years has only been spoken of where deeds of murder and train robbery were mentioned. But his end came at last suddenly and as unheralded as did that of poor Dan Askew, the Clay county farmer murdered in 1875 near the home of Mrs. Samuels, in Clay county, and Billy Westfall, the Rock Island conductor killed at Winston, both dying at the hands of Jesse James. He was killed by one of his own men, trusted and believed in as a friend, and upon whom he had been led to look for help when detectives and county officials sought to

CAPTURE OR KILL HIM.

It has always been said by his friends that none of his companions would betray or kill him, and Mrs. Samuels, his mother, once said, when speaking of his reported death at Short Creek, at the hands of George Shepherd: "And do you believe a one-eyed man could get the drop on Jesse? Why no two men could do it." But at last it came and a boy, not yet out of his teens, did get the drop upon her son and with one shot sent his soul into eternity. He fired once at the outlaw, the ball entering the robber's head behind the left ear and coming out over his eye. Officers have remarked: Some day Jesse James will die with his boots on, and such has been the case. Had he a revolver in his belt, and for an instant suspected that Robert Ford the boy whom he had sheltered, had an idea of betraying him his (Ford's) life would not have been worth a song, and so it was with perfect security that he un-buckled his belt containing four revolvers, and carelessly threw them on the bed. That was the fatal moment, for in an instant

FORD DREW A REVOLVER

and shot him from behind and then waited to see if another bullet was needed to accomplish the outlaw's death. But no more was necessary, and the young man, who had dared openly to start out to kill the hated Missouri terror, did as he said he would, and then calmly joined his brother, Charles Ford, who stood just outside the door, and both re-entered the house and confronted the wife of the dead man, and for a while braved her terrible anger and denunciations. . . .

From. *Kansas City Times*. "The Killing of Jesse James," July 4, 1882

Frank and Jesse James in Their Outlaw Days

Tales of Boots and the Wiles of Women, c. 1882

Andy Adams

Andy Adams (1859–1935) was a working cowboy at the zenith of the great trail drives. Indiana-born, he had helped his family herd cattle and horses on their farm which gave him the experience that you would put to use in Texas and during eight years of trail driving in the 1880s. Afterwards, he drifted from place to place doing a plethora of work in the mercantile business, trail boss, gold-mining, but he began writing as a new-found career at the age of forty-three. Adams wrote seven books between 1903 and 1927. His best known work, The Log of a Cowboy *was published in 1903 and tells of a five-month drive of over 3,000 cattle from Mexico to Montana in 1882. It is from this book that the following excerpt was taken.*

An amusing incident occured during the last night of our camp at these water holes [Indian Lakes]. Coyotes had been hanging around our camp for several days, and during the quiet hours of the night these scavengers of the plains had often ventured in near the wagon in search of scraps of meat or anything edible. Rod Wheat and Ash Borrowstone had made their beds down some distance from the wagon; the coyotes as they circled round the camp came near their bed, and in sniffing about awoke Borrowstone. There was no more danger of attack from these cowards than from field mice, but their presence annoyed Ash, and as he dared not shoot, he threw his boots at the varmints. Imagine his chagrin the next moring to find that one boot had landed among the banked embers of the camp-fire, and was burned to a crisp. It was looked upon as a capital joke by the outfit, as there was no telling when we would reach a store where he could secure another pair.

355

The new trail, after bearing to the westward for several days, turned northward paralleling the old one, and a week later we came into the old trail over a hundred miles north of the Indian Lakes. With the exception of one thirty-mile drive without water, no fault could be found with the new trail. A few days after coming into the old trail, we passed Mason, a point where trail herds usually put in for supplies. As we passed during the middle of the afternoon, the wagon and a number of the boys went into the burg. Quince Forrest and Billy Honeyman were the only two in the outfit for whom there were any letters, with the exception of a letter from Lovell, which was common property. Never having been over the trail before, and not even knowing that it was possible to hear from home, I wasn't expecting any letter; but I felt a little twinge of homesickness that night when Honeyman read us certain portions of his letter, which was from his sister. Forrest's letter was from a sweetheart, and after reading it a few times, he burnt it, and that was all we ever knew of its contents, for he was too foxy to say anything, even if it had not been unfavorable. Borrowstone swaggered around camp that evening in a new pair of boots, which had the Lone Star set in filigree-work in their red tops.

At our last camp at the lakes, The Rebel and I, as partners, had been shamefully beaten in a game of seven-up by Bull Durham and John Officer, and had demanded satisfaction in another trial around the fire that night. We borrowed McCann's lantern, and by the aid of it and the camp-fire had an abundance of light for our game. In the absence of a table, we unrolled a bed and sat down Indian fashion over a game of cards in which all friendship ceased.

The outfit, with the exception of myself, had come from the same neighborhood, and an item in Honeyman's letter causing considerable comment was a wedding which had occurred since the outfit had left. It seemed that a number of the boys had sparked the bride in times past, and now that she was married, their minds naturally became reminiscent over old sweethearts.

"The way I make it out," said Honeyman, in commenting on the news, "is that the girl had met this fellow over in the next county while visiting her cousins the year before. My sister gives it as a horseback opinion that she'd been engaged to this fellow nearly eight months; girls, you know, sabe each other that way. Well, it won't affect my appetite if all the girls I know get married while I'm gone."

"You certainly have never experienced the tender passion," said Fox Quarternight to our horse wrangler, as he lighted his pipe with a brand from the fire. "Now I have. That's the reason why I sympathize with these old beaus of the bride. Of course I was too old to stand any show on her string, and I reckon the fellow who got her ain't so powerful much, except his veneering and being a stranger, which was a big advantage. To be sure, if she took a smile to this stranger, no other fellow could check her with a three-quarter rope and a snubbing post. I've seen girls walk right by a dozen good fellows and fawn over some scrub. My experience teaches me that when there's a woman in it, it's haphazard pot luck with no telling which way the cat will hop. You can't play any system, and merit cuts little figure in general results."

From: *The Log of a Cowboy: A Narrative of the Old Trail Days* (Boston: Houghton Mifflin and Company, Publishers, 1903)

Cowboy Tales around the Camp Fire

The Hazards of Teaching on the Rio Peñasco, c. 1882

Lily Klasner

Born on the Texas frontier in 1862, danger and deprivation marked much of her early life. As Klasner's father was away serving in the Civil War and there was constant danger from roving bands of Commanches, Kiowas, and Lipan Apache Indians, Klasner says that what southern women feared most were "the Jay-hawkers drifting in from the North." After the Civil War, Klasner walked with her family on a long trek to New Mexico. Her father was murdered when she was thirteen and Klasner herself put on a six-gun. She became close friends with John Chisum, "Cattle King of the Pecos," and knew many of the gunslingers and law-men west of the Pecos. She died in 1946 and her manuscript was found more than twenty years later in a trunk in an adobe house in New Mexico. In this narrative, Klasner describes her earliest teaching experiences.

My inclination for teaching showed itself when I was a small girl. There was nothing I liked better than to say to my playmates, "Let's play school," and if they agreed, I always assumed the role of teacher. I felt that this was mine by right, for I was farther advanced than the rest of the children of our family; and those of the Mexican renters who played with us had hardly put their feet onto the road of learning. I will admit that I got a good deal of enjoyment from the punishment my position allowed me to inflict on the others, but at the same time I greatly enjoyed feeling that I was trying to instill some knowledge into the minds of others.

The first chance I had of being a teacher in a real sense came in 1882, when I happened to go away from home for a visit to a family named Jack Wilson that lived on the Upper Peñasco, near what is now Mayhill, New

Mexico. At that time I was nearly grown and rather large for my age. On this portion of the Peñasco, there was quite a settlement of American families, some from Missouri, like the Coes and Mahills, and the others mostly from Texas, like the Jameses, the Bateses, and the Orial Means family. In all these there were quite a number of children and up to that time there were no school opportunities. The public school system was in its infancy in the Territory, and of course, was very laxly managed in an extensive county like that of Lincoln. Of what service were the three commissioners in a county as large as that? A Mr. Bryan, commissioner for that part of the country, lived some distance away on the lower Peñasco, and paid little attention to the upper Peñasco.

While I was at the home of the Wilsons, the families in that section got together and agreed to start a school of their own. They built a schoolhouse and raised enough by subscription to pay a teacher $50 a month for six months. How they selected me as teacher I do not know, but they came to me with the offer and I agreed to teach for them. Mrs Mahill agreed to board me for $10 a month with the understanding that I was to be like one of the family and help with the work morning and evening. This seemed to be the best arrangement I could make for boarding, although the two-mile walk from the Mahills to the school promised to be formidable when the heavy winter snows came.

The log schoolhouse was built by the men of the community quickly enough and equipped with some roughly made tables and benches. My table was a little more substantial than the others, and somebody furnished a chair for my use. About twenty pupils were assembled, and then the school was ready for work.

Of course some of the older boys determined to try me out. They talked a lot about how they would run away from school if I tried to punish them, and then boasted that I could never catch them, for they could outrun me. I confess that my heart sometimes sank into my shoes as I thought of what these boys might do. About five or six of the oldest ones always brought their six-shooters and Winchesters. Though still in their teens they had attained that much of manhood on the frontier. There was reason for them coming armed; they had to ride in from different ranches a long distance away, and there still lurked the fear of Indians. Of course on arrival at school they laid aside their arms and did not put them on until they were ready to start homewards. But it was not reassuring to a greenhorn teacher as I was to think that these boys might make trouble if they became so inclined.

I resolved firmly that I would nip in the bud the first attempt at rebellion, and I succeeded in doing so in a manner that established me in authority. About a week after school commenced, little Frank Mahill got contrary, and refused to make the figure 6 according to directions. He seemed determined to follow his way which was to start at the bottom with the "o" then move upward with the stroke instead of the reverse method which Uncle Ash Upson had taught me and which I was passing on to my students. As he was the youngest and rather spoiled child of Mrs. Mahill with whom I stayed, talked more nicely and coaxingly to him than I might have done had it been anyone else, but with no results. Frank resolutely stuck to his method of making a 6 and I realized that I would have to take issue with him over the matter.

All the other pupils were interested in my tussle with Frank, and it flashed into my mind that I had better give first attention to the door, and with my legs none too steady, I walked over and closed it, locking it as I did so and putting the key into my pocket. I knew somehow that by that action I had conquered the school completely. Without saying a word, I walked back to the desk where Frank stood with his slate, and taking it in my hands, I remarked, "Now, Frank, let's learn how to make those 6's in the right way."

Frank's attitude had been changed, too, and soon he was making his 6's as well as could be expected, starting at the top and rounding out the bottom last. Never later on did I have the least difficulty in exercising proper authority in the school room. The large boys never gave me any of the trouble they had so much boasted of; of course, I had to get after some of the smaller children for minor offenses and sometimes I had to punish them. But on the whole my pupils and I got on very well together, all due, I think, to my having had the courage to lock the door and put the key in my pocket

The Death Sentence of Alfred Packer, April 13, 1883

Melville B. Gerry

Born in Pennsylvania in 1842, Packer meant to serve in the United States Army in the Civil War and enlisted in 1862 but was shortly mustered out due to epilepsy. In the late-fall of 1873 he joined a commercial venture and left Provo, Utah, with a party of twenty-one. They established a winter encampment near Montrose, Colorado. In February 1874, Packer left with five others to head toward Gunnison, Colorado. The party became snowbound and desperate. In April 1874 Packer arrived alone at the Los Pinos Indian Agency near Gunnison. Being questioned as to the whereabouts of his traveling companions, Packer signed a confession that he had killed some of them and eaten them. In August 1874 Packer mysteriously escaped from jail but was recaptured in 1883, nine years after his escape. In later confessions he recanted his earlier confession and claimed that his partners had been killed by another member of the party, whom Packer had to kill in self-defense, but that he still committed cannibalism on the bodies. A jury found him guilty of murder. In the following narrative, Hinsdale District Court Judge Gerry imposes the death sentence. It has been reported that after Judge Gerry read the prepared statement contained in this entry, that Judge Gerry then shouted the following at the condemned man: "Stand up, you man-eating son of a bitch, stand up!" Then pointing a finger at him, the Judge said: "They was seven democrats in Hinsdale County, and you ate five of them, God damn you! I sentence you to be hanged by the neck until you are dead, dead, dead, as a warning against reducing the democratic population of this state." The death sentence, however, was reversed by the Colorado Supreme Court due to a technicality, and Packer was sentenced to forty years imprisonment in a second trial. Packer was paroled in 1901 and died of "senility—trouble & worry" in 1907.

It becomes my duty as the Judge of this Court to enforce the verdict of the jury rendered in your case, and impose on you the judgment which the law fixes as the punishment of the crime you have committed. It is a solemn, painful duty to perform. I would to God the cup might pass from me! You have had a fair and impartial trial. You have been faithfully and earnestly defended by able counsel. The presiding Judge of this Court, upon his oath and his conscience, has labored to be honest and impartial in the trial of your case, and in all doubtful questions presented you have had the benefit of the doubt.

A jury of twelve honest citizens of the county have set in judgment on your case, and upon their oaths they find you guilty of willful and pre-meditated murder—a murder revolting in all its details. In 1874 you in company with five companions passed through this beautiful mountain valley where stands the town of Lake City. At this time the hand of man had not marred the beauties of nature. The picture was fresh from the hand of the Great Artist who created it. You and your companions camped at the banks of a stream as pure and beautiful as ever traced by the finger of God upon the bosom of the earth. Your every surrounding was calculated to impress upon your heart and nature the omnipotence of Deity, and the helplessness of your own feeble life. In this goodly favored spot you conceived your murderous designs.

You and your victims had had a weary march, and when the shadow of the mountains fell upon your little party and night drew her sable cur-tain around you, your unsuspecting victims lay down on the ground and were soon lost in the sleep of the weary, and when thus sweetly uncon-scious of danger from any quarter, and particularly from you, their trusted companion; you cruelly and brutally slew them all. Whether your murderous hand was guided by the misty light of the moon, or the flick-ering blaze of the camp fire, you can only tell. No eye saw the bloody deed performed, no ear save your own caught the groans of your dying victims. You then and there robbed the living of life, and then robbed the dead of the reward of honest toil which they had accumulated, at least so say the jury. To other sickening details of your crime I will not refer. Si-lence is kindness. I do not say these things to harrow your soul, for I know you have drunk the cup of bitterness to its very dregs, and wher-ever you have gone, the sting of your conscience and the goadings of re-morse have an avenging Nemesis which have followed you at every turn in life and painted afresh for your contemplation the picture of the past. I say these things to impress upon your mind the awful solemnity of your situation and the impending doom which you cannot avert. Be not de-ceived, God is not mocked, for whatsoever a man soweth that shall he also reap. You, Alfred Packer, sowed the wind; you must now reap the whirlwind. Society cannot forgive you for the crime you have committed.

It enforces the old Masonic law of a life for a life, and your life must be taken as the penalty of your crime. I am but the instrument of society to impose the punishment which the law provides. What society cannot forgive it will forget. As the days come and go, the story of your crimes will fade from the memory of men.

With God it is different. He will not forget, but will forgive. He pardoned the dying thief on the cross. He is the same God today as then—a God of love and of mercy, of long suffering and for kind forbearance; a God who tempers the wind to the shorn lamb, and promises rest to all the weary and heart-broken children of men; and it is this God I commend you.

Close up your ears to the blandishments of hope. Listen not to its flattering promises of life; but prepare for the dread certainty of death. Prepare to meet thy God; prepare to meet that aged father and mother of whom you have spoken and who still love their dear boy.

For nine long years you have been a wanderer upon the face of the earth, bowed and broken in spirit; no home; no loves; no ties to bind you to earth. You have been indeed, a poor, pitiable waif of humanity. I hope and pray that in the spirit land to which you are so fast and surely drifting, you will find that peace and rest for your weary spirit which this world cannot give.

Alfred Packer, the judgment of the Court is that you be removed from hence to the jail of Hinsdale County, and there be confined until the 19th day of May, A.D. 1883, and that on said 19th day of May 1883, you be taken from thence by the Sheriff of Hinsdale County, to a place of execution prepared for this purpose, at some point within the corporate limits of the town of Lake City, in the said County of Hinsdale, and between the hours of 10 A.M. and 3 P.M. of said day, you then and there, by the said Sheriff, be hung by the neck until you are dead, dead, dead, and may God have mercy upon your soul.

From: *Judge Gerry's Death Sentence of Packer: Hinsdale District Court, Case #1883DC379* courtesy of the Alfred Packer collection at the Colorado State archives

Finding a Small Indian Mummy, c. Summer 1884

James A. McKenna

Pennsylvania-born, James A. McKenna (1851–1941) took a job on a steamboat running between Pittsburgh and St. Louis at the end of the Civil War. Then, in St. Louis, he got work on the steamboat, Far West, that ferried supplies to army outposts on the Missouri River. But McKenna got off at Kansas City and joined up with a wagon train heading for New Mexico. Eventually, he found himself in an area of southern New Mexico known as the "Black Range" which is close to Silver City. In the Black Range McKenna had many adventures, and it was there that McKenna and a partner explored what is now known as the Gila Cliff Dwellings. These ancient dwellings, built by the Anazasi, or Ancient Ones, some seven hundred years ago, were constructed under large cliff overhangs. Some of the most extensive are located in southwestern Colorado, near the four corners area, on the cliff facings of a large mesa called Mesa Verde. A local cowboy named Benjamin Wetherill excavated some of the larger cliff-dwelling sites at Mesa Verde in the late-nineteenth century. Wetherill also found mummified remains like McKenna does in the following story. Bespeaking of his insensitivity toward the Indian indigeous people and the times in which he lived, Wetherill wrote tha the mummies that he found ". . . were not really mummies, but just the dried-up remains of a people without a name" (The Wetherills of the Mesa Verde, edited by Maurine S. Flether). McKenna's story of his exploration of the Gila Cliff Dwellings was extracted from his 1936 book, Black Range Tales.

According to Baxter, when he came to the Gila country shortly after the Civil War, the little valley opposite the Hot Springs showed signs of irrigation ditches, its willow thickets being a hide-out for bears. But after the cattle came all these signs were destroyed. I believe those springs were used by the prehistoric people who had their cliff dwellings about six miles above the springs on the West Fork of the Gila. I went around these cliff dwellings with Baxter, who had been around many pueblos and cave houses in New Mexico, and could talk by the hour on what he had seen.

The cliff was reached by a steep hill that rose to a height of about one hundred and seventy-five feet. In the lower part of this canyon wall of sandstone were four caverns with houses built inside them. These cave dwelling were only one story high, but they appear two stories high, owing to the way they stand on the slope. Entering the eastern cave house by crawling through a small, square door, we explored three houses without going outside to enter them, as passageways led behind wide rock pillars; the fourth cave dwelling to the west we had to reach by a separate opening from the outside. We went through more than twenty compartments, some not over five feet square, none above seven feet high.

In the large cliff house on the West Fork . . . we found many partitions built of rock laid in cement. We thought this cement must have been made of lime and sand, crushed in *metates*, like those still in use among Mexicans and Indians, for grinding corn and other grains and seeds; however, some claim the rocks were laid in adobe mud. Whatever it was, it wore well, for these walls are as strong as the day they were built. Perhaps five hundred years, perhaps five thousand years ago, since no one can tell their age. All the mortar must have been put on by hand as the masonry still bears many finger prints and hand marks. Even the cracks in the floor were sealed with this mortar, and the floors were still in good shape. . . . The roofs also were in good conditions, being held up by pine beams with the bark peeled off. The pine beams were covered with a network of twigs and grasses, and this again with a plaster of adobe mud. T-shaped air holes gave a dim light.

We found no articles made of metal, but many of stone. The hammers and war axes we took note of were nearly all made of a rock not found in the vicinity. A groove was cut through the center in which a split wooden handle was fastened with the sinews of an animal. Other war axes shaped like a mallet were made of a rock called ricolite found near Silver City.

The only ornaments we picked up were of turquoise, generally formed into beads of oblong shape. New Mexico is noted for its high-grade turquoise, but I have never seen any of so fine a quality as that we picked up in the rooms of the cliff dwelling. The beads were strung on animal sinews. Taking in one hand a stone-chipped drill, and in the other a handful of turquoise beads with tiny round holes bored through them one could not but wonder at the skill and patience of these workers in stone. How did they do so well? It has always been a mystery to me. Their arrow-heads, too, were chipped by the hands of artists.

In the upper cliff dwellings we took note of many *ollas*, or water jars, made of red and gray clay, not found in this section. The *ollas* that I found were all decorated with pictures of bear, elk, and deer, and a number of other designs, but there were no birds, flowers, or trees. In the debris we found many pumpkin seeds and some corn on the cob, with a small amount of the flint variety, though most of it looked like popcorn; we also picked up many pink beans and a few striped ones.

In one of the caves was a large hall, or gathering place. . . . An oblong fireplace took up the center of this room. Lying about were many sandals made of bear grass and yucca fiber. Their small size, the small hand prints on the wall, and the small openings between rooms seemed to tell of a race of short people; however, skeletons found in other ruins do not bear out this idea. Under the floors we found bones and skulls. Perhaps if some one learns to read the pictographs on the canyon walls, other burial places may be discovered. In one room, we found a hollow-sounding section, but we had to give up trying to get into it on account of the millions of fleas and mosquitoes we stirred up. . . .

The most interesting thing we found was a perfect mummy with cottonwood fiber woven around it. . . . The length of the figure was about eighteen inches. It lay with knees drawn up and the palms of the hands covering the face. The features were like those of a Chinese child, with high cheek bones and coarse, dark hair. The age of the child at the time of death was thought to be two years. The body was kept for weeks in the show window of a store in Silver City. . . .

Reprinted from *Black Range Tales* by permission of the Rio Grande Press, Inc., © 1936.

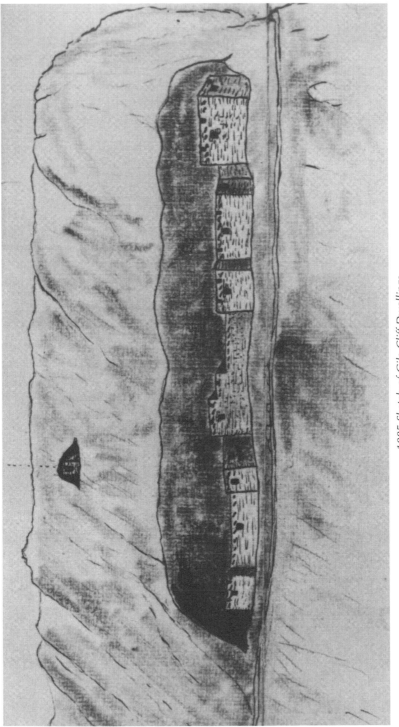

1885 Sketch of Gila Cliff Dwellings

Advice to the Girls of Chillicothe, c. 1885

Charles Lummis

Charles Lummis (1859–1928) was born in Massachusetts and at the age of eighteen, entered Harvard where he met and became lifelong friends with Theodore Roosevelt. In the fall of 1884, twenty-five-year-old Lummis set out on a meandering 143-day "tramp" to Los Angeles where he was to take the job as the city editor for the Los Angeles Times. Along the way, he wrote a series of articles that he dispatched by mail from points along his travels. Further, Lummis wrote similar articles to his former employing newspaper, the Chillicothe, Ohio, Leader. These articles became the basic foundation for his 1892 book, published by Charles Scribner's Sons, A Tramp across the Continent. In the following narrative, excerpted from a modern reprint of his earlier book, Lummis is advocating that unattached young women remaining in Ohio, consider moving West in order to find a husband and happiness.

There is one thing I want to ease my mind of, and if I work in a little of my slang, it isn't because I think the subject a trifling one. It is a little sermon to the girls of Chillicothe. I have often said, and I believe it now, that the old metropolis has a larger proportion of beautiful girls than any other city in the world, and as for their virtues I can say nothing better than that I found my own ideal and mate among them. Now perhaps it would be proper to pretend that all these lovable young ladies are besieged with hosts of lovers, but not being a society liar, I shall not pretend so. I know, as well as you all know, that the conservatism—in English, old-fogyism—of a certain class has kept Chillicothe down so that her boys are driven away from home to make a livelihood, and that the eligible young ladies outnumber the eligible young men about five to one. This is a cruel state of things, and an unnatural one, for the Lord meant that every girl should have one bean anyhow for keeps, and maybe several more for luck. He cut her out, too, for a happy wife and mother; and she knows it. Now get out your arithmetics and see what sort of a show a girl stands of getting married where she is five next to the boys' one. It isn't very hard to reckon.

The West, on the other hand, is full of men—mostly young men—who have come out here from the East, where they were just as good as any of us—and become the makers of this strong, new country. They are men, fine men in body as well as in mind and heart, sturdy, honorable, self-reliant, full of energy and strength, yet tender as only such men can be when it is the time for tenderness, they have become almost a new race. Girls are rarer than other angels, and when one does fold her wings and light down in one of these towns, she can have her pick from the whole population. These men, long separated from mother, sister and home, are not weaned from the human longing for womanly sympathy and companionship, and the desire is intense within them for a home of their own. Why, I could show you, right here, one sweet-faced little New England girl who came out to teach the young . . . She taught school just three days, with the whole male population at her feet, and then married a smart young fellow to whom her preference turned. If you will show me a happier little mother and wife than she is today, I'll agree to turn bachelor myself.

Now I shall not give any advice, for that might be impertinent; but if I were a Chillicothe girl without someone that I thought was a powerful sight better than a brother, I'd make a break for the territories too quick. I'd come out to a place where I was dead sure of a chance to marry a man, and not stay back East and run my slim show of catching on to a dude. Instead of tarrying where the ague would make me shake out of my false teeth when I came to wear them, I'd elope for the finest climate in the world. I'd locate in New Mexico—perhaps right here in Golden—find a man to suit me, let him have me, make him build me a good adobe cottage which I'd fix up as a woman can, and then enjoy life. If he came home some night a millionaire—and that sort of lightning is apt to strike anyone here at any time—it wouldn't worry me, but if he didn't, we could be happy anyhow. There, that's what I'd do—you can do as you like, it's none of my funeral.

Reprinted from *Letters from the Southwest*, James W. Byrkit (editor) by permission of The University of Arizona Press.

Winter Weather, c. 1887

Theodore Roosevelt

Theodore "Teddy" Roosevelt (1858–1919) became the twenty-sixth U.S. President after William McKinley was assassinated in 1901. Roosevelt first headed West in 1883 to hunt buffalo. While in the Dakotas, he purchased a ranch in the Badlands. In 1884 he returned to his ranch for its solitude while grieving the death of his young wife. During this time he authored a number of works about the West. In 1886, he returned to New York and married his childhood sweetheart. He also wrote a series of articles that were turned into the 1888 book, Ranch Life and the Hunting Trail, *from which the narrative below was excerpted.*

When the days have dwindled to their shortest, and the nights seem never ending, then all the great northern plains are changed into an abode of iron desolation. Sometimes furious gales blow out of the north, driving before them the clouds of blinding snow-dust, wrapping the mantle of death round every unsheltered being that faces their unshackled anger. They roar in a thunderous bass as they sweep across the prairie or whirl through the naked cañons; they shiver the great brittle cottonwoods, and beneath their rough touch the icy limbs of the pines that cluster in the gorges sing like the chords of an Eolian harp. Again, in the coldest midwinter weather, not a breath of wind may stir; and then the still, merciless, terrible cold that broods over the earth like the shadow of silent death seems even more dreadful in its gloomy rigor than is the lawless madness of the storms. All the land is like granite: the great rivers stand still in their beds, as if turned to frosted steel. In the long nights there is no sound to break the lifeless silence. Under the ceaseless shifting play of

371

the Northern Lights, or lighted only by the wintry brilliance of the stars, the snow-clad plains stretch out into dead and endless wastes of glimmering white.

Then the great fire-place of the ranch house is choked with blazing logs, and at night we have to sleep under so many blankets that the weight is fairly oppressive. Outside, the shaggy ponies huddle together in the corral, while long icicles hang from their lips, and the hoar-frost whitens the hollow backs of the cattle. For the ranchman the winter is occasionally a pleasant holiday, but more often an irksome period of enforced rest and gloomy foreboding.

In the winter there is much less work than at any other season, but what there is involves great hardship and exposure. Many of the men are discharged after the summer is over, and during much of the cold weather there is little to do except hunt now and then, and in very bitter days lounge listlessly about the house. But some of the men are out in the line camps, and the ranchman has occasionally to make the round of these; and besides that, one or more of the cowboys who are at home ought to be out everyday when the cattle have become weak, so as to pick up and drive in any beast that will otherwise evidently fail to get through the season—a cow that has had an unusually early calf being particularly apt to need attention. The horses shift for themselves and need no help. Often, in winter, the Indians cut down the cottonwood trees and feed the tops to their ponies; but this is not done to keep them from starving, but only to keep them from wandering off in search of grass. Besides, the ponies are very fond of the bark of the young cottonwood shoots, and it is healthy for them.

The men in the line camps lead a hard life, for they have to be out in every kind of weather, and should be especially active and watchful during the storms. The camps are established along some line which it is proposed to make the boundary of the cattle's drift in a given direction. For example, we care very little whether our cattle wander to the Yellowstone; but we strongly object to their drifting east and south-east towards the granger country and the Sioux reservation, especially as when they drift that way they come out on flat, bare plains where there is danger of perishing. Accordingly, the cowmen along the Little Missouri have united in establishing a row of camps to the east of the river, along the line where the broken ground meets the prairie. The camps are usually for two men each, and some fifteen or twenty miles apart; then, in the morning, its two men start out in opposite ways, each riding till he meets his neighbor of the next camp nearest on that side, when he returns. The camp itself is sometimes merely a tent pitched in a sheltered coulée, but ought to be either made of logs or else a dug-out in the ground. A small corral and horse-shed is near by, with enough hay for the ponies, of which each rider has two or three.

In riding over the beat each man drives any cattle that have come near it back into the Bad Lands, and if he sees by the hoof-marks that a few have strayed out over the line very recently, he will follow and fetch them home. They must be shoved well back into the Bad Lands before a great storm strikes them; for if they once begin to drift in masses before an icy gale it is impossible for a small number of men to hold them, and the only thing is to let them go, and then to organize an expedition to follow them as soon as possible. Line riding is very cold work, and dangerous too, when the men have to be out in a blinding snow-storm, or in a savage blizzard that takes the spirit in the thermometer far down below zero. In the worst storms it is impossible for any man to be out.

But other kinds of work besides line riding necessitate exposure to bitter weather. Once, while spending a few days over on Beaver Creek hunting up a lost horse, I happened to meet a cowboy who was out on the same errand, and made friends with him. We started home together across the open prairies, but were caught in a very heavy snow-storm almost immediately after leaving the ranch where we had spent the night. We were soon completely turned round, the great soft flakes—for, luckily, it was not cold—almost blinding us, and we had to travel entirely by compass. After feeling our way along for eight or nine hours, we finally got down into the broken country near Sentinel Butte and came across an empty hut, a welcome sight to men as cold, hungry, and tired as we were. In this hut we passed the night very comfortably, picketing our horses in a sheltered nook near by, with plenty of hay from an old stack. To while away the long evening, I read Hamlet aloud, from a little pocket Shakespeare. The cowboy, a Texan,—one of the best riders I have seen, and also a very intelligent as well as a thoroughly good fellow in every way,—was greatly interested in it and commented most shrewdly on the parts he liked, especially Polonius's advice to Laertes, which he translated into more homely language with great relish, and ended with the just criticism that "old Shakespeare saveyed human natur' some"—savey being a verb presumably adapted into the limited plains' vocabulary from the Spanish.

Even for those who do not have to look up stray horses, and who are not forced to ride the line day in and day out, there is apt to be some hardship and danger in being abroad during the bitter weather; yet a ride in midwinter is certainly fascinating. The great white country wrapped in the powdery snow-drift seems like another land; and the familiar landmarks are so changed that a man must be careful lest he lose his way, for the discomfort of a night in the open during such weather is very great indeed. When the sun is out the glare from the endless white stretches dazzles the eyes; and if the gray snow-clouds hang low and only let a pale light struggle through, the lonely wastes become fairly appalling in their desolation.

There are few moments more pleasant than the home-coming, when, in the gathering darkness, after crossing the last chain of ice-covered buttes, or after coming round the last turn in the wind-swept valley, we see, through the leafless trees, or across the frozen river, the red gleam of the firelight as it shines through the ranch windows and flickers over the trunks of the cottonwoods outside, warming a man's blood by the mere hint of the warmth awaiting him within.

From: *Ranch Life and the Hunting-Trail* (New York: The Century Co., 1888)

Adios to the Coyote Kid, c. 1888

Emmett Dalton

The Dalton Gang, dubbed "The Wild Bunch," were a mix of outlaws consisting of the Dalton brothers—Bob, Emmett, Bill, and Grat—and Charlie Pierce, George Newcomb, Bill Doolin, Charlie Bryant, and Dick Broadwell, alias Texas Jack. The Daltons had worked as deputy marshals but turned to crime after their older brother, Frank, a deputy marshal in Fort Smith was killed in a gun battle in 1887. The Wild Bunch became the scourge of the West as they robbed banks and trains. On October 5, 1892, five gang members rode into Coffeyville, Kansas, with a plan to rob two banks at the same time, but they were recognized and an alarm was raised. Citizen townsmen armed themselves and when the gang tried to escape, a fierce gun battle began in which four citizens and four gang members were killed. Emmett (1871–1937), the sole survivor of the gang was seriously wounded, but recovered and was sentenced to life in prison. He was pardoned by the Kansas governor in 1907, married an old acquaintance, moved to California, and became involved in real estate and the motion picture industry. Emmett published a book about the exploits of the gang, When the Daltons Rode, *and was filmed in a reenactment of the raid on the banks of Coffeyville. Emmett died of natural causes in July 1937 at the age of sixty-six. The following narrative was excerpted from Emmett's book. Nothing more is known about the Coyote Kid other than what Emmett tells us in this story.*

To [the] ranch had come a youngster, a West-struck runaway from Vermont. A strange waif of about eighteen, he bore with a certain swagger the self-proclaimed title of the "Coyote Kid." For a time he attached himself to us. He and I used to wrangle the horses together. We blew discordant tunes on our harmonicas. He must have known who we were, shortly, yet he never peeped. Bob became his idol. Like some shaggy puppy he hung about, wagging friendliness. We paid him to look after our horses. And he appointed himself a sentinel for the band, keeping a weather eye out for strangers. Reluctantly the Coyote Kid told us fragments of his story. Once he showed me part of a letter, much thumbed—"Come home, Son. We'd almost sooner see you dead than tramping around so disreputably amidst godless companions." He seemed ashamed of the missive and begged me not to tell the other boys. The Coyote Kid wanted to be tough, like hundreds of other Kids who filtered through the remotest West to notorious or insignificant destiny. He resented our offer to buy him a railroad ticket back home. A future bad man, perhaps, if time had given him the chance or we had encouraged him.

One evening after we'd been harping "Little Brown Jug" to the mutter of a rising storm, the Coyote Kid rode out across the prairie toward Camp Cantonment to buy us cartridges. Next day we found him in the grass beside his fallen pony. They had been struck dead by lightning. His travels among "godless companions" were over. We buried him there, with the home letter in his faded jeans. Meadow larks nest in the sod above him, and sandhill plums scatter their fragrant petals where he fell. I like to think that he's regaling old St. Peter with ditties on his rusty harmonica.

From: *When the Daltons Rode* (Garden City, NY: Doubleday, Doran & Company, Inc., 1922)

Practicing with the Bow, c. May 1889

Edmund Nequatewa

Nequatewa (1880–1969) was a Hopi Indian whose stories of his early boyhood to young manhood were told to anthropologist, Alfred F. Whiting, in the 1930s. Whiting had Nequatewa's oral history published at that time and it was republished by the University of Arizona Press in 1993 with the title, Born a Chief: The Nineteenth Century Hopi Boyhood of Edmund Nequatewa. *For more than a thousand years, the Hopi Indians have lived in northeastern Arizona. Their origins are shrouded in mystery but they made first contact with Spaniards in the late-1500s and Spanish efforts to convert the Hopi met with limited success. In this vignette, Nequatewa is learning to shoot with the bow and while he hits his mark, he learns that his targets are inappropriate.*

My father was planting a watermelon patch. It must be about a mile east of Shipaulovi, down in the valley. The wind was kind of blowing hard, and my father usually sent me over there every time when the wind blows so I can kind of keep the plants clear of sand so they won't smother. The wind was blowing good and hard, but it kind of calmed down in the afternoon. So I wanted to go over there in the afternoon so father wouldn't be getting me up early in the morning. He always sends me over there early in the morning, but I wanted to go over there in the afternoon. One thing: I always did carry my bow and arrows because I sure did love to see anything I could find to use for a target. I love to shoot at it.

I started down there. One of my aunts, she was just at the stage where she would wear her hair fixed up on the side of her head in a butterfly curl. Mother asked her to go with me so I won't be coming home late, so we could get through before it gets dark.

So we started out, and as we are going along the road, way down below I saw a dove in a peach tree. I said, "Hold on. There is a dove in that
peach tree." She said, "Never mind the dove, we're in a hurry." I just put
up my arrow and let it go. I shot the dove in the center and it fell off the
tree, and I ran over and picked it up.

I don't know what happened, but I pulled too hard on my bow string
and it got loose. I pulled the arrow out of the dove, and I went to fix my
bow string. So I ask this girl to hold the dove. Well, she takes it so easy.
You know how girls are. She was holding the dove so easy, and it wasn't
killed, and so it flew away. I turned around and the dove was going up. I
said, "What you let it go for?" She said, "Oh, it got away." I said, "If I can't
shoot a dove, I'll shoot you." She screamed and ran. I was so mad I just
put up my arrow and took a shot just as she turned around to look back.
The arrow went right through her hair. I lost my arrow. She just screamed
and cried and started running home. She came home with the arrow in
her hair just to prove that I really did take a shot at her.

So I went on to the watermelon patch and worked until it gets dark. I
started home. When I got home, grandfather, my mother's father, was at
the house. He was sure mad, because it was his daughter. This grandfather was married again, so he wasn't living with us anymore. He was mad
because his daughter got shot, but he didn't say anything. But after I had
my supper he asked me what had happened, so I told him about the dove
and how I got mad and she started running so I shot after her.

The old man says, "Boy, you know it is always dangerous to shoot at
someone. You might shoot her in the back of the head, in the ear or her
eyes. Bad boys like you, someone will wish some bad calamity on you, so
you had better watch out." I didn't say anything. Mother didn't say anything. Father didn't say anything. After my grandfather went away, then
my parents talked to me.

"Grandfather was really mad when he first came. He must forget he
was a boy onetime himself. But from now on, don't shoot after anybody.
That is wrong to shoot after a person. It is all right to shoot after birds and
lizards. How would you feel to get shot?"

A few days later a lot of us boys went down into the valley to shoot
birds, and about toward noon we started home. Instead of going up to the
mesa, we went down on the east side of the gap between Mishongnovi
and Shipaulovi to a big cave. We went down into it. There was a bunch
from Mishongnovi and a bunch from Shipaulovi. So we thought we
would play a game down there, and we made two piles of dirt for our targets. We were having a time down there playing a game to see who would
win. Whatever arrows were not in use we stuck on top of the pile of dirt,
sort of just to one side. We Shipaulovi boys won the game once, so we
asked them for their arrows, but they won't give them to us. They prom-

ise to give them to us after the next game if they don't get even with us. So finally we win again, and everybody's arrow was sticking on top of this pile of dirt. So the first boy from our side went ahead and took a shot. This was all planned beforehand when we were running back and forth. We had planned that we would run away with their arrows. One of our best runners was going to take these arrows. We shot to the Mishongnovi side, and we all went back, and this boy ran and picked out all the arrows. Off he went, with us after him.

There was a big sand hill there, and we went crawling up there, with them right after us. We kept throwing handfuls of sand down on these other boys and got sand in their eyes. They couldn't help but stop. So we went on. Just as I was getting up to the rocks, I turn around to see if anyone was coming. Zip! An arrow just went right in my leg, and I just jerked the arrow out. Gosh I was mad. I had only two arrows with me, which were my best ones. I sat right there, and the blood was running down my leg. I was so mad I was determined I'm going to shoot this fellow back. I put my best arrow up, but then I decide to take the one that was in my leg and shoot it and keep my good arrows.

Two fellows were watching me. I thought I would just let the arrow go, but just as it got there one fellow raised up and Bang! I got him right in the shoulder. Well, he just fell over like he was dead, just to make those people think he was dead. By this time there was quite a few people watching from the village. They see this boy was shot, and they tell that it's him, and they came running down. The uncle of this boy came running down, and of course he had heard that I had shot this boy.

When I got on top of the mesa, my great uncle, my mother's mother's brother, came down with his bow and arrows, and this other fellow's uncle, he had a club and said he was going to kill me. My great uncle says, "Hold on." I had the blood dripping down on my leg, and I told him that somebody shot me. So we had to have all those other boys come up, and everybody was holding on to this boy and he was making out like he was so hurt. They pull the arrow and everybody says it's his arrow. I had got the right one!

Well, this boy's uncle says he's going to kill me right then and there, so my uncle says, "If you're man enough, all right." He knows that he won't do it. He says, "Go ahead. I'm here to see you hit him. Don't forget, my arrow is right here. The minute you hit this boy you'll get it." Finally the people began to gather and gather, and we had a big argument. One old man . . . bawled this fellow out, called him all kinds of names. He told him that he wouldn't be man enough to hit me, otherwise he is going to be killed himself. "You're going to be killed if you ever hurt this boy," he told him. My great uncle says, "You give me that club and I'll beat you up with it. Any man that is crazy, who makes such a threat on a boy like this, needs to be beat."

They took me home, and my mother picked up some of these corncobs and an old water jar. She opened up the top and put some live coals inside and then put the corncobs inside and made a lot of smoke. I had to hold the wound against the mouth of the water jar so the smoke will come out into the wound. They always put smoke in the wounds when people had wounds. I couldn't hardly stand it. The other two fellows had to hold me, because if they don't make me, it would get into blood poisoning. They just smoked it, and after that they didn't even put anything on it. The only thing they did, my father had carded some of the wool, and they had washed it and they put that on top of it, but that was all. It didn't even swell up.

A Priest Makes a Sick Call, c. April 1890

James J. Gibbons

To learn more about Father Gibbons, the following excerpt from the December 3, 1931, Denver Post, *gives an excellent biography. The main points are: Born in Providence, R.I., the Rev. James J. Gibbons, whose early life was closely interwoven in the . . . history of Colorado died on December 2ⁿᵈ. He studied for the priesthood at St. Mary's seminary, Baltimore. Following his ordination, he joined the missionary diocese of Colorado in 1885. He was assigned to the Georgetown-Silver Plume parish and was also appointed assistant pastor at Leadville. After spending several years in Leadville, Father Gibbons was assigned to the San Juan district with jurisdiction over the churches at Ouray and Silverton and twenty missions (including Telluride and Rico) and stations scattered through the southwestern Colorado high-country. His remembrances were published in 1898 with the title,* In the San Juan. *The following narrative was excerpted from that book.*

In the winter the whole mountain region lay under a blanket of snow, and the narrow trails beaten out by the patient burro, were the only highways a great part of the season . . . On the Ouray road, (a snowslide) had come down and filled the canon to a depth of fifty or sixty feet with great pines and enormous boulders. Travel was dangerous from Ouray to Red Mountain, and for fourteen miles on the opposite side of the range to Silverton.

In the spring, which at this altitude begins about the 1ˢᵗ of May, only the mail carrier will ride a horse over the trails. Snowslides creep silently at first down the mighty slopes and suddenly, with an awful roar, overwhelm the unsuspecting victim. When the snow begins to thaw, the crust becomes rotten, and horses and burros break through it.

. . . I received a summons to a sick bed from Rico, a mining camp far out in the Dolores country, and over 100 miles from Ouray. The man who bore the despatch had ridden forty-five miles across two ranges of mountains, and over roads where five or six feet of snow, ice, slush and high drifts obstructed his passage. The wires were down and the message did not reach me until Tuesday evening at five o'clock. I lost no time in setting out for Dallas, which is fourteen miles north of Ouray, believing that I might proceed by stage from Dallas to Telluride, and by Trout Lake to Rico. What was my surprise when I found that no stage ran from Telluride to Rico.

I returned from Dallas to Ouray, arriving at seven p.m. and perplexed as to the course to pursue. Saturday, Sunday, Monday and Tuesday—the man must be dead; he was dangerously sick of pneumonia—I could not be home by Sunday. Could I get to Rico at all? These were the thoughts that occupied my mind, as midnight approached. Duty, I exclaimed, and hurrying to the livery I ordered my horse and saddle for half past five in the morning. The Sisters of Mercy packed my vestments for holy mass on the coming Sunday. The holy oils, the chalice, the wine and bread were put away in my grip, and all the necessary preparations were made for the journey.

At five o'clock I said mass in the little stone chapel, and a quarter to six found me seated on a good snow horse, which means one that will take it easy when he sticks in the snow and wait patiently until you dig him out. Old Gray, who had lost one ear in a snowslide, and always played lame when tired, humped his back as he began to climb the mountain, the crest of which marked thirteen miles from home. Here, where the little city of Red Mountain nestles among the pines, I was to turn my faithful friend loose and head him for Ouray, which he rarely failed to find.

We got along very well until we came to the little park near Ironton. It was still quite dark, and the morning was crisp and cold. The snow was hard and the only danger was in the deep holes in the road. Old Gray managed to escape for a long time, but at last, despite his cautious movements, slipped and fell into a hole, out of which he could not rise, and as he lay on my leg I could not dismount and help him. He made two or three gentle efforts to get up, and as a trained horse will do, not succeeding remained quiet. My position was embarrassing and painful; much of the horse's weight was on my leg, grinding me into the frozen ice and snow. I believe it was my long ulster alone that saved the bone from breaking. I kept tugging and twisting the old horse's nose and ear, but he lay stiff as a log in the snow. What was I to do? I was growing faint from pain, and running my hand into my overcoat pocket I discovered my hunting knife, which I had recently cleaned. I cut the crust around my hip, and after nearly an hour's scraping and punching, I was enabled to get from under old Gray, who, during all my labors never stirred. Once free myself, I soon had him up. By this time it was daylight, and I was on the alert for the rest of the journey.

On my arrival at Red Mountain I sent my gray friend home, and strapping my pack on my shoulders, set out for Silverton, thirteen miles down grade. The sun was hot and reflected its burning rays from the seething masses of snow on the mountain sides. When I reached the depot the bell was ringing for the outgoing train to Durango. Boarding the train I rode to Rockwood, which is forty-five miles from Rico.

The stage left there every morning at nine, and when the roads were good, generally made connections with the train going to Durango. Fancy my chagrin when I learned that it took the stage two days to reach Rico! At that season of the year, the roads being bad, sometimes you traveled in a wagon, at other times in a sleigh, and sometimes you were forced to walk. You had to push the wagon or the sleigh to help the fagged horses up the slippery hills, and by way of change you spent hours digging the almost smothered horses out of the soft snow or mending broken harness with rope, twine, or wire. It was the last straw on the camel's back to have to pay seven dollars for the privilege of riding on the stage.

With two days more on the road, I began to think that the sick man was not only dead, but buried. To render the situation more exasperating I had to remain over night in Rockwood in a hotel made of slabs and logs through which the bitter cold winds came at will. The only attraction of the chamber in which I slept in my leggings, overshoes and great coat, was a square of gaudy carpet on the floor, which seemed to mock rather than give any comfort. In the morning about eight I met the manager of the stage line and begged for a horse. He had no horse to spare, but he had a good strong mule; on its right knee, however, there was a bunch about as large as a man's head, and if I had no objections, I might have the mule to ride to Rico. The price would be the same as on the stage, and he would wager ten dollars that the mule would carry me surely, if slowly, to my journey's end before nine that night. And he did carry me slowly, and as will be seen, very slowly.

I took the obliging manager at his word and was soon seated in my McClellan saddle with my vestments strapped on in regular marching order. The day was beautiful. The sun was already warm and little streams trickled down the cliffs and hills. I knew the road and the short cuts so well that I thought I could not make a mistake, but experience taught me that pride goes before a fall. I saw a short cut which I believed led to the main road a mile from Rockwood. Why not take it? I was in a hurry; time was precious. Upon taking this road I found instead of turning to the left, as I had supposed it would, it veered to the right more and more, and presently I discovered that I was going back to Silverton.

Coming to what is called in the West a hogback, I had a view of the surrounding country, and saw the road a mile off. I would not turn back and go over the same road again, but cross the country through the soft snow and fallen timber. I followed the hogback for half a mile, and the traveling was fair, but at the bottom of a little valley into which I descended, I found the snow deep and much water. With a determination born of courage and a strong mule, I pushed ahead, when all of a sudden one of my sources of security failed and the mule disappeared, leaving visible only his head, shoulders and embossed knee.

I had broken through the ice; I was in a lagoon. In a moment I was out of my saddle and standing up to my hips in water and mud. The mule, with all his shortcomings, was a good one, and with a powerful lunge came forth from his watery grave. I was in a predicament and rather excited, and the mule was trembling. I looked around for some way out. I saw a house in the distance and a man gesticulating. I waved my hand to him and he approached. He proved to be a Mr. Nary, who assisted me in getting out of the swamp and brought me to his house. To say that the priest and mule were well attended would be putting it mildly. Hay and oats were given to the mule, and of course the priest received a royal welcome. My clothes dried, and a good dinner enjoyed, I was in the saddle again at one in the afternoon with three or four miles to my credit, but still forty miles from my destination. The afternoon was uneventful, the mule putting in some solid work on the bad roads. At dusk I was within fifteen miles of Rico and forging my way along as fast as I could.

The awful darkness, which fell like a pall over the canon and on the misty waters of the Dolores, I shall not forget. The silence was broken at times by the hoarse roar of the snowslide, the short bark of the coyote, and the dismal wail of the mountain lion from some neighboring cliff. But the only fear I had was that the mule might fall.

I was riding over ground consecrated by the hardships of the first Franciscans, who hundreds of years before followed the star of empire westward and named the sparkling stream Dolores, sorrowful. Was it for the sense of loneliness which came to the missionaries as they passed the silent ruins of the Mancos, the empty dwellings on the cliff, and the desolate country which once fed happy thousands, they named the stream, Dolores? At last, worn out by my long ride, my limbs cramped and my muscles rigid from constant tension, I beheld lights here and there far up the Dolores, and my heart was filled with joy. The mule seemed to quicken his pace and we were soon at the hotel.

It took but a few minutes to locate the sick man, whom I found recovering, at the turning point of a bad case of pneumonia. I met the doctor and Nick Hunt, who had carried the despatch over that fearful road, and was nursing the sick man and keeping up the courage of his friend until the priest should arrive. I heard the sick man's confession and then inquired about the welfare of the community.

From: *In the San Juan* (Telluride, CO: St. Patrick's Parish, 1898)

The Death of Sitting Bull, December 16, 1890

James McLaughlin

Born into the Hunkpapa Sioux clan in 1831, Sitting Bull became a famous med-
icine man of the Lakota tribe. Shortly before the battle on the Little Big Horn with
Custer, Sitting Bull had a vision in which he saw his people victorious over the
white soldiers. After the battle, Sitting Bull and his followers went to Canada. In
1881 Sitting Bull returned to the United States and capitulated. He was held
prisoner for two years and was released on the Standing Rock Reservation in
South Dakota. In 1885 he joined Buffalo Bill's Wild West Show. In 1890 he was
a part of the "Ghost Dancers," an Indian ritual in which it was believed that dead
Indians would come back to life and destroy the whites. The author of the follow-
ing narrative was the Indian Agent at the Standing Rock Reservation at the time
of Sitting Bull's death.

On December 12th the following telegram was received by the Post
Commander of Fort Yates, who furnished me with a copy:

"Headquarters, Department of Dakota St. Paul, Minn. December 12th,
1890 To Commanding Officer, Fort Yates, North Dakota: —The Division
commander has directed that you make it your especial duty to secure the
person of Sitting Bull. Call on Indian Agent to cooperate and render such
assistance as will best promote the purpose in view. Acknowledge receipt,
and if not perfectly clear, report back. By command of General Ruger.
(Signed M. BARBER, Assistant Adjutant General)"

Upon receipt of the foregoing telegram the Post Commander sent for
me, and held a consultation as to the best means to effect the desired arrest. It was contrary to my judgment to attempt the arrest at any time
other than upon one of the bi-weekly ration days when there would be

but a few Indians in Sitting Bull's neighborhood, thus lessening the chances of opposition or excitement of his followers. The Post Commander saw the wisdom of my reasoning, and consented to defer the arrest until Saturday morning, December 20th, with the distinct understanding, however, that the Indian police keep Sitting Bull and his followers under strict surveillance to prevent their leaving the reservation, and report promptly any suspicious movements among them.

Everything was arranged for the arrest to be made on December 20th; but on December 14th, at 4 P.M., a policeman arrived at the Agency from Grand River, who brought me a letter from Lieutenant of Police Henry Bull Head, the officer in charge of the force on Grand River, stating that Sitting Bull was making preparations to leave the reservation; that he had fitted his horses for a long and hard ride, and that if he got the start of them, he being well mounted, the police would be unable to overtake him, and he, therefore, wanted permission to make the arrest at once. I had just finished reading Lieut. Bull Head's letter, and commenced questioning the courier who brought it, when Col. Drum, the Post Commander, came into my office to ascertain if I had received any news from Grand River. I handed him the letter which I had just received, and after reading it, he said that the arrest could not be deferred longer, but must be made without further delay; and immediate action was then decided upon, the plan being for the police to make the arrest at break of day the following morning, and two troops of the 8th Cavalry to leave the post at midnight, with orders to proceed on the road to Grand River until they met the police with their prisoner, whom they were to escort back to the post; they would thus be within supporting distance of the police, if necessary, and prevent any attempted rescue of Sitting Bull by his followers. I desired to have the police make the arrest, fully believing that they could do so without bloodshed, while in the crazed condition of the Ghost Dancers, the military could not; furthermore, the police accomplishing the arrest would have a salutary effect upon all the Indians, and allay much of the then existing uneasiness among the whites. I, therefore, sent a courier to Lieut. Bull Head, advising him of the disposition to be made of the cavalry command which was to cooperate with him, and directed him to make the arrest at daylight the following morning.

Acting under these orders, a force of thirty-nine policemen and four volunteers (one of whom was Sitting Bull's brother-in-law, "Gray Eagle") entered the camp at daybreak on December 16th, proceeding direct to Sitting Bull's house, which ten of them entered, and Lieut. Bull Head announced to him the object of their mission. Sitting Bull accepted his arrest quietly at first, and commenced dressing for the journey to the Agency, during which ceremony (which consumed considerable time) his son, "Crow Foot," who was in the house, commenced berating his father for accepting the arrest and consenting to go with the police; whereupon he (Sitting Bull) got stubborn and refused to accompany them.

By this time he was fully dressed, and the policemen took him out of the house; but, upon getting outside, they found themselves completely surrounded by Sitting Bull's followers, all armed and excited. The policemen reasoned with the crowd, gradually forcing them back, thus increasing the open circle considerably; but Sitting Bull kept calling upon his followers to rescue him from the police; that if the two principal men, "Bull Head" and "Shave Head," were killed the others would run away, and he finally called out for them to commence the attack, whereupon "Catch the Bear" and "Strike the Kettle," two of Sitting Bull's men, dashed through the crowd and fired. Lieut. "Bull Head" was standing on one side of Sitting Bull and 1st Sergt. "Shave Head" on the other, with 2d Sergt. "Red Tomahawk" behind, to prevent his escaping; "Catch the Bear's" shot struck Bull Head in the right side, and he instantly wheeled and shot Sitting Bull, hitting him in the left side, between the tenth and eleventh ribs, and "Strike the Kettle's" shot having passed through Shave Head's abdomen, all three fell together. "Catch the Bear," who fired the first shot, was immediately shot down by private of police "Lone Man," and the fight then became general—in fact, a hand-to-hand conflict—forty-three policemen and volunteers against about one hundred and fifty crazed Ghost Dancers.

The fight lasted about half an hour, but all the casualties, except that of Special Policeman John Armstrong, occurred in the first few minutes. The police soon drove the Indians from around the adjacent buildings, and then charged and drove them into the adjoining woods, about forty rods distant, and it was in this charge that John Armstrong was killed by an Indian secreted in a clump of brush. During the fight women attacked the police with knives and clubs, but in every instance they simply disarmed them and placed them under guard in the houses near by until the troops arrived, after which they were given their freedom. . . .

From: *Account of the Death of Sitting Bull and the Circumstances Attending It* from a letter to the Office of Indian Rights Association, Philadelphia, January 12th, 1891

Sitting Bull in 1885

The End of a Dream, December 29, 1890

Black Elk

Following the death of Sitting Bull on December 15, 1890, Chief Big Foot and his Minnicoujou band set out for Pine Ridge. They were intercepted by the 7ᵗʰ Cavalry and brought, under a white flag of truce, to Wounded Knee. On the morning of December 29ᵗʰ, soldiers prepared to search the band for weapons. A rifle was fired, setting off intense shooting that left more than 250 Indians, most of them unarmed, dead. A cousin to Crazy Horse, Black Elk, narrated the following events to John G. Neihardt in May 1931, and this, and other stories make up the book, Black Elk Speaks.

In the morning I went out after my horses, and while I was out I heard shooting off toward the east, and I knew from the sound that it must be wagon-guns (cannon) going off. The sounds went right through my body, and I felt that something terrible would happen.

When I reached camp with the horses, a man rode up to me and said: "Hey-hey-hey! The people that are coming are fired on! I know it!"

I saddled up my buckskin and put on my sacred shirt. It was one I had made to be worn by no one but myself . . . I painted my face all red, and in my hair I put one eagle feather for the One Above.

It did not take me long to get ready, for I could still hear the shooting over there.

I started out alone on the old road that ran across the hills to Wounded Knee. I had no gun. I carried only the sacred bow of the west that I had seen in my great vision. I had gone only a little way when a band of young men came galloping after me. The first two who came up were Loves War and Iron Wasichu. I asked what they were going to do, and they said they

389

were just going to see where the shooting was. Then others were coming up, and some older men.

We rode fast, and there were about twenty of us now. The shooting was getting louder. A horseback from over there came galloping very fast toward us and he said: "Hey-hey-hey! They have murdered them!" Then he whipped his horse and rode away faster toward Pine Ridge.

In a little while we had come to the top of the ridge where, looking to the east, you can see for the first time the . . . burial ground on the little hill . . . Just south of the burying ground on the little hill a deep dry gulch runs about east and west, very crooked, and it rises westward to nearly the top of the ridge where we were. . . . We stopped on the ridge not far from the head of the dry gulch. Wagon guns were still going off over there on the little hill, and they were going off again where they hit along the gulch. There was much shooting down yonder, and there were many cries, and we could see cavalrymen scattered over the hills ahead of us. Cavalrymen were riding along the gulch and shooting into it, where the women and children were running away and trying to hide in the gullies and the stunted pines.

A little way ahead of us, just below the head of the dry gulch, there were some women and children who were huddled under a clay bank, and some cavalrymen were there pointing guns at them. We stopped back behind the ridge, and I said to the others: "Take courage. These are our relatives. We will try to get them back."

Then I rode over the ridge and the others after me, and we were crying: "Take courage! It is time to fight!" The soldiers who were guarding our relatives shot at us and then ran away fast, and some more cavalrymen on the other side of the gulch did too. We got our relatives and sent them across the ridge to the northwest where they would be safe.

I had no gun, and when we were charging, I just held the sacred bow out in front of me with my right hand. The bullets did not hit us at all.

We found a little baby lying all alone near the head of the gulch. I could not pick her up just then, but I got her later and some of my people adopted her. I just wrapped her up tighter in a shawl that was around her and left her there. It was a safe place, and I had other work to do.

The soldiers had run eastward over the hills where there were some more soldiers, and they were off their horses and lying down. I told the others to stay back, and I charged upon them holding the sacred bow out toward them with my right hand. They all shot at me, and I could hear bullets all around me, but I ran my horse right close to them, and then swung around. Some soldiers across the gulch began shooting at me too, but I got back to the others and was not hurt at all.

By now many other Lakotas, who had heard the shooting, were coming up from Pine Ridge, and we all charged on the soldiers. They ran eastward toward where the trouble began. We followed down along the dry gulch, and what we saw was terrible. Dead and wounded women and children and little babies were scattered all along there where they had been trying to run away. The soldiers had followed along the gulch, as they ran, and murdered them in there. Sometimes they were in heaps because they had huddled together, and some were scattered all along. Sometimes bunches of them had been killed and torn to pieces where the wagon guns hit them. I saw a little baby trying to suck its mother, but she was bloody and dead.

There were two little boys at one place in this gulch. They had guns and they had been killing soldiers all by themselves. We could see the soldiers they had killed. They boys were all alone there, and they were not hurt. These were very brave little boys.

When we drove the soldiers back, they dug themselves in, and we were not enough people to drive them out from there. In the evening they marched off up Wounded Knee Creek, and then we saw all that they had done there.

Men and women and children were heaped and scattered all over the flat at the bottom of the little hill . . . and westward up the dry gulch all the way to the high ridge, the dead women and children and babies were scattered. . . .

It was a good winter day when all this happened. The sun was shining. But after the soldiers marched away from their dirty work, a heavy snow began to fall. The wind came up in the night. There was a big blizzard, and it grew very cold. The snow drifted deep in the crooked gulch, and it was one long grave of butchered women and children and babies, who had never done any harm and were only trying to run away. . . .

And so it was all over.

I did not know then how much was ended. When I look back now from this high hill of my old age, I can still see the butchered women and children lying heaped and scattered all along the crooked gulch as plain as when I saw them with eyes still young. And I can see that something else died there in the bloody mud, and was buried in the blizzard. A people's dream died there. It was a beautiful dream.

And I, to whom so great a vision was given in my youth,—you see me now a pitiful old man who has done nothing, for the nation's hoop is broken and scattered. There is no center any longer, and the sacred tree is dead.

8-26-08

Scene Two Days after the Tragedy at Wounded Knee

Bibliography

Adams, Andy. *The Log of a Cowboy: A Narrative of the Old Trail Days* (Boston: Houghton Mifflin Company, Publishers, 1903)

Adams, Grizzly. *The Adventures of James Capen Adams, Mountaineer and Grizzly Bear Hunter of California*, by Theodore H. Hittle (Boston: 1861)

Beckwourth, James P. *The Life and Adventures of James P. Beckwourth, Mountaineer, Scout, and Pioneer, and Chief of the Crow Nation Indians*, as dictated to T. D. Bonner (New York: Harper and Brothers, 1856)

Beidler, X. X. *Beidler Vigilante*, Helen Fitzgerald Sanders and William H. Bertsche, Jr. (editors) (Norman, OK: University of Oklahoma Press, 1957)

Betzinez, Jason. *I Fought With Geronimo* with Wilbur Sturtevant Nye (Lincoln, NE: University of Nebraska Press, 1987)

Bird, Isabella L. *A Lady's Life in the Rocky Mountains* (New York: G. P. Putnam's Sons, Publishers, 1881)

Black Elk. *Black Elk Speaks* (as told through John G. Neihardt) (New York: Morrow & Company, Publishers, 1932)

Black Hills Pioneer. "Assassination of Wild Bill . . . " (Black Hills, SD, August 5, 1876)

Boyd, Frances Anne Mullen. *Cavalry Life in Tent and Field* (New York: J. S. Tait, 1894)

Brackenridge, Henry Marie. *Views of Louisiana, together with a Journal of a Voyage up the Missouri River, in 1811* (Pittsburg, PA: Cramer, Spear and Eichbaum, Publishers, 1814)

Bradbury, John. *Travels in the Interior of American, in the Years 1809, 1810, and 1811* (London: Sherwood, Neely, and Jones, Publishers, 1819)

Brady, Cyrus Townsend. *Recollections of a Missionary in the Great West* (New York: Charles Scribner's Sons, 1900)

Breiver, Charles. Report on the "Burial of the Bones on the Mountain Meadows," from Appendix VI of Anna Jean Backus *Mountain Meadows Witness: The Life and*

Times of Bishop Philip Klingensmith (Spokane, WA: The Arthur H. Clark Company, 1995)

Brewerton, George Douglas. *A Ride with Kit Carson through the Great American Desert and the Rocky Mountains* (New York: Harper & Brothers, 1853)

Carson, Kit. *Kit Carson's Own Story of His Life*, Blanche C. Grant (editor) (Taos, NM: 1926)

Carrington, Henry B. *The Indian Question* (Mattituck, NY: J. M. Carroll & Company, 1909)

Carrington, Margaret Irvin. *Ab-sa-ra-ka: Home of the Crows* (Philadelphia: J. B. Lippincott and Company, Publishers, 1868)

de Castañeda, Pedro. *The Journey of Coronado*, translated by George Parker Winship, from earlier Spanish and English translations (New York: Dover Publications, Inc., 1990)

Catlin, George. *Life Among the Indians* (London: Gall & Inglis, Publishers, 1875)

Chisholm, James. *South Pass 1868* (Lincoln, NE: University of Nebraska Press, 1960)

Clum, John. *Apache Days & Tombstone Nights*, Neil B. Carmony (editor) (Silver City, NM: High Lonesome Books, 1997)

Cody, William F. *Buffalo Bill's Own Story of His Life and Deeds* (Chicago: Homewood Press, 1917)

Collins, John S. *My Experiences in the West*, Colton Storm (editor) (Chicago: The Lakeside Press, R. R. Donnelley & Sons Company, 1970)

Conner, Daniel Ellis. *A Confederate in the Colorado Gold Fields*, Donald J. Berthrong and Odessa Davenport (editors) (Norman, OK: University of Oklahoma Press, 1970)

Cook, James Henry. *Fifty Years on the Old Frontier as Cowboy, Hunter, Guide, Scout, and Ranchman* (New Haven, CT: Yale University Press, 1923)

Cremony, John C. *Life Among the Apaches: Interpreter to the U.S. Boundary Commission, Under the Hon. John R. Batlett, in 1849, '50 and '51, and Late Major of California Volunteer Cavalry, Operating in Arizona, New Mexico, Texas and Western Arkansas* (San Francisco, 1868)

Crockett, Davy. *The Life of David Crockett, etc.* (New York: A. L. Burt Company, 1902)

Custer, Elizabeth B. *Boots and Saddles: or Life in Dakota With General Custer* (New York: Harper Publishing Co., 1885)

Custer, George Armstrong. Letter to Judge Kidder on the Death of His Son, dated August 23, 1867, is contained in E. A. Brininstool, *Troopers With Custer: Historic Incidents of the Battle of the Little Big Horn* (Lincoln, NE: University of Nebraska Press, 1989)

Custer, George Armstrong. *My Life on the Plains, or Personal Experiences with Indians* (New York: Heldon & Company, 1874)

Dalton, Emmett (in collaboration with Jack Jungmeyer). *When the Daltons Rode* (Garden City, NY: Doubleday, Doran & Company, Inc., 1922)

Darley, George M. *Pioneering in the San Juan: Personal Reminiscences of Work Done in Southwestern Colorado During the "Great San Juan Excitement"* (Chicago: Fleming H. Revell Company, Publishers, 1899)

DeBarthe, Joe. *Life and Adventures of Frank Grouard* (St. Joseph, MO: published by Joe DeBarthe, 1894)

Drannan, William F. *Capt. William F. Drannan, Chief of Scouts As Pilot to Emigrant and Government Trains, Across the Plains of the Wild West of Fifty Years Ago* (Chicago: Thos. W. Jackson Publishing Company, 1910)

Edwards, Frank S. *A Campaign in New Mexico With Colonel Doniphan* (Philadelphia: Carey and Hart, Publishers, 1847)

Ewert, Theodore. *Private Theodore Ewert's Diary of the Black Hills Expedition of 1874*, John M. Carroll and Lawrence A. Frost (editors) (Piscataway, NJ: Consultant Resources Incorporated, 1976)

Farmer, James E. *My Life With the Army In The West*, Dale F. Giese (editor) (Santa Fe, NM: Stagecoach Press, 1993)

Ferris, Warren Angus. *Life in the Rocky Mountains*, published in a series of installments in the *Western Literary Messenger* (Buffalo, NY: Chadbourne & Co., from July 13, 1842 to May 4, 1844).

Fletcher, Baylis John *Up the Trail in '79*, Wayne Gard (editor and introduction) (Norman, OK: University of Oklahoma Press, 1968)

Flipper, Henry O. *Negro Frontiersman: The Western Memoirs of Henry O. Flipper* (El Paso, TX: Texas Western College Press, 1963)

Forsyth, George A. *Thrilling Days in Army Life* (New York: Harper and Brothers, 1900)

Fowler, Jacob. *The Journal of Jacob Fowler*, Elliott Coues (editor) (Lincoln, NE: University of Nebraska Press, 1970)

Fugate, James M. *James M. Fugate's Adventures, 1853*, and reprinted in *On the Santa Fe Trail*, Marc Simmons (editor) (Lawrence, KS: University Press of Kansas, 1986)

Garrard, Lewis H. *Wah-To-Yah and the Taos Trail* (Cincinnati, OH: A. S. Barnes and Company, Publishers, 1850)

Garrett, Pat F. *The Authentic Life of Billy, the Kid* (Santa Fe, NM: New Mexican Printing and Publishing Company, 1882)

Geronimo. *Geronimo's Story of His Life* (New York: Duffield Publishers, 1906)

Gerry, Melville B. *Judge Gerry's Death Sentence of Packer: Hinsdale District Court, Case #1883DC379* (Denver: Alfred Packer collection at the Colorado State archives)

Gibbons, James J. *In the San Juan* (Telluride, CO: St. Patrick's Parish, Telluride, Colorado, 1898)

Grant, George D. "Captain Grant's Report from Devil's Gate," printed in the *Deseret News*, November 19, 1856

Hardin, John Wesley. *The Life of John Wesley Hardin, from the Original Manuscript as Written by Himself* (Seguin, TX: Smith & Moore, Publishers, 1896)

Haslin, Robert. From William Lightfoot Visscher, *A Thrilling and Truthful History of The Pony Express or Blazing The Westward Way and Other Sketches and Incidents of Those Stirring Times* (Chicago: Rand, McNall & Co., 1908)

Haun, Catherine. Story from an entry of Catherine Haun's 1849 Manuscript Diary (San Marino, CA: The Huntington Library)

Heard, Isaac. *History of the Sioux War and Massacre* (St. Paul, MN: St. Paul Press, December 24, 1863)

Horn, Sarah Ann. *Comanche Bondage: Dr. John Charles Beales's Settlement of La Villa de Dolores on Las Moras Creek in Southern Texas of the 1830s* by Carl Coke Rister (editor) and Don Worcester (introduction) (Lincoln, NE: University of Nebraska Press, 1989)

Horn, Tom. *Life of Tom Horn, Government Scout and Interpreter, Written by Himself: A Vindication* (Denver: Louthan Book Company, 1904)

Howard, Oliver Otis. "Supplementary Report: Non-Treating Nez Perce Campaign," December 26, 1877, *In Report of the Secretary of War*, 1877

Irving, Washington. *The Adventures of Captain Bonneville* (Chicago: Belford, Clarke & Company, Publishers, 1848)

Jackson, Alfred T. *The Diary of a Forty-Niner*, Chauncey L. Canfield (editor) (San Francisco: Morgan Shepard Company, 1908)

James, Thomas. *Three Years Among the Indians and Mexicans* (St. Louis: Missouri Historical Society, 1916)

Jennings, N.A. *A Texas Ranger* (New York: Charles Scribner's Sons, 1899)

Just, Emma Thompson. *Letters of Long Ago*, Agnes Just Reid (editor) and Brigham D. Madsen (introduction). (Salt Lake City, UT: University of Utah Tanner Trust Fund, 1973)

Kansas City Times. "The Killing of Jesse James," July 4, 1882, reprinted in *Dust to Dust: Obituaries of the Gunfighters*, Jerry J. Gaddy (editor) (Ft. Collins, CO: The Old Army Press, 1977)

Kearny, Steven. Speech reprinted from W. H. Emory *Notes of a Military Reconnaissance, from Fort Leavenworth, in Missouri, to San Diego, in California, including part of the Arkansas, Del Norte, and Gila Rivers* (Washington, DC: 30th Congress, 1st Session, 1848)

Kelly, Fanny. *Narrative of My Captivity Among the Sioux Indians* (Hartford, CT: Mutual Publishing Company, 1871)

Kern, Edward M. Letter to 'Mary' dated February 10, 1849, from *Fremont's Fourth Expedition*, LeRoy R. Hafen and Ann W. Hafen (editors and introductions) (Glendale, CA: The Arthur H. Clark Company, 1960)

Klasner, Lily. *My Girlhood Among Outlaws*, Eve Ball (editor) (Tucson, AZ: The University of Arizona Press, 1972)

Larpenteur, Charles. *Forty Years a Fur Trader on the Upper Missouri*, Paul L. Hedren (introduction) (Lincoln, NE: University of Nebraska Press, 1989)

Laurence, Mary Leefe. *Daughter of the Regiment*, Thomas T. Smith (editor) (Lincoln, NE: University of Nebraska Press, 1996)

Left Handed. *Son of Old Man Hat*, A Navaho Autobiography recorded by Walter Dyk, Edward Sapir (foreword) (Lincoln, NE: University of Nebraska Press, 1967)

Lemmon, Ed. *Boss Cowman: The Recollections of Ed Lemmon, 1857–1946* (Lincoln, NE: University of Nebraska Press, 1969)

Leonard, Zenas. *The Adventures of Zenas Leonard, Fur Trader and Trapper, 1831–1836* (Cleveland, OH: W. F. Wagner, 1904)

Lewis, Meriwether. *Original Journals of the Lewis and Clark Expedition*, Reuben Gold Thwaites (editor) (New York: Dodd, Mead & Company, 1904)

Love, Nat. *A True History of Slavery Days, Life on the Great Cattle Ranges and On the Plains of the 'Wild and Woolly' West, Based on Facts, and Personal Experiences of the Author* (Los Angeles: Wayside Press, 1907)

Lummis, Charles. *Letters from the Southwest*, James W. Byrkit (editor) (Tucson, AZ: The University of Arizona Press, 1989)

MacKenna, Benjamín Vicuña. From *We Were 49ers! Chilean Accounts of the California Gold Rush*, Edwin A. Beilharz and Carlos U. López (translators and editors) (Pasadena, CA: Ward Ritchie Press, 1976)

Magoffin, Susan Shelby. *Down the Sante Fé Trail and into Mexico* (New Haven, CT: Yale University Press, 1926)

Majors, Alexander. *Seventy Years on the Frontier: Alexander Majors' Memoirs of a Lifetime on the Border* (Chicago: Rand, McNally & Company, 1893)

Marcy, Randolph B. *The Prairie Traveler: A Hand-Book for Overland Expedition, with Maps, Illustrations and Itineraries of the Principal Routes Between the Mississippi and the Pacific* (Washington: Published by authority of the War Department, 1859)

Mayer, Frank H. with Charles B. Roth. *The Buffalo Harvest* (Denver: Sage Books, 1958)

McComas, Evans S. *A Journal of Travel*, Martin Schmitt (editor) (Portland, OR: Champoeg Press, 1954)

McConnell, William J. *Frontier Law: A Story of Vigilante Days*, Senator William E. Borah (introduction) (Chicago: World Book Company, 1926)

McKenna, James A. *Black Range Tales*, Shane Leslie (introduction) (Glorietta, NM: The Rio Grand Press, Inc., 1936)

McLaughlin, James. *Account of the Death of Sitting Bull and the Circumstances Attending It* from a letter written to the Office of Indian Rights Association, Philadelphia, January 19, 1891.

Möllhausen, Baldwin. *Diary of a Journey from the Mississippi to the Coasts of the Pacific*, Peter A. Fritzell (introduction) (New York: Johnson Reprint Corporation, 1969)

Mountain Charley (a.k.a. Mrs. E. J. Guerin). *Mountain Charley, or the Adventures of Mrs. E. J. Guerin, Who Was Thirteen Years in Male Attire*, Fred W. Mazzulla and William Kostka (introduction) (Norman, OK: University of Oklahoma Press, 1968)

Nequatewa, Edmund. *Born a Chief: The Nineteenth Century Hopi Boyhood of Edmund Nequatewa* told to Alfred F. Whiting, P. David Seaman (editor) (Tucson, AZ: The University of Arizona Press, 1993)

Oatman, Olive. *Captivity of the Oatman Girls* (Carlton & Porter, Publishers, 1857)

Owens-Adair, Bethenia. *Gleanings From a Pioneer Woman Physician's Life* (Portland, OR: Mann & Beach, Printers, 1906)

Ormsby, Waterman L. The article, "Overland to California," published by the *New York Herald*, Thursday, November 11, 1858, and reprinted in *The Butterfield Overland Mail*, Lyle H. Wright and Josephine M. Bynum (editors) (San Marino, CA: The Huntington Library, 1998)

Parker, Samuel, Rev. *Journal of an Exploring Tour Beyond the Rocky Mountains, Under the Direction of the A.B.C.F.M. Performed in the Years 1835, '36, and '37; Containing a Description of the Geography, Geology, Climate, and Productions; and the Number, Manners, and Customs of the Natives With a Map of Oregon Territory* (Minneapolis: Ross & Haines, reprinted in 1967 in limited edition from the 1838 edition)

Parkman, Francis, Jr. *The Oregon Trail: Sketches of the Prairie and Rocky-Mountain Life* (Boston: Little, Brown and Company, 1892)

Pickett, Joseph W. *Memoirs of Joseph W. Pickett, Missionary Superintendent in Southern Iowa and in the Rocky Mountains for the American Home Missionary Society* (Boston: Congregational Publishing Society, 1880)

Pike, James. *The Scout and Ranger: Being the Personal Adventures of Corporal Pike of the Fourth Ohio Cavalry as a Texas Ranger, in the Indian Wars, Delineating Western Adventure; Afterward a Scout and Spy, in Tennessee, Alabama, Georgia, and the Carolinas, Under Generals Mitchell, Rosecrans, Stanley, Sheridan, Lytle, Thomas, Crook, and Sherman* (New York: J. R. Hawley & Co., 1865)

Pike, Zebulon. *The Journals of Zebulon Montgomery Pike*, Donald Jackson (editor) (Norman, OK: University of Oklahoma Press, 1966)

Powell, John Wesley. *Exploration of the Colorado River of the West and Its Tributaries. Explored in 1869, 1870, 1871, and 1872, under the Direction of the Secretary of the Smithsonian Institution* (Washington: Smithsonian Institution, 1875)

Purple, Edwin Ruthven. *Perilous Passage: A Narrative of the Montana Gold Rush, 1862–1863*, Kenneth N. Owens (editor) (Helena, MT: Montana Historical Society Press, 1995)

Reed, Virginia. "The Letter" contained in George R. Stewart, *Ordeal by Hunger: The Story of the Donner Party* (Cambridge, MA: The Riverside Press, 1936)

Reid, Samuel Chester. *The Scouting Expeditions of McCulloch's Texas Rangers; or the Summer and Fall Campaign of the Army of the United States in Mexico—1846; Including Skirmishes with the Mexicans and an Accurate Detail of the Storming of Monterey; Also, the Daring Scouts at Buena Visa Together with Anecdotes, Incidents, Descriptions of Country, and Sketches of the Lives of the Celebrated Partisan Chief, Hays, McCulloch, and Walker* (Philadelphia: John E. Potter and Company, 1859)

Riggs, Stephen R. *Mary and I: Forty Years With the Sioux* (Chicago: Congregational S.S. and Publishing Society, 1887)

Roe, Frances Marie Antoinette Mack. *Army Letters from an Officer's Wife, 1871–1888* (New York: D. Appleton, Publishers, 1909)

Roosevelt, Theodore. *Ranch Life and the Hunting-Trail* (New York: The Century Co., 1888)

Russell, Osborne. *Journal of a trapper: or, Nine years in the Rocky Mountains, 1834–1843: being a general description of the country, climate, rivers, lakes, mountains, etc., and a view of the life by a hunter in those regions* (Boise, ID: Syms-York, Publishers, 1914)

Ruxton, George Frederick. *Adventures in Mexico and the Rocky Mountains* (London, 1847)

Sanford, Mollie Dorsey. *Mollie: The Journal of Mollie Dorsey Sanford in Nebraska and Colorado Territories, 1857–1866*, Donald F. Danker (introduction and notes) (Lincoln, NE: University of Nebraska Press, 1976)

Scharmann, Hermann B., Sr. *Scharmann's Overland Journey to California*, Margaret Hoff Zimmermann and Erich W. Zimmermann (translators) (Freeport, NY: Books for Library Press, 1918)

Schultz, James Willard. *My Life as an Indian* (New York: Doubleday, 1907)

Seymour, Silas. *Incidents of a Trip Through the Great Platte Valley, to the Rocky Mountains and Laramie Plains, in the Fall of 1866, With a Synoptical Statement of the Various Pacific Railroads, and an Account of the Great Union Pacific Railroad Excursion to the One Hundredth Meridian of Longitude* (New York: D. Van Nostrand, 1867)

de Smet, Pierre-Jean. *Life, Letters and Travels of Father Pierre-Jean de Smet, S.J., 1801–1873*, Hiram Martin Chittenden and Alfred Talbot Richardson (editors) (New York: Francis P. Harper, Publishers, 1905)

Smith, Henry. "Early Reminiscences Number 10, Scraps from a Diary" (*Seattle Sunday Star*, October 29, 1887)

Smith, John S. *Congressional Testimony of Mr. John S. Smith* (Washington: U. S. Government Printing Office, March 14, 1865)

Smyth, R. J. *Personal Reminiscences of Fort Phil Kearney and the Wagon Box Fight* from Cyrus Townsend Brady's 1904 *Indian Fights and Fighters* (Lincoln, NE: University of Nebraska Press, 1971)

Stanley, Henry Morton. *My Early Travels and Adventures* (New York: Scribner's, 1895)

Thomas American Horse. From Edward Kadlecek and Mabell Kadlecek, *To Kill an Eagle: Indian Views on the Last Days of Crazy Horse* (Boulder, CO: Johnson Books, 1981)

Toponce, Alexander. *Reminiscences of Alexander Toponce* (Salt Lake City, UT: Katie Toponce, Century Printing, 1923)

Townsend, John Kirk. *Narrative of a Journey Across the Rocky Mountains to the Columbia River* (originally published in 1839 and reprinted by the University of Nebraska Press, 1978)

de Vaca, Alvar Nuñez Cabeza. *The Journey of Alvar Nuñez Cabeza de Vaca*, translated by Fanny Bandelier (1905), and *Adventures in the Unknown Interior of America*, translated and edited by Cyclone Covey from the original 1542 edition and from later English translations (Albuquerque, NM: University of New Mexico Press, 1998)

Van Oden, Aaron. *Texas Ranger's Diary & Scrapbook*, Ann Jensen (editor) (Dallas, TX: The Kaleidograph Press, 1936)

Whiting, William Henry Chase. *Exploring Southwestern Trails*, Ralph P. Bieber and Averam B. Bender (editors) (Glendale, CA: The Arthur H. Clark Company, 1938)

Wislizenus, F. A. *A Journey to the Rocky Mountains in 1839* (St. Louis, MO: Missouri Historical Society, 1912)

Wooden Leg. *A Warrior Who Fought Custer*, Thomas B. Marquis (interpreter and editor) (Chicago: Midwest Company, Publishers, 1931)

Wyeth, John B. (written for him by Benjamin Waterhouse). *Oregon, or A Short History of a Long Journey from the Atlantic Ocean to the Region of the Pacific by Land, drawn up from the Notes and Oral Information of John B. Wyeth, One of the Party who left Mr. Nathaniel J. Wyeth, July 28th 1832, Four Days March Beyond the Ridge of the Rocky Mountains and the Only One Who Has Returned to New England* (Cambridge, MA, 1833)

Younger, Cole. *The Story of Cole Younger* (Chicago: The Henneberry Press, 1903)

Most of the extracts contained in this anthology are in the public domain or permission has been granted by a publishing company or copyright holder to reprint the material. In a few cases, however, copyright holders could not be located after a diligent search effort was undertaken. Either these are out-of-business or have been absorbed into other companies such that they could not be located. The editor and publisher apologize for any errors or omissions in this book and would be grateful for notification of any corrections that should be incorporated into future editions of this volume.

About the Author

Dr. Richard Scott is a professor at the Metropolitan State College of Denver where he resides with his fellow professor wife, Judy. Judy and Richard have four children. Richard has been a J. William Fulbright Scholar to Rhodes University in South Africa and to the Portuguese Catholic University in Portugal. He is working on several more books about historical incidents in the West.

Tombstone Desperados—David Scott, Salvatore DeFatta and Richard Scott

401